Annie Rialland, Rachid Ridouane and Harry van der Hulst (Eds.)
**Features in Phonology and Phonetics**

# Phonology and Phonetics

Editor
Aditi Lahiri

## Volume 21

# Features in Phonology and Phonetics

Posthumous Writings by Nick Clements and Coauthors

Edited by
Annie Rialland, Rachid Ridouane
and Harry van der Hulst

DE GRUYTER
MOUTON

ISBN 978-3-11-055520-2
e-ISBN (PDF) 978-3-11-039998-1
e-ISBN (EPUB) 978-3-11-040010-6
ISSN 1861-4191

**Library of Congress Cataloging-in-Publication Data**
A CIP catalog record for this book has been applied for at the Library of Congress.

**Bibliografische Information der Deutschen Nationalbibliothek**
The Deutsche Nationalbibliothek lists this publication in the Deutschen
Nationalbibliografie; detailed bibliographic data are available on the internet http://
dnb.dnb.de.

© 2017 Walter de Gruyter GmbH, Berlin/Boston
This volume is text- and page-identical with the hardback published in 2015.
Typesetting: Frank Benno Junghanns, Berlin
Printing and binding: CPI books GmbH, Leck

♾ Printed on acid-free paper
Printed in Germany

www.degruyter.com

# Contents

Preface —— vii
Curriculum vitae of George N. Clements —— ix
Contributors —— x


Part 1
Introduction

Annie Rialland, Rachid Ridouane and Harry van der Hulst
**Features in Phonology and Phonetics:
The contributions of George N. Clements** —— 3

**Appendix: Publications of George N. Clements** —— 17


Part 2
Unpublished manuscripts

George N. Clements
**The hierarchical representation of vowel height** —— 25

George N. Clements and Rajesh Khatiwada
**Cooccurrence constraints on aspirates in Nepali** —— 127


Part 3
Contributions on individual features

Hyunsoon Kim and George N. Clements
**The feature [tense]** —— 159

Hyunsoon Kim, George N. Clements and Martine Toda
**The feature [strident]** —— 179

George N. Clements, Jacqueline Vaissière, Angélique Amelot and Julie Montagu
**The feature [nasal]** —— 195

Jean-Marc Beltzung, Cédric Patin and George N. Clements
**The feature [ATR] —— 217**

Chakir Zeroual and George N. Clements
**The feature [pharyngeal] —— 247**

**Index —— 277**

# Preface

It is one of the great sadnesses of my life that Nick Clements died "before his time." It was one of the great privileges of my life to have known and worked with him. I wish I could somehow extend that privilege to all of you. This meager preface is the best I can do.

Nick was the gentlest of people. I can honestly say that, as someone who has been spared that quality, I never heard a harsh word from him, even when the topic of conversation was about critics of our joint work together. Where I might have wished a plague of boils, Nick gave attention and respect. Our joint work was the better for it, of course. That was Nick's way.

Nick was a very private person. So it was only after long swathes of time together that I learned how remarkably diverse he was. As a young man he was a classical music DJ with the occasional dip into sports casting. He told me that his job was to whip the play-by-play action into a froth of excitement from descriptions that came mechanically in over a ticker tape machine miles away from the actual ballpark. I wish I could have done that.

Once when Nick came back home to the United States for medical care, he entrusted a painting to me for safekeeping. It was a copy of a painting originally

thought to have been by Giorgone. The copy was extraordinary, especially the drapery in the background.

The painting hung in my office for several months while Nick was operated on for the removal of a serious tumor. It remained there while he underwent a lengthy rehabilitation that left him walking with a cane he swore he would come to discard. He did.

As it turned out, the painting, originally attributed to Giorgone, has since been recognized as an early work of Titian. I think Nick was drawn to it, even though he didn't know at the time that it was a Titian, because his eye told him it was superb. He had tremendous taste as a student of art and subsequently as a scientist.

Nick gave up art for linguistics. Lucky for the one; perhaps not so for the other. He became a consummate linguist. His work was a model of insight, creativity, sophistication, judiciousness and care. This will be apparent to everyone who reads this collection. If his articles were objects, Faberge eggs come to mind.

If I had to find a single word to describe the early Nick, the Nick with whom I wrote *CV Phonology*, that word would be "unflappable." When Nick moved to Paris, married Annie Rialland and had two children, William and Célia, he added "serenity" to that description. It was an unbeatable combination. It stood him in great stead during the ultimate crisis of his life. In the end he kept friends at bay. He wanted to spare them.

Nick was clearly at his happiest in Paris with Annie, William, Célia and his colleagues at the Laboratory for Phonetics and Phonology with whom he worked for over sixteen years while he served as Director of Research at the Centre National de la Recherche Scientifique (CNRS). Some of his most fruitful scholarship was done during this period. His inquiry into the origin of phonological features began in earnest here. He has planted the seeds. His colleagues will tend the harvest.

After Nick died his son, William, sent me a photograph that he had taken of Nick in a Parisian nightclub. It was of his father playing piano in a small ensemble. A jazz musician myself, I had no idea that Nick played the piano. It was one more layer pealed away.

The photograph left me with a smile and a question. If only Nick had lived, how many more layers would there have been? How much greater would be our loss?

Samuel Jay Keyser<br>
Cambridge, MA<br>
April 13, 2013

# Curriculum Vitae of George N. Clements
(1940–2009)

## Education

1973    Ph.D., School of Oriental and African Studies (University of London) Thesis: The Verbal Syntax of Ewe.
1968    Certificate, Centre de Linguistique Quantitative, Faculté des Sciences, Université de Paris.
1962    B.A. Yale University, New Haven, CT. Phi Beta Kappa Society.

## Academic positions

1997–2009    Research Director (DR1), CNRS
1992–1997    Research Director (DR2), CNRS
1987–1991    Professor of Linguistics, Cornell University, Ithaca, New York, USA
1982–1986    Associate Professor, Cornell University, Ithaca, New York, USA
1975–1982    Assistant/Associate Professor, Harvard University, Cambridge, MA (USA)
1973–1974    Teaching Assistant, Lecturer, Department of Foreign Languages and Linguistics, MIT, Cambridge, MA, (USA)
1971–1973    Chargé de cours, English language and literature, Université de Paris 7 (Jussieu) et Université de Paris 8 (Vincennes)

For a complete CV, see Nick's personal website http://nickclements.free.fr/

# Contributors

**Angélique Amelot**
Laboratoire de Phonétique et Phonologie,
UMR 7018 (CNRS/Sorbonne Nouvelle)
angelique.amelot@univ-paris3.fr

**Jean-Marc Beltzung**
Laboratoire de linguistique de Nantes
(LLING), EA 3827, Université de Nantes
Jean-Marc.Beltzung@univ-nantes.fr

**George N. Clements**
Laboratoire de Phonétique et Phonologie,
UMR 7018 (CNRS/Sorbonne Nouvelle)

**Rajesh Khatiwada**
Laboratoire de Phonétique et Phonologie,
UMR 7018 (CNRS/Sorbonne Nouvelle)
rajesh.khatiwada@univ-paris3.fr

**Hyunsoom Kim**
Department of English, Hongik University,
Sangsoo-dong 72-1, Mapo-gu,
Seoul 121-791, Republic of Korea
hyunsoomkim@hotmail.com

**Julie Montagu**
Laboratoire de Phonétique et Phonologie,
UMR 7018 (CNRS/Sorbonne Nouvelle)
julie_montagu@hayoo.com

**Cédric Patin**
Savoirs, Textes, Langage,
UMR 8163, (CNRS/Université Lille 3)
cedric.patin@gmail.com

**Annie Rialland**
Laboratoire de Phonétique et Phonologie,
UMR 7018 (CNRS/Sorbonne Nouvelle)
annie.rialland@univ-paris3.fr

**Rachid Ridouane**
Laboratoire de Phonétique et Phonologie,
UMR 7018 (CNRS/Sorbonne Nouvelle)
rachid.ridouane@univ-paris3.fr

**Martine Toda**
Laboratoire de Phonétique et Phonologie,
UMR 7018 (CNRS/Sorbonne Nouvelle)
martine.toda@cnrs.fr

**Jacqueline Vaissière**
Laboratoire de Phonétique et Phonologie,
UMR 7018 (CNRS/Sorbonne Nouvelle)
jacqueline.vaissiere@univ-paris3.fr

**Harry van der Hulst**
Department of Linguistics,
University of Connecticut
harry.van.der.hulst@uconn.edu

**Chakir Zeroual**
Faculté Polydisciplinaire de Taza,
Taza-Morocco, and Laboratoire de
Phonétique et Phonologie,
UMR 7018 (CNRS/Sorbonne Nouvelle)
chakirzeroual@yahoo.fr

Part 1

**Introduction**

Annie Rialland, Rachid Ridouane and Harry van der Hulst
# Features in Phonology and Phonetics: The contributions of George N. Clements

Our primary goals in this introduction is to place Nick Clements' contribution to Feature Theory in a historical and contemporary context and introduce some of his unpublished manuscripts as well as new work with colleagues collected in this book.

## 1 Breaking the phoneme into features

To emphasize to beginning students that linguistics is an empirical science we like to point out that, as in physics, much of our work aims at identifying the ultimate building blocks of our subject. This search takes many different forms. Semanticists look for concepts that qualify as conceptual primitives, while syntacticians look for basic categories below the levels of the traditional parts of speech. Ongoing work often is more likely to lead to further questions than to definite answers. What is the set of primitives in either domain? How are semantic concepts and syntactic categories related? Are the latter autonomous or reducible to the former? Are the primes in either domain universal, present in all languages or, at least, available to all of them? And if so, where do they come from and where do they exist? Do users of languages, or linguists for that matter, construct these categories *de novo*, each time one of them learns or analyzes a language? Or are they part of an innate endowment, anchored in the human genome? While these are undoubtedly the most fundamental questions that can be raised, the field of linguistics is still in a state where none of them has generally accepted answers.

In the early days of phonology, the abstract building blocks of the size of speech sound were called *phonemes*, a term that reflects the claim that these units are the basic building blocks at the phonological level, putting the idea that phonemes are analyzable in smaller ingredients on hold. The recognition of abstract units, of whatever size, entailed questions that are analogous to the questions that we raised earlier concerning syntax and semantics. Importantly, it was now inevitable to ask the question how phonological units (phonemes) relate to phonetic units. Indeed, some see this relation as analogous to that between syntax and semantics. However, it turned out to be far from simple to correlate each phonological unit with a phonetic event of some sort, since nothing in the articulation or the perception of speech seems to point to a counterpart of discrete phonemes. Notoriously, speech is continuous. Clearly there was and is a mismatch between the basic units of speech (articulatory movements and their acoustic consequences) and phonemes and to this day proponents of the phoneme notion are being suspected of being under the spell of the alphabetic bias of the International Phonetic Alphabet (IPA). But leaving aside for the moment whether phonemes 'exist', and if they do, where, further developments alleviated the mismatch by digging deeper on the phonological side. The early phonologists, notably Nikolai Trubetzkoy, highlighted the fact that classifications of phonological oppositions point to distinctive phonetic properties *below* the level of the phoneme, i.e. the 'features' that were anticipated in the IPA diacritics. Then, Roman Jakobson made the bold proposal that these properties correlate with subunits of the phonemes thus giving proper recognition of phonological features. From the beginning, phonological features were meant to correlate with phonetic properties that are potentially distinctive (or contrastive) in at least one language, although they could function non-distinctively in other languages. A well-known example is '[aspiration]' which is distinctive in Thai and allophonic in English. Jakobson's ideas culminated in Jakobson, Fant and Halle (1952) and Jakobson and Halle (1956) in which a small set of distinctive features was posited. These authors dealt with the duality of speech (production and perception) by providing an articulatory and acoustic definition for each feature. Of these, Jakobson held the latter to be more fundamental because, as he argued, the acoustic aspect of speech is shared by both speaker and hearer. The proposed system found its way in Generative Phonology in Chomsky and Halle (1968)'s The Sound Pattern of English (SPE), where it was decided to put emphasis on the articulatory correlates of their features. The articulatory primacy was also supported by proponents of the so-called *motor theory of speech perception* (Liberman and Mattingly 1985). Thus, 20th century phonology came to be dominated by a view of phonology which acknowledged, at the very least phonemes as well as a universal set of distinctive features. Additionally, various writers or schools made room for higher-order units such as syllables and various kinds of larger stretches. At the same time, we find views that omit the phoneme level and construct larger units, roughly syllable sized, directly from articulatory buildings blocks, a view that we find in modern times in Articulatory Phonology (Browman and Goldstein 1986), as well as other non-segmental phonologies.

## 2 The internal organization of features

The field of phonology has moved along productively on the assumption that distinctive features are a genuine and minimal part of the phonological vocabulary. Indeed, following the SPE model (and other models that built on Jakobson's insights), much of the field today assumes that phonological representations consist of linear strings of phonemes (although that term was tainted for a while, and for the wrong reasons[1]), each phoneme being an unordered set of features.

In the early 1970's, when Nick Clements had become an active participant in the field, various modifications of this view were proposed, leading to a number of enrichments of the phonological representation 'outside the phoneme' and 'inside the phoneme' (see van der Hulst and Smith 1982 for an early overview of these developments). Firstly, outside the phoneme, it was recognized that some sort of grouping of phonemes ('syllable structure') was needed. Secondly, these syllables, or similar units, themselves needed a grouping into even higher levels such as *feet*. Nick's work mainly focused on what was happening *inside* the phonemes.[2] In 1975, John Goldsmith revived the idea that tones have a tendency to lead a life of their own, an idea that was not unfamiliar to many students of tonal languages, and, theoretically acknowledged in the prosodic school of John Rupert Firth. Goldsmith proposed a transparent notational apparatus to formalize this idea which gave rise to *Autosegmental Phonology*. Clements (1980, 1977) presented a significant extension of the autosegmental theory to the domain of *vowel harmony*, setting a trend to liberate all features from the SPE segmental harness which, then, necessitated recognition of a *skeletal tier* to which all features on their respective tiers refer. Properties and use of the skeletal tier, as the terminal units of syllabic structure, form the subject of Clements and Keyser (1983), an influential study of a wide variety of phonological phenomena.

The mid 1980s witnesses a further development of the world within the phoneme in which Nick played a pivotal role: the idea of feature grouping (see Clements 1985, 1999). The basic idea here is that a segment is not an unordered feature bundle, but displays a hierarchical-geometrical structure in which features are grouped into classes. While such feature classifications were familiar from phonetics and indeed would be implicit in pedagogical explanations

---

[1] Generative phonology rejected the phonemic level *as enforced by biuniquess*. Rejecting this level simply means that a distinction between a morphophonemic and a phonemic level disappears. The resulting level can then be called the phonemic level. Nonetheless, after features had been added to phonology, phonemes were no longer the basic building blocks of phonology.
[2] This is not to say that he did not contribute to extra-phonemic domains such as syllable structure (see Clements and Keyser 1983), the related issue of sonority (Clements 2009). Nick also developed a new theory on reduplicative copying (1985).

of the set of features, Nick's work demonstrated that feature grouping had to be acknowledged *in* the phonology. When nasal consonants assimilate to the place properties of following consonants, we do not want to write separate rules for each place adjustment, but rather capture the generalization that nasal copy the place node of the following consonant, no matter which features are dominated by this node. This was a very powerful idea that changed the way that phonological processes were understood and represented.[3] The combination of autosegmental phonology and feature geometry led to a whole new three-dimensional conception of phonological representations in which tiers (rather than features) were hierarchically grouped and phonological operations could effect individual features or feature classes.

Continuously, Nick developed the grouping notion in conjunction with homing in on a set of phonological features and their hierarchical relationships. This work incorporated the notion that some features (like those for the major articulators) are unary, while others are binary; see Clements and Hume (1995). In some cases, Nick proposed new features or feature organization. His work on major class features introduced the feature [approximant] (Clements 1990, 1992, Osu and Clements 2009). Another example can be found in his 1990 study (which is contained in the present volume) of vowel harmony processes involving tongue root, tongue height or aperture which he proposed to unify in a model that would allow multiple tiers for the feature [open].

At the same time, Nick also continued to address the fundamental issues that were always 'lurking in the background'. One such issue concerns the question whether all features that are necessary for phonetic interpretation are specified at all levels of representation. Early on in generative phonology much attention was given to the claim that redundant feature values, i.e. values that can be predicted on the basis of other values, can be left unspecified at the lexical level, provided that the predictabilities are encoded in redundancy rules, which at some point before the derivation reaches the surface are filled in. The use of underspecification was criticized in Stanley (1967) as potentially leading to ternarity and therefore traded in for full specification in SPE.[4] In the early 1980s underspecification, if properly constrained so as to avoid ternarity, could be reinstated (Ringen 1977, Kiparsky 1982) and the further-reaching claim was made that more economy could be achieved by designating one value for each feature as 'the default value' which could then also be left unspecified, leading

---

[3] Similar ideas had been or were being explored in Anderson and Jones (1974) and Sagey (1986).

[4] Full specification demanded the presence of all redundant values, but not of feature specifications that, in a traditional sense, would be called allophonic.

to what was called 'radical underspecification' (Archangeli 1984). In his more recent work, Nick tackled the problem of under- or non-specification head on, trying to develop a set of explicit criteria for specification of feature values at various levels and going beyond technical issues of redundancy. In his paper on 'representational economy' (Clements 2001), he argues in detail that only those features need to be ever specified that play a role in the expression of phonological generalizations. These would not just be specifications that are distinctive, but also those that are active in one way or another..

While attention for phonemic inventories has always been minimal in generative phonology, Nick also investigated the relationship between features and inventories in his work on feature economy, returning to important findings in the work of André Martinet. In Clements (2009) he develops a set of feature-based principles that account for the major trends in the structure of phoneme inventories:

i. *Feature Bounding*: features place an upper bound on the number of potentially contrastive categories in a language.
ii. *Feature Economy*: features tend to be combined maximally.
iii. *Marked Feature Avoidance*: certain feature values tend to be avoided.
iv. *Robustness*: highly-valued feature contrasts tend to be employed before less highly-valued contrasts.
v. *Phonological Enhancement*: marked features are often introduced to reinforce weak perceptual contrasts.

These 5 principles interact to define broad properties of sound systems, such as symmetry and the tendency of sounds to be dispersed in auditory space. Further phonetically-based principles fine-tune the realization of phonological categories at the phonetic level. It is suggested that these general properties of sound systems may have their explanation in the nature of early language acquisition. In motivating and explaining these principles Nick characteristically made connections between different strands of research in phonology, phonetics and typological studies. He based his findings, as always, on solid empirical grounds, in this case by extensive use of the expanded UPSID database containing 451 phoneme inventories.

Before discussing some more recent avenues in Nick's work, we conclude this section with remarking that his work, while aiming to establish a very precise inventory of features, including their relations and phonetic interpretations, based on broad empirical (and often original) descriptive work, would often reflect, sometimes directly, on some of the broader and foundational issues surrounding the nature of features and feature theory with reference to the question whether features are innate or learned, Nick sides with the innateness view point. Features for him are primarily cognitive units, i.e. believed to be in the mind of the talker, and not to be transparently reflected in the vocal-tract actions that do causally structure the signal (e.g., Hammarberg 1976; Pierrehumbert 1990; Fowler 1986). In Clements (1993), Nick reflects on the nature of phonological primitives. He held features to be innate, universal and specific to humans, thus not as derived through generalizations based on phonetic similarity and analogy (Blevins 2004, Mielke 2008).

## 3 Where do features come from?

That the notion of phonological features has gained almost complete acceptance within linguistics does not entail that there was general acceptance of a specific set of features, although the task here seems somewhat more tangible than the task of establishing a set of semantic or syntactic features (which many semanticists and syntacticians have given up on). While no commonly agreed set has been established, it is also still undecided where features come from and where they exist. Are features constructed in the process of language acquisition due to general cognitive principles of categorization (Blevins 2004, Mielke 2008) or is there an innate set of such primes that evolved for the specific purpose of language? While Chomsky and Halle (1968) emphasize the innateness (and thus also universality) of features, even linguists who would take a more 'developmental' view, would generally agree that features are an indispensable tool for phonological analysis, not only by linguists but also by native speakers who seem to cast generalizations in terms of features, which must therefore have some sort of cognitive status, even if not innate. In fact, we could say the same thing for phonemes which, while in doubt for some phonologists, remain indispensable as tools for phonological analysis, both by linguists and native language users; the literature on the 'psychological reality' of phonemes is vast (see Silverman 2006 for a recent critic of the phoneme.). It is interesting that while, for example, speech errors provide good evidence for phoneme-based substitutions, feature-based substitutions are much less clear (Fromkin 1973). We must conclude that generally accepted answers to the issue of which features are needed, their innateness or the nature of phonetic correlates cannot be supplied and while it is clear that discussion is ongoing, Nick's work provides a rich array of potential answers and directions for further research.

A central issue in Nick's recent work concerns the relation distinctive features have to measurable physical properties. Even though most linguists and phoneticians agree that features are defined in terms of concrete physical and auditory properties, there is little agreement on exactly how they are defined. Historically speaking, there have been two main approaches to the phonetic implementation of distinctive features, one emphasizing their acoustic/auditory properties and the other their articulatory properties. According to the tradition launched by Jakobson, Fant and Halle (1952), features are defined primarily in acoustic terms, each feature being assigned a unique, invariant acoustic correlate. Features could be extracted by listeners from the speech stream through the detection of these correlates. In this view, the articulatory stage of speech is viewed as the means used to obtain each pair of acoustically contrastive effects: *"we speak to be heard in order to be understood"* (Jakobson, Fant and Halle 1952: 13). This approach has not been abandoned, and some researchers emphasize that *"speech perception is hearing sounds, not tongues"* (Ohala 1996). According to a second tradition initiated by Chomsky and Halle (1968), features are primarily defined in the articulatory domain. This approach is grounded in the *motor theory of speech perception* (Liberman and Mattingly 1985), and underlies some more recent theoretical approaches such as *Articulatory Phonology* (Browman and Goldstein 1986). In this view, objects of speech perception are the intended phonetic gestures of the speaker, viewed as the elementary events of speech production and perception. The emphasis on the articulatory properties of distinctive features provides furthermore a better account for some recurrent phonological processes across languages (such as place assimilation).

Based on phonetic fieldwork and the study of the sounds of a wide variety of languages, Ladefoged (1971), in a criticism of the Jakobsonian and the SPE feature systems, proposed a new system that was meant to account for a variety of phonation and articulation types previously unknown in the phonetic literature. Claiming that neither a purely acoustic/auditory nor a purely articulatory account is self-sufficient, Ladefoged proposed two disjoint feature sets: a set grouping sounds together because of their auditory similarity and a set grouping sounds because of their articulatory similarity. While such an approach may have its appeal, it is unclear whether some of the novel features that Ladefoged proposed (e.g. [click], [tap], and [wide]) satisfy the requirements expected of a feature system: expressing the content and structure of phoneme inventories, delimiting the number of theoretically possible speech sound contrasts within and across languages, and accounting for common phonological patterns found across languages (Clements and Hallé 2010).

K. N. Stevens and his colleagues at The Massachusetts Institute of Technology (MIT) have developed another approach within the framework of *Quantal Theory of speech* (Stevens 1972, 1989, 2003, Stevens and Keyser 2010). The main originality of this approach is the equal status it accords to the acoustic and articulatory dimensions of spoken language, overcoming the tradition competition between these two apparently incompatible approaches. Features are defined with respect to certain articulatory dimensions within which small shifts in the position of the tongue, lips, or vocal folds do not have major consequences for perception. The central claim is that there are regions in which the relationship between an articulatory configuration and its corresponding acoustic output is not linear:

> "For some types of articulatory parameters, there are ranges of values … for which the acoustic signal has well-defined attributes, and these ranges are bounded by regions in which the properties of the signal are relatively insensitive to perturbations in the articulation. The acoustic attributes of the signal within one of these plateau-like regions appear to define the acoustic correlates of a phonetic feature. (Stevens 1972: 64)

In this view, these stable regions form the basis for a universal set of distinctive features, each of which corresponds to an articulatory-acoustic coupling within which the auditory system is insensitive to small articulatory movements.[5] Parallel to Quantal Theory, Stevens and colleagues have developed a language-specific process referred to as *enhancement* (see Stevens et al. 1986, Stevens and Keyser 1989, Keyser and Stevens 2006), according to which features in danger of losing their perceptual saliency can be reinforced by additional gestures or redundant features, such as lip rounding in back vowels like [u]. Thus, the surface representation of an utterance includes not only the feature-defining acoustic and articulatory attributes but also an array of articulatory gestures and their acoustic consequences that enhance the perceptual saliency of the defining attributes. The defining acoustic attributes of a feature are a direct consequence of its articulatory definition. These are considered to be language-independent. The enhancing attributes of a feature are additional cues that aid in its identification. These may vary from language to language (Stevens and Keyser 2010).

Because it places phonology on solid, testable phonetic grounds, Quantal Theory is one of the recent models which has best succeeded in integrating phonetics and phonology. It has also inspired related approaches, such as the theory of distinctive regions and modes (Carré and Mrayati 1990). However, Quantal Theory has not been submitted to a complete, rigorous empirical testing. Clements, together with some of his colleagues and students, proposed to undertake such testing within the project *"Phonetic bases of distinctive features: quantal*

---

**5** Another explanation for why languages heavily favor certain articulatory and acoustic pairings in constructing their phoneme systems while avoiding others is that preferred contrasts maximize acoustic distinctiveness while minimizing articulatory effort (Liljencrants and Lindblom 1972).

*theory"* funded by the French Ministère délégué de la Recherche under the ACI-Prosodie program (2004–2007).

Quantal theory has raised a certain number of controversies (see the special issue of *Journal of Phonetics* 17 (1989)). A first criticism concerns its inability to explain the fact that certain sounds and sound inventories are much more frequent across languages than others. Other criticisms have borne more particularly on the nature of the fit between Quantal Theory and the facts which it is supposed to explain. The project coordinated by Nick was most particularly interested in the following questions:

- What is the exact acoustic and articulatory definition of each feature?
- Can these definitions be confirmed at the perceptual level?
- Can a quantal definition be given to each feature?
- Is quantal theory as valid for vowel features as for consonant features?
- Are both values of binary features (such as nasal/oral) quantal?
- To what degree do acoustic correlates vary according to phonological context, style, speaker, or language?
- Do acoustic correlates vary according to the class of sounds in question (for example, stops *vs.* fricatives, obstruents *vs.* sonorants, or consonants *vs.* vowels)?

The study of these and similar questions form the main subjects of Nick's recent contributions. Clements proposed and edited, with P. Hallé, a special issue of *Journal of Phonetics* 38(1), published in 2010. The papers collected in this issue emanated, for the most part, from a conference organized by Nick on the theme *"Phonetic Bases of Distinctive Features"* held at the Carré des Sciences, Ministère Délégué de la Recherche, Paris, on July 3, 2006. The volume provided an up-to-date overview of the phonetic bases of distinctive feature theory and highlighted the considerable evolution of the theory since the early work of the 1950s and 1960s, due to the development of new theoretical models on the one hand and to empirical studies that have developed our understanding of the diversity of cues that may be associated with any given feature on the other. The contributions to this issue dealt with various aspects, including biological bases of universal feature definitions, feature theory and variation, and features in lexical access.

Clements also edited with R. Ridouane a book on *"Where do phonological features come from? Cognitive, physical and developmental bases of distinctive speech categories"*, published in 2011. Most of the papers collected in this volume grew out of the conference *"Where Do Features Come From?"* held at Sorbonne University, Paris, October 4–5, 2007, co-organized by Clements and Ridouane. Following on the issues dealt with in the special issue of Journal of Phonetics

38(1), papers in this volume explored how distinctive speech categories originate and how they are cognitively organized and phonetically implemented. In addition, it explored the role features play in language acquisition and how they emerge in language development.

## 4 Summary of themes

In addition to the purely scientific goals of the project *"Phonetic bases of distinctive features: quantal theory"*, one of Nick's objectives was to create a 'features research group' with the specific aim of providing a thorough description for some of the most common features. Two studies from this research group have been published in a volume following a conference at the University of Chicago's Paris Center in June of 2009, organized in tribute to Nick's contributions to the field of phonology. The first study entitled *"Do we need tone features?"* (Clements, Michaud and Patin 2011) was concerned with whether tone is different from other phonological features and concluded that tonal features may well be motivated in our studies of tonal system, but the type of motivation is different in kind from that which is familiar from the study of other aspects of phonology. The other study entitled *"Language-independent bases of distinctive features"* (Ridouane, Clements and Khatiwada 2011) provided a language-independent phonetic definition of the feature [spread glottis], and showed that an articulatory definition of this feature in terms of a single common glottal configuration or gesture would be insufficient to account for the full range of speech sounds characterized by this feature; an acoustic definition is also necessary.

A selection of additional papers written by members of the 'features research group' is included in this collection. They deal with the following distinctive features: [ATR], [nasal], [pharyngeal], [strident], and [tense]. A protocol was established by Nick to homogenize the contributions on each feature. Specifically, authors were asked to first provide a brief bibliography of the main sources on the feature as well as a historical overview of the feature (who first proposed it, its status within the current models, critics, etc.). Then a more developed presentation of the linguistic use of the feature is provided, specifying both lexical and phonological functions of the feature. The rest of the contribution is devoted to the phonetic implementation of the feature. Depending on the feature, the authors provide its articulatory, acoustic and auditory definitions, its temporal alignment in different segments it defines, whether the definition provided is quantal or not, and the way the feature may enhance or be enhanced by additional cues. A basic assumption in these studies is that a segment can be said to bear a feature [F] at the phonetic level only if it satisfies both its articulatory and acoustic definitions. In other words, for a feature [F] to be recovered from a speech event, not only must its articulatory condition be met, but its acoustic definition must be satisfied, or failing that its enhancing attributes must be present.

This volume includes in addition two previously unpublished manuscripts. *"The hierarchical representation of vowel height"*, written in the early 90's, is concerned with how vowel height could be formally characterized in phonological representations. More specifically, it questions how the phonological nature of vowel height is expressed in feature terms, and how these features are formally organized within an autosegmental approach. In this extremely thorough contribution Nick proposed an account in terms of an 'aperture' theory of vowel height, in which different vowel categories were distinguished in terms of a single, hierarchically subdivided feature category [open], used to implement height distinctions. We decided to include this manuscript in this volume because it proposes a model that directly addresses problems that were and still are inherent in models of vowel height, and because it offers well-motivated solutions. For instance, by characterizing vowel height in terms of a single phonological feature, it directly accounts for the fact that vowel height maps into a unitary phonetic parameter, with well-defined acoustic and articulatory correlates. We believe that by publishing this manuscript in this volume, this work will receive the attention it deserves.

The second manuscript entitled *"Cooccurrence constraints on aspirates in Nepali"*, co-authored with Rajesh Khatiwada, examines cooccurrence restrictions on aspirated consonants in Nepali. Similar to other Indo-Aryan languages, such as Hindi, Nepali has as many as four series of stops: voiceless unaspirated, voiced unaspirated, voiceless aspirated, and voiced aspirated. Based on an exhaustive search of the 26,073 entries in Turner's Comparative and Etymological Dictionary of the Nepali Language (1931), the study reveals that only a small number of noncompound words contain two aspirates, and that the vast majority of these are either reduplications or loanwords. When these sectors of the lexicon are excluded, the number of diaspirate roots is vanishingly small. The cooccurrence constraints on aspirates are not predictable from the individual frequencies of the phonemes concerned, since the number of observed $C^hVC^h$ sequences is significantly less than what would be predicted on a statistical basis. These facts support the view that aspiration takes the root as its domain in Nepali, though its location within the root is unpredictable and must be lexically specified. The distribution of aspiration in Nepali is compared to that of Sanskrit and examined within the typological framework of MacEachern (1999).

## 5 Conclusion

In this brief introduction we have not been able to do full justice to the enormous amount of work that Nick Clements produced on the subject of phonological features (let alone on the many other subjects he worked and wrote on), nor have we documented his influence of phonological theory in general and the work that many others have done and continue to do on phonological features. Nonetheless, we hope that the preceding sections have touched upon some general aspects of his work, especially work that he was engaged in until just before his untimely death. His vast body of published work as well as the work that is collected in this volume will speak for themselves. Nick was always and will continue to be a positive force in phonology.

## References

Anderson, M. John and Charles Jones. 1974. Three theses concerning phonological representations. *Journal of Linguistics* 10: 1–26.

Archangeli, Diana. 1984. *Underspecification in Yawelmani Phonology and Morphology*. PhD Dissertation, MIT.

Blevins, Juliette. 2004. *Evolutionary Phonology: The Emergence of Sound Patterns*. Cambridge: Cambridge University Press.

Browman, P. Catherine and Louis Goldstein. 1986. Towards an articulatory phonology. In C. Ewen and J. Anderson (eds.), *Phonology Yearbook* 3, 219–252. Cambridge: Cambridge University Press.

Carré, René and Mohamed Mrayati. 1990. Articulatory-acoustic-phonetic relations and modeling, regions and modes. In W. J. Hardcastle and A. Marchal (eds.), *Speech production and speech modelling*, 211–240. Dordrecht: Kluwer Academic Publishers.

Chomksy, Noam and Morris Halle. 1968. *The Sound Pattern of English*. New York: Harper and Row.

Clements, G. Nick. 1977. The autosegmental treatment of vowel harmony. In W.U. Dressler and O.E. Pfeiffer (eds.), *Phonologica 1976*, 111–119. Innsbruck: Innsbrucker Beiträge zur Sprachwissenschaft.

Clements, G. Nick. 1980. *Vowel harmony in nonlinear generative phonology: an autosegmental model*. Bloomington: Indiana University Linguistics Club.

Clements, G. Nick. 1985. The problem of transfer in nonlinear morphology. *Cornell Working Papers in Linguistics*: 1–36.

Clements, G. Nick. 1990. The role of the sonority cycle in core syllabification. In M. Beckman and J. Kingston (eds.), *Papers in Laboratory Phonology* 1, 283–333. Cambridge: Cambridge University Press.

Clements, G. Nick. 1992. Phonological Primes: Features or Gestures? *Phonetica* 49: 181–93.

Clements, G. Nick. 1993. Underspecification or nonspecification? In M. Bernstein and A. Kathol (eds.), *ESCOL'93, Proceedings of the Tenth Eastern States Conference on Linguistics*, 58–80. Cornell University, Ithaca, USA.

Clements, G. Nick. 1998. The sonority cycle and syllable organization. In W.U. Dressler, H.C. Luschützky, O. Pfeiffer, and J. Rennison (eds.), *Phonologica*, 63–76. Cambridge University Press, Cambridge.

Clements, G. Nick. 1999. The geometry of phonological features. In J. Goldsmith, (ed.), *Phonological Theory: the Essential Readings*, 201–223. Oxford: Blackwell.

Clements, G. Nick. 2001. Representational economy in constraint-based phonology. In T. Alan Hall (ed.), *Distinctive Feature Theory*, 71–146. Berlin & New York: De Gruyter Mouton.

Clements, G. Nick. 2009. The role of features in phonological inventories. In Eric Raimy and Charles Cairns, (eds.), *Contemporary Views on Architecture and Representations in Phonological Theory*: 19–68. Cambridge, MA: MIT Press.

Clements, G. Nick, Alexis Michaud and Cédric Patin. 2011. Do we need tone features? In J. Goldsmith, E. Hume and L. Wetzels (eds.), *Tones and Features: Phonetic and Phonological Perspectives*, 3–24. Berlin & New York: De Gruyter Mouton.

Clements, G. Nick and Elizabeth Hume. 1995. The Internal Organization of Speech Sounds. In John Goldsmith (ed.), *Handbook of Phonological Theory*, 245–306. Basil Blackwell, Oxford.

Clements G. Nick and Pierre Hallé (eds.). 2010. Phonetic Bases of Distinctive Features. Special issue of *Journal of Phonetics* 38 (1).

Clements, G. Nick and Rachid Ridouane (eds.). 2011. *Where do phonological features come from? Cognitive, physical and developmental bases of distinctive speech categories*. Amsterdam: John Benjamins.

Clements, G. Nick and Samuel J. Keyser. 1983. *CV Phonology: a Generative Theory of the Syllable*. Linguistic Inquiry Monograph. Cambridge, MA: MIT Press.

Fowler, Carol A. 1986. An event approach to the study of speech perception from a direct realist perspective. *Journal of Phonetics* 14: 3–28.

Fromkin, Victoria A. (ed.). 1973. *Speech Errors as Linguistic Evidence*. The Hague: Mouton.

Godsmith, John. 1975. An Autosegmental typology of tone. In Ellen Kaisse (ed.), *Proceedings from the Fifth North Eastern Linguistics Society*, Harvard University.

Hammarberg Robert. 1976. The metaphysics of coarticulation. *Journal of Phonetics* 4: 353–363.

Jakobson, Roman and Morris Halle. 1956. *Fundamentals of language*. The Hague: Mouton.

Jakobson, Roman, Gunnar Fant and Morris Halle. 1952. *Preliminaries to Speech Analysis*. Cambridge, MA: MIT Acoustics Laboratory.

Keyser, S. Jay and Kenneth N. Stevens. 2006. Enhancement and overlap in the speech chain. *Language* 82 (1): 33–63.

Kiparsky, Paul. 1982. From Cyclic Phonology to Lexical Phonology. In Harry van der Hulst and Norval Smith (eds.): 131–175.

Ladefoged, Peter. 1971. *Preliminaries to Linguistic Phonetics*. Chicago: University of Chicago Press.

Liberman Alvin M. and Ignatius G. Mattingly. 1985. The motor theory of speech perception revised. *Cognition* 21: 1–36.

Liljencrants, Johan and Bjorn Lindblom. 1972. Numerical simulation of vowel quality systems: The role of perceptual contrast. *Language* 48: 839–862.

MacEachern, Margaret. 1999. *Laryngeal co-occurrence restrictions*. New York: Garland.

Mielke, Jeff. 2008. *The Emergence of Distinctive Features*. Oxford: Oxford University Press.

Ohala, John. 1996. Speech perception is hearing sounds, not tongues. *Journal of the Acoustical Society of America* 99 (3): 1718–1725.

Osu, Sylvester and George N. Clements. 2009. Les nasales en ikwere. *Corela* 1. Online publication http://corela.edel.univ-poitiers.fr/index.php?id=134 (accessed on February 2014).

Pierrehumbert, Janet. 1990. Phonological and phonetic representation. *Journal of Phonetics* 18: 375–394.

Ridouane, Rachid, George N. Clements and Rajesh Khatiwada. 2011. Language-independent bases of distinctive features. In J. Goldsmith, E. Hume and L. Wetzels (eds.), *Tones and Features: Phonetic and Phonological Perspectives*, 260–287. Berlin & New York: De Gruyter Mouton.

Ringen, Catherine. 1977. *Vowel Harmony: Theoretical Implications*. PhD Dissertation, Indiana University

Sagey, Elizabeth. 1986. *The Representation of Features and Relations in Nonlinear Phonology*. PhD Dissertation, Department of Linguistics, MIT.

Silverman, Daniel. 2006. *A Critical Introduction to Phonology: of Sound, Mind, and Body*. Continuum Critical Introductions to Linguistics. London/New York: Continuum.

Stanley, Richard. 1967. Redundancy rules in phonology. *Language* 43: 393–436.

Stevens, N. Kenneth. 1972. The quantal nature of speech: evidence from articulatory-acoustic data. In E. E. David, Jr. and P. B. Denes (eds.), *Human Communication: a unified view*, 51–66. New York: McGraw-Hill.

Stevens, N. Kenneth. 1989. On the quantal nature of speech. *Journal of Phonetics* 17: 3–45.

Stevens, N. Kenneth. 2003. Acoustic and perceptual evidence for universal phonological features. *Proceedings of the 15th International Congress of Phonetic Sciences*, 33–38. Barcelona, Spain.

Stevens, N. Kenneth and Samuel J. Keyser. 1989. Primary features and their enhancement in consonants. *Language* 65: 81–106.

Stevens, N. Kenneth and Samuel J. Keyser. 2010. Quantal theory, enhancement and overlap. *Journal of Phonetics* 38: 10–19.

Stevens, N. Kenneth, Samuel J. Keyser and Haruko Kawasaki. 1986. Toward a phonetic and phonological theory of redundant features. In J. Perkell and D. Klatt, (eds.), *Symposium on Invariance and Variability of Speech Processes*: 432–469. Hillsdale: Lawrence Erlbaum.

Turner, Ralph Lilley. 1931. *A Comparative and Etymological Dictionary of the Nepali Language*. London: Routledge and Kegan Paul.

van der Hulst, Harry and Norval Smith (eds.). 1982. The structure of phonological representations (Parts I and II). Dordrecht: Foris.

# Appendix

## Publications of George N. Clements

### Books, monographs and edited collections

2011. Clements, G. Nick and Rachid Ridouane (eds.). *Where do Phonological Features Come From? Cognitive, Physical and Developmental Bases of Distinctive Speech Categories.* Amsterdam: John Benjamins.
2010. Clements, G. Nick and Pierre Hallé (eds.). Phonetic bases of distinctive features. Special issue of *Journal of Phonetics* 38 (1).
1984. Clements, G. Nick and John Goldsmith (eds.) *Autosegmental Studies in Bantu Tone.* Berlin & New York: Mouton de Gruyter.
1983. Clements, G. Nick and Samuel J. Keyser. *CV Phonology: a Generative Theory of the Syllable.* Linguistic Inquiry Monograph 9. Cambridge, MA: MIT Press.
1983. Morris Halle and George N. Clements. *Problem Book in Phonology.* Cambridge, MA: MIT Press and Bradford Books. (Spanish translation: Problemas de Fonología. edición española a cargo de A. Alonso Cortés. Minerva Ediciones. Madrid. 1991)
1982. Clements, G. Nick. *Compensatory Lengthening: an Independent Mechanism of Phonological Change.* Bloomington: Indiana University Linguistics Club.
1980. Clements, G. Nick. *Vowel Harmony in Nonlinear Generative Phonology: an Autosegmental Model.* Bloomington: Indiana University Linguistics Club.

### Journal articles

2009. Sylvester Osu and Clements, G. Nick. Les nasales en ikwere. *Corela 7.* Numéro 1. Available online: http://edel.univpoitiers.fr/corela/document.php?id=2110.
2005. Clements, G. Nick and Sylvester Osu. Nasal harmony in Ikwere. a language with no phonemic nasal consonants. *Journal of African Languages and Linguistics* 26 (2): 165–200.
2003. Clements, G. Nick. Feature economy in sound systems. *Phonology* 20 (3): 287–333
2003. Yetunde, Laniran and Clements, G. Nick. Downstep and high tone raising: interacting factors in Yoruba tone production. *Journal of Phonetics* 31 (2): 203–250.
2000. Clements, G. Nick. Phonological monophthongs, phonetic diphthongs: evidence from English. *Les Cahiers de l'ICP. Bulletin de la Communication Parlée* 5: 57–75.
2000. Clements, G. Nick. Some antecedents of nonlinear phonology. *Folia Linguistica* 34 (1–2): 29–55.
2000. Clements, G. Nick. In defense of serialism. *The Linguistic Review* 17 (2–4): 81–97.
1992. Clements, G. Nick. Phonological Primes: Features or Gestures? *Phonetica* 49: 181–193.
1990. Clements, G. Nick and Remi Sonaiya. Underlying feature specification in Yoruba. *Studies in the Linguistic Sciences* 20 (1): 89–103.
1989. Clements, G. Nick. African linguistics and its contributions to linguistic theory. *Studies in the Linguistic Sciences* 19 (2): 3–39
1985. Clements, G. Nick. The geometry of phonological features. *Phonology Yearbook* 2: 225–252.
1984. Clements, G. Nick. Binding domains in Kikuyu. *Studies in the Linguistic Sciences* 14 (2): 37–56.

1984. Clements, G. Nick. Vowel harmony in Akan: a consideration of Stewart's word structure conditions. *Studies in African Linguistics* 15 (3): 321–337.
1983. Clements, G. Nick, J. McCloskey, J. Maling, and A. Zaenen. String-vacuous rule application. *Linguistic Inquiry* 14 (1): 1–17.
1982. Clements, G. Nick. A remark on the Elsewhere Condition. *Linguistic Inquiry* 13 (4): 682–685.
1981. Clements, G. Nick. An outline of Luganda syllable structure. *Studies in African Linguistics*. Supplement 7, 12–16.
1980. Clements, G. Nick. A note on local ordering. *Islenskt mal og almenn malfrae* 2, 15–23.
1980. Clements, G. Nick and John Goldsmith. What is downstep? A reply to Clark. *Studies in African Linguistics* 11 (2): 239–254.
1979. Clements, G. Nick. Review article: A tonal grammar of Etsako (B. Elimelech). *Journal of African Languages and Linguistics* 1 (1): 95–108.
1979. Clements, G. Nick and Kevin C. Ford. Kikuyu tone shift and its synchronic consequences. *Linguistic Inquiry* 10 (2): 179–210.
1979. Clements, G. Nick. The description of terraced-level tone languages. *Language* 55 (3): 536–558.
1975. Clements, G. Nick. The logophoric pronoun in Ewe: its role in discourse. *Journal of West African Languages* 10 (2): 141–177.
1975. Clements, G. Nick. Analogical Reanalysis in Syntax: the Case of Ewe Tree-grafting. *Linguistic Inquiry* 6 (1): 3–51.
1974. Clements, G. Nick. Vowel Harmony in Ewe. *Studies in African Linguistics* 5 (3): 281–301.

## Encyclopaedia chapters

2006. Clements, G. Nick. Feature organization. In Keith Brown (ed.), *The Encyclopedia of Language and Linguistics*, 2ᵉ edition, vol. 4, 433–441. Oxford: Elsevier Limited.
1999. Clements, G. Nick. Phonology. In Robert A. Wilson and Frank C. Keil. (eds.), *MIT Encyclopedia of Cognitive Science*, 634–637. Cambridge, MA: MIT Press.
1994. Clements, G. Nick. Nonlinear Phonology. In R.E. Asher (ed.), *The Encyclopedia of Language and Linguistics* vol. 5, 2824–2832. Oxford & New York: Pergamon Press.
1992. Clements, G. Nick. Autosegmental Phonology. In William Bright. (ed.), *Oxford International Encyclopedia of Linguistics* vol. 1, 146–150. Oxford & New York: Oxford University Press.

## Book chapters

2011. Clements, G. Nick, Alexis Michaud and Cédric Patin. Do we need tone features? In J. Goldsmith. E. Hume, and L. Wetzels (eds.), *Tones and Features: Phonetic and Phonological Perspectives,* 3–24. Berlin & New York: De Gruyter Mouton.
2011. Ridouane Rachid, George N. Clements, and Rajesh Khatiwada. Language-independent bases of distinctive features. In J. Goldsmith, E. Hume and L. Wetzels (eds.), *Tones and Features: Phonetic and Phonological Perspectives,* 260–287. Berlin & New York: De Gruyter Mouton.
2009. Clements, G. Nick, The role of features in speech sound inventories. In Eric Raimy and Charles Cairns (eds.), *Contemporary Views on Architecture and Representations in Phonological Theory*, 19–68. Cambridge, MA: MIT Press.

2009. Clements, G. Nick. Does sonority have a phonetic basis? Comments on the chapter by Vaux. In Eric Raimy and Charles Cairns (eds.), *Contemporary Views on Architecture and Representations in Phonological Theory*, 165–175. Cambridge, MA: MIT Press.
2008. Clements, G. Nick and Annie Rialland. Africa as a phonological area. In Bernd Heine and Derek Nurse (eds.), *A Linguistic Geography of Africa*, 36–85. Cambridge: Cambridge University Press.
2007. Clements, G. Nick. L'Évitement de la marque: une nouvelle approche a l'étude des universaux dans les inventaires phonémiques. In Elisabeth Delais-Roussarie and Laurence Labrune (eds.), *Des sons et des sens: données et modèles en phonologie et en morphologie*, 25–47. Paris & London: Hermès.
2003. Clements, G. Nick and Sylvester Osu. Ikwere nasal harmony in typological. perspective. In Patrick Sauzet and Anne Zribi-Hertz (eds.), *Typologie des langues d'Afrique et universaux de la grammaire*, vol. II, 70–95. Paris: L'Harmattan.
2003. Clements, G. Nick. Les diphtongues brèves en anglais: fonction phonétique du trait tendu/relâché. In Jean-Pierre Angoujard and Sophie Wauquier-Gravelines (eds.), *Phonologie: Champs et Perspectives*, 35–55. Lyon: ENS Editions.
2002. Clements, G. Nick and Sylvester Osu. Explosives. implosives. and nonexplosives: the linguistic function of air pressure differences in stops. In Carlos Gussenhoven and Natasha Warner (eds.), *Laboratory Phonology 7*, 299–350. Berlin & New York: Mouton de Gruyter.
2001. Clements, G. Nick. Representational economy in constraint-based phonology. In T. Alan Hall (ed.), *Distinctive Feature Theory*, 71–146. Berlin & New York: Mouton de Gruyter.
2000. Clements, G. Nick. The geometry of phonological features. In Charles W. Kreidler (ed.), *Phonology: Critical Concepts*, vol. 2, 143–171. London: Routledge. (from The Geometry of Phonological Features. Phonology Yearbook 2. 1985).
2000. Clements, G. Nick. Phonology. In B. Heine and D. Nurse (eds.), *African Languages: an Introduction*, 123–160. Cambridge: Cambridge University Press. [French translation Phonologie. In Bernd Heine and Derek Nurse (eds.), *Les langues africaines*, 149–192. Edition française sous la direction de H. Tourneux. Paris: Karthala. 2004].
1999. Clements, G. Nick. The Geometry of Phonological Features. In J. Goldsmith (ed.), *Phonological Theory: the Essential Readings*, 201–223. Oxford: Blackwell.
1999. Clements, G. Nick and Samuel Jay Keyser. From CV phonology: a generative theory of the syllable. In J. Goldsmith (ed.), *Phonological Theory: the Essential Readings*, 185–200. Oxford: Blackwell.
1997. Clements, G. Nick. Berber Syllabification: Derivations or Constraints? In I. M. Roca (ed.), *Derivations and Constraints in Phonology*, 289–330. Oxford: Oxford University Press.
1996. Clements, G. Nick and Susan R. Hertz. An integrated approach to phonology and phonetics. In J. Durand and B. Laks (eds.), *Current Trends in Phonology*, 143–174. CNRS, Paris-X. & University of Salford: University of Salford Publications.
1995. Clements, G. Nick and Elizabeth Hume. The internal organization of speech sounds. In John Goldsmith (ed.), *Handbook of Phonological Theory*, 245–306. Oxford: Basil Blackwell.
1993. Clements, G. Nick. Un modèle hiérarchique de l'aperture vocalique: le cas bantou. In B. Laks and M. Plénat (eds.), *De natura sonorum*, 23–64. St. Denis: Presses Universitaires de Vincennes.
1993. Clements, G. Nick. Lieu d'articulation des consonnes et de voyelles: une théorie unifée. In B. Laks and A. Rialland (eds.), *L'Architecture des représentations phonologiques*, 101–145. Paris: Editions du CNRS.

1992. Clements, G. Nick. Comments on Chapter 7 [J.J. Ohala: 'The segment: primitive or derived?']. In G. J. Docherty and D. R. Ladd (eds.), *Papers in Laboratory Phonology II: Gesture, Segment, Prosody*, 183–189. Cambridge: Cambridge University Press.

1992. Clements, G. Nick. The sonority cycle and syllable organization. In W. U. Dressler, H. C. Luschützky, O. Pfeiffer and J. Rennison (eds.), *Phonologica 1988*, 63–76. Cambridge: Cambridge University Press.

1991. Clements, G. Nick. Downdrift in a tone language with four tone levels. In J. Kelly (ed.), *A Festschrift for Jack Carnochan, York Papers in Linguistics* 15, 33–40. York: Dept. of Language and Linguistic Science, University of York.

1990. Clements, G. Nick. The Status of Register in Intonation Theory: Comments on the Papers by Ladd and by Inkelas and Leben. In J. Kingston and M. Beckman (eds.), *Papers in Laboratory Phonology I: Between the Grammar and the Physics of Speech*, 58–72. Cambridge: Cambridge University Press.

1990. Clements, G. Nick. The role of the sonority cycle in core syllabification. In M. Beckman and J. Kingston (eds.), *Papers in Laboratory Phonology 1*, 283–333. Cambridge: Cambridge University Press.

1986. Clements, G. Nick. Compensatory lengthening and consonant gemination in Luganda. In L. Wetzels and E. Sezer (eds.), *Studies in Compensatory Lengthening*, 37–77. Dordrecht: Foris Publications.

1986. Clements, G. Nick. Syllabification and epenthesis in the Barra dialect of Gaelic. In K. Bogers, H. van der Hulst and M. Mous (eds.), *The Phonological Representation of Suprasegmentals (Studies Dedicated to J. M. Stewart)*, 317–336. Dordrecht: Foris Publications.

1985. Clements, G. Nick. Akan vowel harmony: a Nonlinear Analysis. In D.L. Goyvaerts. (ed.), *African Linguistics: Essays in Honor of W.M.K. Semikenke*, 55–98. Amsterdam: John Benjamins.

1984. Clements, G. Nick and John Goldsmith. Introduction. In Clements, G. N. and J. Goldsmith (eds.), *Autosegmental Studies in Bantu Tone*, 1–18. Dordrecht: Foris Publications.

1984. Clements, G. Nick. Principles of tone assignment in Kikuyu. In Clements, G. N. and J. Goldsmith (eds.), *Autosegmental Studies in Bantu Tone*, 281–340. Dordrecht: Foris Publications.

1983. Clements, G. Nick. The hierarchical representation of tone features. In I. R. Dihoff (ed.), *Current Approaches to African Linguistics, vol. I*, 145–176. Dordrecht: Foris Publications.

1982. Clements, G. Nick and Engin Sezer. Vowel and consonant disharmony in Turkish. In H. van der Hulst and N. Smith (eds.), *The Structure of Phonological Representations (Part II)*, 213–255. Dordrecht: Foris Publications.

1981. Clements, G. Nick. A hierarchical model of tone. In W.U. Dressler, O.E. Pfeiffer, and J. Rennison (eds.), *Phonologica 1980* (Innsbrucker Beiträge zur Sprachwissenschaft, vol. 36), 69–75. Innsbruck: Institut für Sprachwissenschaft.

1981. Clements, G. Nick and Kevin C. Ford. On the phonological status of downstep in Kikuyu. In D. L. Goyvaerts (ed.), *Phonology in the 1980's*, 309–357. Ghent: Story-Scientia.

1979. Clements, G. Nick. Super-equi and the intervention constraint. In D.J. Napoli and E.N. Rando (eds.), *Syntactic Argumentation*, 301–317. Washington, D.C.: Georgetown University Press.

1978. Clements, G. Nick. Tone and syntax in Ewe. In D. J. Napoli (ed.), *Elements of Tone, Stress, and Intonation*, 21–99. Washington, D.C.: Georgetown University Press.

1977. Clements, G. Nick. Four tones from three: the extra-high tone in Anlo Ewe. In P. F. A. Kotey and H. Der-Houssikian (eds.), *Language and Linguistic Problems in Africa*, 168–191. Columbia, SC: Hornbeam Press.

1977. Clements, G. Nick. The Autosegmental treatment of vowel harmony. In W.U.. Dressler and O.E. Pfeiffer (eds.), *Phonologica 1976* (Innsbrucker Beiträge zur Sprachwissenschaft, vol. 19), 111–119. Innsbruck: Institut für Sprachwissenschaft.

## Conference papers

2008. Rachid Ridouane and G.N.Clements. Bases phonétique du trait [glotte ouvert]: données berbères. *Proceedings of Journées d'Etudes sur la Parole 27* (JEP 27). Avignon.

2007. Clements, G. Nick and Rajesh Khatiwada. Phonetic realization of contrastively aspirated affricates in Nepali. *Proceedings of ICPhS 16*, 629–632. Saarbrücken. Germany.

2006. Clements, G. Nick and Rachid Ridouane. Quantal phonetics and distinctive features: a Review. In Antonis Botinis (ed.), *Proceedings of the ISCA Tutorial and Research Workshop on Experimental Linguistics*, 28–30. Athens: University of Athens

2006. Clements, G. Nick and Rachid Ridouane. Distinctive feature enhancement: a review. In Antonis Botinis (ed.). Proceedings of the ISCA Tutorial and Research Workshop on Experimental Linguistics. 28–30 August 2006. 97–100. Athens: University of Athens.

2003. Clements, G. Nick. Testing feature economy. In María Josep Solé, Daniel Recasens and Joaquín Romero (eds.), *Proceedings of the 15th International Congress of Phonetic Sciences*, 2785–2788. Barcelona: Futurgraphic.

2003. Clements, G. Nick. Feature economy as a phonological universal. In María Josep Solé, Daniel Recasens and Joaquín Romero (eds.), *Proceedings of the 15th International Congress of Phonetic Sciences*, 371–374. Barcelona: Futurgraphic.

2002. Clements, G. Nick and Sylvester Osu. Patterns of nasality and obstruence in Ikwere, an African language with nasal harmony. In Ana Suelly, A. C. Cabral and Aryon D. Rodrigues (eds.), *Línguas Indígenas Brasileiras: Fonologia. Gramática e História*, 41–60 (Atas do 1º Encontro Internacional do Grupo de Trabalho sobre Linguas Indígenas da ANPOLL). Universidade Federal do Pará: Editora Universitaria. Tome 1.

1999. Clements, G. Nick. Affricates as noncontoured stops. In O. Fujimura, B. Joseph and B. Palek (eds.), *Proceedings of LP '98: Item order in language and speech*, 271–299. Prague: The Karolinum Press.

1995. Clements, G. Nick and Yetunde Laniran. A long-distance dependency in Yoruba tone realization. In K. Elenius and P. Branderud (eds.), *Proceedings of the 13th International Congress of Phonetic Sciences*, 734–737. Stockholm.

1995. Clements, G. Nick, Susan R. Hertz, and Bertrand Lauret. A representational basis for modelling English vowel duration. In K. Elenius and P. Branderud (eds.), *Proceedings of the 13th International Congress of Phonetic Sciences*, 46–49. Stockholm.

1995. Clements, G. Nick. Constraint-based approaches to phonology. In K. Elenius and P. Branderud (eds.), *Proceedings of the 13th International Congress of Phonetic Sciences*, 66–73. Stockholm.

1993. Clements, G. Nick. Underspecification or nonspecification? In M. Bernstein and A. Kathol (eds.), *ESCOL '9, Proceedings of the Tenth Eastern States Conference on Linguistics*, 58–80. Ithaca, NY: DMLL Publications, Cornell University.

1991. Clements, G. Nick. Vowel height assimilation in Bantu languages. In K. Hubbard (ed.), *Proceedings of the 17th Annual Meeting of the Berkeley Linguistics Society*, 25–64. Berkeley: University of California.

1991. Clements, G. Nick and Susan R. Hertz. Nonlinear Phonology and Acoustic Interpretation. *Proceedings of the 12th International Congress on Phonetic Sciences*, 364–373. Aix-en-Provence (France).

1988. Clements, G. Nick. Toward a substantive theory of feature specification. *Papers from the 18th Annual Meeting of the North Eastern Linguistic Society* (NELS 18), 79–93.
1987. Clements, G. Nick. Phonological feature representation and the description of intrusive stops. In A. Bosch, B. Need, and E. Schiller (eds.), *Papers from the Parassesion on Autosegmental and Metrical Phonology*. Chicago Linguistic Society. Chicago: University of Chicago.
1977. Clements, G. Nick. Neutral vowels in Hungarian vowel harmony: an autosegmental interpretation. In J. Kegl, D. Nash and A. Zaenen (eds.), *Proceedings of NELS 7*, 49–64.
1977. Clements, G. Nick. Tone as speech melody: a new theory of terracing. In A. Ford, J. Reighard and R. Singh (eds.), *Montreal Working Papers in Linguistics 6*, 49–66.
1976. Clements, G. Nick. Palatalization: Linking or assimilation? In S.S. Mufwene, C.A. Walker and S.B. Steever (eds.), *Chicago Linguistics Society* 12, 96–109.

## Book reviews

2001. Clements, G. Nick. Review of "Le maxi du Bénin et sud-Togo : description. phonologique (F. Gbeto)" and "Les emprunts linguistiques d'origine européene en fon (nouveau kwa. gbe : Bénin) (F. Gbéto)". *The Journal of African Languages and Linguistics* 22 (2): 181–187.
1996. Clements, G. Nick. Review of "The Phonology of Tone: the Representation of Tonal Register" (eds. H. van der Hulst and K. Snider). *Language* 72 (4): 847–852.
1982. Clements, G. Nick. Review of Tone: a Linguistic Survey (ed. V. Fromkin). *Lingua 53*: 334–342.

## Working papers

1996. Clements, G. Nick and Susan R. Hertz. An integrated model of phonetic representation in grammar. In L. Lavoie (ed.), *Working Papers of the Cornell Phonetics Laboratory* 11, 43–116.
1993. Clements, G. Nick. Nonlinear phonology and its antecedents. *Travaux de l'Institut de Phonétique de Paris*, nouvelle série, no. 1, 31–53.
1991. Clements, G. Nick. Place of articulation in consonants and vowels: a unified theory. *Working Papers of the Cornell Phonetics Laboratory* 5, 77–123.
1991. Clements, G. Nick and E. Hume (eds.), *Working Papers of the Cornell Phonetics Laboratory*, no. 5. Ithaca. NY (USA): Department of Modern Languages and Linguistics. Cornell University.
1988. Clements, G. Nick (ed), *Working papers of the Cornell phonetics laboratory*, no. 2. Department of modern languages and linguistics. Ithaca, NY: Cornell University.
1985. Clements, G. Nick. The problem of transfer in nonlinear morphology. *Cornell Working Papers in Linguistics*, 1–36.
1984. Clements, G. Nick. A nonlinear model of tone. *Papers in Ghanaian Linguistics* 4, 28–59.
1981. Clements, G. Nick (ed.). *Harvard studies in phonology* 2. Bloomington: Indiana University Linguistics Club.
1981. Clements, G. Nick and Samuel Jay Keyser. A three-tiered theory of the syllable. *Occasional paper 19*. Center for Cognitive Science, MIT.
1977. Clements, G. Nick (ed.). *Harvard studies in phonology* 1. Cambridge, MA: Department of Linguistics, Harvard University.

Part 2

**Unpublished manuscripts**

George N. Clements
# The hierarchical representation of vowel height

November 1990, Cornell University

## 1 Overview

A major goal of phonological theory is to determine the primitive atomic units, or features, that play a basic role in the mental representation of speech sounds. We will be concerned here with one aspect of this question: how is vowel height formally characterized in phonological representations? More specifically, what features are most appropriate to express the phonological nature of vowel height? And how are these features formally organized in terms of multitiered phonological representations of the sort proposed in the recent development of autosegmental phonology (Goldsmith 1976, Clements 1985a, 1987a, 1989a, Sagey 1986, McCarthy 1986, 1988 and others)?

The basic idea that will be developed here is quite simple. Vowel height – a physical parameter involving the degree of openness, or aperture of the oral cavity during vowel production – is phonologically represented in terms of a single, hierarchically subdivided feature category which, following Milliken (1988), I will term [open]. Rather than analyzing vowel height into several formally distinct features, we claim that vowels are characterized in terms of a single feature category, corresponding to a single physical parameter.

This study offers evidence that the parameter of vowel height is divided into a number of hierarchically embedded *registers*. The primary division partitions the vowel space into two primary registers, higher vs. lower. Languages with just two degrees of vowel height, such as Classical Arabic with its three vowels /i u a/, can be described in terms of these primary registers alone. In languages with three degrees of height, such as Latin with its five vowels /i u e o a/, one of these primary registers is further divided into a higher vs. lower *secondary register*. In languages with more than three degrees of height, further subdivision take place until all degrees of height have been accounted for.

The schema given in (1) below may help the reader in visualizing this conception. This schema, which has the form of a binary branching decision tree, represents vowel height in a system with two primary height registers. The higher primary register is subdivided into two secondary registers, and the lower of these is further subdivided into two tertiary registers. This schema describes a system in which one or more low vowels are opposed to a set of nonlow vowels. Within the nonlow set, a set of high vowels is opposed to a set of nonhigh vowels, and within the latter, a set of higher mid vowels is opposed to a set of lower mid vowels. Thus, the schema describes a four-height system with the vowels /i u e o ɛ ɔ a/:

(1) primary registers:

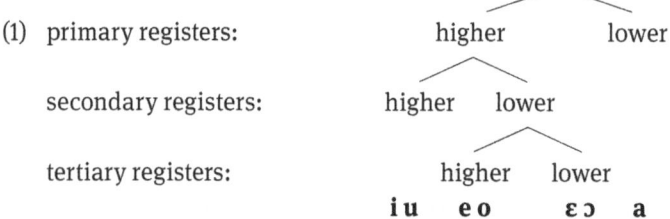

secondary registers:

tertiary registers:

Notice that within the uniform physical dimension of vowel aperture, each "cut" or subdivision is a binary one. This property allows us to analyze vowel aperture in terms of multiple occurrences of the single binary feature [open], in which [−open] corresponds to occurrences of "higher" in the tree and [+open] to occurrences of "lower."

This conception can be formalized in terms of multitiered feature representations in the following way. Occurrences of the binary feature [open] are assigned to tiers which are arrayed in a certain rank order. These ordered tiers will be designated by the names $open_1$, $open_2$, and so forth. Each such tier maps into a register in (1) in the obvious way. Thus $open_1$ corresponds to the primary register, $open_2$ to the secondary register, and so forth. All occurrences of [open] link directly to a single node, termed the Aperture node. We thus have partial tree representations such as the following, in which particular vowel heights are determined by the values assigned to each occurrence of [open]:

(2) Aperture

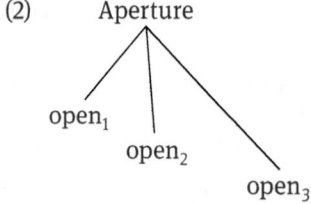

We will elaborate on this conception and provide phonological motivation for it in the later discussion.

This conception of tree geometry departs in a significant way from that given in earlier studies, such as those cited above. Earlier works have generally assumed a principle according to which each feature category is assigned to one and only one tier. This principle, termed the Unitary Feature Tier Hypothesis by Selkirk (1988a), is stated as follows by Goldsmith (1979: 203):

(3)  *Unitary Feature Tier Hypothesis:*
No feature may appear on more than one tier.

The present model allows certain features, such as [open], to appear on more than one tier.

There is some precedent for this move elsewhere in the theory. In certain studies of tone, the feature [high tone] has been assigned to different tiers corresponding to whether it designates tone level or tone register (Clements 1983; Hyman 1986 to appear; Snider 1988; Inkelas 1989; Inkelas and Leben 1990). Such proposals are designed to capture the generalization that the same phonetic dimension, $F_0$, may function in two different ways in tone systems. As we will see below, much of the motivation for such treatments of tone carries over to the study of vowel height. Second, it has been argued in recent work that place of articulation features must be assigned to two separate "planes" or substructures, one corresponding to primary (or consonantal) place of articulation and the other to secondary (or vocalic) place of articulation (Clements 1989a). Under this proposal, for example, [labial] is arrayed on one tier in the representation of consonants (where it is usually implemented as labial constriction) and on another in the representation of vowels (where it is usually implemented as lip rounding). Such a separation of tiers expresses the fact that occurrences of [labial] in consonants may interact freely across vowels in assimilation and dissimilation processes, while occurrences of [labial] in vowels may interact across consonants, regardless of their identity. (See also Selkirk (1988b) for a somewhat different version of this conception). By recognizing separate tiers for vowel and consonant place features, we express such apparently nonlocal effects without proliferating place features, and without violating general conditions of locality. Again, this proposal involves a violation of the Unitary Feature Tier Hypothesis.

Thus there is a certain amount of independent motivation for eliminating (3) as an axiom of the theory. Most importantly, the mode of representation in (2) proves to have a number of desirable empirical consequences, as we will see below.

The conception briefly outlined above will be further developed in the remainder of this study, and applied to a variety of language data. Section 2 reviews previous analyses of vowel height. Section 3 outlines a hierarchical model, and show how it fits into a larger general theory of feature representation and rule application. Sections 4 and 5 give evidence for some of the basic predictions of the theory in the area of assimilatory rules, and explore the phonology of the five-height vowel system of Sotho in some detail. Section 6 applies the theory to the phenomenon of stepwise or scalar diphthongization as found in certain Swedish dialects. Section 7 examines the physical attributes of vowel height and discusses the relation of vowel height to the feature [ATR], and section 8 presents a general summary.

# 2 Previous Analyses of Vowel Height

This section presents a review of earlier proposals for the phonological analysis of vowel height within generative phonology and other contemporary traditions. We will consider three major treatments of vowel height that have been actively discussed in the recent literature: binary feature approaches (section 2.1), multivalued feature approaches (section 2.2), and one-valued feature approaches (section 2.3).

## 2.1 Binary Vowel Height Features

Standard generative phonology proposes that all phonological features are binary at the level of systematic (underlying) phonological representation (SPE = Chomsky and Halle 1968). However, it has proven difficult to find a fully adequate set of binary features for vowel height. The most familiar feature system, that of SPE, proposes two vowel height features [high], [low], which combine to define three heights as follows:

(4)
|  | i,u | e,o | a |
|---|---|---|---|
| high: | + | – | – |
| low: | – | – | + |

But these features have an anomalous status in the SPE feature system, for a number of reasons.

First, these features require a universal constraint ruling out the logically possible, but physiologically impossible combination *[+high,+low]. In contrast, most other SPE features are freely combinable. It is often taken as a desideratum of feature theory that all logically possible feature combinations should be empirically realizable (see e.g. Hulst (1989)).

Second, while other features are defined in terms of distinct articulatory and acoustic correlates, the features [high] and [low] are defined in terms of the same articulatory parameter (often described as the height of the tongue body) and the same acoustic parameter (first formant frequency). Thus the three vowel heights they define represent steps along a uniform physical scale, rather than independent articulatory categories with distinct acoustic values.

Third, the two features [high], [low] are by themselves insufficient to define vowel systems employing more than three vowel heights, such as French or many West African languages with the phonemic vowels /i e ɛ a ɔ o u/ among others. Some treatments of these languages have assigned the same height to the vowels /ɛ ɔ a/, treating them all as [+low] at the phonological level (see e.g. Schane 1968 for French, and Oyelaran 1970 for Yoruba). While this approach is appropriate for languages in which /a/ functions phonologically as if it belonged to the same height as /ɛ ɔ/ (see discussion of Gbe below), in other languages /a/ behaves differently from /ɛ ɔ/ in regard to height-related rules (see discussion of Bantu below). Furthermore, this analysis does not account for languages with minimal contrasts between lower mid vowels and low vowels, such as /ɛ æ / or /ʌ a/ (see Maddieson 1984 for examples). Thus, it appears that we need some means to distinguish more than three vowel heights.

In response to this problem, some phonologists have used the SPE feature [tense] to account for additional tongue heights, using it for example to distinguish the higher and lower mid vowels of French (Plénat 1987). However, in their discussion of this feature Chomsky and Halle state that [tense] does not designate differences in vowel height properly speaking, but rather differences in muscular tension, amplitude, length, and displacement of the articulators from the neutral vocal tract configuration. They say (SPE: 68–69):

> Phonetically the difference between tense and lax sounds can best be characterized as a difference in the manner in which the articulatory gesture is executed. A tense sound is executed deliberately so that the articulating organs actually attain their various target configurations; in producing a lax sound, on the other hand, the gesture is executed rapidly and with reduced amplitude. Tense vowels are, therefore, distinguished from the corresponding lax vowels by being more intense, of longer duration, and articulated with a greater deviation of the vocal cavity from its neutral (rest) position.

With Sievers, they warn against confusing the tense/lax distinction with vowel height distinctions (pp. 324–325). The claim inherent in the SPE feature system, then, is that there can be at most three "pure" vowel heights in a language, and that if we examine systems with four or more vowel heights more closely, we will find that some of the apparent height distinctions can be more accurately attributed to differences in muscular tension, duration, and so forth.[1]

---

[1] A somewhat different account of [tense] is proposed by Wood (1975), who regards its primary correlate as a relatively narrow constriction at the place of maximal constriction. See discussion in note 2 below.

Implicit in most modern approaches to feature theory is the view that different features map into specific, distinct correlates that are defined uniformly for all languages. For purposes of further reference, I will call this constraint the Phonetic Distinctness Criterion, and state it in two parts:

(5) *The Phonetic Distinctness Criterion:*
   a. Each feature is defined in a uniform way across languages.
   b. No two features are defined in terms of identical acoustic or articulatory correlates.

(5a) precludes the possibility that a given feature could be defined in arbitrarily different ways in different languages. (5b) precludes the possibility that two features could have the same acoustic or articulatory definition (although it does not exclude the possibility that two features could have overlapping definitions, i.e. that they could have partly similar and partly different correlates). (5) places an important constraint on the descriptive power of phonological theory, as it greatly reduces the class of phonological descriptions that can be assigned to any given phonetic sequence.

If we accept this criterion, however, it is clear that the feature [tense] cannot be used to supplement [high] and [low] in all languages with four vowel heights. In many Romance and African languages, the vowels /i e ɛ/ and /u o ɔ/ form phonetically parallel series, involving similar, progressive distinctions in first formant frequency and tongue body position. Representative x-ray tracings for the vowels of French and the West African language Ngwe at mid-point in their production are given in Figure 1 below, after Brichler-Labaeye (1970) and Ladefoged (1968). (Note that Ngwe has minimal contrasts between /ɛ æ/ and /ɒ a/, precluding the use of [+low] for the lower mid vowels.)

It will be seen that in both languages, the articulatory difference between /i e/ is similar to the difference between /e ɛ /, and the same is true of the difference between /u o/ and /o ɔ/, at least as far as their steady state position is concerned. There is no articulatory discontinuity between any two vowel heights: vowels are produced along a uniform scale in which successively lower vowels have a lower tongue body position and a narrower pharyngeal cavity.[2] Similarly, the acoustic correlates of [high] and [tense] in French and many other four-height languages are identical, involving first formant ($F_1$) frequency alone. It should

---

[2] These data are equally problematical if we accept the account of [tense] given by Wood (1975) (see note 1). The cross-sectional area of the vocal tract at the place of maximal constriction in front vowels is successively more open as we proceed from higher to lower vowels, while it is very similar for all back vowels.

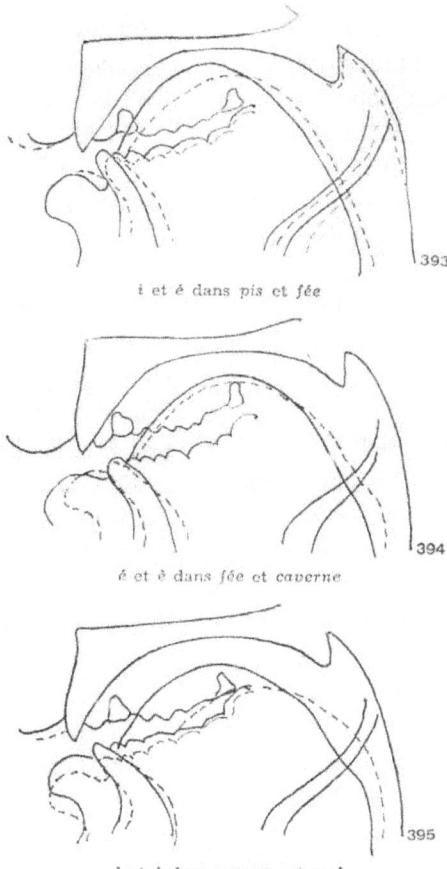

**Figure 1a.** Superimposed X-ray tracings of the French vowels [i] and [e] (top figure), [e] and [ɛ] (middle figure), and [ɛ] and [a] (bottom figure. After Brichler-Labaeye (1970: 250).

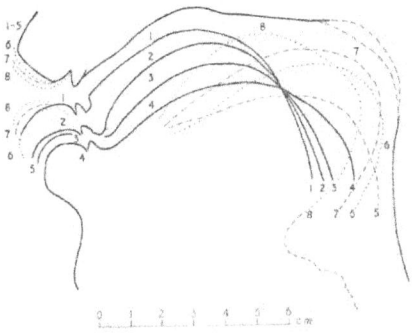

**Figure 1b.** Superimposed X-ray tracings of eight Ngwe vowels. Key: 1 = [i], 2 = [e], 3 = [ɛ], 4 = [æ], 5 = [ɑ], 6 = [ɔ], 7 = [o], 8 = [u]. After Ladefoged (1968: 34).

be pointed out that in more recent work, the feature [tense] has fallen into disfavor, since many of the oppositions it was proposed to deal with, e.g. in the English vowel system, appear to be better treated in terms of underlying length (Anderson and Jones 1977, Halle and Mohanan 1985).

Another feature which has been used to account for supplementary vowel heights is advanced tongue root (ATR), also known as Expanded Pharynx (Lindau 1979). This feature was first proposed to account for vowel harmony in certain African languages such as Akan and Igbo, in which vowels of the two harmonic series are primarily distinguished by the relatively advanced vs. relatively retracted position of the tongue root (Stewart 1967, Ladefoged 1968). It was subsequently quite widely extended to languages having more than three tongue heights (see e.g. Perkell 1971). However, this extended use of [ATR] often leads to violations of the Phonetic Distinctness Criterion (5), since in many languages with four vowel heights, tongue root position covaries with tongue height in approximately equal steps, and the only consistent acoustic correlate of [ATR], like that of [high], is $F_1$ frequency (Lindau 1979). For these and similar reasons, Hyman has recently suggested that [ATR] might be understood as a "cover feature possibly involving different gestures in different languages (height, quality, pharyngealization, centralizing, flattening, etc.)" (Hyman 1988: 266). However, that such a proposal would force us to exempt "cover features" (however they are to be defined as a class) from the Phonetic Distinctness Criterion (5). In the following discussion we will outline an alternative which allows us to maintain the Phonetic Distinctness Criterion for all features, including those responsible for vowel height. We return to an examination of the status of [ATR] in section 7.2.

## 2.2 Multivalued Vowel Height Features

Problems such as these have led to a number of alternative proposals for treating vowel height. In one view, vowel height is regarded as a multivalued feature with up to four (or eventually more) values. This view has an antecedent in the work of Trubetzkoy (1939), who proposed that vowels can be distinguished along the three dimensions of localization, degree of aperture, and resonance. In Trubetzkoy's view, vowel aperture forms a system of *gradual oppositions* whose terms are characterized by different degrees of the same property, in this case vowel height. Similarly, in current treatments of vowel height as a multivalued feature, each vowel is characterized by a value of the feature [high]: in a four-height system, for instance, high vowels can be assigned the value [4 high], upper mid vowels [3 high], lower mid vowels [2 high], and low vowels [1 high] (see, for example, Ladefoged 1971, Lindau 1978).

This approach addresses most of the problems discussed above in a straightforward fashion. First, it eliminates the need to stipulate that [+high] and [+low] do not combine, since high and low tongue position are separate points along a single scale. Second, it expresses the fact that tongue height forms a uniform articulatory and acoustic parameter, since again, only one feature with a uniform physical definition is involved. Third, it allows the description of systems with four or more vowel heights without artifice, since [high] can have as many values as there are distinct vowel heights in a language.

In addition, multivalued approaches allow a direct expression of rules that have the effect of moving vowels up or down one degree on the height scale. Thus, for example, in the three-height system of a variety of Gbe (to be discussed in more detail in section 5.1), mid stem vowels become high and low stem vowels become mid before the suffix vowel /-i/, as shown below; as a concomitant effect, unrounded vowels are fronted:[3]

(6) a. Gbe vowels:  
    3 high:     i        u  
    2 high:     e    ə    o  
    1 high:     ɛ    a    ɔ  

b. Stem Vowel Raising: before [i],  
    e ⟶ i     ə ⟶ i     o ⟶ u  
               a ⟶ e     ɔ ⟶ o

High stem vowels /i u/ are unaffected. Stated more simply, the rule makes vowels one degree higher before higher vowels[4]. This rule can be stated in a multivalued feature framework as follows:

(7)    V    ⟶    [n+1 high]  /  __   + V      (m > n)  
      [n high]                       [m high]

In standard feature theory, on the other hand, this rule must be expressed in terms of paired variables, as follows:

(8)       V                                    V  
     [−high, αlow]    ⟶    [−low, −αhigh]  /  __   + [+high]

This rule is observationally adequate, but unsatisfactory for theoretical reasons similar to those pointed out by Chomsky and Halle in SPE, Chapter 9. The

---

[3] The vowel /ɛ/ does not occur in the variety of Gbe under discussion, although it occurs in other Gbe dialects; see further discussion below.

[4] No mid vowels occur as suffix vowels, except for a marginal case to be discussed below; thus we find no examples with a low stem vowel followed by a mid suffix vowel.

problem with paired variables is that widely recurring pairings such as that of [high] and [low] in (8) are not distinguishable from rare or nonoccurring ones. For instance, they allow us to formulate rules such as the following, which is formally just as simple as the rule in (8):

(9)         V                                                   V
    [–high, αback]  ⟶  [–back, –αhigh]  /  ___ + [+high]

By this rule, nonhigh vowels become front and front vowels become high before high vowels. Applying to the vowel system in (6), it would map /ə o/ into /e/, /a ɔ/ into /ɛ/, and /e ɛ/ into /i/. But rules like this, and many others that can be devised by similar substitutions into (8), seem unattested. Only the features [high] and [low] seem to require the use of paired variables. These observations suggest that vowel height is not adequately characterized in standard feature theory.

In spite of these apparent advantages, most phonologists have been reluctant to adopt the proposal that vowel height is a multivalued feature. For one thing, it is not evident that other features require more than two values. Trubetzkoy himself regarded gradual oppositions as a "relatively rare" type, best exemplified by vowel aperture and "musical height" (tone), and crucial phonological evidence for multivalued oppositions realized along a single articulatory/acoustic parameter has been very difficult to motivate convincingly outside vowel height and tone[5]. For instance, while Ladefoged and Maddieson (1990) argue for a ternary analysis of the front/back dimension on the basis of evidence that languages may have minimal oppositions between front, central and back vowels, these oppositions can be plausibly analyzed in terms of the place features [coronal] and [dorsal], and other proposals for multivalued features seem equally susceptible to reanalysis in terms of the unified theory of consonant and vowel features proposed in Clements (1989a). Thus a multivalued feature [high] appears to represent an anomaly within the context of otherwise binary feature systems.

More importantly, this system does a less adequate job than the binary system of capturing natural classes and natural rule types. Thus, multivalued feature theory treats each value of the feature [high] as equally simple, and thus equally likely to figure in phonological rules. However, we rarely if ever find rules such as V ⟶ [2 high] / ___ [2 high], for example, which if applying in a system such as that of Gbe (cf. (6a)) would map both high and low vowels into mid vowels as shown in (10):[6]

---

[5] Tone itself is analyzed as a binary hierarchical feature in Clements (1983).
[6] The same objection can be made to a proposal by Wang (1968) to replace [low] with [mid].

(10) V ⟶ [2 high] / __ [2 high]:
     i, ɛ  ⟶  e
     u, ɔ  ⟶  o
     a     ⟶  ə

The rarity of such a rule is not explained under a multivalued feature system, which predicts that it should be as common as a rule which spread [1 high] or [3 high]. Its rarity is explainable in binary feature theories, however, by the fact that spreading rules normally spread single features such as [+high] or [−high]; the rule required to express the process illustrated in (10) would have to spread the two features [−high −low].

A further problem, pointed out by Hayes (1988), is that the treatment of vowel height as a multivalued feature raises difficulties for the expression of rules of partial height assimilation, such as those causing low vowels to become mid before high vowels. It has usually been assumed that such rules can be formulated as follows:

(11) [3 high] ⟶ [2 high] / __ [1 high]    (a ⟶ e / __ i, a ⟶ o / __ u)

Such rules can be easily expressed in traditional representational frameworks. However, in autosegmental theories of feature representation, such as the one assumed here, they can no longer be easily described, since spreading of the multivalued feature [1 high] necessarily results in *total* assimilation:

(12)    V     V           (a ⟶ i / __ i, a ⟶ u / __ u)
        ╪╲╲╲╲│
     [3 high] [1 high]

Exactly the same problem arises in the autosegmental formulation of the rule in (7). There appears to be no way to express partial height assimilation without the introduction of otherwise unmotivated rules or conventions. To put it another way, the formalism strongly predicts that all height assimilations should be *total* assimilations. Thus there seems to be no principled way of integrating multivalued vowel height theory within autosegmental phonology.[7]

---

[7] See Durand (1990: 81–88) for further discussion and critique of multivalued features.

## 2.3 One-valued Vowel Height Features

A second alternative to binary treatments of vowel height is exemplified in the theory of one-valued features or *particles* developed by Sanford Schane in various publications (Schane 1984a, 1984b, 1987). In this theory, vowels are viewed as consisting of combinations of the elementary particles *a, i, u*, designating the parameters of openness, palatality, and labiality, respectively.[8] Following Schane (1987), I give particle representations for some representative vowels below:

(13)
| vowels:    | a | i | e | ɛ | æ | u | o | ɔ | y | ø | œ |
|------------|---|---|---|---|---|---|---|---|---|---|---|
| particles: | a | i | i | i | i | u | u | u | i | i | i |
|            |   |   | a | a | a |   | a | a | u | u | u |
|            |   |   |   | a | a |   |   | a |   | a | a |
|            |   |   |   |   | a |   |   |   |   |   | a |

As (13) shows, all nonhigh vowels contain the particle *a*, all front vowels contain *i*, and all rounded vowels contain *u*. The "simple" vowels [a, i, u] are represented by the single particles *a, i, u*, respectively. More complex vowels are characterized as various combinations of these: front rounded vowels contain both *i* and *u*, higher mid vowels have one occurrence of *a*, and lower mid vowels have two occurrences of *a*. In general, the more complex the vowel, the greater the number of particles required to characterize it. In this system, vowel height can acquire a potentially unbounded number of grades, due to the ability of the particle *a* to occur a potentially infinite number of times in the representation of a vowel.

Like the multivalued feature theory, such "one-valued" feature systems have apparent advantages over binary ones. First, all particles are compatible with each other: each can combine with the others, and thus no stipulated feature cooccurrence restrictions are required such as the one required to exclude [+high,+low]. Second, since only one feature, the particle *a*, is proposed for the dimension of vowel height, we account in a straightforward way for the fact that vowel height constitutes a uniform articulatory and acoustic dimension. Third,

---

**8** Related theories of vowel features making use of *a, u, i* (also termed *components* or *elements*), but differing in the syntax by which these features combine, have been proposed by Anderson and Jones (1977), Rennison (1984), Kaye, Lowenstamm, and Vergnaud (1985), and Anderson and Ewen (1987), among others. I will discuss only Schane's theory here, since only this version allows us to account for diphthongization rules of the Swedish type (to be discussed below) in a straightforward way (Schane 1984b: 137, 142). However, most of the following discussion applies to other one-valued feature theories as well.

systems with four or more vowel heights are easily accounted for by allowing the particle *a* to "stack" in a potentially unbounded manner.

A particularly interesting argument in favor of this type of system has been has been based on facts of vowel fusion. The particle analysis of fusion is summarized by Schane (1984a, 40) as follows: "the common change whereby [ai] monophthongizes to [e] and [au] to [o] I call...fusion, because the separately occurring particles...fuse or combine into a single complex particle...The very notion of fusion implies that a resulting complex particle contains all and only the particles of the input." Thus the fusion of [a] and [i] combines the particles characterizing each, giving a composite vowel whose representation is simply the union of the representations of the source vowels:

(14) vowels: a + i → e
 particle representation: a i a, i

No special conventions or redundancy rules are needed. See Schane (1987) for a further study of Sanskrit vowel fusion in this framework. We return to a discussion of fusion and its relevance for feature analysis in section 3.3.

In spite of these apparent advantages, one-valued feature systems have certain drawbacks as well. First, there is a technical problem that has not been satisfactorily resolved, and which seems to reflect a more fundamental problem in the theory. In the four-height system presented in (13), [æ] and [a] have quite different feature characterizations, and it is not apparent that [æ] is simply the front counterpart to [a]. Moreover, the notation suggests that [æ] and [ɛ] are lower than [a], since they are characterized by more occurrences of the particle *a*.

This problem could be addressed by assigning [a] three occurrences of *a*. As a general principle, [a] would have to be assigned a number of *a*-particles equal to the number of vowel heights in a given language minus 1, as shown below:

(15) a. two-height system:    particle representation:
  i   u      i    u
   a        a
 b. three-height system:
  i   u      i    u
  e   o     ia   ua
   a        aa
 c. four-height system:
  i   u      i    u
  e   o     ia   ua
  ɛ   ø     iaa  uaa
   a        aaa

However, this solution has other drawbacks. First, it leads to the view that while [i] and [u] can be given uniform representations across languages, the representation of [a] systematically varies according to the number of vowel heights. In standard theories, of course, [a] always has the uniform representation [–high, +low]. Second, it forces us to abandon one of the central claims of particle theory, that the markedness of a vowel varies in proportion to the number of particles required to characterize it. Schane offers this claim as one of the principle advantages of particle theory:

> Particle notation automatically contains within itself a built-in 'markedness' metric: number of particles determines degree of complexity. Thus, [a], [i], and [u], with one particle each, are the least marked vowels...Particle notation provides a direct mirroring of degree of markedness. A more marked segment visually has more components than a less marked one. (Schane 1984b: 143)

Thus if we assigned three occurrences of *a* to the vowel [a] in a system like (14c), we would implicitly claim that it is a highly marked vowel.[9] But this seems incorrect: [a] is usually considered the least marked vowel across languages, regardless of the number of vowel heights, on the basis of its frequency, optimal sonority properties, ease of acquisition, and similar criteria.

A further problem with one-valued feature systems based on the particles *i, u, a* is that they do not characterize all natural classes of vowels needed to express phonological generalizations. Specifically, while feature characterizations like those in (13) characterize the classes of nonhigh vowels, rounded vowels, and front vowels, they provide no straightforward way of capturing the classes of high vowels, low vowels, back vowels, mid vowels, and unrounded vowels. One might suppose that this problem could be solved by allowing specific reference to absent values. Thus, the class of high vowels could be defined as the class of all vowels *not* characterized by the particle *a*, the class of back vowels as those not characterized by *i*, and so forth.[10]

But such a proposal would not solve the full range of problems. First, it provides no way of referring to the low vowels /a æ/ as a natural class in systems like (13). Second, it still provides us with no way of accounting for "opaque" occurrences of high, back, or unrounded vowels which block rules of harmony or

---

**9** This, in fact, is Schane's own solution. He proposes a "law of maximum aperture" according to which [a] must have at least as many particles as the lowest tonality vowels (Schane 1984a: 139). This proposal, in conjunction with the markedness claims cited above, predicts that the markedness of [a] in a vowel system increases in proportion to the number of degrees of vowel height it contains, a surprising claim not elsewhere justified or discussed by Schane.
**10** See Durand (1990: 289–290) for a proposal to extend the notation in this direction.

assimilation; this behavior can be explained by prelinking the features [+high], [+back], etc. in question to the opaque segment (see e.g. Clements and Sezer 1982 for an analysis of Turkish along these lines). Third, it does not allow us to express a well-attested class of "polarity" rules in which the feature [high] or [low] switches values. One familiar example is the Perfective/Imperfective Stem Ablaut rule of Classical Arabic (SPE 356, McCarthy 1981) and modern Arabic vernaculars (Herzallah 1990). Another is found in Spanish where a low thematic vowel is replaced by a nonlow vowel in the subjunctive (*canta* 'he sings' (indic.), *cante* (subj.)) and a nonlow thematic vowel is replaced by a low vowel in the subjunctive (*come* 'he eats' (indic.), *coma* (subj.)). A third occurs in a variety of Gta, a South Munda language spoken in Orissa state, India. In this language, echo-words are formed from univocalic vowel roots as follows (Mahapatra 1976: 829):

(16) a. /o, u, i, e/ — /a/

  por ⟶ paṭ 'to burn'
  pūk ⟶ pāk 'to blow'
  cir ⟶ car 'to split'
  beṭ ⟶ baṭ 'to meet'

 b. /a/ — /u/

  baj ⟶ buj 'to fry'

What is common to these changes is that the value of [low] is reversed. In all these cases, we find rules which involve a relation between [αlow] in one term and [−αlow] in another, requiring both values to be specified.

Fourth, from a theoretical point of view, giving rules the power to refer to absent values allows them to refer to non-natural classes (Clements 1987b). Thus, for example, a rule referring to the class of segments *not* characterized by the particle *i* refers to a nonnatural class, since it refers to all segments except for front vowels and palatalized consonants; it is unlikely that any rule crucially refers to this set of segments in any language.[11]

A particularly difficult problem for particle theory concerns the treatment of assimilation. On the view that assimilation is universally characterized as autosegmental spreading, it does not allow us to account for the fact that feature

---

**11** Furthermore, in theories not containing the Redundancy Rule Ordering Constraint of Archangeli and Pulleyblank 1986, such a rule would also be able to refer to all segments whose specification for *i* happens to be redundant, and thus unspecified, at the point at which the rule applies. This constraint is stated by Archangeli and Pulleyblank as follows:

A default or complement [or redundancy – GNC] rule assigning [aF], where "a" is "+" or "−", is automatically assigned to the first component in which reference is made to [aF].

values other than those expressible as particles, e.g. high and back, may function as assimilatory triggers. Of particular importance to the present study, the theory has no way of expressing the fact that lower vowels commonly assimilate to higher vowels. Many examples of assimilatory vowel raising are given in this study, but it would be appropriate to examine a further case here. In the Northern Salentino dialect of Italian as described by Calabrese (1987), in certain morphological categories such as the plural and masculine higher mid vowels become high (17a) and lower mid vowels are diphthongized (17b) before syllables containing high vowels:[12]

(17) a. higher mid vowels:
| | | | | |
|---|---|---|---|---|
| 'wall' | pareti | SG | pariti | PL |
| 'month' | mesi | SG | misi | PL |
| 'season' | stasoni | SG | stasuni | PL |
| 'hairy' | pilosa | F | pilusu | M |

b. lower mid vowels:
| | | | | |
|---|---|---|---|---|
| 'foot' | pɛti | SG | piɛti | PL |
| 'strong' | fɔrti | SG | fuɛrti | PL |
| 'good' | bɔna | F | buɛnu | M |
| 'slow' | lɛnta | F | liɛntu | M |

Calabrese argues that these alternations result from a rule spreading [+high] onto stressed mid vowels; if the result is a [+high] lax vowel, as in the forms in (17b), a further rule applies spelling it out as a diphthong. Particle theory has no natural way of expressing this rule. Since there is no particle corresponding to [+high], no particle is available for spreading, or for triggering the subsequent spell-out rule. In sum, although feature systems based on the elementary particles *a*, *i*, *u* vary in their specifics from one writer to another, they all share the property of making it difficult or impossible to capture at least some natural classes of vowels and some natural rule types, including assimilatory vowel raising.

Perhaps the major difficulty with systems of this type, however, is that they have not so far been successfully integrated into a viable general conception of feature theory. Most proponents of such systems have attempted to develop a more comprehensive view of features in which one-valued "particles" replace standard binary features across the board; see especially Anderson and Ewen (1987), which is the most comprehensive presentation of one-valued feature theory up to now. But such systems have not so far been put to the test of accounting for a

---

12 All forms have penultimate stress.

wide range of complex phonological phenomena, including those involving relations between consonants and vowels. A theory that proposes one set of features (or particles) for vowels (such as *i u a*) and another set for consonants will have serious difficulties in accounting for natural classes of consonants and vowels and in describing their mutual relations correctly.[13]

The approach I will take to vowel height will draw upon some of the basic insights of all the theories discussed above. It will retain the view that all features are binary, allowing us to capture natural classes, to express the fact that both values of features can spread, and to state rules of partial assimilation, etc. However, it will allow vowel height to be treated as one of a class of hierarchical features, corresponding to Trubetzkoy's "gradual oppositions." Like the nonbinary feature systems discussed above, it will express the generalization that vowel height forms a uniform articulatory and acoustic parameter with a potentially unbounded number of values. This insight seems basically correct, and forms a criterion against which any theory of vowel height must be evaluated.

# 3 The Hierarchical Representation of Vowel Height

In the preceding discussion we have argued that from a physical-phonetic point of view, vowel height forms a uniform articulatory and acoustic parameter with a potentially unbounded number of values. It is a striking fact that just these properties characterize tone, a phonological feature interpreted in terms of the uniform acoustic dimension of fundamental frequency ($F_0$).[14] As noted above, Trubetzkoy regarded vowel height and tone (which he termed "musical height" or "register") to constitute the most common types of multivalued or "gradual" oppositions. In section 3.1 we consider the parallel between vowel height and tone more closely. In section 3.2 we develop a formal analysis of vowel height in hierarchical terms.

## 3.1 The Hierarchical Representation of Tone

Tone, like vowel height, raises problems for a traditional (nonhierarchical) binary analysis. Given the fact that tone forms a uniform acoustic dimension and that tone languages can show three or more lexically contrastive level tones,

---

[13] See Clements (1989a) for further discussion. Smith (in press) offers suggestions on how the one-valued features *a, i, u* might be generalized to consonants.
[14] The articulatory basis of tone production in most tone languages is still poorly understood.

tone contrasts cannot be captured by two binary features without violating the Phonetic Distinctness Criterion (5).[15] Indeed, tone systems may show not only three, but four and even five phonologically distinct tone levels (for languages with 5 and more levels, see e.g. Bearth and Zemp 1967, Weidert 1981).

For these and other reasons, tone has been treated as a *hierarchical* feature which, in its lexical function, organizes the acoustic dimension of $F_0$ into a hierarchically organized series of registers and subregisters (see Clements 1983, Hyman 1986 and others). In this view, simple tone systems with two tone levels divide the total range into two primary registers, higher and lower, while more complex systems with three or more tone levels create further subregisters in the way suggested in (1) above for vowel height.

Such a model accounts directly for the facts noted above. As only one feature is involved, we account for the fact that tone maps into a uniform acoustic dimension without violating the Phonetic Distinctness Criterion. Since there is no upper bound on the number of hierarchical subdivisions that a language may have, tone registers can be successively subdivided to the extent required in any language. The upper bound on such subdivision is not set by the formalism, but is determined by the limits on the human ability to perceive tone distinctions under normal conditions of speech; in this view, the fact that tone systems seldom if ever distinguish among more than five tone levels is a fact about constraints on speech perception, rather than about feature theory as such.[16]

Further evidence for a hierarchical view of tone comes from the fact that tone rules sometimes require reference to the notions "higher than" and "lower than" in a way that cannot be naturally expressed in terms of binary features like [upper] and [high tone]. For example, in the Yala dialect of Ikom with the three tone levels L (low), M (mid), and H (high), downstep is inserted between two tones just in case the first is lower than the second (Armstrong 1968). Thus, downstep is inserted in the tone sequences LM, LH, and MH, and no others. This rule can be easily expressed within a hierarchical system of tone representation if we assume the tonal representations given in (18a), where *h* designates relatively a high tone and *l* designates a relatively low tone (the characterization of H tone on register$_2$ is nondistinctive and is therefore not specified):

---

**15** Thus the model proposed by Yip (1980b), which also treats tone hierarchically, distinguishes between a register feature [upper] and a formally distinct tone level feature [high tone] both mapping into a single acoustic dimension, $F_0$.

**16** Similarly in formal syntax, the fact that human languages show an aversion to multiple center-embedding is usually attributed to the theory of speech processing rather than to constraints on formal grammar as such.

(18) a.

|  | L | M | H |
|---|---|---|---|
| register₁: | l | l | h |
| register₂: | l | h |  |

b.

| L | M | | L | H | | M | H |
|---|---|---|---|---|---|---|---|
| l | l | | l | h | | l | h |
| l | h | | l |  | | h |  |

The downstep rule can be stated: insert downstep between any two tones characterized by the sequence [l h] on any tier. This sequence occurs just in the tone sequences LM, LH, and MH, as we see in (18b). This formalism directly expresses the generalization "lower tones downstep higher tones."[17]

The evidence given above might also appear to support a multivalued characterization of tone height, but further evidence suggests that only the hierarchical, binary account is correct. In a number of languages, we find that nonadjacent tone levels group into natural classes. Evidence from Chinese is given by Yip (1980b), and evidence can be cited from African languages as well. Thus in the Anlo [àŋlɔ̀] dialect of Ewe, a Gbe language, if we name the tones A, B, C, D from highest to lowest, we find that the alternating pairs are {A,B}, {C,D}, and {A,C}, as shown by the operation of highly productive tone rules. These alternations can be directly accounted for if we characterize the four tones as follows:

(19)

|  | A | B | C | D |
|---|---|---|---|---|
| register₁: | h | h | l | l |
| register₂: | h | l | h | l |

This analysis assigns tones to four pairs sharing at least one tone feature on one row: {A,B}, {C,D}, {A,C}, and {B,D}. As mentioned, three of these pairs are related by alternations, including the nonadjacent pair {A, C}. The pairs that share no tone feature within a register, namely {B,C} and {A,D}, do not alternate.[18]

---

[17] In some languages, what at first appears to be downstep can sometimes be better characterized as automatic time-dependent declination, independent of the particular nature of the tonal string (Pierrehumbert 1980). This analysis is not available for Yala Ikom, in which (temporally unrealized) floating tones trigger the downstep rule just as do linked tones. See Armstrong (1968) for further discussion.

[18] See Yip (1980b), Clements (1983) for further examples of nonadjacent tone height assimilations in four-height systems, and Hyman (1986) for discussion of apparent {BC} assimilations, which he reanalyzes in terms of floating tones and underspecification.

## 3.2 A Hierarchical Model of Vowel Height

Let us now explore the consequences of assuming that vowel height, like tone, is hierarchical in nature. Section 3.2.1 presents the notion of vowel height register. Section 3.2.2 considers the status of vowel height in multitiered phonological representations, and section 3.2.3 discusses the formalization of height-related rules.

### 3.2.1 Vowel Height Registers

In the hierarchical model, a single binary-valued feature of relative vowel height, termed [open], divides all the vowels of a given language into two primary registers, a higher register and a lower one. If no further subdivision takes place, this basic division creates a two-height system such as /ɨ a/ or /i u a/. If further subdivision takes place, a system with three vowel heights is created such as /i u e o a/. Additional subdivisions will create systems with four or more vowel heights, as shown in the tree in (20).

(20) open:

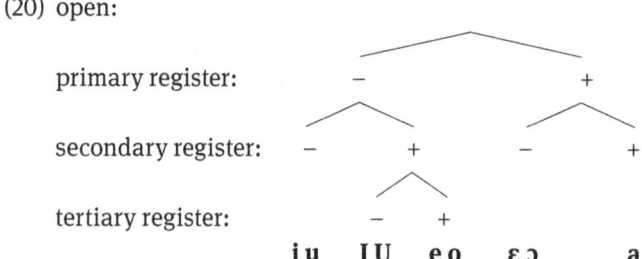

primary register:

secondary register:

tertiary register:

           i u   I U   e o   ɛ ɔ     a

Such representations characterize some vowels as being more closely related than others. For example, vowels that belong to the same primary register are more closely related than vowels that belong to different primary registers, vowels that belong to the same primary and secondary registers are more closely related than vowels that do not, and so forth. Thus [I U] and [e o] in (20), which belong to the same primary and secondary registers, are more closely related than [**I U**] and [i u], which share only the primary register.

A basic claim of representations like (20) is that the more closely two vowels are related in the hierarchy, the more closely they are related phonologically. Phonological relatedness is shown in the way vowel heights pattern in phonological systems. For example, closely related vowel heights tend to be more subject to rules of mutual assimilation (raising and lowering), the underlying contrast between them may be subject to phonotactic restrictions, they tend to characterize a smaller number of lexical contrasts, and they often historically from splits in more basic registers, just as secondary tone registers often arise from splits in primary registers.

### 3.2.3 Three-height Vowel Systems

Given the discussion so far, we would expect that systems with three or more vowel heights will be able to organize thier vowel heights in different hierarchical patterns. Thus, for example, there should be two ways to characterize a three-height system as shown in (21a,b). Here and below I use the notation A, B, C, ... to designate vowel heights from highest to lowest, so that in a three-height system /i u e o a/ the letter A designates the high vowels /i u/, B designates the mid vowels /e o/, and C designates the low vowel /a/.

(21) a.　　　　　　　　　　　　　b.

(A　B)　C　　　　　　　A　(B　C)

The first of these figures depicts a system in which the low vowel is opposed to mid and high vowels at the primary level of hierarchical division, giving the grouping ((A B) C), and the second shows a system in which high vowels are opposed to mid and low vowels, giving the grouping (A (B C)). We may formalize these analyses in terms of the feature [open] as follows ('+' represents [+open] and '−' represents [−open]):

(22)　　　　a. ((A　B)　C)　　　b. (A　(B　C))
　open$_1$:　　　−　−　+　　　　　−　+　+
　open$_2$:　　　−　+　　　　　　　　　−　+

In these matrices, specification of a vowel for [open$_1$] assigns it a value on the primary register tier, and specification for [open$_2$] assigns it a value on the secondary register tier. These matrices are a shorthand notation for fully explicit autosegmental representations in which feature values are assigned to independent tiers (see below), and will be used whenever the details of tier structure are not directly relevant to the discussion.

In many three-height systems, there is evidence that the preferred grouping is the one given in (21a) and (22a). This is shown by phonological rules which neutralize the opposition between high and mid vowels in certain contexts, while leaving low vowels intact. Thus in many Bantu languages with three vowel heights, mid and high vowels alternate with each other while low vowels are relatively stable (see Katamba 1989 for an account of Luganda). Similarly, in the Pasiego dialect of Spanish, mid and high vowels alternate with each other while low vowels do not (McCarthy 1984). I take such facts to indicate that the first hierarchical subdivision takes place within the higher of the two primary registers in these languages, yielding a preferred grouping ((A B) C) in which the low vowel is opposed to both the mid and high vowels, as shown in (21a) and (22a).

These examples involve languages with three phonetic vowel heights and three phonological heights. However, the number of phonetic vowel height in a language need not be the same as the number of phonological vowel heights, and the question: "how many phonological vowel heights does a given language have?" is not always an easy one to answer. Some surface vowel heights do not function as independent heights in the phonological rule system. Thus, for example, in the vowel system of modern Turkish we find three phonetic vowel heights, as follows:

(23) Turkish surface vowels:

i ü ɨ u
e ö   o
  a

Note, however, that /a/ does not contrast minimally with any mid vowel. Furthermore, /a/ behaves in strict parallel to the other nonhigh vowels with respect to vowel harmony and other rules (see e.g. Clements and Sezer 1982); to assign it a separate underlying height of its own would introduce needless complication into the statement of phonological rules. We can simplify the description of Turkish by recognizing only two underlying vowel heights, as shown in (24):

(24) Turkish underlying vowels:

high:     i   ü   ɨ   u
nonhigh:  e   ö   a   o

The third phonetic height can be derived by a late rule.[19]

---

[19] Other languages allow similar arguments to be made for treating one phonetic height as derived. For example, the short vowels in Yokuts with three phonetic vowel heights [i u o a] are best analyzed as having two phonological heights (see e.g. Kenstowicz and Kisseberth 1979, Archangeli 1985), and the system /i u e o ə ɛ ɔ a/ of Gbe with four phonetic vowel heights is best analyzed as having three phonological heights, as is argued in Clements (1974) and below.

In other languages, however, phonetic low vowels can be shown to constitute an independent phonological height of their own. In some cases, this follows directly from the fact that they show minimal height contrasts with mid vowels, as in English and Danish /ɛ/ vs. /æ/, or English and Cantonese /a/ vs. /ʌ/. In other cases where direct contrasts are lacking, the arguments depend on the behavior of low vowels with respect to phonological rules. An example from Spanish will illustrate. Spanish has the following system, with three phonetic and phonological vowel heights:

(25) Spanish vowels:
   height 3:   i     u
   height 2:   e     o
   height 1:      a

In Spanish, we cannot cite minimal phonemic contrasts to show that /a/ constitutes a separate vowel height on its own. However, such an analysis is supported by the phonological rule system. Thus, under certain conditions the mid vowels /e o/ diphthongize to [ie] and [ue], respectively, while the low vowel never diphthongizes; this requires diphthongization to be formulated on the class of [–low] vowels. Similarly, mid stem vowels (but not low stem vowels) alternate with high vowels in a subclass of verbs as shown by forms like *sentir* 'to feel', *sintieron* 'they felt' and *poder* 'to be able, *pudieron* 'they were able.' We have already mentioned that mid and high vowels alternate with each other to the exclusion of low vowels in the Pasiego dialect. It would be possible, of course, to distinguish the mid vowels from the low vowel by referring to the feature complex [α round αback], but we would be unable to explain why just this complex and no other recurs in the description of Spanish vowels.

## 3.2.3 Four-height Vowel Systems

Let us now consider the analysis of systems with four phonological heights. In one common pattern, further subdivision of the pattern in (21a) and (22a) appears to take place in the lower of the secondary registers, giving the grouping ((A (B C)) D). Thus in several Romance and African languages with four phonological vowel heights, the higher and lower mid vowels (B, C) appear to be closely related to each other phonologically. In French, for example, upper mid vowels and lower mid vowels contrast in only a small set of contexts, while high vowels and low vowels contrast with mid vowels in nearly all contexts. Furthermore, the upper vs. lower mid vowel contrast accounts for only a few lexical oppositions, and is tending to disappear in many varieties of French. These and other facts suggest a hierarchical organization of the type ((A (B C)) D).[20] Similarly, vowel height contrasts found in oral vowels are often neutralized in nasal vowels, and in four-height systems it is often the two mid vowel heights that are neutralized, as in the West African language Dan (Bearth and Zemp 1967).

There is, however, another common pattern found in many Bantu seven-vowel systems in which four high vowels /i u I U/ are opposed to three nonhigh vowels /ɛ ɔ a/. Several languages of this type will be discussed below. In these cases it seems appropriate to assume that the primary registral distinction sets the low vowels (D) apart from all others, as in French, while the secondary split opposes the two high vowel series (A,B) to a single mid vowel series (C).

The French and Bantu types of system are represented in (26a,b) below. In both systems, the primary register division separates low vowels from all others. In (26a), however, vowel heights B and C are grouped together at the secondary level, while in (26b) vowel heights A and B are grouped together.

(26)  a. ((A  (B  C))  D)      b. (((A  B)  C)  D)

|       | (A | (B | C)) | D) | ((A | B) | C) | D) |
|-------|----|----|-----|----|-----|----|----|----|
| open₁: | −  | −  | −   | +  | −   | −  | −  | +  |
| open₂: | −  | +  | +   |    | −   | −  | +  |    |
| open₃: |    | −  | +   |    | −   | +  |    |    |

In subsequent discussion, feature displays such as those in (26) will be often be given in a fully-specified form, in which redundant values are filled in by the following default rules:

(27) a.  Ø ⟶ +/+ ___
     b.  Ø ⟶ −/___ −

That is, empty cells on any row in a vowel height matrix such as those in (26) are assigned plus specifications after plus specifications and minus specifications before minus specifications. These rules have the effect of mapping the redundancy-free matrices in (26a) and (26b) into the fully-specified matrices (28a) and (28b), respectively:

---

**20** See also Bichakjian (1986) for a similar analysis, making use of a registral feature [raised] to cross-classify [high] and [low] in the mid vowels. Specifically, Bichakjian argues for the organization (A (B C) D), in which a preliminary ternary cut among high, mid and low vowels is then subdivided into a secondary division among low vowels.

(28)       a. ((A    (B    C))   D)    b. (((A    B)    C)   D)
open₁:       −     −     −    +        −     −     −    +
open₂:       −     +     +    +        −     −     +    +
open₃:       −     −     +    +        −     +     +    +

The rules in (28) are not arbitrary, but express the hypothesis that vowels tend to fill the height dimension in such a way as to maximize the articulatory and acoustic distance between them (cf. Liljencrants and Lindblom 1972). Thus the values introduced by the rules of (28), by assigning vowels to the periphery of each subregister, have the effect of dispersing vowels maximally within the height dimension.[21]

A further, logically possible grouping is one in which both primary registers subdivide into secondary registers, giving the relationship ((A B) (C D)). In terms of features, this is expressed as in (29):

(29)           ((A    B)    (C    D))
open₁:          −     −     +     +
open₂:          −     +     −     +

In such systems, the higher two heights would be opposed to the lower two heights. We return to a consideration of possible systems of this type in section 7.2.

To summarize, it is proposed that [open] is a hierarchical feature which organizes the height or aperture dimension into a set of hierarchically related registers. Simple two-height vowel systems such as /i u a/ involve two primary registers [−open] and [+open], designating relatively higher vs. lower vowels. Three-height systems such as /i u e o a/ commonly involve a split of the [−open] register into two secondary registers, establishing a contrast between high and mid vowels. Additional splits may create systems of four heights and more. Systems of four and more vowel heights are examined in some detail in the following sections. Before considering them, however, we turn to the question of how the feature [open] is arrayed in multitiered feature representations.

---

[21] It will be noted that the redundancy rules in ($28) apply according to specifications present in other phonemes in the system, rather than uniquely in the phoneme to which the rule applies. If this claim is correct, default rules for hierarchical features (tone, vowel height) have a different formal character from those for other features, which normally apply in a context-free fashion, without reference to other phonemes in the system.

### 3.2.4 The Geometry of Vowel Height

There are a number of ways in which the hierarchical conception of vowel height outlined above can be integrated within a multitiered feature model, each representing a separate hypothesis or submodel within the hierarchical theory of register presented in the preceding discussion. I will outline a particular proposal in the following discussion, although other conceptions are possible as well, equally consistent with the basic claims of the hierarchical model.

The approach I will adopt here draws upon related, independent proposals by Hyman (1988) and Odden (1989a). Hyman points out that close functional relationships between features can be expressed in autosegmental terms by placing the features under a single class node, and suggests on the basis of evidence from the West African language Esimbi that the two height features [high], [low] may be assigned to a single height node. He proposes the structure shown in (30) (Hyman 1988: 269):

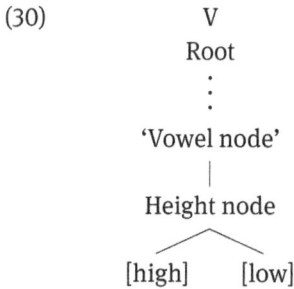

(30)

We will discuss Hyman's analysis of Esimbi in section 5.2 below.

Odden (1989a) reviews a range of evidence bearing on the question of which vowel features form natural classes in phonological rules. He observes that while [back] and [round] on the one hand, and [high], [low], and [ATR] on the other, tend to function as single units in assimilation rules, subsets of features drawn from each of these two groups do not function together; thus we do not find rules in which [back] and [high] assimilate together to the exclusion of the other features, for instance. In order to capture this generalization, Odden proposes that each of the two groups is linked under a separate class node in phonological representations. He calls these nodes the back/round node and the height node, respectively, and suggests that they link directly under the place node. Since the back/round node dominates place features of vowels just as the (C-)place node does in consonants, I will call it the V-place node.

Drawing on these proposals, I will regard vowel height as a separate subtree in the feature characterization of vowels, rooted in a class node which I term *aper-*

*ture*. I hypothesize that the aperture node links directly to a node that I will term the *vocalic* node. The vocalic node also dominates the V-place (Vocalic place) node to which vowel place features such as [labial] attach. The vocalic node itself links to the place (or C-place) node, which dominates not only the vocalic node in vowels and glides but also consonant place features in consonants. I further suggest, more speculatively, that each occurrence of [±open] under the Aperture node is assigned to a separate autosegmental tier. These tiers are ranked, and conventionally numbered 1, 2, ..., *n*, where *n* is the number of registral divisions. This conception gives the following partial tree structure for the vowel /ø/ in a four-height system of the type characterized in (26a):

(31) Partial representation of the vowel [ɔ]:

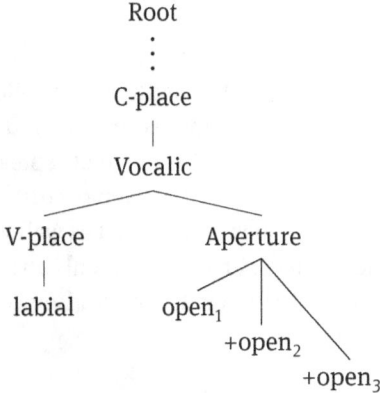

Representations such as (31) predict that features grouped under single nodes in the tree should be able to undergo phonological rules of spreading, delinking, and the like, while features that are not grouped under single nodes will not. For instance, it predicts that each aperture feature will be able to spread individually, or that all can spread together as a single unit, giving total height assimilation. It also predicts that each vocalic place feature can spread individually, or that all can spread as a unit, giving total place assimilation. It further predicts that the aperture and vocalic place features can spread as a unit exclusively of higher-level features, describing total vowel assimilation (exclusive of features like [nasal] or tone). The following sections will offer evidence supporting these predictions.[22]

---

[22] We will not be directly concerned with testing the third of these predictions, since it is not directly relevant to the rest of our claims. This prediction entails that vowels may show total assimilation across consonants, including those specified for the place node, and is not

The present proposal directly encodes the proposals of Hyman and Odden, and is adequate to cover the data discussed in the rest of this study. However, there is at least one other way of arraying the feature [open] consistently with the hierarchical model. In the *coplanar* model proposed by Archangeli (1984, 1985), it can be assumed that lower-ranked occurrences of [open] link under higher-ranked ones, in the following manner:

(32)  Vocalic
      |
      open$_1$
      |
      open$_2$
      |
      (etc.)

An attractive aspect of this mode of representation is that it directly encodes the hierarchical ranking of aperture features, making it unecessary to stipulate a rank order among tiers. The major difference between this mode of representation and the one suggested in (31) is that it predicts that if a given occurrence of [open] spreads, all lower-ranked occurrences of [open] will spread as well. Given the organization in (31), on the other hand, each occurrence of [open] can spread independently of the others. I have not so far found evidence deciding conclusively between these two types of representation.

### 3.2.5 Rule Application to Hierarchical Tiers

For the most part, rules applying on hierarchical tiers apply just as they do on other tiers. However, the placement of [open] on several tiers raises the question

---

uncontroversial. Thus Odden (1989a) notes that rules of total vowel spreading are rare, and Steriade (1987b) argues that they are restricted to sequences of adjacent vowels or vowels separated by laryngeal glides, i.e. to vowel sequences not separated by independently-specified consonantal place features. However, enough genuine cases of transconsonantal Vocalic node spreading seem to be attested to justify recognition of the vocalic node as a separate entity in representations. One case is proposed from Yawelmani Yokuts by Archangeli and Pulleyblank (1986), although these data have been subjected to other analyses. In Maltese, short vowels /i e a o/ metathesize across consonants at all places of articulation (Hume 1990). In Kolami, the epenthetic vowel inserted in CVC__C contexts is an exact copy of the preceding vowel, regardless of the intervening consonant (Emenau 1955, Kenstowicz and Pyle 1973, Steriade 1982). These and other examples will be discussed elsewhere.

of how a rule mentioning [open] applies if it is satisfied on several tiers at the same time.

It will be assumed that rules may specify operations over tiers without identifying their rank.[23] Thus, a vowel raising rule may simply state that an occurrence of [−open] spreads onto a node characterized as [+open], as shown in (33):

(33) Aperture   Aperture

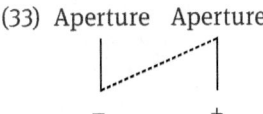

    −        +

As stated, this rule is defined on any tier (necessarily, an [open] tier) on which the sequence of values "− +" occurs. It is thus defined on both tiers in the following representation:

(34)

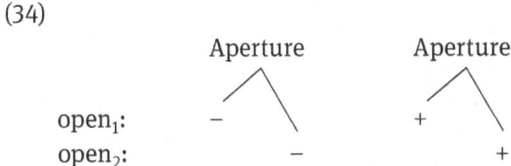

In linear phonology, when a rule is defined on more than one segment in a representation we must state whether the rule is directional, and if so, whether it applies from left to right or right to left. Similarly in the case of (34), we must decide whether rule (33) should be allowed to apply on both tiers or on just one, and in the latter case, which one.

Rules like (33) describes a process in which a vowel is raised one degree in height after any higher vowel. If we reversed the feature values, it would describe the lowering of a vowel one degree in height after any lower vowel. Now let us assume a system of three vowel heights as given, for example, in (22a), in which A, B, C represent high, mid and low vowels respectively, with redundant values filled to give (35):

(35)         A    B    C
    $open_1$:   −    −    +
    $open_2$:   −    +    +

---

[23] This assumption is independently motivated by the downstep rule of Yala (Ikom), discussed earlier, which applies to sequences of tone features without regard to the tier they are located on.

If it is to have the desired effect of raising a vowel one degree in height after any higher vowel, (33) must spread [−open] on tier 1 in the sequences BC and AC, and tier 2 in the sequence AB. This is shown in the representations below:

(36) 

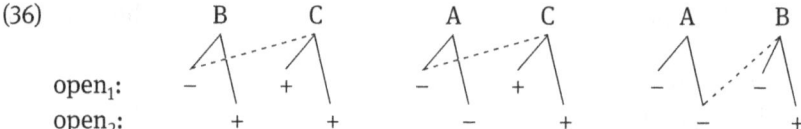

|  | B | C | A | C | A | B |
|---|---|---|---|---|---|---|
| open₁: | − | + | − | + | − | − |
| open₂: | + | + | − | + | − | + |

Notice, in particular, that we may spread only once, on tier 1, in the sequence AC, since if we spread on tier 2 as well, we would incorrectly map the low vowel C into the high vowel A instead of into the mid vowel B. To achieve the correct result, it appears that we must allow the spreading rule (33) to apply in a top-down, noniterative fashion; that is, we apply it from the highest-ranked tier downward, stopping as soon as the rule has applied once. For similar reasons, to express the parallel vowel lowering process, a rule identical to (33) but with the feature values reversed must apply in a bottom-up, noniterative fashion.

I tentatively take these modes of application to be the unmarked (and perhaps only possible) way of applying rules formulated on unranked hierarchical tiers. More generally, let us say that if the affected value (e.g. the value borne by the target in a spreading rule) is plus, the rule applies top-down, while if it is minus, it applies bottom-up, in both cases non-iteratively. This requirement guarantees that rules formulated on unranked [open] tiers will change vowel height by single degrees only, given feature specifications like those in (35). This convention is the counterpart to the one required in multivalued feature frameworks to allow rules to specify changes of the form "n+1" and "n−1." Thus, the Gbe rule stated earlier in terms of the multivalued feature [high] in (7) can now be now formulated as the mirror image of rule (33) above, as follows:

(37) Aperture  + Aperture

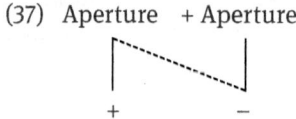

+          −

We will see several further examples of such rules in the later discussion.

A final assumption, assumed throughout this study, is that branching configurations are ill-formed except at the level of the timing tier, or skeleton. This is expressed as the No Branching Condition, as follows:

(38) *No Branching Condition:*

The configuration

B    C

is ill-formed, where A is any class node and B, C are on the same tier.

This principle represents the claim that segments have no internal branching structure. In other words, wherever a feature appears to "contour" across a single segment, we are actually dealing with a complex segment having two sequenced Root nodes linked to a single timing tier slot (see Clements 1989b for further discussion and motivation). When a rule creates a violation of this condition, the violation is eliminated by a convention which deletes the earlier or "older" of the two branches. Thus, for example, when (37) applies to a representation, the older of the two branches under the first Aperture node, namely the one terminating in [+open], is automatically deleted. This convention is stated as follows:

(39) *Branch Pruning Convention:*

If a rule creates a branching configuration under a class node, remove the older of the two branches.

## 3.3 Underspecification of Vowel Features

We consider here the question of underspecification, that is, the extent to which vowel features (including [open]) are fully specified in underlying representation. In this study I assume a version of the theory of distinctive feature specification, according to which segments are underlyingly specified only for the features required to uniquely identify them and distinguish them from all other segments in the inventory. Such representations will be called *redundancy-free*. Segments may acquire redundant feature specifications as a result of derivational processes, including redundancy rules which fill in redundant values. Versions of such a theory are offered in Halle 1959, Steriade 1987a, and Clements 1987b. For concreteness, I will assume the latter, though differences among these theories do not appear to be crucial to the present discussion.

Schane (1973) has proposed that the features present in the redundancy-free representation of vowels normally or always include the marked values of [back] and [round], i.e. [–back] and [+round]. Thus [i, e] are characterized as [–back] and [u, o] as [+round] even if one of these features can be predicted from the other. This proposal can be adapted into the unified system of vowel and consonant features presented in Clements (1989a) by replacing [–back] with [+coronal] and [+round] with [+labial], bringing the feature representation of vowels into line with that of consonants.

On these assumptions, the fully-specified feature representation of the three-height vowel system /i u a/ as found in languages like Sanskrit is given as in (40a), and the redundancy-free representation is given as in (40b).

(40)

|         | a. | i | u | a | b. | i | u | a |
|---------|----|---|---|---|----|---|---|---|
| coronal |    | + | – | – |    | + |   |   |
| labial  |    | – | + | – |    |   | + |   |
| open    |    | – | – | + |    |   |   | + |

It will be noted that the incorporation of Schane's proposal does not violate the principle of distinctive feature specification. In (40b), all vowels are specified only for those features required to identify them and distinguish them from all others in the system. Thus, [i] is the only [+coronal] vowel in the system, [u] is the only [+labial] vowel, and [a] is the only [+open] vowel. Indeed, by specifying only marked values of these three features (necessarily the plus-values, in the theory of Clements (1989a), we satisfy the requirements of distinctive feature specification in the simplest possible way.

Given these representations, we can easily express fusion processes of the type discussed earlier in connection with particle representations of vowel height (cf. (14)). Recall that in a common type of fusion process, such as is found in Sanskrit, [ai] monophthongizes to [e] and [au] monophthongizes to [o]. In particle theory, this is expressed as the set-theoretical union of the particles *i, u, a*. Similarly, given the representations in (40b) fusion effects the union of the values [+coronal], [+labial], and [+open]. Thus if [a] and [i] come into contact through fusion of the two Vocalic nodes dominating them, the resulting vowel [e] is the union of their representations:

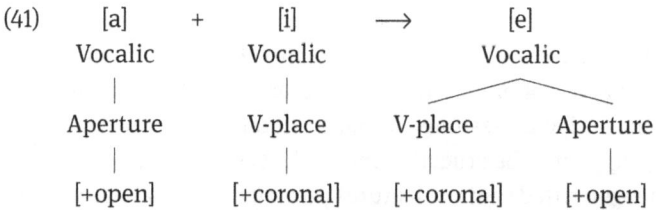

[o] results from the union of [a] and [u] in just the same way. We achieve this result since in this particular case, our representations are isomorphic to those proposed by particle theory. We differ from particle theory, of course, in allow-

ing that each vowel feature can acquire a second value derivationally, thereby accounting for natural classes and natural rule types in a way that particle theory cannot. Thus the present theory appears to inherit the advantages of particle theory without inheriting its disadvantages.

## 4 Vowel Place Assimilation

As we have seen, the model illustrated in (31) claims that place features of vowels form a node in the feature tree (*V-place*) independent of aperture, just as place features of consonants link to a node (*C-place*) independent of consonantal stricture. One prediction of the theory, then, is that we should find rules of total place assimilation spreading vocalic place features such as [labial], [coronal], [dorsal][24] as a unit, while vowel height is unaffected. These rules have the following form shown in (42):

(42) *Total place assimilation:*

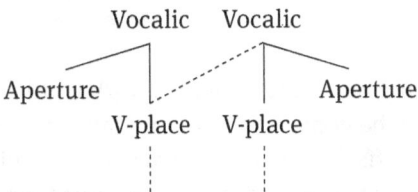

This prediction is important to establishing the independence of the aperture features, since even if the Aperture node did not exist, the existence of a V-place node shows that place features have a different formal status from aperture features, and thus provides preliminary evidence in favor of the formal independence of the latter. Several rules of the type shown in (42) are discussed by Odden (1989a). We will examine one of Odden's cases here, and add a further example from a Gbe language in the following section.

In Eastern Cheremis, /e/ in final position partially assimilates to a preceding nonlow vowel in the same word. The following examples illustrate this process with the 3SG possessed suffix, whose base form is /-še ~ že/.[25] As (43a) shows, the

---

[24] The present study assumes the theory of place features presented in Clements (1989a), though as far as the present paper is concerned, conventional vowel features such as [back] and [round] could be assumed just as well.
[25] The initial consonant of this suffix alternates regularly according to the nature of the immediately preceding consonant by a rule that is not of concern here.

final vowel of this suffix is realized as [o] if the first preceding full vowel is [u] or [o] and as [ö] if the first preceding full vowel is [ü] or [ö]; otherwise it is realized as [e]. Example (43b) shows that the reduced vowel [ə] may intervene between the trigger and the target; (43b) and (43c) also show that morpheme-final /e/ is reduced to [ə] internally. (43c) and (43d) show that if the first preceding full vowel is unrounded, the final vowel does not alternate. (43d) also shows that it is the first preceding full vowel that determines the shape of the final vowel, not the word-initial vowel. These generalizations can be amply illustrated with other suffixes, and are largely exceptionless (see Sebeok and Ingemann 1961).

(43) *nominative:*      *3SG possessed:*

|   |   | nominative | 3SG possessed |   |
|---|---|---|---|---|
| a. |   | surt | surt-šo | 'house' |
|   |   | boz | boz-šo | 'wagon' |
|   |   | üp | üp-šö | 'hair' |
|   |   | šör | šör-žö | 'milk' |
| b. |   | korno /korne/ | kornə-žo | 'road, way' |
| c. |   | erge | ergə-že | 'boy' |
| d. |   | burgem | burgem-že | 'clothing' |
|   |   | oza | oza-že | 'water' |

An intervening reduced vowel need not necessarily alternate with a full vowel, as they do in these examples, but may be nonalternating (and thus presumably underlying) schwas; cf. the inessive suffix /-əšte/, whose final vowel assimilates to the initial vowel of the word in forms like *pört-əštö* 'house', *pört-əšto* 'tree', and *buj-əšto* 'head.'

The assimilation rule not only applies to suffix vowels, but also accounts for a pervasive gap in the distribution of final /e/ in nonalternating forms. Thus, with only four exceptions in the lexicon provided by Sebeok and Ingemann,[26] [o] or [ö] occur to the exclusion of [e] in word-final position under the same conditions as those in which assimilation takes place: *korno* 'road' (cf. (43b)), *ludo* 'duck', *kürtnö* 'iron', *puldərčo* 'quail', *požkədfo* 'neighbor', *pügəlmö* 'cone', etc. Thus the rule in question appears to have the status of a lexical, word-level rule.

The theoretical interest of this rule, as Odden points out, is that it affects the place features [labial] and [coronal] (i.e. the standard features [round] and [back]) while not affecting [open]. Note that [labial] and [open] are both minimally distinctive in the vowel system, so that [labial] crucially spreads while

---

[26] As a subgeneralization, all the exceptions have /u/ as their initial vowel: *kue* 'birch', *šue* 'sparse', *kuze* 'how', and *uke* 'there is/are not'.

[open] crucially does not. We may therefore conclude that the rule in question is a rule of total place assimilation, spreading the V-place node.

To explain the transparency of reduced vowels, I will assume, following Odden, that reduced vowels lack place and aperture features, and thus also (in the present system) lack the V-place, Aperture and Vocalic nodes. This analysis is supported not only by the /e/-reduction rule, which can be analyzed as deleting the Vocalic node, but also by the fact that /ə/ rejects stress onto the first preceding full vowel to its left, or if there is none, to the first vowel (Hayes 1985), explainable under the assumption that vowels without Vocalic nodes do not have sufficient "weight" to be stressed. Since consonants also lack the V-place and Vocalic nodes (cf. (31)), they are also transparent to assimilation.[27] Under these assumptions, the rule can be formulated as follows (ω = prosodic word):

(44) *Eastern Cheremis Vowel Assimilation:*

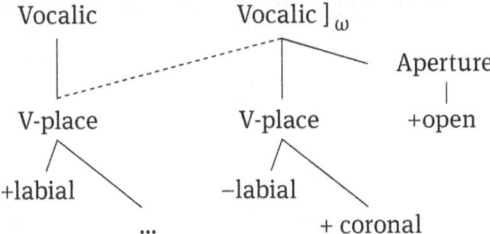

This rule applies to a sequence of two Vocalic nodes adjacent on their tier, of which the first dominates the feature [+labial] and the second all the features of [e]; if the second Vocalic node is final in the word, the V-place node of the first spreads onto it. The output is subject to the Branch Pruning Convention (39), which deletes the V-place node under the second Vocalic node.

Further examples of rules spreading the V-place node given by Odden include Tunica, Wikchamni Yokuts, and Macushi. In the next section we will see phonological rules in Gbe that spread both the V-place node and the Aperture node.

---

[27] This statement is strictly true only of consonants that do not bear secondary articulations; consonants with secondary articulations interact with vowel features. See Clements (1989c) for an analysis of secondary articulation in the present framework.

# 5 Vowel Height Assimilation

The model in (31) also predicts that the Aperture node can spread, taking with it all its dependent height features. This process results in total height assimilation. This process is schematized as follows:

(45) *Total height assimilation:*

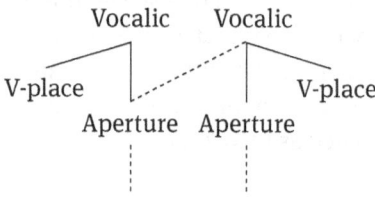

We consider examples of rules of this type in this section.

## 5.1 Height Assimilation in Gbe

Our first example will come from Ewe and other members of the Gbe language group spoken in Ghana, Togo, and the Republic of Benin. Gbe vowels have one of three phonological degrees of height, as shown in (6) above, and more completely in (46). (46) is a pandialectal vowel chart; most Gbe dialects do not have all the vowels in (46) underlyingly, lacking one or two vowels of the set /e ə ɛ / and/or their nasal counterparts /ə̃ ɛ̃/.

(46) *Gbe vowels:*

|   | oral |   |   | nasal |   |   |
|---|---|---|---|---|---|---|
| height$_3$: | i |   | u | ĩ |   | ũ |
| height$_2$: | e | ə | o |   | ə̃ |   |
| height$_1$: | ɛ | a | ɔ | ɛ̃ | ã | ɔ̃ |

/a/ is not analyzed as forming a fourth phonological vowel height in Gbe, since it always patterns with /ɛ ɔ/ in height-sensitive phonological rules, and never shows any phonological evidence of constituting a fourth height (see Clements 1974 for fuller discussion).

We first consider evidence for the V-place node, parallel to that discussed just above for Eastern Cheremis. In a Ghanaian variety of Gbe described by Westermann (1930: 193–195) and Capo (1986), the definite article suffix /-a/ assimilates to a preceding stem vowel in terms of backness and roundness. Thus we find (tones omitted; examples from Westermann):

(47) bli + a  →  bli-ɛ  'the corn'
     du + a  →  du-ɔ  'the town'
     te + a  →  te-ɛ  'the yam'
     to + a  →  to-ɔ  'the mountain'
     kø + a  →  kɔ-ɔ  'the knot'
     ga + a  →  ga-a  'the money'

The underlying form of the article must be /-a/, since [a] may surface before the plural suffix -wo in examples like [azi-a-wo] ~ [azi-ɛ-wo] 'the groundnuts' where assimilation is optional. The optionality of the rule, together with its morphological conditioning, provides good evidence that it is a single rule rather than two independent rules with similar effects. Assuming the analysis of height in (46),[28] the rule in question simply spreads backness and roundness, i.e. all the features under the V-place node, as in the Eastern Cheremis case.

Gbe also presents evidence for the Aperture node. In most Gbe dialects, a rule of Suffix Vowel Assimilation causes the suffix vowel /-i/ to agree with the preceding stem vowel in height (see Capo 1985a, revising the analysis of this suffix given in Clements 1974). Suffix Vowel Assimilation is fed by a dialect-variable rule of Stem Vowel Assimilation, which causes some stem vowels to assimilate partly or entirely to the height of the suffix vowel. These rules are illustrated by the forms in (48). Underlying vowels are given at left, and surface realizations are given in the following columns for three representative varieties of Ewe (Adangbe, Kpando, Aŋlɔ) and one of Fon (Danxome). (Blanks indicate that the stem vowel shown at the beginning of the row is absent in the dialect in question; optional variants are given in parentheses. Nasal vowels behave like oral vowels of the same height.)

---

**28** This feature analysis is not crucial to the analysis of the forms under discussion here. If we treated /a/ as being one degree lower in height than /ɛ ɔ/, the spreading rule will create the intermediate vowels [æ ɒ], which can then be mapped into [ɛ ɔ] under structure-preserving redundancy rules.

(48) *Suffix vowel assimilation in Gbe dialects:*

| underlying: | Adangbe: | Kpando: | Aŋlɔ: | Danxome: |
|---|---|---|---|---|
| /i+i/ | i+i | i+i | i+i | i+i |
| /u+i/ | u+i | u+i | u+i | u+i |
| /e+i/ | e+e | e+e (i+i) | – | e+e |
| /ə+i/ | e+e | – | i+i | – |
| /o+i/ | o+e | o+e (u+i) | u+i | o+e |
| /ɛ+i/ | ɛ+ɛ | – | – | ɛ+ɛ |
| /a+i/ | ɛ+ɛ | ɛ+ɛ | e+e | ɛ+ɛ |
| /ɔ+i/ | ɔ+ɛ | ɔ+ɛ | o+e | ɔ+ɛ |

We see three rules operating here:

1. *Stem Vowel Fronting.* Central stem vowels /əa/ are fronted before the suffix vowel /-i/ (all dialects).
2. *Stem Vowel Raising.* Stem vowels assimilate partly or entirely to the *underlying* height of the suffix vowel (some dialects only):
    Kpando: /e o/ raise to /i u/ (optional)
    Aŋlɔ: /e o/ raise to [i u], and /a ɔ/ raise to [e o] (obligatory)
3. *Suffix Vowel Assimilation:* The suffix vowel assimilates to the *surface* height of the stem vowel (all dialects).

Notice that Stem Vowel Raising must crucially apply before Suffix Vowel Assimilation, since they stand in a feeding relationship.

Before proposing an analysis, let us consider the analysis of vowel height more closely. Clements (1974) proposed to treat the three vowel heights of Ewe in terms of the two standard features [high], [ATR] as follows:

(49)

| | i | u | e | ə | o | ɛ | a | ɔ |
|---|---|---|---|---|---|---|---|---|
| high | + | + | – | – | – | – | – | – |
| ATR | + | + | + | + | + | – | – | – |

This feature analysis is not implausible, since it not only accounts for phonemic contrasts in a natural way, it also defines natural classes in Ewe and other Gbe dialects correctly. The use of [ATR] is consistent with the presence of this feature in geographically proximate and genetically related languages such as Akan (Stewart 1967). However, I was unable to offer any direct evidence for the appropriateness of the feature [ATR], as opposed to [low] or some other vowel height feature; in particular, apart from the alternations shown in (48), Gbe languages give no evidence of ATR-type vowel harmony such as we find elsewhere in West Africa.

Stewart (1983) criticized this analysis on historical grounds, arguing that [a] must have constituted a distinct fourth vowel height in proto-Gbe since it did not pattern with the mid vowels in his reconstructed ATR-based vowel harmony system; he saw no reason to assume that a reanalysis took place subsequently. In a reply, Capo (1985b) pointed out that the three-height analysis of Gbe languages (including Ewe) is justified synchronically since it accounts correctly for vowel alternations across all dialects. However, he proposed to revise the analysis given in (49) by replacing the feature [ATR] with [low], reflecting the intuition that Suffix Vowel Assimilation involves a single parameter of tongue height. He proposed to restate the rule in terms of the features [high] and [low] as follows (Capo 1985a):

(50) V $\longrightarrow$ [–high, αlow] / [–high, αlow] + —

This revision does not entirely succeed in formalizing Capo's intuition, however, since as we have seen, standard feature theory does not express the fact that the features [high] and [low] define two poles of a single phonological and phonetic dimension. The problem is solved, however, once we adopt the view that vowel height is characterized in terms of a single, hierarchically-represented feature [open]. Ewe vowels may be described as shown in the (fully-specified) matrix in (51):

(51)

|          | i | u | e | ə | o | ɛ | a | ɔ |
|----------|---|---|---|---|---|---|---|---|
| coronal  | + | − | + | − | − | + | − | − |
| labial   | − | + | − | − | + | − | − | + |
| open$_1$ | − | − | − | − | − | + | + | + |
| open$_2$ | − | − | + | + | + | + | + | + |

Suffix Vowel Assimilation can now be expressed as the spreading of the Aperture node from the first vowel to the second, as shown in (52):

(52) *Gbe Suffix Vowel Assimilation:*

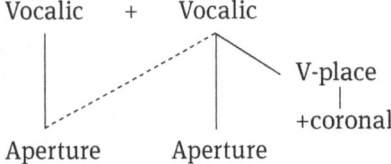

As the V-place node is not affected, thus the suffix vowel retains its coronal (front) articulation. This analysis preserves the advantages of my 1974 treatment, while incorporating the essential insight underlying Capo's proposal. Similar rules of height assimilation are found in several languages of the Central Togo group (Clements 1974), and can be treated in the same way.

Consider now the rule of Stem Vowel Raising illustrated in (48). The Kpando version of this rule, which is the most prevalent version across dialects, raises mid vowels to high, while a generalized version of this rule, found in the Aŋlø dialect, also raises /a ø/ to [e o]. Given the features in (51), the Kpando form of the rule can be stated as one which spreads [−open$_2$] from the high suffix vowel to mid stem vowels:

(53) *Kpando Stem Vowel Raising:*

$$
\begin{array}{c}
-\text{open}_1 \\
| \\
\text{Aperture} + \text{Aperture} \\
\phantom{xx}\diagdown\phantom{xxxxxx} \\
+\text{open}_2 \quad\quad -\text{open}_2
\end{array}
$$

The Aŋlɔ version of the rule, which raises a nonhigh stem vowel one degree in height before a higher suffix vowel, was stated earlier in (37), which represents a formal generalization of (53). We emphasize once again that the hierarchical model of vowel height provides a straightforward notation for capturing the generalization underlying this rule.[29]

Stem Vowel Raising is taken to its furthest extreme in the Hwe dialect, illustrated in (54) below (Capo 1985a):

---

[29] As stated, rule ($37*$) should also raise low vowels to mid before mid suffix vowels. However, such sequences do not normally occur inside the word. The only relevant suffix is the syntactic focus particle /e/ which usually does not trigger either stem vowel raising or suffix vowel assimilation, cf. [vi e] 'it's a child', [ɲɔ̃ ẽ] 'it's me', [əmɔ̃ ẽ] 'it's a path', [akpa e] 'it's a sprat.' However, both rules apply in a few high-frequency grammatical sequences such as [nũka e] 'what is it?' (slow speech) alternating with [nuke e] (fast speech), in which a weak (clitic) boundary can be assumed; here we see that [é] does in fact raise to [e] before the suffix [e], as the rule predicts.

(54)    oral vowels:            nasal vowels:
        underlying:  surface:   underlying:  surface:
        i + i        i + i      ĩ + i        ĩ + ĩ
        u + i        u + i      ũ + i        ũ + ĩ
        e + i        i + i       –            –
        o + i        u + i       –            –
         –            –         ɛ̃ + i        ĩ + ĩ
        ɔ + i        ɔ + ɛ      ɔ̃ + i        ũ + ĩ
        a + i        ɛ + ɛ      ã + i        ĩ + ĩ

Hwe has Stem Vowel Fronting and Suffix Vowel Assimilation as in other dialects. Where it differs is in the way its Stem Vowel Raising rule applies to nasal vowels, raising them all to high. This can be expressed as a rule of total height assimilation spreading the Aperture node from the suffix vowel onto nasal stem vowels, once again supporting a treatment in which aperture features are linked under a common node.[30]

For ease of exposition, we have not given our feature representations in underspecified form, as is required by the theory of distinctive specification theory (Section 3.3). However, underspecified feature representations will give the correct results for all the rules discussed above. To see this, consider the redundancy-free feature specifications corresponding to those in the fully-specified matrix given in (51):

(55)        | i | u | e | ə | o | ɛ | a | ɔ |
|---|---|---|---|---|---|---|---|---|
| coronal | + |   |   | + |   | + | – |   |
| labial  |   | + |   |   | + | – |   | + |
| $open_1$ |   |   | – | – | – | + | + | + |
| $open_2$ | – | – | + | + | + |   |   |   |

These specifications are the minimal ones required to uniquely identify each vowel, and distinguish it from all others in the system. Notice that each vowel is specified for at least one value of [open]. It follows that all vowels have an Aperture node, and can trigger Suffix Vowel Assimilation (52), as we require. Further, all vowels are specified for the aperture features necessary for the operation of

---

[30] This formulation of the rule predicts that mid nasal vowels, if present, would also raise to high. This prediction cannot be directly tested. Thus we cannot rule out an alternative formulation in which the feature [–$open_2$] spreads leftward onto low nasal vowels, creating vowels with the specification [+$open_1$, –$open_2$] which then undergo the redundancy rule [–$open_2$] → [–$open_1$].

Stem Vowel Raising (53). In order to apply the generalized version of Stem Vowel Raising (37), however, we must assume that the redundant value [−open$_1$] has been inserted in the suffix vowel [i] by the time the rule applies. This would follow either from an extrinsic ordering of the redundancy rule before Stem Vowel Raising, or from the Redundancy Rule Ordering Constraint of Archangeli and Pulleyblank (1986) (see note 10). Thus all rules apply correctly even if we assume the underlying feature representations given in (55).

On the other hand, the Gbe data do rule out an analysis in which the suffix vowel is totally unspecified for height features at the time Suffix Vowel Assimilation applies, and height features spread onto it from the stem vowel to the left.[31] Since the suffix vowel conditions Stem Vowel Raising, its height must be specified at the point at which Stem Vowel Raising applies, prior to Suffix Vowel Assimilation.

To summarize the major conclusions of this section, we have seen that in several Ewe (and other Gbe) dialects, vowel place features and vowel height features can each spread as a unit. In contrast, there appears to be no evidence in any variety of Gbe that other subsets of vowel features, e.g. [+open$_1$] and [+labial], can spread together. This patterning supports the view that V-place and Aperture are nodes in phonological representations. Finally, by assuming a hierarchical organization of the feature [open], we account for the scalar nature of Stem Vowel Raising in its most general version (37).

## 5.2 Height Assimilation in Bantu[32]

The previous section examined a group of languages exhibiting three phonological vowel heights. We now turn to a linguistic unit, Bantu, many of whose members appear to have four phonological vowel heights. Bantu vowels tend to be produced with equal tenseness and duration in similar contexts, and do not generally involve a phonetically independent dimension of tongue root advancing of the sort found in many African languages with vowel harmony systems, such as Akan and Igbo.[33] Thus the postulation of features such as [ATR] or [tense] to describe Bantu vowel height distinctions is unmotivated in a theory

---

31 Such an analysis is proposed by Abaglo and Archangeli (1989).
32 This part provided the basis for the article: Vowel Height Assimilation in Bantu Languages. In G. N. Clements (1991), *Proceedings of the 17th Annual Meeting of the Berkeley Linguistics Society*, 25–64. [Note of the editors.]
33 A possible exception is Nen (also known as Tunen); see Hulst, Mous and Smith (1986) and references therein.

assuming the Phonetic Distinctness Criterion (5). For this reason, four-height Bantu systems provide a particularly interesting "laboratory" for the study of vowel height phonology.

We first consider height assimilation in Kimatuumbi, a Bantu language discussed in recent work by Odden (1989a,b). In this language, the initial vowel of stems is one of the set /i u I U ɛ ɔ a/, while medial vowels are drawn from the reduced set /i u a/. I give Kimatuumbi vowels below with their analysis in terms of the feature [open]. This analysis assumes that Kimatuumbi, like other Bantu languages with four vowel heights, has the left-branching hierarchical structure (((A B) C) D) characterized earlier in (26b) and (28b).

(56)  a. stem-initial:                                b. stem-medial:

|        | i | u | I | U | ɛ | ɔ | a | | i | u | a |
|--------|---|---|---|---|---|---|---|---|---|---|---|
| $open_1$ | − | − | − | − | − | − | + | | − | − | + |
| $open_2$ | − | − | − | − | + | + | + | |   |   |   |
| $open_3$ | − | − | + | + | + | + | + | |   |   |   |

Let us first consider the neutralization of vowel height found in medial position (56b). Height neutralization of this sort, in which mid vowels are eliminated in favor of peripheral (high and low) vowels, are quite common across languages. As Katamba has noted, "Languages with a five vowel phoneme system consisting of /i e a o u/, if they have rules which neutralize vowel distinctions in certain environments, tend to maintain the opposition between /i a u/ in the places of neutralization" (Katamba 1989: 109). Such neutralizations are not restricted to five-vowel systems, as the Kimatuumbi examples show.

Goldsmith (1987), noting further examples of this type, proposes that an adequate phonological theory should be able to account for them in terms of simple operations on representations: "When there are positions of limited distribution, the subclass of available segments should be simply expressible using the same assumptions about features, modifying only the minimum and maximum number of associations permitted in that position." In the spirit of Goldsmith's remarks, we will propose that non-primary vowel height registers can be prohibited in certain contexts by constraints on the maximal number of elements that can be linked to the aperture node. In the case of Kimatuumbi, the reduced system (56b) can be derived by a constraint prohibiting underlying configurations with two or more occurrences of [open] under the Aperture node:

(57)      * Aperture          (in stem-medial position)
             ╱╲
          open  open

(57) claims that only the primary height register [±open$_1$] may occur contrastively in medial position, and thus correctly derives the fact that only /i u a/ appear in this context.

Consider now the Kimatuumbi height assimilation rule. This rule assimilates a nonlow vowel to the height of a nonlow vowel in the preceding syllable.[34] As a regular exception, /u/ does not assimilate to /ɛ/. Where the assimilation rule does not apply, as after a low vowel, /i/ and /u/ are realized as such. Thus we find the following realizations (see Odden (1988a, 1989) for examples and further discussion; tones are omitted):

(58) *Kimatuumbi height assimilation:*

| underlying: | surface: | example (stem): | |
|---|---|---|---|
| i + i | i + i | yipilya | 'thatch with for' |
| i + u | i + u | libulwa | 'be ground' |
| u + i | u + i | utika | 'be pullable' |
| u + u | u + u | yupulwa | 'be served' |
| I + i | I + I | twIIkIlwa | 'be lifted' (of a load) |
| I + u | I + U | tIkUlya | 'break with' |
| U + i | U + I | UUgIlwa | 'be bathed' |
| U + u | U + U | kUmbUlya | 'beat with' |
| ɛ + i | ɛ + ɛ | chɛɛngɛya | 'make build' |
| ɛ + u | ɛ + u | kwɛmulya | 'comb' |
| ɔ + i | ɔ + ɛ | bɔɔlɛlwa | 'be de-barked' |
| ɔ + u | ɔ + ɔ | bɔmɔlwa | 'be destroyed' |
| a + i | a + i | asimilwa | 'be borrowed' |
| a + u | a + u | tyamulya | 'sneeze on' |

We cannot describe this process as a single rule using the traditional features [high] and [ATR], since these features do not form a unique constituent in feature trees (cf. Sagey 1986). If we adopt the hierarchical feature [open] as proposed in (56), however, the assimilation rule will resemble the one in Ewe except for the condition that both trigger and target must be nonlow (i.e., [–open]). The rule can be stated as in (59). (Since consonants are not characterized for the aperture or Vocalic nodes, they will not block assimilation.)[35]

---

[34] The fact that this rule is restricted to nonlow vowels justifies treating low vowels as a separate phonological height. Similar arguments apply in most other Bantu languages.

[35] As in the case of Gbe discussed in the previous section, this rule will operate correctly even if we assume underspecified representations at the point at which the rule applies.

(59) *Kimatuumbi height assimilation:*

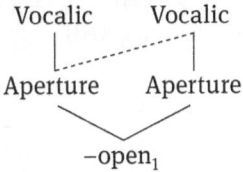

Consider next Kinande, whose seven-vowel system is similar to that of Kimatuumbi and which has a similar rule of total height assimilation as well. The following discussion draws on a recent account by Hyman (1989), which is based in turn on earlier work by Mutake (1986) and Schlindwein (1987).

In addition to its Kimatuumbi-like total height assimilation rule, Kinande has a rule of partial assimilation according to which vowels rise one degree in height before one of the higher high vowels [i u], except for word-initial vowels, which are not affected. By this rule [I U] become [i u] and [ɛ ɔ] become [e o], in the latter case creating a new, derived vowel height. Examples are given below. Underlying representations of roots are given at right. /ɛ-/ and /ɔ-/ are augment prefixes, and /rI-/ and /mU-/ are class prefixes.[36] By the rule in question, high vowel roots cause assimilation in both class prefixes (60a), and the high vowel agentive suffix /-i / causes assimilation in both mid vowel roots and the prefix / mU-/ (column 2 of (60b,c)).

(60) a. ɛ-ri-lim-a 'to exterminate'   ɔ-mu-lim-i 'exterminator' /lim-/
       ɛ-ri-huk-a 'to cook'           ɔ-mu-huk-i 'cook'         /huk-/
    b. ɛ-rI-lIm-a 'to cultivate'      ɔ-mu-lim-i 'farmer'       /lIm-/
       ɛ-rI-hUm-a 'to beat'           ɔ-mu-hum-i 'beater'       /hUm-/
    c. ɛ-rI-hɛk-a 'to carry'          ɔ-mu-hek-i 'porter'       /hɛk-/
       ɛ-rI-bɔh-a 'to tie'            ɔ-mu-boh-i 'tier'         /bɔh-/
    d. ɛ-rI-kar-a 'to force'          ɔ-mu-kar-i 'forcer'       /kar-/

The final example in this set, (60d), seems to show that the low vowel /a/ does not undergo the rule itself, but somehow allows assimilation to pass through it to the preceding vowel. Hyman argues that the low vowel actually does undergo the rule, and that its surface realization results from a low-level rule which assigns raised low vowels the value [ʌ:] if long, and [a] if short; cf. the comparable form *o-mu-kʌ:li* 'woman,' with overt assimilation of the long low vowel.

---

[36] The underlying value of the vowel in /mU-/ is established by forms like ɔ-*mU-tahI*, in which there is no following higher high vowel to trigger assimilation.

In Hyman's analysis, the assimilation rule spreads the feature [ATR] leftward across the word, excluding word-initial vowels. This treatment assumes a feature analysis such as the following (derived vowels are bracketed):

(61)

|      | i | u | I | U | [e] | [o] | ɛ | ɔ | [ʌ] | a |
|------|---|---|---|---|-----|-----|---|---|-----|---|
| high | + | + | + | + | –   | –   | – | – | –   | – |
| low  | – | – | – | – | –   | –   | – | – | +   | + |
| ATR  | + | + | – | – | +   | +   | – | – | +   | – |

This analysis is problematical for our account. As already mentioned, Kinande has a rule of total height assimilation similar in relevant respects to the one in Kimatuumbi. This is illustrated in the forms below, where it accounts for alternants of the applied suffix /-Ir/:

(62)  ε-ri-lim-ir-a      'to exterminate for'
      ε-ri-huk-ir-a      'to cook for'
      ε-rI-lIm-Ir-a      'to cultivate for'
      ε-rI-hUm-Ir-a      'to beat for'
      ε-rI-hεk-εr-a      'to carry for'
      ε-rI-bɔh-εr-a      'to tie for'
      ε-rI-kar-Ir-a      'to force for'

Hyman argues that the first two examples in (62), involving assimilation of the lower high vowel /I/ of the applied suffix to the higher high vowels /i u/, cannot be subsumed under the partial assimilation rule just described as a mirror image case since in all other contexts it applies only from right-to-left. He proposes that all the assimilations in (62) are due to an independent rule of (total) height assimilation applying to stem-medial vowels such as that of the applied suffix /-Ir/. Again, however, in order to account for height assimilation in these cases under the feature analysis in (61) we would have to spread two features [high], [ATR], which do not occur under a separate node of their own in the framework of Sagey (1986). One solution to this problem would be to link [ATR] to the Height (Aperture) node, essentially as proposed by Odden (1989a). However, while this would allow us to describe the facts correctly, it would severely violate the spirit of the present account of feature theory. If [ATR] is an articulatorily-defined feature, it should be assigned to the place node and not to the aperture node. On the other hand, if [ATR] is not phonetically distinct from [high], we would be led to a violation of the Phonetic Distinctness Criterion (5).

As an alternative, let us consider that all vowel height distinctions are characterized by the feature [open] just as in Kimatuumbi. Thus the feature analysis is as given in (63):

(63)           i    u    I    U    ε    ɔ    a

| | i | u | I | U | ε | ɔ | a |
|---|---|---|---|---|---|---|---|
| $open_1$ | − | − | − | − | − | − | + |
| $open_2$ | − | − | − | − | + | + | + |
| $open_3$ | − | − | + | + | + | + | + |

Given this analysis, left-to-right (total) assimilation can be described by the same rule as is required in Kimatuumbi (59), and the right-to-left partial assimilation rule illustrated in (60) can be described by a rule spreading [−$open_3$] as follows:

(64)  Aperture    Aperture

           ┌┄┄┄┄┄┄┄┄┐
       +$open_3$    −$open_3$

In addition to mapping [I U] into [i u], this rule creates the three derived vowels [e o ʌ] characterized as shown in the feature chart of Kinande surface vowels below:

(65)

| | i | u | I | U | [e] | [o] | ε | ɔ | [ʌ] | a |
|---|---|---|---|---|---|---|---|---|---|---|
| $open_1$ | − | − | − | − | − | − | − | − | + | + |
| $open_2$ | − | − | − | − | + | + | + | + | + | + |
| $open_3$ | − | − | + | + | − | − | + | + | − | + |

Comparing this chart to the one in (61), we see that it is isomorphic to it under the equivalences [+high] : [−$open_2$], [+low] : [+$open_1$], [+ATR] : [−$open_3$]. Thus both analyses characterize the same set of natural classes. However, under the hierarchical approach, it is not necessary to use [ATR] to crossclassify the vowel heights characterized by the other aperture features, since the feature [open] can be used for this purpose.

This analysis of Kinande is of particular interest since (if correct) it shows that vowel height is not simply a scale with a number of fixed values, as is implied in multivalued theories of vowel height. Such theories are unable to express partial assimilation rules such as the Kinande rule without considerable arbitrariness.[37] But such rules are expressed naturally in a hierarchical theory,

---

[37] If the notation V → n+1 is to be used, the underlying vowel heights of Kinande would have to be discontinuous: 5, 4, 2, 1.

and do not require recourse to an essentially diacritic use of the feature [ATR]. The Kinande data are equally problematical for one-valued feature theories such as particle theory, which cannot express assimilation to the feature [+high] (here, [–open$_3$]) in terms of independently-motivated principles of autosegmental phonology; as we have noted, these theories, which offer no counterpart to the feature [+high], strongly predict that such processes should not exist. Such theories are required to use an [ATR] particle to express the partial height assimilation rule, but then cannot explain why this feature should link together with aperture particles under a single node to the exclusion of other particles, as is required by the total height assimilation rule.

We conclude this section with a discussion of Esimbi, a Broad Bantu language spoken in Cameroon, analyzed by Hyman (1988) who draws upon earlier descriptions by Stallcup (1980a,b). This language is of particular interest for its "scalar" rule determining prefix height. We begin with a brief description of significant features of its interesting vocalic phonology, and then turn to a discussion of the rule in question.

The basic generalizations are as follows. Seven surface vowels [i u e o ɛ ɔ a] are found in prefixes but only three surface vowels [i ɨ u] occur in stems.[38] Vowel prefixes show one of three alternating patterns: I = [i ~ e ~ ɛ], U = [u ~ o ~ ɔ], A = [o ~ ɛ ~ ɔ ~ a], the correct alternant being determined by the stem. There are three types of stems, which we might call "high", "mid," and "low" due to their influence on prefixes; the class to which a stem belongs is phonologically unpredictable on synchronic grounds. Prefix alternations are summarized below for each of the three possible prefix vowels and each of the eight possible stem vowels (note that stems have only one surface vowel quality regardless of their length):

(66) Esimbi prefix alternations (after Hyman 1988: 258):

| prefix: | | /I-/ | /U-/ | /A-/ |
|---|---|---|---|---|
| 'high' stems: | /i/ | i-Ci | u-Ci | o-Ci |
| | /u/ | i-Cu | u-Cu | o-Cu |
| 'mid' stems: | /e/ | e-Ci | o-Ci | ɛ-Ci |
| | /o/ | e-Cu | o-Cu | ɔ-Cu |
| | /ɨ/ | e-Cɨ | o-Cɨ | ɔ-Cɨ |
| 'low' stems: | /ɛ/ | ɛ-Ci | ɔ-Ci | a-Ci |
| | /ɔ/ | ɛ-Cu | ɔ-Cu | a-Cu |
| | /a/ | ɛ-Cɨ | ɔ-Cɨ | a-Cɨ |

---

[38] I follow Hyman in transcribing the second series of vowels as [e o], but it would be more consistent with our earlier practice to transcribe them as [ɪ ʊ] given the feature analysis in (69) below.

Let us consider the prefix vowels /I-/ and /U-/ first. As (66) shows, these prefixes are realized as high vowels after "high" stems, mid vowels after "mid" stems, and low vowels after "low" stems. In Hyman's analysis, stem vowels are underlyingly characterized for one of three degrees of vowel height: thus "high" stems have underlying high vowels, "mid" stems underlying mid vowels, and "low" stems underlying low vowels. This analysis is given between slants in the left-hand column of (66). The underlying height features of the stem are shifted to the prefix by a rule of Height Transfer, and determine its surface height. Stem vowels, which at this point have no height features, are subject to a default rule assigning the value [+high] to vowels that are underspecified for height. Stem and prefix vowels are underlyingly characterized for one of the two place of articulation features [−back] and [+round], in the obvious way. The surface form of each vowel is therefore determined by summing its intrinsic place features and its derived height features.

The facts described so far make a strong argument for recognizing a separate Height (or Aperture) node, as Hyman himself points out. The rule of Height Transfer can be regarded as autosegmentally delinking the Height node from the stem and relinking it to the prefix. This accounts for the fact that all height features are transferred at the same time.

The analysis of the prefix /A-/ is more complex, as the data in (66) show. Although the surface alternant of this vowel is always predictable from the stem vowel, its realization does not involve simple assimilation. The basic observations to be made are given below:

(67) a. When the stem vowel is high /i u/, /A-/ is realized upper mid
 b. When the stem vowel is upper mid /e o ə/, /A-/ is realized lower mid
 c. When the stem vowel is lower mid /ɛ ɔ/ or low /a/, /A-/ is realized low

In other words, when the height of the stem vowel is transferred onto /A-/, this height is lowered by one step: high to upper mid, mid to lower mid, and lower mid to low (vacuously, low remains low). In Hyman's analysis, place features are assigned to /A-/ by independent, secondary processes.

The problem, then, is to account for the stepwise lowering effect of the prefix /A-/ in a principled way. Hyman offer two solutions, one making use of standard feature representations and the feature [ATR], and the second making use of the Height node. For reasons that will be clear from the preceding discussion, we will consider only the second here. According to this analysis, each stem is assigned a single underlying floating Height node bearing appropriate specifications for [high] and [low]. The prefixes /I-/ and /U-/ do not have an underlying Height node, since their height is determined by the height of the stem, but the

/A-/ prefix bears a Height node specified as [–high]. When the stem Height node is transferred to this prefix, its own Height node delinks, giving a representation in which a floating [–high] Height node precedes the (new) Height node of the prefix. This is shown for the underlying sequence /A-Cɛ/ below:

(68)

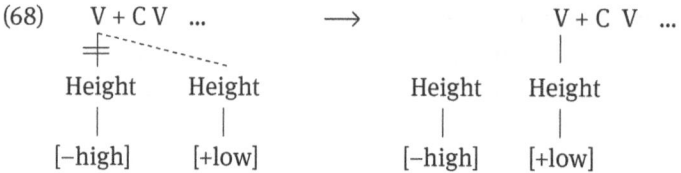

Hyman then asks: "Could this floating [–high] be a *vocalic downstep* marker, causing height lowering just as a floating L tone causes tonal downstep?" (p. 270).

This is a simple and elegant analysis, and one which I believe to be correct in its essentials on the basis of Hyman's evidence. In spite of this, I believe that Hyman's question should be answered in the negative. I will argue below that the floating Height node is not a trigger for downstep, but for stepwise height assimilation. If it were really the equivalent of a downstep trigger, we would expect all subsequent vowels to be one degree lower in height until downstep is "reset." In particular, if the domain of downstep is larger than the word, we would expect not only the immediately following stem but also all subsequent words in the domain to be lowered one degree in height. Furthermore, we would expect successive downsteps in this domain to be cumulative, just as they are in tone languages, predicting that there is no principled limit on the number of vowel heights in Esimbi. As far as we can tell from Hyman's discussion, this is not the case: there are only four phonetic vowel heights in Esimbi, and the domain of height lowering is the immediately following stem and nothing more. We could technically account for this fact in a downstep analysis by identifying the domain of downstep as the word, but this amounts to admitting that the crucial evidence for a downstep analysis is lacking.

Let us consider an alternative account making use of the hierarchical feature analysis developed earlier, already illustrated for other Bantu languages. I propose that the full feature analysis of Esimbi vowels is the following:

(69) *Feature analysis of Esimbi vowels:*

|          | i | ɨ | u | e | o | ə | ɛ | ɔ | a |
|----------|---|---|---|---|---|---|---|---|---|
| coronal  | + | – | – | + | – | – | + | – | – |
| labial   | – | – | + | – | + | – | – | + | – |
| open₁    | – | – | – | – | – | – | – | – | + |
| open₂    | – | – | – | – | – | – | + | + | + |
| open₃    | – | – | – | + | + | + | + | + | + |

Note that Esimbi is analysed as having a four-height system with the organization (((A B) C) D), just as we have proposed for other Bantu four-height systems. Height transfer works essentially as in Hyman's analysis. If the stem vowel is /a/, the prefixes /I-/ and /U-/ will be mapped into the intermediate vowels [æ] and [ʊ], respectively, and these will be subsequently converted into the correct [ɛ] and [ɔ] by the following redundancy rules:

(70) [+coronal] (=[–back])  ⟶  [–open₁]
     [+labial] (=[+round])  ⟶  [–open₁]

I assume that the underlying representation of /A-/ is simply that of the vowel /a/ in (69). When the Aperture node of this vowel is delinked, we have the following set of representations for /A-/ followed by high, higher mid, and lower mid vowels, respectively (the bracketed Ap[erture] node represents the floating node):

(71)                /a + i, u /:        /a + e, o, ə/:       /a + ɛ, ɔ /:

                  [Ap]     Ap         [Ap]      Ap         [Ap]      Ap
open₁:             +        –           +        –           +        –
open₂:             +        –           –        –           +        +
open₃:             +        –           +        +           +        +

At this point, the following rule of partial height assimilation applies:

(72) Esimbi Prefix Height Assimilation:

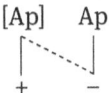

This rule states that [+open] characterizing a floating Aperture node spreads onto an Aperture node characterized by [–open]. As no particular tier is specified, this rule is defined on any tier which satisfies its description (necessarily an [open] tier, since no other features link to the Aperture node). Recall now the convention on rule application to hierarchical tiers proposed in section 3.2.3 above: when applications to more than one ranked tier are possible, and the target is minus-specified, the rule applies bottom-up and non-iteratively. Applying (72) to the representations in (71) in this fashion, we have the following results:

(73)

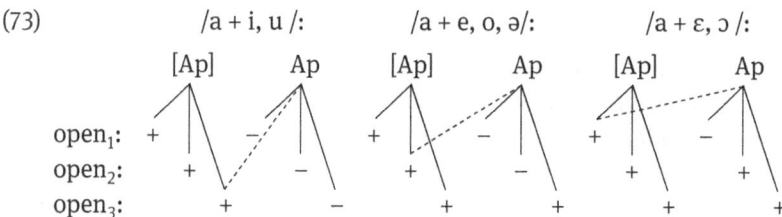

Assuming the Branch Pruning Convention (39), this rule correctly derives all alternants of /A-/ as far as their height is concerned.[39,40] In sum, we have shown that a variety of intricate height-related phenomena in Bantu languages can be accounted for in a straightforward way in terms of the hierarchical theory of vowel height proposed here. We have been able to maintain a uniform analysis of vowel height in all the four-height Bantu languages under discussion assuming the grouping (((A B) C) D), in which the primary division opposes a low vowel to the nonlow vowels, and a secondary division opposes a mid series to two high vowel series. This analysis therefore claims that such Bantu languages have two series of high vowels, one series of mid vowels, and one low vowel. It is interesting that this analysis is identical to the Proto-Bantu vowel system proposed by Meinhof (1932) and Guthrie (1967) on the basis of phonetic criteria, comparative evidence and historical sound changes.

---

**39** I assume, with Hyman, that place features are determined by independent rules of little interest to the present discussion.

**40** Two comments are in order. First, if we assume that redundant features are absent in underlying representations, as is required by all current underspecification theories, they must be filled in by the time (72) applies, either by extrinsic ordering of redundancy rules or by the Redundancy Rule Ordering Constraint (see note 10). Second, the present analysis does not crucially require that the Aperture node triggering the assimilation be floating at the time the assimilation rule (72) applies. This rule could equally well apply before Height Transfer, since there are no other sequences of /a + V/ to which it could apply. This would be consistent with the generally well-supported view that segmental features delinked by rules are immediately deleted by a general convention.

## 5.3 Vowel Raising in the Sotho Languages

One of the world's most complex systems of vowel height is found in the Sotho group of Bantu languages, spoken in southern Africa. These languages have five (or arguably, six) phonological vowel heights as well as a thoroughgoing system of partial height assimilation. This section presents an analysis of the vowel system of one of the members of this group, Sesotho (or Southern Sotho).[41] John Harris (1987) offers an insightful analysis of several important phonological rules of this language. We follow Harris's general account, while introducing new data and offering a new interpretation of vowel height.

Sesotho has six phonetically distinct vowel heights, as shown in (74) below.[42]

(74) *Sesotho surface vowels:*

    6.    i    u
    5.    i̗    u̗
    4.    I    U
    3.    e    o
    2.    ɛ    ɔ
    1.       a

Of these six heights, the second is clearly nonphonemic: vowels of height 5 are derived from vowels of height 4 by a regular rule of High Vowel Raising, which will be discussed below. This leaves us with a system of five phonemic vowel heights. In this respect Sesotho superficially resembles languages with three basic vowel heights crossclassified by the feature [tense] (as in some analyses of English) or [ATR] (as in recent analyses of Akan and other West African languages). However, these resemblances are misleading. Sesotho gives no phonetic evidence for treating the five phonemic vowel heights in terms of anything but a uniform phonetic parameter of vowel height. All vowels tend to be of equal

---

41 The Sotho languages include Tswana, Northern Sotho, and Southern Sotho (also known as Sesotho) (see Doke 1954 for a general descripttion of the group as a whole). Southern Sotho phonology is described in considerable detail in Doke and Mofokeng's grammar (1957) and Kunene's doctoral dissertation (1961), and further exemplified in Mabile and Dieterlen's dictionary (1961). Nearly identical vowel systems are found in the other Sotho languages; for discussion of Tswana see Cole (1949, 1955), and for Northern Sotho see Ziervogel (1967). In the early stages of the preparation of the present account I had the benefit of many working discussions of Sesotho phonology with Evelyn Khabanyane, a resident of Motsethabong district, Welkom, South Africa.
42 Standard orthography does not distinguish all vowel heights; the transcription system used here is based on that of Kunene (1961).

duration in similar contexts, and fall along a single, uniform scale as far as first and second formant values are concerned (Khabanyane 1990). Furthermore, Sesotho does not have a system of "cross-height" vowel harmony pairing its different vowel heights into overlapping sets, as do Akan and many other languages with [ATR]-type vowel harmony. Indeed, as we will see, its phonological system cannot be understood in terms of an analysis making crucial use of the feature [ATR].

We begin with an impressionistic phonetic description. Not surprisingly, Sesotho vowels are acoustically and perceptually very close to each other. Kunene's vowel chart (Kunene 1961) is given below.

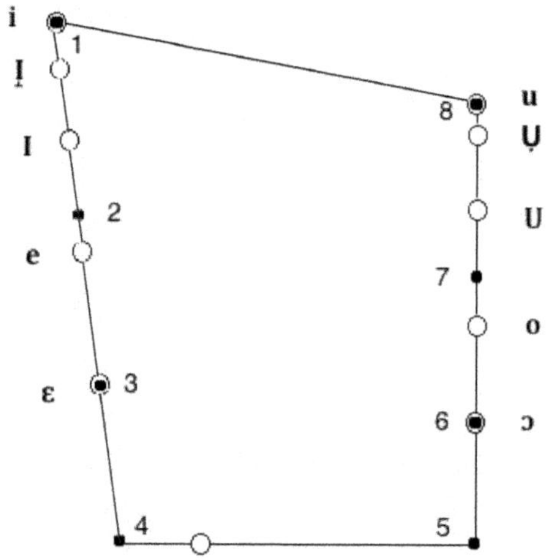


**Figure 2.** Chart showing Sesotho vowels in relation to Cardinal Vowels. Dots indicate the positions of the Cardinal vowels, numbered 1 to 8, while circles indicate the positions of Sesotho vowels. Adapted from Kunene (1961: 11).

According to Kunene, the tongue position of [i] is practically the same as that of C.V. (cardinal vowel) 1. The two lower high front vowels, [Ị] and [I], lie between C.V. 1 and C.V. 2, but [Ị] is much closer to 1 than to 2, while [I] is about twice as far from C.V. 1 as it is from C.V. 2. The tongue position of [e] is slightly lower than that of C.V. 2, and that of [ε] is about the same as C.V. 3. Back vowels are distributed in the same way. Vowel charts such as the one in Figure 2 are interpreted as representing the position of the highest point of the tongue, but in practice they are usually based on the phonetician's subjective impressions of auditory distance among vowels as manifested in first and second formant frequencies (Lindau 1978, Fischer-Jørgensen 1985). In fact, the judgements recorded in Figure 2 mesh quite well with the formant measurements presented in Khabanyane (1990), which show heights 1 and 2 well separated from the others acoustically, and the remaining heights clustered closely together.

The distinction between corresponding height 5 and height 6 vowels is difficult to perceive, even for listeners with phonetic training. Khabanyane's measurements show small mean first formant differences between corresponding height 5 and 6 vowels, ranging between 20 and 80 Hz. However, these differences are apparently perceptible. In the very similar vowel system of Tswana, Cole reports that minimal pairs such as [–bidit&#817;sẹ] 'call' (perfect stem) and [–bi&#817;dit&#817;sẹ 'beat' (perfect stem) or [lʊʃʊŋ] 'mosu bush thicket' (locative) and [lʊʃʊ̣ŋ] 'death' (locative) are reliably distinguished by speakers (1949: 115). One might expect comparable pairs to be distinguishable in Sesotho.

Historically, heights 1, 2, 4 and 6 are inherited directly from the four-height system of Proto-Bantu generally reconstructed as /i u I U ɛ ɔ a/,[43] and are cognate to the vowels transcribed with the cognate symbols in the discussion of Kimatuumbi and Kinande above. Heights 3 and 5 are Sotho innovations, created by the rules of vowel raising discussed below. Of these, height 3 vowels appear to represent the older innovation, as they appear in similar contexts in several neighboring Bantu languages, and are phonemic (in the sense of classical phonemics). This is shown by the following Sesotho examples, giving representative minimal and near-minimal pairs involving heights 2 and 3:[44]

(75) height$_2$ /ɛ ɔ/:            height$_3$ /e o/:

pɛrɛ 'horse'                      pere 'pear'
bɔna 'it'                         bona 'this one'
hlɔtsɛ 'piece of dry skin or leather'   hlotsa 'to limp'
lIhɔtlɔ 'bare patch of skin on animal'  mUhotle 'coot' (species)
hɔtɛla 'to burn'                  hotele 'hotel'
mUɛtsɛ 'back, side of animal'     mUetso 'way of doing'
pɔsɔ 'error'                      fosa 'to err'

The height 5 vowels, in contrast, appear to be more recent, as they arise in the postlexical phonology by exceptionless rules that are mostly free of grammatical or morphological conditioning.

Let us first consider the rule of Mid Vowel Raising, which raises lower mid vowels (height 2) to upper mid (height 3). This rule applies under a complex

---

[43] These vowels are frequently transcribed /i̧ u̧ i u e o a/ in the Bantuist tradition.
[44] In these and the following examples, tone, which does not interact with vowel raising, is omitted.

variety of conditions, some of which are purely phonological and some of which are morphological. In the most general case, it applies whenever a lower mid vowel is followed by a high vowel in the next syllable. Thus it shifts [ɛ ɔ] to [e o] respectively when the following syllable contains any of the vowels [i u I U]. Mid Vowel Raising accounts for the morpheme-internal upper mid vowels in (76), and for the alternations in (77a,b).

(76) lI-qheku   'old person'
     tepU       'spider's web'
     foufal-a   'go blind'
     notshi     'bee'

(77) verb stems with the suffix -a:        related forms with high vowel suffixes:

    a.  -sɛba      'gossip'          mU-sebi       'gossiper'
        -bɛtla     'sharpen'         -betluwe      'has been sharpened'
        -rɔka      'praise'          sI-roki       'poet'
        -bɔla      'rot'             sI-bodu       'rotten thing'
        -bɛtla     'sharpen'         sUbetlI       'not to sharpen'
        -ɛpa       'to dig'          -epUlla       'to dig out'
        -bɔna      'see'             -bonI         'have seen'
        -kɔba      'bend'            -kobUlla      'unbend'

    b.  -tɛtɛma    'shake, tremble'  -tetemisa     'cause to shake'
        -hlɔhlɔna  'to itch'         sU hlohlonI   'not to itch'
        -kɔbɛhɛla  'curve towards'   -kobehelI     'not to curve towards'

As the last set of examples (77b) shows, Mid Vowel Raising is unbounded, applying to each vowel in a string of syllables containing lower mid vowels as long as the last one is followed by a syllable with a high vowel.

Mid Vowel Raising also applies to /ɛ ɔ/ followed by syllabic [ŋ], which occurs as a locative suffix and as a stem-final consonant. Harris (1987) argues convincingly that the locative suffix has the more abstract form /-iŋ/ or /-Iŋ/ at the time Mid Vowel Raising applies; therefore this case can be subsumed under the preceding one.[45] Examples are given in (77):

---

[45] We will show below that the underlying form of this suffix must be /-iŋ/.

(78) a.  [ŋ] as a locative suffix:

|  |  |  |  |
|---|---|---|---|
| lIsapɔ | 'bone' | lIsapoŋ | (locative) |
| kɔpanɔ | 'meeting, assembly' | kɔpanoŋ | (locative) |
| sIlɛpɛ | 'axe' | sIlepeŋ | (locative) |
| pɛpɛnɛnɛ | 'open space' | pepeneneŋ | (locative) |
| phɔfɔlɔ | 'animal' | phofoloŋ | (locative) |
| thɛkɔ | 'price' | thekoŋ | (locative) |
| sIhɔlɛ | 'deformed person' | sIholeŋ | (locative) |

b.  [ŋ] as a stem-final consonant:

| beŋ | 'masters' |
|---|---|
| dihloŋ | 'shame' |
| lInoŋ | 'vulture' |
| kxhokoŋ | 'gnu' |

Many of these examples provide further confirmation that assimilation is unbounded.

Further phonological contexts for Mid Vowel Raising are the sequence [n̪ n], the palatal nasal [ʃ], and [s] alone or in the clusters [ts], [n̪ tsh], but only if this is part of a causative, intensive, or perfect suffix. Harris shows that these contexts also contain high vowels at the point where Mid Vowel Raising applies, which are subsequently deleted by a variety of lexical rules (see Harris 1987: 277–286 for further discussion).

The cases examined so far show that Mid Vowel Raising is conditioned by high vowels in a following syllable. In addition, there is some evidence that Mid Vowel Raising is triggered by the upper mid vowels [e o] as well. This is shown first by the fact that the rule applies iteratively, i.e. in a self-feeding fashion, in examples like -tetemisa, -hlohlonI, and kobehelI in (77). On the first iteration, the rule affects the second of the two mid vowels, changing e.g. underlying /tɛtɛmisa/ to [tɛtemisa]; in the second iteration [e] triggers the reapplication of the rule to the first vowel, giving the surface form [tetemisa]. One might consider an alternative analysis in which the two mid vowels share a single Aperture node as a result of the Obligatory Contour Principle (OCP) (McCarthy 1986), applying in this case to reduce identical adjacent Aperture nodes to one. In this analysis, the assimilation would be one-step, and would therefore not offer crucial evidence that upper mid vowels are triggers. However, there is some evidence that the OCP is not operative as a general constraining principle in Sesotho segmental phonology. Harris (1987) argues that Sesotho has a rule which deletes high front vowels between a voiced coronal and a coronal:

(79) High Front Vowel Deletion
[−cons, +high, −back] ⟶ ø / [+voiced, +cor] ___ [+cor]

This rule creates OCP violations at the segmental level in examples like /nɔn-il-ɛ/ → non-in-ɛ → non-n-ɛ [noṇne] 'be fat', and at the [coronal] feature level in examples like /bɔn-is-a/ → bon-is-a → bon-s-a → [boṇtsha] 'show.' If the OCP is applicable to the Aperture tier, it would have to be as a special case; although such an analysis cannot be ruled out in principle, I know of no independent evidence suggesting that it is correct.

We could make a stronger argument for the claim that upper mid vowels are Mid Vowel Raising triggers if we could show that underlying occurrences of these vowels, or occurrences created by independent rules prior to the operation of Mid Vowel Raising, also trigger the rule. Such evidence is available. We find many words with [e o] in word-final position, where Mid Vowel Raising is not defined. Examples are given in (80).[46]

(80) sIfate       'tree'
     ntate        'father'
     Itswe        'besides'
     mU̱suwe      'teacher'
     kI̱fuwe      (name)
     sI̱ruwe      (type of plant)
     pilo         'soot'
     Masilo       (name)
     Nkilo        (name of rat)
     sI̱tulo      'chair' (< Afr. *stoel*)
     kulo         'bullet' (< Afr. *koeël*)

There are two ways of analyzing these forms. One is to assume that the upper mid vowels are not underlying, but are derived by a rule of Final Mid Vowel Raising applying to a small set of lexically marked forms. Since this rule has many exceptions, however, it would be more straightforward to assume that these vowels are underlying. In this analysis, the vowels /e o/ have acquired marginal (systematic) phonemic status in Sesotho in final position. It does not matter for our

---

[46] Harris, though not noting examples of this kind, observes a variable postphonological rule according to which mid vowels may vary along a phonetic continuum between lower mid and upper mid, e.g. sɪfatɛ ~ sɪfate 'tree' (1987: 277). Apparently, the rule illustrated in (80), which applies to only a small set of words, represents a lexicalization of this principle, perhaps restricted to certain dialects.

purposes which of these two analyses we accept, however, since it is sufficient for our argument that the mid vowels are not created by Mid Vowel Raising.

We can now make an independent argument that upper mid vowels are Mid Vowel Raising triggers. A larger study of the Sesotho lexicon shows that the vowels [ɛ ɔ] and [e o] do not occur in adjacent syllables.[47] This is due in part to a further rule which raises lower mid vowels to upper mid in syllables following upper mid vowels. By this rule, for example, the subjective suffix /-ɛ/ and the noun-forming suffix /-ɔ/ are realized as [e o], as shown in the following forms:

(81) besa     'roast'    bese    (present subjunctive)
     tlotsa   'anoint'   tlotse  (present subjunctive)
     etsa     'do'       mUetso  'way of doing'
     tlotsa   'anoint'   tlotso  'anointing'

In these examples, it is clear that the suffix vowel assimilates to the upper mid vowels of the prefinal syllables, where they are either underlying, or perhaps conditioned by the following s or s-cluster. But this cannot be the explanation for the word-internal vowels [e o] in (82):

(82) thepe         'kind of vegetable'
     lelele        'long, tall'
     maŋolo        'fertilizer'
     sIbele        'rumor'
     sIhlekehleke  'island'
     mUkoloko      'procession'
     lIqitolo      'one with tricks'
     shweshwe      'type of wild flower'
     sIkolo        'school' (< Eng.)
     koro          'wheat' (< Afr. *koring* )
     bUleke        'tin can' (< Afr. *blik* )

In these examples, there is no way of deriving the word-internal upper mid vowels from lower mid vowel sources by independently-motivated rules. And if we assumed that these vowels are underlying, we would fail to express the generalization that upper mid vowels do not occur word-internally unless followed

---

**47** Doke and Mofokeng (p. 6) cite two exceptions to this statement, *fosɛha* 'miss the mark' (neut.) and *etsɛha* 'do' (neut.). Apparently, the neuter suffix *-éh* constitutes an exception to progressive raising, perhaps due to the influence of the [h], as glottals are known to have a lowering influence on vowels in other languages.

by a high vowel or an upper mid vowel in the next syllable. In short, the simplest analysis is to assume that these vowels are derived by Mid Vowel Raising, triggered in this case by upper mid vowels.⁴⁸

To summarize the discussion so far, we have seen that Mid Vowel Raising raises lower mid vowels to upper mid when followed by either a high vowel or an upper mid vowel in the next syllable. More succinctly, we can say that it raises lower mid vowels by one degree in height when followed by a higher vowel. But how can we express this generalization in formal terms?

Mid Vowel Raising presents a thorny descriptive problem for standard theories of vowel height, as Harris points out. While a "classical" binary feature theory using features like [high], [low], and [ATR] can describe the facts correctly, it cannot do so insightfully. Thus, assuming a feature analysis like the following (height 5 vowels are omitted for purposes of the present discussion):

(83) Sesotho vowel features (using [ATR])

|      | i | u | I | U | e | o | ɛ | ɔ | a |
|------|---|---|---|---|---|---|---|---|---|
| high | + | + | + | + | – | – | – | – | – |
| low  | – | – | – | – | – | – | – | – | + |
| ATR  | + | + | – | – | + | + | – | – | – |

The rule raising [ɛ ɔ] before higher vowels could be stated as follows:

(84) Mid Vowel Raising (standard features):

$$\begin{bmatrix} -\text{high} \\ -\text{low} \end{bmatrix} \rightarrow [+\text{ATR}] \Big/ \_\_ \begin{Bmatrix} +\text{high} \\ +\text{ATR} \end{Bmatrix}$$

However, this rule fails to characterize Mid Vowel Raising as an assimilation rule, since not all triggering vowels are [+ATR]. As Harris puts it, we want to say

---

**48** Apart from the phonologically-conditioned cases discussed above, upper mid vowels occur in a variety of morphologically-determined contexts, including the following (Harris 1987):
    a. plural prefix of class 1a nouns;
    b. demonstrative concords;
    c. relative concords;
    d. tense-aspect-modality markers ('deficient verbs')

Harris argues convincingly that these values are assigned by a default rule applying to minor-category grammatical forms inserted in the syntax. Assuming that this analysis is correct, these form do not shed further light on the Mid Vowel Raising rule, and we will accordingly have nothing further to say about them here.

that whatever property is shared by [i u I U e o] gets spread onto mid vowels [ɛ ɔ] to yield [e o]: but in this analysis, no single feature is shared by the set [i u I U e o] to the exclusion of [ɛ ɔ].

As an alternative, Harris proposes a feature analysis in which the lower mid vowels and low vowels are assigned to the same surface height, [+low], so that [i u I U e o] now share the feature [−low]. [ATR] is used only to distinguish the two high vowel series. This analysis is given below:

(85) Sesotho surface vowels (Harris 1987):

|          | i | u | I | U | e | o | ɛ | ɔ | a |
|----------|---|---|---|---|---|---|---|---|---|
| high     | + | + | + | + | − | − | − | − | − |
| low      | − | − | − | − | − | + | + | + |   |
| rounded  | − | + | − | + | − | + | − | + | − |
| back     | − | + | − | + | − | + | − | + | + |
| ATR      | + | + | − | − | − | − | − | − | − |

In Harris' analysis, nonhigh vowels are not specified for [low] prior to the operation of Mid Vowel Raising, which amounts to saying that the contrast between upper and lower mid vowels does not exist underlyingly. Mid Vowel Raising is formulated as a rule that spreads [−low] onto all vowels other than [a], as follows:[49]

(86) Mid Vowel Raising (Harris 1987):

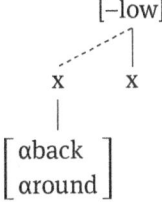

A later redundancy rule fills in the value [+low] on vowels that have not yet received a specification for [low], that is, nonhigh vowels that do not lie in the domain of (86).

Given Harris' assumptions, this analysis describes the facts correctly and completely. Nevertheless, there are certain problems to which we turn now.

---

[49] Harris's x s can be understood as representing the Vocalic node in the present framework, and [αback, αround] as standing for a specified V-place node, which is presumably absent in the representation of /a/.

First of all, it is forced to classify the low vowel /a/ as belonging to the same height as the lower mid vowels, in spite of the fact that it consistently fails to pattern with these vowels in phonological rules. This requires us to stipulate the feature cluster [αback, αround][50] in the rule, which has no function other than to exclude the low vowel from the domain of the rule. It is unexplained why these features, in particular, should play a crucial role in conditioning a rule of height assimilation.

Furthermore, the Sotho vowel system as analysed in (85) is typologically deviant from the point of view of other Bantu systems, and inconsistent with phonetic realization. We have already noted that other Bantu systems with the seven vowels /i u I U ɛ ɔ a/ organize them into the four-height pattern (((A B) C) D), with two high vowel series, one mid vowel series and one low vowel series; we have also pointed out that this analysis is usually attributed to Proto-Bantu. A quite different system is assumed for Sesotho in Harris's analysis, in which /ɛ ɔ a/ all count as low vowels throughout the later stages of the phonology. We could propose late realization rules that would map this system into one in which [e o] are [+ATR,−low] and [ɛ ɔ] are [−ATR, −low], consistently with phonetic realizations (in which [a] is well separated from [ɛ ɔ], cf. Khabanynane 1990), but these rules obviously detract from the overall simplicity of the analysis. Finally, the crucial reliance on [ATR] in this analysis represents a violation of the Phonetic Distinctness Criterion (5), making it unavailable to us even in principle.

Let us then consider an alternative analysis making use of the hierarchical theory of vowel height developed above. On the basis of the evidence discussed earlier, I will assume an underlying 9-vowel system for Sesotho, as shown in the full feature representations given below:

| (87) | i | u | I | U | e | o | ɛ | ɔ | a |
|---|---|---|---|---|---|---|---|---|---|
| $open_1$ | − | − | − | − | − | − | − | − | + |
| $open_2$ | − | − | − | − | + | + | + | + | + |
| $open_3$ | − | − | + | + | + | + | + | + | + |
| $open_4$ | − | − | − | − | − | − | + | + | + |

We see that the vowel system characterized by the first three register distinctions, [$open_1$], [$open_2$] and [$open_3$], is formally identical to those of four-height Bantu languages such as Kimatuumbi and Kinande. Sesotho differs from these languages in introducing a fourth distinction, [$open_4$], which divides the mid vowels into two categories, upper and lower. As the most "fragile" of the registers, the one with the lowest functional load, we assign it the lowest hierarchical

---

[50] Or equivalently in our framework, the V-place node; see the note above.

rank. Our claim is thus that at the level of its most basic height distinctions, the Sesotho system is identical to that of most Bantu four-height systems.

Mid Vowel Raising can be expressed as a rule spreading [−open$_4$] onto preceding [−open$_1$] vowels, as shown in (88):[51]

(88) Mid Vowel Raising (final version):

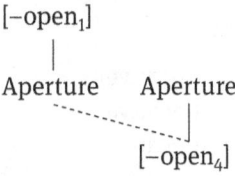

In many respects, this analysis is similar to Harris's. In particular, the feature [−open$_4$] plays the same role as the feature [−low] in his analysis, characterizing [i u I U e o] as a natural class as opposed to [ɛ ɔ a]. However, the analysis in (87), unlike Harris's, allows us to separate the low vowel [a] from the lower mid vowels [ɛ ɔ] in underlying representation, eliminating the problems arising from the absence of a distinction between these two series in Harris's system. In particular, rule (88) is naturally conditioned to apply only to [−open$_1$] vowels, reflecting the fact that rules of partial height assimilation are often restricted to particular height registers (cf. the analysis of Kimatuumbi given earlier).

We now consider the rule of High Vowel Raising, which raises height$_4$ (lower high) vowels to height$_5$ (mid high) vowels. As described by Kunene (1961) and Khabanyane (1986), this rule applies under the following conditions:

(89) a. before a syllable containing one of the vowels [i u] of height 6;
b. before the syllabic nasal [ŋ];
c. after a syllable containing one of the height 6 vowels [i u] of identical backness to the affected vowel.

The first two rules apply in an unbounded fashion, while the third affects only one vowel. These cases are illustrated in (90a)-(90c), respectively.

---

51 As in the earlier discussion of Gbe and Kinande, if we assume underspecified underlying representations, relevant features must be filled in by the time ($88) applies, either by extrinsic ordering of redundancy rules or as a result of the Redundancy Rule Ordering Constraint.

(90) a. i. verbs:
-bIla          'boil'           -bIdile (perfect)   -bIdisa (causative)
-nUka          'season'         -nUkile (perfect)   -nUkisa (causative)
ii. nouns:
mUrUbisi       'owl'
mUlIlIri       'vagabond'
sIfuba         'chest'
mUruti         'teacher, minister'

b. sIbI            'sin'           sIbIŋ        (locative)
bUhUlUhUlU     'long ago'      bUhUlUhUlUŋ  (locative)
sIrUpI         'thigh'         sIrUpIŋ      (locative)

c. mUrifI          'clay pot'
-rumUla        'tease, provoke'
-phuthUlUha    'become unfolded'

Given the subtlety of the distinction between the two highest degrees of height, one might ask whether the mid high (height 5) vowels arise through gradient implementation rules, instead of discrete phonological rules. If this were true, they could be ignored as far as the phonological rule system is concerned. Unfortunately, a thorough phonetic investigation of this question has not yet been carried out. But a gradient rule analysis seems to be suggested by Kunene's observation that "raising is often more pronounced, and therefore more easily observable, where [–I] is followed in the next syllable by [i], and [U] by [u], than in cases where [–I] is followed by [u] and [U] by [i]" (Kunene 1961: 15). Further support for this view comes from Khabanyane's observation that the rule illustrated in (90b) does not affect the first in a string of more than one vowel (Khabanynane 1986); this might suggest that we are dealing with a gradient implementation rule whose "window" extends over several syllables, affecting vowels most strongly in syllables closest to the conditioning vowel.

On the other hand, there is some evidence to suggest that the rule is truly phonological in nature. First of all, we have already reported Harris's analysis of the syllabic nasal [ŋ] as consisting of the sequence /-iŋ/ or /-Iŋ/ at the point at which Mid Vowel Raising takes place. We can explain the fact that this nasal is also a trigger for High Vowel Raising if we assume that it has the representation /-iŋ/ at the point at which this rule takes place. On this analysis, High Vowel Raising is always triggered by one of the high vowels [i u], giving us a natural analysis. On the assumption that rules applying before discrete phonological rules are themselves phonological, at least in the unmarked case, it follows that High Vowel Raising is phonological, since it precedes the phonological rule mapping /-iŋ/ into syllabic [ŋ].

Further evidence sugesting that High Vowel Raising may be phonological in nature comes from certain forms noted by Khabanyane (1986). The negative suffix /-I / is realized as [– Į] under the following circumstances:[52]

(91) the negative suffix /-I / is realized as:
    a.  [-Į] before a noun object:

| hU sĮ is-Į bana | 'not to take children away' |
|---|---|
|  | (is- 'cause to go' + -I 'negative') |
| hU sI phŲphŲth-Į mUthU | 'not to shake off a person' |
| ha a kŲp-Į mmɛ | 'he does not ask mother' |

    b.  [-Į] after a vowel of height 6:

| hU sĮ is-Į | 'not to take away' |
|---|---|
| hU sĮ dul -Į | 'not to sit' |

    c.  [-I] elsewhere:

| hU sI phŲphŲth-I | 'not to shake off' |
|---|---|
| ha a kŲp-I | 'he does not ask' |
| hU sI sɛb-I | 'not to gossip' |
| hU sI kɔkɔt-I | 'not to knock' |

The second and third examples in (91a) show that raising is unbounded within the word, even when the negative suffix is realized as the height 4 vowel [I] in final position (91c). This suggests that the basic, or default value of the negative suffix may be /Į/, which triggers High Vowel Raising in preceding lower high vowels and is subsequently lowered to [I] in phrase-final position after a vowel of height 5 or lower. This analysis, if correct, suggests that High Vowel Raising may be a phonological rule. If grammatical conditioning is characteristic of phonological but not phonetic rules, as is widely believed, then High Vowel Raising must be phonological in nature, since it is conditioned by the presence or absence of a following object. The fact that High Vowel Raising is rendered opaque by the rule of phrase-final lowering applying to the forms in (91c) also suggests that the rule may be phonological, if phonetic assimilation processes are transparent on the surface, as I have suggested elsewhere (Clements 1985b).

These arguments cannot be considered conclusive, since at present there does not exist a general theory of phonetic implementation rules, at least outside the domain of tone and intonation. However, we will pursue the consequences of treating High Vowel Raising as a phonological rule in the interest of seeing what further assumptions are required in our model to deal with this phenomenon.

---

[52] The rule which I state and illustrate in ($91) is based upon examples given by Khabanyane (1986), and has not been elsewhere reported in the literature.

As a phonological rule, High Vowel Raising must split an existing vowel height, the second from highest, into two subsidiary levels. The second from highest vowel height, the one containing /I U/, is created at the third level of hierarchical division ([$\text{open}_3$]) according to the feature characterization in (87); or more accurately, it is the lower tertiary register of the higher secondary register of the higher primary register. Therefore, the rule in question must split this tertiary register into two further subregisters, creating a new hierarchical level [$\text{open}_5$], and then spread the higher value of this new subregister ([+$\text{open}_5$]) onto high ([–$\text{open}_2$]) vowels lying in its domain.

Formally, the rule first "sets the stage" for the split by copying the values of [$\text{open}_3$] under the high vowels ([–$\text{open}_2$]) on the new [$\text{open}_5$] tier. This gives us the following expanded set of tiers:

(92)

| | i | u | I | U | e | o | ɛ | ɔ | a |
|---|---|---|---|---|---|---|---|---|---|
| $\text{open}_1$ | – | – | – | – | – | – | – | – | + |
| $\text{open}_2$ | – | – | – | – | + | + | + | + | + |
| $\text{open}_3$ | – | – | + | + | + | + | + | + | + |
| $\text{open}_4$ | – | – | – | – | – | – | + | + | + |
| $\text{open}_5$ | – | – | + | + | | | | | |

We can now state High Vowel Raising as a rule that spreads the newly created feature [–$\text{open}_5$] onto [–$\text{open}_2$] vowels:

(93) High Vowel Raising (splits [+$\text{open}_3$]):

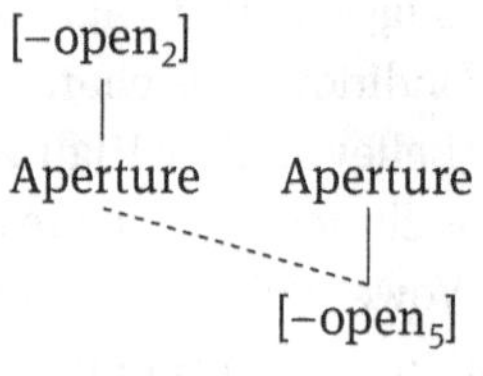
[–open2]
Aperture
Aperture
[–open5]

After High Vowel Raising applies, we have the derived six-height surface system given below:

(94)

| | i | u | Ị | Ụ | I | U | e | o | ɛ | ɔ | a |
|---|---|---|---|---|---|---|---|---|---|---|---|
| $\text{open}_1$ | – | – | – | – | – | – | – | – | – | – | + |
| $\text{open}_2$ | – | – | – | – | – | – | + | + | + | + | + |
| $\text{open}_3$ | – | – | + | + | + | + | + | + | + | + | + |
| $\text{open}_4$ | – | – | – | – | – | – | – | – | + | + | + |
| $\text{open}_5$ | – | – | – | – | + | + | (+) | (+) | (+) | (+) | (+) |

We may assume, though noncrucially, that the redundancy rules given in (27) apply to fill in the parenthesized values on the [open$_5$] tier.

We may finally consider whether it is possible to collapse Mid Vowel Raising and High Vowel Raising into a single, comprehensive rule. This rule would say something like: "raise a vowel one degree in height before a higher vowel." Elegant as this proposition may be, it proves to be inadequate. The reason for this is that vowels of height 1 and height 3 are never raised before higher vowels.[53] This is shown by representative examples like the following (Kunene 1961, Mabile and Dieterlen 1961):

(95) a.  /a/ followed by higher vowels:
    rata          'love'
    mU-rati     'lover'
    rat-isa     'cause to love'
    rat-I        'not to love'
    ba-tlile    'they have come (and are here)'
    ha-ba-buI  'they do not speak'

b.  /e, o/ followed by higher vowels:
    etsa           'do'
    mU-etsi      'doer'
    mU-ets-uwa  'victim'
    ets-isa      'cause to do'
    ets-Ulla    'to undo'
    fosa          'err'
    mU-fosi     'one who errs'
    bU-fosi     'fallibility'
    mU-fos-uwa  'one at the prejudice of whom a mistake has been committed'
    fos-isa     'cause to miss'
    e-chitja   'hornless' (class 9)
    o-mUhUlU  'big' (class 3)

Further evidence that the rules cannot be collapsed comes from the fact that they apply under different conditions. Thus Mid Vowel Raising applies before lexical rules such as High Front Vowel Deletion (79), while High Vowel Raising is a later, perhaps postlexical rule. We are thus dealing with two independent rules, Mid Vowel Raising and High Vowel Raising, having similar effects.

---

[53] However, /a/ is raised to [ɛ] or [e] by an independent rule before an immediately abutting underlying /i/ (Harris 1987).

In sum, we have shown that the complexities of the Sotho vowel system can be expressed in terms of a straightforward application of the model developed earlier. We have proposed an underlying vowel system very similar to those proposed for other Bantu languages, differing only in the introduction of an additional register characterizing Sesotho as a language with five underlying vowel heights. Our analysis directly expresses the generalization that the vowels [I U] and [ɛ ɔ] are raised one degree in height before a syllable containing a higher vowel. And not the least of our results is that by abandoning the features [high], [low] and [ATR] in favor of a single, hierarchical feature [open], we have achieved a better fit to the facts of phonetic realization.

## 6 Height Diphthongization

As a further problem for standard treatments of vowel height, some linguists have pointed to the existence of a class of diphthongization rules which treat vowel height as a scalar phenomenon, causing the first or second mora of a vowel to be raised or lowered by one step on the height scale. For example, in a variety of Swedish spoken in southern and western Scania (including the towns of Malmö and Lund), we find a diphthongization process in which the first mora of a stressed long vowel is lowered one degree in height. This rule has the following effect (Bruce 1970); the first three columns give front vowels, and the last column back vowels.

(96) /i:/ ⟶ ei      /y:/ ⟶ øy      /ʉ:/ ⟶ øʉ      /u:/ ⟶ eu
     /e:/ ⟶ ɛe      /ø:/ ⟶ œø                     /o:/ ⟶ ɛo
     /ɛ:/ ⟶ æɛ                                    /ɑ:/ ⟶ æɒ

As we see, the first mora of each vowel drops one degree in height.[54] This rule is supported not only by cross-dialectal comparison but by dialect-internal alter-

---

54 I follow Bruce (1970) in transcribing the diphthongized variant of /ɑ:/ as [æɑ]. Bruce, who uses the symbol [Å] to designate a rounded lower mid back vowel, reports that the exact phonetic value of this part of the diphthong is uncertain. He remarks: "the interpretation of the diphthongization of the vowel /ɑ/ as [æɑ] or even extremely [æo] is in my opinion more adequate than the traditional [ɑu]" (8). An examination of his spectrograms and formant chart reveals that that first formant of the second half of this diphthong is substantially higher than that of either [o] or [u] in [ɛo] and [eu], suggesting that it could be regarded as a lower mid vowel [ɔ]. Bruce's data are from a speaker of the Malmö dialect; spectrograms of a speaker from Lund, reproduced in Figure 3 below, suggest that this diphthong has two contextual variants: [æɑ] internally and [au] finally.

nations. First, as this type of diphthongization is considered substandard, it can be partly or entirely suppressed in more formal speech registers, giving rise to stylistically-conditioned alternations. Second, as diphthongization is applicable only in open syllables, we find phonologically conditioned alternations such as [veit] 'white' vs. [vit-t] 'white-NEUT', [lɛed-a] 'lead-INF' vs. [led-də] 'lead-PAST' (Hayes 1990).

Bruce (1970) and Lindau (1978) argue that the diphthongizations in (96) cannot be adequately treated within a binary feature system, and propose rules making use of a multivalued height feature. Swedish is not an isolated case, as similar diphthongization rules are found in the three-height system of Eastern dialects of Finnish (Kiparsky 1968) and in the four-height system of Quebec French, discussed in detail by Dumas (1981). Hayes (1990) argues that such processes not only represent a serious problem for binary feature theories, but call for a revision of hierarchical approaches to feature representation such as those proposed in works such as Clements (1985a) and Sagey (1986). We address these issues in this section.

Let us first examine the acoustic properties of Scanian diphthongs. Formant measurements are given in Figure 3, after a study by Jessen (1990).[55] Figure 3a gives values of the diphthongs in word-internal position, and Figure 3b gives values in final position.

These figures confirm that the diphthongs fall into two sets, which we may call front and back, according to their final target value. Front diphthongs show a falling $F_1$ and a slightly rising $F_2$, as we would expect of diphthongs that rise in height. Back diphthongs show not only a falling $F_1$ but a dramatically falling $F_2$, consistent with the view that they involve a shift of the tongue body from the front to the back of the oral cavity as well as a rise in tongue height. Figure 3b shows similar acoustic characteristics, except that the low back diphthong [æɑ] rises toward a value close to that for [u]; we take this to be a special phrase-final variant of this vowel. Together, Figures 3a and 3b give good support for the transcriptions in (96), and suggest two generalizations: back vowels acquire an initial fronted component, and all vowels acquire an initial lowered component.

---

[55] These measurements are based upon recordings of one speaker of the Lund dialect, Mona Lindau, generously made available to us by Bruce Hayes. Two tokens of each vowel were produced in each context. The values in the figures are averages of these tokens. A study of spectrograms shows that the diphthongs generally show two steady-state portions separated by transitions; the values shown in the figures are taken toward the beginning and end of each diphthong. Obviously, no firm conclusions can be drawn from a small data set such as this, but given its general agreement with the data given by Bruce, we believe that it gives a reliable (if approximate) picture of the acoustic properties of Scanian diphthongs. For further data (including spectrograms) and discussion, see Jessen (1990).

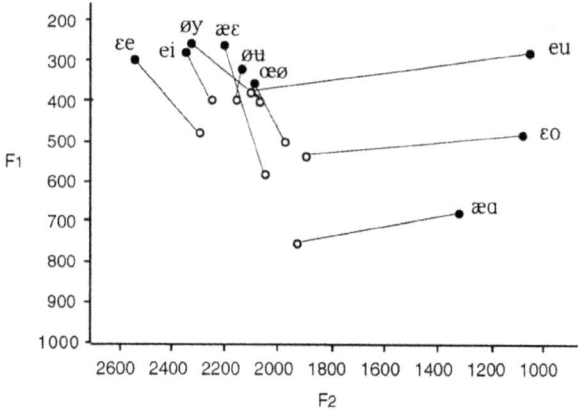

**Figure 3a.** Diphthongs in the Lund dialect of Swedish, spoken medially in the context [r__ta] (after data provided in Jessen 1990). Open circles = beginning points, closed circles = endpoints

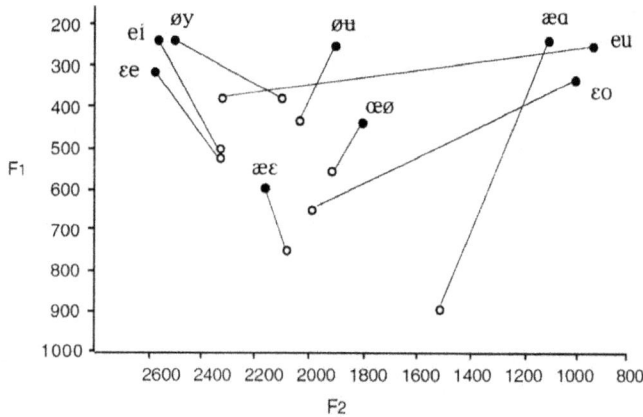

**Figure 3b.** Diphthongs in the Lund dialect of Swedish, spoken in prepausal position (after data provided in Jessen 1990). Open circles = beginning points, closed circles = endpoints.

To see why these data are problematical for standard binary feature frameworks, let us see how proponents of such a framework might attempt to deal with them. First, one might object that the diphthongization rule is a phonetic rule, rather than a phonological one; in this case, it would not bear on phonological feature representation. However, it is becoming increasingly clear that phonetic rules do bear on phonological representation. For example, Pierrehumbert and Beckman (1988) have shown that phonetic realization provides evidence for the nature of autosegmental feature specification in Japanese, and Keating (1988) has argued that phonetic realization can provide evidence for segmental feature representation as well. Thus the fact that a given phenomenon is phonetic in nature does not mean that it is irrelevant to phonological representation. It is the goal of much recent work in the area of the phonology/phonetics interface to find a representational system for phonology that provides the basis for simple phonetic implementation rules. In the case of Swedish dipthongization, one might argue that a nonstandard feature representation provides a better input to the phonetics – one allowing simpler realization rules – than a standard framework involving the features [high] and [low].

There is, however, some evidence that scalar diphthongization processes can take place in the phonology. In Swedish, as shown in the transcriptions in (96), diphthongization feeds a further rule that unrounds the fronted first mora of back diphthongs,[56] and in the Eastern dialects of Finnish described by Kiparsky (1968) diphthongization feeds a redundancy rule which makes nonlow back vowels round. These rules have the character of "enhancement rules" as described by Stevens et al. (1986). In Quebec French, with a complex height diphthongization rule similar to that of Swedish, the lowered first mora of the derived diphthong triggers a later process of vowel assimilation just as do vowels lowered by other rules (Dumas 1981: 28). Thus it appears that the diphthongs created by scalar raising and lowering rules can provide input to further phonological rules, suggesting that they are phonological themselves.

As a second strategy for maintaining the standard feature analysis of height, it might be proposed that the feature involved in lowering is not [high] or [low] but [tense]. Specifically, it might be proposed that Swedish long vowels are basically tense, and that the diphthongization rule laxes the first mora. If such a proposal is to avoid using features in a phonetically arbitrary way, it would have to be supported by a demonstration that [tense] provides a better account of the phonetic properties of the diphthongs than [high] and [low]. However, if the feature [tense] is defined more or less as in SPE (see section 2.1), the evidence seems to point in the opposite direction. Bruce (1970: 6) points out that short vowels as opposed to the long (diphthongizing) ones are usually more "extreme" in the sense that their position on the vowel chart is further away from the neutral vowel position than that of their long counterparts (i.e. the target of the second portion of the diphthong), and suggests that the usual correlation of tenseness with length may be reversed in this variety of Swedish. Further, whether we take the neutral

---

[56] Hayes (1990) transcribes diphthongized front rounded vowels with initial unrounded moras in the Lund dialect. However, according to his tapes and to Hayes (p.c.), these moras could just as well be regarded as rounded. See Jessen (1990) for discussion and analysis suggesting that they are in fact rounded.

position to be that of [e] (as in SPE) or of [ə] (as in a common alternative practice), it is clear from the data in Figure 3 that the initial parts of the diphthongs do not all tend toward the neutral vowel. Indeed the first moras of the low vowels [æɛ] and [æʊ] are actually *further* from the neutral position than the second. Similar problems with the use of [tense] to describe diphthongization in Quebec French are described by Dumas (1981: 12–16, 29–35). [57]

Thirdly, one might accept that diphthongization is a phonological rule making use of the features [high] and [low], and exploit paired feature variables to write the rule. This is the strategy proposed by Yip (1980a), who argues that the Scanian facts can be accounted for in terms of [high] and [low] on certain further assumptions concerning the analysis of the Swedish vowel system. Given these assumptions, the rule can be written making use of paired variables as follows:

(97) V ⟶ [–high, –αlow] / ____ [αhigh]

We have already questioned, however, whether rules of this type are appropriate. As was mentioned in the discussion of (8), the problem with paired variables is that widely recurring pairings such as that of [high] and [low] are not distinguishable from rare or nonoccurring ones. What is specific to the gradient diphthongization rules that we find in Swedish, Finnish and Quebec French is that only vowel height is affected across the board, while other features are affected only in a few vowels, if any. This generalization cannot be captured in terms of the standard framework, in which [high] and [low] have the same formal status as all other features.

In sum, the problems facing a feature analysis making use of [high] and [low] seem real, and I will explore an alternative account in the following discussion. I will first consider the nature of diphthongization as a general process, and then propose an analysis of Swedish diphthongization.

---

[57] As far as Swedish is concerned, the definition of [tense] given by Wood (1975), according to which tense vowels are more constricted at the place of major constriction than the corresponding lax vowel, fares better than the traditional definition. In the front vowel series, where the major constriction is at the hard palate, the first member of each diphthong is more open, and thus less constricted, than the second. In particular, if we reinterpret /ɛː/ as a tense low vowel /æt:/, then its diphthongized realization [æɛ] can be interpreted as a more open (laxer) vowel [æl] followed by a less open (tenser) vowel [æt]. In the back series, where the major constriction is velopharyngeal, the first member of each diphthong is less constricted than the second by virtue of the fact that it is a front (palatal) vowel. While Wood's definition of [tense] gives good results in this case, it cannot be generalized to the type of diphthongization found in Quebec French and Finnish. Further, Wood's feature [tense] has not so far been justified on phonological grounds, that is in terms of its ability to define natural classes correctly.

Traditional theory often uses the term "breaking" to describe diphthongization processes. This term expresses the idea that single, homogenous segments are "broken" or divided into two heterogenous ones. Andersen (1972) and Stampe (1972) suggest that what initially triggers the diphthongization of a segment is the appearance of variation along some phonetic parameter, such as tongue height, internal to that segment. When that variation becomes salient enough to be reinterpretated as phonological, the segment is reanalyzed as bearing two different, sequenced values of a single feature; at this point, it has achieved the status of a phonological sequence. As Andersen correctly points out, this view cannot be directly expressed in theories of phonological representation which treat phonemes as feature matrices with no ordered subparts. At best, such theories would allow us to characterize phonological diphthongization in terms of two successive rules, one reanalyzing a monophthong as a sequence of identical short vowels, and the second raising or lowering one of the short vowels, as follows: i: → ii → ei. But such an analysis seems unsatisfactory; since diphthongization is a common phonological process, an adequate theory should be capable of formalizing it in terms of a single elementary rule type, instead of two.

It might appear that this problem could be solved if we analyzed long vowels as sequences of short identical vowels to start with; under this analysis, the first of the two steps would be unnecessary. This advantage is illusory, however, for two reasons. First, it is now well established that long segments consist of single feature matrices linked to two positions on the timing tier, or skeleton (Kenstowicz 1982, Prince 1984, Clements 1986, Hayes 1986, Schein and Steriade 1986). We cannot make a special exception to this principle just for vowels that undergo diphthongization.

Second, while this analysis provides an elegant account of the diphthongization of long vowels, it does not extend to the diphthongization of short vowels. This type of diphthongization, while rare, does exist. Three examples are given below.

1. /æ/ must be analyzed as an underlying short vowel in English, for several reasons. First, unlike long vowels, it does not usually attract stress in penultimate position, and regularly weakens to shwa when unstressed (98a). Second, unlike long vowels, it does not undergo Vowel Shift, and thus does not alternate with short vowels in Trisyllabic Shortening environments; compare examples like *lax, laxity* in (98b) with pairs like *sane, sanity* in which underlying long /ǣ/ shortens to [æ̆] before the suffix *-ity*, and is raised to [ē] by Vowel Shift otherwise. Third, like other short vowels, it undergoes lengthening and subsequent Vowel Shift in lengthening environments (98c). Fourth, like other short vowels, it may occur before a following tautosyllabic cluster ending in a noncoronal consonant; long vowels do not occur in this environment (98d).

(98) a.  biography (cf. biogr[æ]phic, with the prestressing suffix -*ic*)
         galaxy (cf. gal[æ]ctic)
         complimentary (cf. compliment[æ]rity)
         syllable (cf. syll[æ]bify)
     b.  lax  laxity  laxative
         gas  gaseous  gasify
         class  classify  classical
         mandate mandatory
     c.  Iran   Iranian
         manic  mania
         titanic  titanium
     d.  clasp, ask, talc, tank, fang
         cf. *[kleysp], *[iysk], *[tuwlk], *[tawŋk], *[fayŋ], etc.

In many dialects of American English, however, "tense" allophones of /æ/ diphthongize to [ɛ.ə], [e.ə] or [i.ə] in words like *man, lamb*; see Labov, Yaeger and Steiner (1972) for extensive discussion.

  2. Rising diphthongs were created from tonic short open *e* and *o* in the early development of modern Romance languages from Vulgar Latin. However, vowel length was not phonemic in these languages when these developments took place. Some examples follow (Meyer-Lübke 1890):

(99) Lat.    Fr.      It.     Sp.
     pĕtra   piedre   pietra  piedra
     pĕde    piet     piede   pied
     nŏva    nueve    nuova   nueva
     mŏrit   muert    muore   muere

Thus in Spanish, for example, the short open vowels *ę̆, *ǫ̆ diphthongized to [i̯e u̯o] under stress, and in a later development the latter shifted to [u̯e] (Menéndez Pidal 1973). Although the vowels underlying the Spanish diphthongs may have undergone subsequent reanalysis (see Harris 1985 for a synchronic analysis in which the diphthongizing vowels are followed by empty skeletal slots in underlying representation), there is no independent reason to believe that they or other tonic vowels were phonologically long, i.e. bimoraic, at the point when they first diphthongized (see Malkiel 1984). Indeed, since diphthongization took place in closed as well as open syllables (*fuerte, fuente*), a phonological lengthening rule would have been phonologically unnatural, as it would have made stressed heavy syllables extra-heavy.

3. Another example of short vowel diphthongization comes from the Malmö dialect of Swedish described just above. Bruce writes: "the short vowels – at least the more close ones, are also sometimes diphthongized. In the short vowels the diphthongization lies in the final part of the vowel...the target is reached at once, after which there is, or may be, a gliding off the target towards a more open and central vowel position" (Bruce 1970: 5–6). An example is *bott* /but/ 'lived', realized as [buət].

Thus although it is true that the diphthongization of short vowels is rarer than that of long vowels, it does occur, and we must be able to account for it. Its relative rarity can be explained by reference to phonetics: formant frequency variations internal to a vowel are more salient (and so more liable to be reanalyzed as phonological diphthongization) if they are longer in duration. Thus we would expect such reanalysis to occur not only in phonologically long vowels but also in short vowels of relatively long duration. This is just what we find in the examples discussed above. Thus, /æ/ has the longest duration of all short vowels in American English (Peterson and Lehiste 1960), and this is the only short vowel that undergoes phonologically significant diphthongization in English.[58] In Romance, vowels are regularly assigned increased duration under stress even when there is no phonemic length. Thus in modern Spanish, stressed short vowels have substantially greater duration than the corresponding unstressed vowels, and duration is a significant factor in stress perception (for a thorough study and further references, see Solé Sabater, n.d.). As for the Scanian Swedish cases, Bruce remarks that short vowels in this dialect appear to have nearly the same intrinsic duration as long vowels; according to Bruce, short vowels are distinguished from their long counterparts not primarily by duration but by their different mode of diphthongization, involving an offglide from the target. In sum, it seems that the precondition for diphthongization is *phonetic* length rather than phonological length. If this is true, phonological theory must be able to characterize diphthongization as a process involving phonologically short vowels as well as long vowels.[59]

If diphthongization cannot be formulated upon sequences of identical short vowels, then, how can we characterize it as a unitary process? A natural solution can be found if we adopt certain further assumptions regarding rule application, which appear to be well motivated on independent grounds. I will assume,

---

[58] In some dialects, though, /ɔ/ is following the pattern of /æ/ (Labov, Yaeger and Steiner 1972); but /ɔ/ is the longest short vowel after / æ /, according to the measurements given by Peterson and Lehiste (1960).

[59] Hayes (1990) proposes that phonological theory should exclude the description of short vowel diphthongization in principle. However, the evidence cited above seems sufficient to show that such processes are possible, and occur in relatively well-studied languages.

following Andersen's basic conception, that diphthongization has the effect of resequencing a unitary feature as two. Let us call this basic operation *splitting*. Splitting rules have the effect shown in (100), and can be stated as in (100b):

(100) a.  
```
   X              X                X
   |      →      ╱╲       or      ╱╲
   αF          +F  -F            -F  +F
```

b. [αF] → + −   or   [αF] → − +

Splitting rules create configurations in which the splitting feature [F] is sequenced under its parent node.

It will be noticed, however, that (100a) violates the No Branching Condition stated in (38). Previously, we saw that some violations of this condition could be eliminated by the Branch Pruning Convention (39), which deletes the older of the two branches. In the present case, however, this convention is inapplicable, since both of the branches have the same "age." Consequently, another strategy is required to eliminate the branching configuration. The applicable convention is the Node Fission Convention, which we state as follows:

(101) *Node Fission Convention:*

Given a branching configuration of the form:

where B, C are on the same tier, split A into two segments $A_1 A_2$ of the same category as A such that

i. $A_1$ dominates B,
ii. $A_2$ dominates C, and
iii. $A_1$, $A_2$ each dominate separate tokens of all other features originally dominated by A.

(101) applies to the output of splitting rules, reapplying as often as necessary in order to insure that the ultimate output contains no violations of the No Branching Condition (38).

Let us see how this model applies to a hypothetical case such as [i] → [ei]. We require a rule that splits [−open] as follows:

(102) [−open] → + −

The vowel [i] has the partial representation shown in (103).

(103)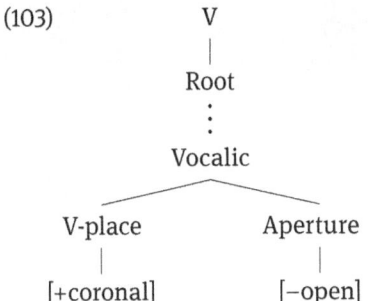

(Notice that this representation does not involve a violation of the No Branching Condition (38), since V-place and Aperture lie on different tiers.) The rule applies to (103) to create the derived representation shown in (104):

(104)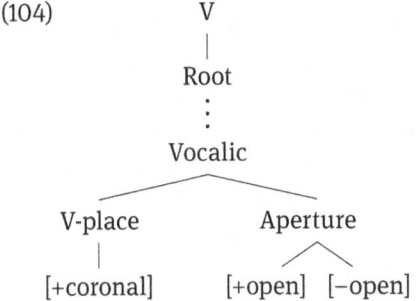

This representation violates the No Branching Condition on the [open] tier, however. The Node Fission Convention (101) therefore applies and splits the aperture node into two, yielding the representation:

(105)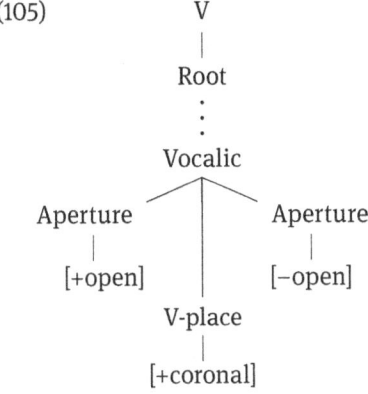

This structure still violates the No Branching Condition on the Aperture tier, however, and the Node Fission Convention reapplies "up the tree" until eventually the highest node (the skeletal slot) is reached:

(106)

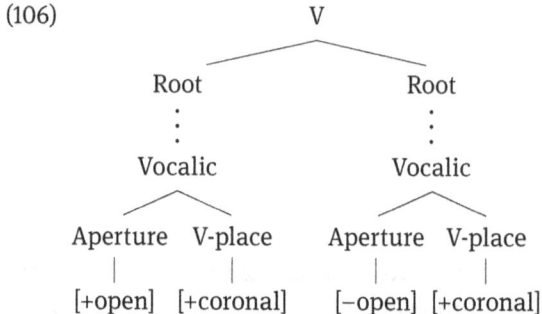

It will be seen that the Node Fission Convention has created two discrete structures under the V-node. It can thus be viewed as the converse of the Shared Features Convention, which requires separate segments that come to share features to collapse into single segments to the maximal extent possible (Steriade 1982, Clements 1985a).[60] In this particular case we have derived a short diphthong, consisting of two discrete subtrees linked to a single timing tier node. If the diphthongizing vowel had been long, i.e. linked to two separate V-nodes in the input, then each root node would be dominated by a separate V-node in the output.

It will be noticed that the Node Fission Convention creates OCP violations on all feature tiers except the one containing the original splitting feature. This might at first sight seem to be an undesirable consequence. However, some evidence that it may be correct comes from the fact that diphthongs arising from splitting (breaking) rules often undergo subsequent dissimilatory rules involving features such as backness and rounding (in our terms, [coronal] and [labial]). Thus when the English vowel /i:/ underwent height diphthongization as part of the English Great Vowel Shift, it later dissimilated in backness as well, becoming [ay] in most dialects. Similarly, rounding dissimilation took place in the last stage of the Spanish diphthongization process [o] > [uo] > [ue], and we find an analogous delabialization rule applying to the output of Swedish diphthongization, which is discussed below. Many similar examples can be given. These facts can be explained on the assumption that Node Fission creates across-the-board

---

**60** I assume that the Shared Features Convention is subject to the No Branching Condition, i.e. that class nodes are merged only when they dominate identical features (Clements 1985a, 240).

OCP violations, which may then be resolved in different languages on a case-by-case basis.[61]

To summarize, we have developed a single formalism for the expression of diphthongization rules, which expresses the diphthongization of short vowels and long vowels as a unitary phenomenon defined by the elementary operation of feature splitting. The output of splitting undergoes an automatic convention of Node Fission which divides it into two discrete segments; thus, a single "feature bundle" is reanalyzed as a sequence of two feature bundles. Let us now consider how this model extends to "scalar" diphthongization rules of the Swedish type (cf. (96)). It will be recalled that this rule lowers the initial part of long vowels by one degree on the height scale. Let us assume the following surface assignments of [open], defining four heights:

(107)

| | i | y | ʉ | u | e | ø | o | ɛ | ɒ | [æ] |
|---|---|---|---|---|---|---|---|---|---|---|
| $open_1$ | – | – | – | – | – | – | – | – | – | + |
| $open_2$ | – | – | – | – | – | – | – | + | + | + |
| $open_3$ | – | – | – | – | + | + | + | + | + | + |

Let us assume, furthermore, that (102) is the diphthongization rule of Swedish, where it is restricted to long vowels in open syllables. This rule, as stated, is not defined on any particular [open] tier. It will be recalled from the previous discussion that the algorithm for rule application to unspecified tiers requires that rules apply bottom-up and noniteratively when the affected value of [open] is minus, i.e. just once, in the lowest possible register. Applying rule (102) to the vowels in (107) in this way gives the following results:[62]

(108) high vowels /iː yː ʉː uː/: $[-open_3]$ ⟶ $[+open_3]\ [-open_3]$
higher mid vowels /eː øː oː/: $[-open_2]$ ⟶ $[+open_2]\ [-open_2]$
lower mid vowels /ɛː ɒː/: $[-open_1]$ ⟶ $[+open_1]\ [-open_1]$

The rule splits the appropriate feature [open] of each vowel into two, of which the second retains its original value [–open] and the first is [+open]. The result is the following:

---

[61] This scenario is consistent with Yip's view that the OCP sets up a "pressure to change" resolved in language-particular ways, rather than triggering universal repair mechanisms that apply automatically to all violations whenever they arise (Yip 1988).

[62] As in several cases discussed earlier, as some of the relevant occurrences of [-open] are redundant, they must be inserted into representations by the time rule (102) applies.

(109)

|  | i | y | ɨ | u | e | ø | o | ɛ | ɒ | [æ] |
|---|---|---|---|---|---|---|---|---|---|---|
| open₁ | − | − | − | − | − | − | − | ± | ± | + |
| open₂ | − | − | − | − | ± | ± | ± | + | + | + |
| open₃ | ± | ± | ± | ± | + | + | + | + | + | + |

In each case, the splitting process triggers the "ripple" effect illustrated in the earlier derivation by which higher-level class nodes are successively split into two by the Node Fission Convention until we reach the Root node. This effect is illustrated as follows, for front vowels:

(110)  a. intput:          b. output:

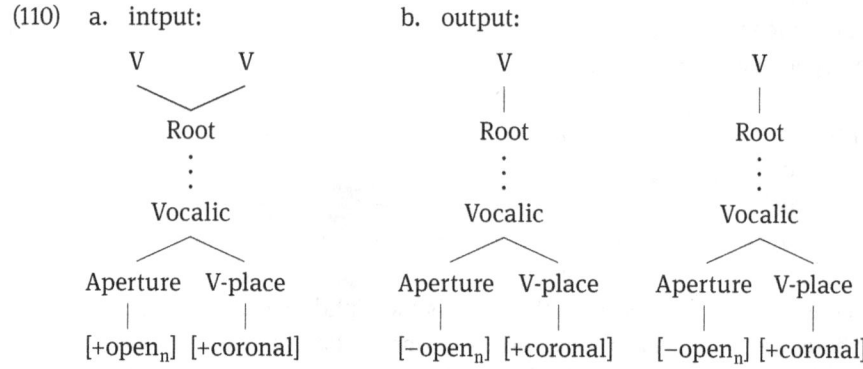

on some tier.

A subsidiary effect of Scanian diphthongization is to unround the first part of the long back rounded diphthongs [eu ɛo]. This can be expressed as the following dissimilation rule:

(111)   [−coronal]
            |
        V-place     V-place
           ≠           |
        [+labial]   [+labial]

This rule feeds the default rule spelling out the default value of [labial] as minus, and a redundancy rule stating that all unrounded vowels in Swedish are front:

(112)  a. [    ]  →  [−labial]
       b. [−labial]  →  [+coronal]

The full set of derivations goes as follows:

(113)  i:   y:   ʉ:   u:   e:   ø:   o:   ɛ:   ɒ:      underlying
       ei   øy   øʉ   ou   ɛe   œø   ɔo   æɛ   æɒ      rule (102)
                      əu             ʌo                rule (111)
                      eu             ɛo                rules (112 a,b)

It will be seen that given the principles assumed in these derivations, which are general in scope and universal in application, the diphthongization rule of Swedish can be described within a model of diphthongization which extends readily to diphthongizations of many other types (see Andersen 1972 for further examples). No principles or devices specific to diphthongization are required, other than the provision of the elementary operation "split [F]" itself, which is on a par with operations like "delink [F]" and "insert [F]." It is possible that the process of feature splitting illustrated above can be generalized to other phenomena that are not normally treated as diphthongization, although this question cannot be pursued here.

In sum, we have seen that diphthongization in the Scanian dialects of Swedish, often taken as an argument for a multivalued height feature, can be expressed in simple, theoretically well-motivated terms under the hierarchical view of vowel height developed above. A further result of the analysis proposed here is that diphthongization can be simply expressed in terms of the theory of tree geometry proposed in Clements (1985) and other studies, without the formal modifications to the theory proposed by Hayes (1990). It appears that other cases of apparent "diphthongization paradoxes" discussed by Hayes can be handled in the same way.[63]

# 7 The Phonetic Basis of Vowel Height

We have argued that feature theory must meet the Phonetic Distinctness Criterion (5), which requires that all features have distinct universal physical correlates, both acoustic and articulatory. This condition has played an important role in our argumentation, forcing us for instance to rule out the use of features like [tense] and [ATR] to describe vowel distinctions that are phonetically indistinguishable from vowel height distinctions. It is appropriate at this point to ask

---

[63] Hayes suggests, for example, that the Icelandic preaspiration rule (Thráinsson 1978) can be viewed as a type of diphthongization. See Clements (1989d) for an analysis of Icelandic preaspiration in terms of the theory proposed here. Cases of context-sensitive diphthongization, in which a feature spreads from a neighboring segment to create a feature sequence internal to a segment, can also be expressed in terms of the Node Fission Convention.

what the physical correlates of the feature [open] are. While the acoustic definition of vowel height is a relatively straightforward matter – there being much evidence that vowel height maps primarily into the acoustic dimension of first formant ($F_1$) frequency – the question of defining vowel height in articulatory terms has been a matter of long-standing controversy.

Section 7.1 reviews two types of approaches to this problem, one attempting to define vowel height in terms of the highest point of the tongue, and the second defining it in terms of global vocal tract cavity configurations. We argue that the second approach provides the more adequate basis for relating vowel articulation to acoustic output. We review major findings regarding the relation between $F_1$ frequency and vocal tract cavity configurations, and propose a phonetic definition of [open] based on these findings. Section 7.2 examines the status of the feature [ATR] in the light of these findings, and shows that it can be regarded as a way of implementing the feature [open] rather than an independent feature.

## 7.1 Physical Correlates of Vowel Height

The major problem in finding an adequate articulatory definition of vowel height is to single out the basic mechanism underlying variation in vowel height and distinguish it from its subsidiary effects. In the classical tradition, deriving from Jones (1909), vowel height was defined in terms of the highest point of the tongue. This definition offered a good first approximation to an understanding of vowel height, and had the practical advantage that it defined vowel height in terms of an observable property at a time when x-ray photography was not yet available. However, it runs into problems when we attempt to apply it to the data resulting from x-ray studies of vowels in many languages, as is admitted even by its proponents. Ladefoged (1968) found that neither the highest point of the tongue nor an acoustic chart plotting $F_1$ against $F_2$ give a good fit to perceived auditory distances among vowels in the West African language Ngwe. Lindau (1978) measured vowel height for five speakers of American English in terms of the distance between the highest part of the tongue and the hard palate, and compared the articulatory chart obtained in this way with the arrangement of the vowels on an auditory chart. While her data showed that the articulatory chart provided as good a fit to the auditory data as an acoustic chart of these vowels did, both measures reveal discrepancies, especially in the mid-vowel region.

Another potential problem for the classical definition is that some high vowels turn out to have lower tongue heights than some nonhigh vowels. For instance, Lindau's data showed that the mid vowel [e] has a higher tongue position than the high vowel [I] for some speakers of American English. But as several phonologists have pointed out, this objection can be addressed if we view tongue height not as an absolute property, but as a relative one. Such a view requires only that a high vowel have a higher tongue position than a *corresponding* nonhigh vowel, that is, one belonging to the same series, or which shares all other features. Thus since the vowels [e] and [I] differ not only in height but also in phonological length (or tenseness) in English, they are not directly comparable.

While the classical definition of vowel height may be useful for practical purposes of vowel classification, it is not ultimately satisfying from a theoretical point of view since it is difficult to see what the position of the highest point of the tongue should have to do with first formant frequency. A related weakness of this definition is that it attaches no significance to tongue root constriction and the volume of the pharyngeal cavity in vowel production. But as Fischer-Jørgensen aptly points out (1985: 85):

> What remains of the criticism [of the classical system of vowel description – GNC] is that the pharynx cavity, which could not be observed when the classical system was set up, has been neglected. The description does not take account of the fact that the most narrow constriction for [a] and [ɒ] and generally for [o ɔ] is in the pharynx, and as degree and place of constriction in the total vocal tract are essential for the calculation of the acoustic output, the classical system is not the most adequate starting point for such calculations.

A different approach to vowel description has attempted to characterize the properties of vowels in terms of models of the total vocal tract configuration, from the glottis to the lips. Most of these models have been based upon the study of x-rays of vocal tract configurations during vowel production. One of the earliest and most influential is that of Stevens and House (1955), who observed that we can specify the acoustical performance of the vocal tract if we know the cross-sectional area at all points along the tract. They specify this area in terms of three independent parameters: the location of the center of the tongue constriction, the minimal cross-sectional area at this point, and the dimensions in the vicinity of the lips. This model provides a relatively accurate way of estimating formant frequencies of English vowels, although it provides no separate parameter corresponding to vowel height.

Another explicit vocal tract model is that of Fant (1970) which represents vocal tract cavities in terms of a double Helmholz resonator in which the anterior resonator corresponds to the front cavity and the posterior resonator to the back cavity. This model allows a mathematical prediction of the resonance frequencies of vowels based on estimates of vocal tract cavity and constriction sizes. Fant estimated the vocal tract configurations of each of the Russian vowels [i e ɨ u o a] and compared them with their formant frequencies. He found that the frequency of $F_1$ is generally dependent more on the back (i.e. pharyngeal) cavity volume than on the volume of the other cavities, except for [a], whose $F_1$ value is affected equally by changes in the front and back cavity volumes. The $F_1$ frequency of the vowels [i e ɨ] was found to be almost completely determined by the back cavity volume as well as by the narrowest section of the front cavity (p. 121).[64]

Fant's study is one of the first to bring to light the importance of back cavity volume in estimating $F_1$ frequency, the primary acoustic correlate of vowel height. The affiliation between $F_1$ frequency and back cavity volume is directly observable, as we can informally verify in the following way. If we silently articulate the vowels [i e ɛ æ ɒ ɔ o u] in that order, while exciting the natural resonance frequency of the back cavity by snapping a finger sharply against the side of the larynx while keeping the glottis closed, we observe that a clear note is produced whose pitch rises as the series [i e ɛ æ] is produced but falls again as [ɑ ɔ o u] are articulated. This rise and fall corresponds to differences in back cavity volume among the vowels, and is explained by the principle that all else being equal, the natural frequency of a resonator increases as its volume becomes smaller and decreases as its volume becomes larger.[65]

There is also an affiliation between front cavity volume and $F_2$ frequency. But it is important to point out that the relationship between formant frequencies and vocal tract cavities is not a simple or direct one. One reason for this is that in actual vowel production, the two cavities are not isolated from each other, but are connected by smaller passages (constrictions) whose size determines the amount of coupling between the cavities. At one extreme, the constriction is so narrow that the two cavities influence each other very little, while at the other the constriction is so large that the vocal tract approaches the shape of a single uniform tube. Stevens and House (1955) and Fant (1970) found that such variations have a direct influence on formant frequency.[66] A further problem is that

---

[64] Fant adds that his model underestimates the $F_1$ frequency/back cavity affiliation to some degree (p. 127).

[65] This technique for making the first formant audible was taught to me by John Kelly, and is described by Catford (1988).

[66] On the basis of additional modelling drawing on perceptual criteria derived from the study of synthesized vowels, Fant found that $F_1$ rises as the back cavity becomes smaller, $F_2$ rises as the front cavity becomes smaller, and both $F_1$ and $F_2$ rise as the extent of the lingual or labial constriction decreases. In back rounded vowels, as the location of the pharyngeal constriction is lowered, the back cavity volume gradually decreases (raising $F_1$), while at the same time the labial constriction decreases (raising $F_1$ and $F_2$) and (not observed in Fant's data, but shown in other x-ray studies) the front cavity volume increases (lowering $F_2$). Thus the two effects on $F_2$ tend to cancel each other out, and the net effect of the lowering of back rounded vowels is a raising of $F_1$. In unrounded vowels, lowering of the tongue body not only decreases the degree of tongue constriction at the palate (raising $F_1$ and $F_2$) but also increases the front cavity volume (lowering $F_2$), so that here too the net effect of lowering tends to be a raising of $F_1$.

cavity volume and degree of constriction can seldom be varied independently, and in actual vowel production these parameters show a good deal of covariation. In particular, enlarging the back cavity tends to raise and front the tongue body and narrow the constriction of front and high vowels, while enlarging the front cavity has the opposite effect. Furthermore, labial constriction tends to decrease as the jaw and tongue body are lowered.

The importance of back cavity volume and degree of constriction in determining $F_1$ frequency has been supported in more recent studies as well. Wood (1975) reports results from an analogue model of the vocal tract based on studies of x-rays of several languages. He finds that both retracting the tongue root (decreasing back cavity volume) and widening the tongue constriction at the place of articulation raise $F_1$, though these effects are most prominent in front and high vowels. Widening the tongue constriction also lowers $F_2$ in front vowels and raises $F_2$ in back vowels. Maeda (in press), in a study of French vowel articulation, finds that tongue shape can be described in terms of a small number of independent articulatory parameters including jaw movement and horizontal tongue body displacement, among others. Jaw opening involves the concomitant lowering of the tongue in the buccal region and retracting of the tongue in the pharynx. Computer modelling shows that this complex of movements tends to raise $F_1$ in the back rounded vowels [u o] and both raise $F_1$ and lower $F_2$ in the unrounded vowels [i e a].

To summarize the discussion so far, available studies show that $F_1$ frequency may be raised and lowered by several different articulatory mechanisms, which are summarized below:

(114)  $F_1$ rises as:                    $F_1$ falls as:

   the jaw is lowered              the jaw is raised
   back cavity volume decreases    back cavity volume increases
   dorsal constriction is widened  dorsal constriction is narrowed
   labial constriction is widened  labial constriction is narrowed

Given this wealth of articulatory resources for producing the same acoustic effect, one reasonably asks whether all play an equal or fixed role in vowel height realization. There is evidence that some of these gestures can substitute for the absence, or low amplitude of others. In a series of bite-block experiments, Lindblom et al. (1971) and Gay et al. (1981) found that speakers compensate for artificially fixed jaw positions by making appropriate adjustments in tongue position in order to achieve fixed acoustic vowel targets. Lindau's x-rays of four Akan speakers (1979), to which we return below, show that her subjects differ in the proportion to which they use tongue root retraction and tongue body lowering to achieve distinctions in vowel height. Maeda (in press) shows that his French subjects exploit the trade-off relation between jaw lowering and tongue body adjustments in actual speech. These observations show that $F_1$ modulations can be achieved in several ways, and suggest a "goal-oriented" rather than articulator-oriented view of speech production, as least as far as vowel height is concerned.

It seems reasonable, therefore, to view the vowel height feature as a linguistic property which pairs ideal auditory/acoustic goals with specific vocal tract area functions.[67] The definition of features in terms of auditory/ acoustic goals is supported by the observation that the articulatory configurations favored by human languages correspond to stable acoustic regions (Stevens 1989). The linking of such goals to vocal tract area function s instead of to specific articulator movements is also supported compensatory articulation phenomena of the sort mentioned just above. We thus view the physiological aspect of phonological features such as vowel height primarily in terms of variations in the size and shape of vocal tract cavities, rather than in terms of the activity of particular articulators as such. In this view, different articulations "count" as realizations of a given phonological feature only if they all define an auditory/acoustic goal by means of the appropriate (set of) vocal tract configurations.

The feature [open] can now be defined in the following way:

(115) [+open] vowels are realized with a decrease in pharyngeal cavity volume or a widening of the tongue constriction relative to [−open] vowels; from an acoustic point of view, they are realized with a higher $F_1$ frequency.

By not specifying the exact articulatory maneuvers by which these vocal tract cavity adjustments and their acoustic effect on $F_1$ are achieved, this definition allows for the compensatory articulation phenomena noted above. The feature [open] can be regarded as acoustically-motivated in the sense that we can define it more simply in acoustic terms than in articulatory terms. However, it is not an "acoustic feature" pure and simple since if the definition is correct, $F_1$ raising can only be carried out by the appropriate tongue body movements and not e.g. by decreasing a labial constriction.

The definition proposed in (115) is well supported by published x-ray studies of vowels in many different languages, which show that lower vowels tend not only to have lower tongue heights but also smaller back cavity volumes and wider tongue constrictions than their higher counterparts. The relationship

---

[67] Or more accurately, with sets of such functions, since features like [open] and [continuant] are realized with different area functions at different places of articulation.

between vowel height and cavity volume in French has been noted by Brichler-Labaeye (1970: 106), who reports that the vowels [i e ɛ a] are distinguished, in descending order, by

> abaissement et recul de la langue et, de ce fait, agrandissement progressif de la cavité buccale, accompagné d'une diminution du volume de la cavité pharyngale; en même temps, augmentation de l'angle des maxillaires et de l'ouverture labiale.

This description is supported by the x-rays of superimposed vowels published on pp. 250–252 of this work, and applies to the other vowel series as well.[68] In the variety of Breton spoken in Argol, Bothorel found that the height of front vowels correlates better with pharynx volume than with other measures of vowel height such as the location of the highest point of the tongue and the amount of jaw opening (Bothorel 1982: 192–196). In other languages, evidence of a regular correspondence between vowel height and back cavity volume is found in figures given by Ladefoged (1968) for Ngwe (reproduced in Figure 1 above), by Perkell (1971) for English, by Lindau (1979) for Akan, and by Traill (1985) for !Xóõ Bushman. The relation between vowel height and constriction width is also quite regular, though as a common exception [o] often has a wider constriction than [ɔ]; Wood (1975) suggests that this may be due to the physiological antagonism between the muscular gestures required to advance the tongue root in the lower pharynx while narrowing the constriction in the upper pharynx required in the production of [o]. He suggests that the spectral disadvantages resulting from this anomaly may be offset by some other factor, such as an increase in lip rounding.

The definition of vowel height in (115) has a significant advantage over the classical definition in that it allows us to understand why vowel height should correlate with $F_1$ frequency instead of with some other acoustic correlate. But it also allows us to understand why vowel height should vary with the position of the highest point of the tongue. By our definition, one way of producing a high vowel is to increase the volume of the pharyngeal cavity. The primary and most widely-exploited means of expanding the pharyngeal cavity is by advancing the root of the tongue (Lindau 1979). It has been widely observed that since the tongue is a constant mass, advancing the tongue root will have the consequence of raising the tongue body, causing the dorsum to approach the hard or soft palate (see Wood 1975: 115, Lindau 1979: 171, Hall and Hall 1980: 207, Jacobson 1980: 185). As a result, the highest point of the tongue will necessarily be dis-

---

[68] Other x-ray studies of French support this description; see Delattre (1968), Bothorel et al. (1986), and earlier sources cited by Brichler-Labaeye (1970).

placed upward. A second way of producing a high vowel, by our definition, is to narrow the constriction at the place of articulation, and this will again raise the highest point of the tongue in the high and front vowels. Our definition therefore accounts directly for the traditional observation that higher vowels have higher tongue heights, while relating this observation to more general vocal tract configurations which provide a basis for explaining the acoustic properties of vowel height.

## 7.2 [ATR] Revisited

We now return to a question raised toward the beginning of this study: how does the proposed feature [ATR] interact with vowel height, which we have now characterized in terms of the hierarchical feature [open]? In particular, is [ATR] needed in phonological theory?

Historically speaking, the primary motivation for recognizing [ATR] as a phonological feature has come from the phenomenon of "cross-height" vowel harmony, in which vowels of different, noncontiguous heights fall into separate harmonic sets (Stewart 1967). This type of system is illustrated in the following chart of Akan vowels:

(116)  Akan vowels:  set membership:
    $height_5$:    i    u      set 1
    $height_4$:    I    U      set 2
    $height_3$:    e    o      set 1
    $height_2$:    ɛ    ɔ      set 2
    $height_1$:      a        set 2

All vowels occurring in a harmonic span must be members of one set or the other. This type of vowel harmony could not be characterized in terms of vowel height in earlier theories, since such theories had no way of characterizing noncontiguous height categories. It should now be clear, however, that by allowing a hierarchical arrangement of the feature [open] we are able to account for the "cross-height" nature of ATR harmony systems in a straightforward way. Thus we have already seen that the partial height assimilation rule of Kinande (64) maps [I U] into [i u], [ɛ ɔ] into [e o], and [a] into [ʌ] in much the same way that typical ATR-based harmony rules do. The surface vowel system of Kinande was characterized as follows in (65), repeated below:

(117) (=(65))

| | i | u | I | U | [e] | [o] | ɛ | ɔ | [ʌ] | a |
|---|---|---|---|---|---|---|---|---|---|---|
| open$_1$ | − | − | − | − | − | − | − | − | + | + |
| open$_2$ | − | − | − | − | + | + | + | + | + | + |
| open$_3$ | − | − | + | + | − | − | + | + | − | + |

In this characterization, [open] at the third hierarchical level cross-classifies [open] at the two other levels in a way that is isomorphic to the way [ATR] is used for this purpose. Even if the Kinande system did not exist, the present system would predict that it should, since under our assumptions there is no way to prevent the creation of systems like (117) other than by arbitrary stipulation.

It follows that the special properties of "cross-height" vowel harmony systems like that of Akan can be described in a straightforward way if we assume that [open] is assigned to vowels as follows:

(118)

| | i | u | I | U | e | o | ɛ | ɔ | a |
|---|---|---|---|---|---|---|---|---|---|---|
| open$_1$ | − | − | − | − | − | − | − | − | + |
| open$_2$ | − | − | − | − | + | + | + | + | + |
| open$_3$ | − | − | + | + | − | − | + | + | + |

In this classification, [+ATR] vowels are characterized as [−open$_3$] and [−ATR] vowels as [+open$_3$]. This classification is analogous to that proposed for Kinande in all relevant respects: in both cases, the assignment of [open$_3$] to a vowel assigns it to the appropriate subregister within the set of [±open$_2$] vowels, i.e. high or nonhigh vowels. A comparison with tone register is once again enlightening. If we abstract from the low vowel /a/, which is external to the system of vowel harmony as such (Clements 1985b), the basic "high" vs. "nonhigh" distinction characterized by [open$_2$] may be compared to the primary "upper" and "lower" registers of many East Asian tone languages, while the further distinction internal to each of these registers characterized by [open$_3$] is comparable to the secondary "high" vs. "low" distinction internal to each tone register (see Yip 1980b).[69]

Although this approach accounts for the phonological properties of ATR harmony systems, we must also ask whether it accounts for its phonetic properties as well. The answer seems to be that it does. If we accept the phonetic definition of [open] proposed in (115), we see that [open] and [ATR] have essentially the same properties.

---

[69] However, the Akan system differs from that of some Asian languages in using the subsidiary register feature [open3] as its long-domain or prosodic feature; in contrast, in Asian languages making use of register as well as subsidiary tone height distinctions, we usually find register functioning as a morpheme-domain feature (cf. Yip).

Thus from an acoustic point of view, both features are realized by variations in $F_1$ frequency. Lindau (1979) found in her phonetic study of [ATR] in Akan that [+ATR] vowels had higher $F_1$ frequencies than their [−ATR] counterparts. Her formant chart also shows that $F_2$ is higher in [+ATR] front vowels (as well as high back vowels) than in the corresponding [−ATR] vowels (p. 167), but again we find similar differences between [−open] and [+open] front vowels. $F_2$ frequency tends to fall as we step down through the series [i e ɛ å], as is reflected in the skewed left edge of the trapezoid traditionally used to represent two-dimensional vowel space (see e.g. Figure 2). Thus there appears to be no consistent difference between the acoustic effects associated with these two features.

The acoustic similarities are paralelled by close articulatory similarities. If the definition of [open] given in (115) is correct, both features are realized by variations in pharyngeal cavity size and narrowness of the tongue constriction. While the literature on ATR vowel systems emphasizes tongue root advancement and other factors involved in overall pharyngeal cavity expansion, it also consistently notes that [+ATR] vowels are produced with higher tongue body positions. As noted above, this effect can be straightforwardly explained by the fact that as the tongue root is advanced, the tongue body (as a constant mass) is necessarily forced upward and forward, narrowing the tongue constriction. Thus Lindau (1979) reports that [+ATR] front vowels in Akan have narrower palatal constrictions than their [−ATR] counterparts "in many cases," though the differences vary in degree from speaker to speaker. We have already seen evidence from experimental modelling that narrowing the tongue constriction also lowers $F_1$. Thus tongue raising can be viewed as a further way of implementing [ATR], in conjunction with tongue root advancement. In sum, even though the feature [ATR] has been described as making greater use of pharyngeal cavity variation than tongue-height typically does, the differences between the two features seem to be a matter of degree rather than kind. Given the close acoustic and articulatory relation between these two features, the Phonetic Distinctness Criterion (5), if taken seriously, argues strongly that we consider them as variant implementations of a single feature whose correlates are essentially those given in (115).

We must, however, consider a serious objection to this analysis. Lindau (1979) argues, on the basis of statistical analysis, that pharynx width is a better predictor of membership in the two vowel harmony categories in Akan than tongue height is. She takes this result to show that tongue height does not contribute independently to distinguishing the two sets of vowels in Akan, viewing it as an artifact of the correlation between tongue height and pharynx width. She argues further that even though tongue root advancing accompanies tongue body raising in languages like English, it does not form an independent control parameter in these languages. Similar results are reported by Jackson (1988).

It must be recalled, however, that Akan and English differ in an important phonological respect: Akan has a cross-height vowel harmony system while English does not. As a result, these languages use vowel height variation in fundamentally different ways. This fact, by itself, may be sufficient to explain the different implementations of [open] in the two systems. In vowel harmony systems, by definition, a single feature has a uniform value throughout the span of harmony, usually the word. In most types of vowel harmony, the harmonic feature is implemented in a uniform way throughout the span. Thus in labial harmony systems, for instance, all vowels are produced with either rounded or unrounded lips, while in backness harmony systems all vowels are produced with either a palatal or dorsal tongue constriction. Consider now the implementation of harmony in a system based on vowel height. If height is to be implemented in a uniform way throughout each harmony span, it must be implemented in terms of tongue root position, since the tongue root can be more or less "anchored" in a given position independently of where the tongue body is positioned (though cf. the earlier remarks on mid back vowels). If it were implemented in terms of tongue body placement, and tongue root advancement were reserved exclusively for the production of high vs. nonhigh vowels, the tongue body would still have to move back and forth to produce back vs. front vowels, and thus could not be "anchored" in any given position throughout the domain. To put it another way, of the two ways of implementing vowel height, one is "articulator-free," remaining constant regardless of the place of articulation of the vowel concerned, while the other is "articulator-bound." If vowel height is to be implemented in a uniform way throughout the harmony domain, as are other features, then it is the "articulator-free" implementation (involving tongue root position) that must be selected.

We may conclude, therefore, that there are no obstacles, either phonological or phonetic, to regarding "cross-height" vowel harmony as based on vowel height, as the term itself implies. But if [ATR] is not required for cross-height vowel harmony, there is little reason to use it for characterizing vowel height in other types of vowels, in which no independent evidence for an independent tongue root parameter has ever been adduced. Indeed, there is a bonus to the total elimination of [ATR] from the feature system. Up to the present, it has been an anomaly that of all the vowel features known to be used in the world's languages, only the (traditional) features [back], [round], and [ATR] clearly serve as the basis for prototypical vowel harmony systems: strikingly, no evidence has ever been brought forward showing that a height feature, such as [high] or [low], can serve as the basis for true vowel harmony. We are now in a position to offer an explanation for this gap, consistent with the theory of vowel height developed here: so-called ATR harmony is nothing other than height harmony, implemented primarily in terms of tongue root position.

What could count as potential counterevidence to the proposal to eliminate [ATR] in favor of [open] across the board? Phonetic counterevidence would come from a demonstration that vowel height does in fact have a consistently different set of physical correlates from [ATR], contrary to the results of the literature reviewed above. Phonological counterevidence would consist of the demonstration that in some language, [ATR] functions as if it were linked to a node other than the Aperture node. As will be recalled, however, Odden (1989a) has found that the feature ATR generally patterns with [high] (and perhaps [low]) in vowel systems, and has suggested that it be placed under the Aperture node (his Height node) together with these features. We have reviewed some further evidence in favor of this view above. This is exactly what we would expect if ATR is in fact a way of implementing [open], but would be anomalous if [ATR] is an independent, articulator-defined feature. At present there seems to be no clear evidence that ATR patterns under any node other than the Aperture node in any language.

We note, nevertheless, that [ATR] overlaps to a certain extent with the feature [pharyngeal], which functions as a vowel feature in some languages. Thus, Herzallah (1990) argues that [pharyngeal] is a derived feature of vowels in Palestinian Arabic, where it arises both from vowel assimilation to pharyngeal consonants, and from a redundancy rule assigning [+pharyngeal] to [+open] vowels. From a phonetic point of view, too, the tongue root retraction found in [−ATR] vowels appears to be quite similar to that found in pharyngeal consonants (Lindau 1978: 553, 1979: 175–176).[70] In several Caucasian and Khoisan languages, a feature of pharyngeal constriction crossclassifies all vowels, including vowels at contrastive heights (for discussion and references see Ladefoged and Maddieson 1990). Based on this evidence, it seems likely that some apparent occurrences of [ATR] may turn out to be implementations of [pharyngeal] rather than [open]. However, in no case does it seem necessary to postulate [ATR] as a feature in addition to both [open] and [pharyngeal].[71]

---

[70] Though not in emphatic consonants, which are articulated higher in the pharynx. Herzallah proposes that emphatics are to be analyzed as simultaneously [+pharyngeal] and [+dorsal]. See McCarthy (1989a) for fuller discussion of the feature [pharyngeal].

[71] The definition of [open] given in ($115) is similar to a definition of [tense] proposed by Wood (1975). Wood finds that tense vowels have a narrower constriction at the place of articulation than their lax counterparts, and also notes that they tend to have more advanced tongue root positions, though he argues that the latter factor is acoustically less significant. As we have seen, the effect of these gestures on $F_1$ frequency is uniformly to lower it, and so we will regard this apparent feature as simply another way of implementing [open], having the same status as ATR.

# 8 Summary and Conclusions

Let us review our major results. We have presented a theory in which vowel height is characterized in terms of a hierarchical, binary feature [open]. Occurrences of [open] are assigned to different ranked tiers. The highest-ranked tier divides vowel height into two primary registers, higher and lower, and lower-ranked tiers divide the height dimension into successive subregisters. Although it allows the expression of scalar processes, the feature [open] is not a multi-valued or scalar feature in the sense of Ladefoged (1971), since [open] is binary-specified on each tier. Not is it a single-valued feature or particle in the sense of Schane (1984a,b) and others, since it is at least potentially binary on each tier, subject to underspecification.

Developing suggestions by Hyman and Odden, we have suggested that separate occurrences of [open] link to the Aperture node which itself links to the Vocalic node, as shown in (31) (in a variant of this proposal, they form a chain linked directly to the Vocalic node as shown in (32)). This model allows the direct expression of rules of partial and total height assimilation within a restrictive autosegmental theory of assimilation. Together with a proposed algorithm for rule application, it allows the expression of rules that apply in a stepwise fashion; and with certain additional conventions governing derivational well-formedness, it extends to a treatment of scalar diphthongization rules found in languages like Swedish. We have finally seen that the hierarchically-defined feature [open] may subsume the feature [ATR], and underlie so-called ATR vowel harmony systems.

This model directly addresses problems that are inherent in earlier models of vowel height, and offers well-motivated solutions. First of all, by characterizing vowel height in terms of a single phonological feature, we directly account for the fact that vowel height maps into a unitary phonetic parameter, with well-defined acoustic and articulatory correlates. Second, the model accounts directly for the fact that vowel systems may have more than three vowel heights, without requiring the arbitrary, essentially diacritic use of features like [tense] and [ATR] to account for the additional heights. Third, it seems that the system does not require redundancy rules to rule out universally ill-formed combinations of [±open]; all combinations of [+open] and [−open] are well-formed in principle, and we have examined systems making use of many of the logically possible combinations. Fourth, this feature system accounts readily for natural classes of vowels, and allows us to express recurrent rule types that cannot be adequately expressed in other theories, including total and partial height assimilation and stepwise diphthongization. By allowing binary feature specifications, we are able to describe both raising and lowering rules in terms of the same theory of assimilation. Fifth, by assigning the feature [open] to a class node of its own we are able to express the phonological independence of vowel height with respect to place of articulation. Sixth, the system forms part of a larger theory of features which provides for the hierarchical arrangement of features (notably, tone) which are defined in terms of a uniform physical scale.

If these conclusions are correct, the hierarchical feature [open] can replace the standard vowel height features [high], [low]. We have also reviewed several problems in the use of [ATR] to express vowel height relationships, and have proposed that this feature can be replaced by [open] to express "cross-height" vowel harmony and other types of height-related phenomena. In so doing we can explain certain anomalies in current treatments, such as the fact that tongue root advancing has only been found to be an independent control mechanism in languages with ATR-type vowel harmony, and that vowel harmony systems appear to use [ATR] to the exclusion of [high] and [low].

These results have a more general implication for feature theory. In the past, while most linguists have tacitly assumed some form of the Phonetic Distinctness Criterion (5), they have often turned a blind eye to problems that arise in applying it to features such as vowel height. By insisting that this criterion has no exceptions, we have been forced to reject analyses of height-related phenomena involving illegitimate uses of features like [tense] and [ATR], and have tried to find alternative analyses consistent with it. Consequently we have been able to obtain simple descriptions of a number of puzzling phenomena that have gone without satisfactory explanation up to now. This result confirms the heuristic value of the Phonetic Distinctness Criterion, and provides a strong argument for incorporating it as a general constraint on feature theory.

If these conclusions are correct, we must abandon the view that all features conform to a single type (e.g., binary and non-hierarchical). There is so far no persuasive evidence that features other than vowel height (and perhaps tone) function in the hierarchical manner described here. But this result should not be surprising, in view of the fact that formal distinctions are now emerging elsewhere in the feature system. It is now widely accepted, for example, that place of articulation features such as [labial] and [coronal] function in a unary rather than a binary manner, at least in consonant systems (see e.g. Sagey 1986, McCarthy 1988); thus there appear to be no rules of the form "spread [–labial] from one consonant to another" or "disallow sequences of [–coronal] obstruents," such as one would expect to find if these features were truly binary. Other features, however, such as the major class features [sonorant] or the minor place of articulation features [anterior] and [distributed], appear to function in a binary fashion. Current study appears to be leading to the view that phonological features are not homogeneous, but fall into formally distinct subsets corresponding to differences in the way they function in rule systems.

## Acknowledgements

This study has benefited from the lengthy comments on an earlier draft version sent to me by Larry Hyman and David Odden, which have helped me avoid several errors and find a better formulation both of the theory and of particular analyses. Thanks are also due to Morris Halle, Elizabeth Hume and Leo Wetzels for useful comments and criticisms, and to Alan Prince for oral comments on a earlier version of this study presented at the MIT Conference on Feature and Underspecification Theories, October 8–10, 1989. I have tried to address the issues raised by Prof. Prince at appropriate points of the present text. Research was supported in part by NSF grant INT-8807437.

## References

Abaglo, P. and D. Archangeli. 1989. Language-particular underspecification: Gengbe /e/ and Yoruba /i/. *Linguistic Inquiry* 20 (3): 457–480.
Andersen, H. 1972. Diphthongization. *Language* 48: 11–50.
Anderson, J. M. and C. J. Ewen. 1987. *Principles of Dependency Phonology*. Cambridge: Cambridge University Press.
Anderson, J. M. and C. Jones. 1977. *Phonological Structure and the History of English*. Amsterdam: North-Holland.
Archangeli, D. 1984. *Underspecification in Yawelmani Phonology and Morphology*. MIT PhD dissertation, published by Garland Publishing, N.Y.
Archangeli, D. 1985. Yokuts harmony: evidence for coplanar representations in nonlinear phonology. *Linguistic Inquiry* 16: 335–372.
Archangeli, D. and D. Pulleyblank. 1986. The content and structure of phonological representations. Ms., University of Arizona and University of Ottawa.
Armstrong, R. G. 1968. Yala (Ikom): a Terraced-level language with three tones. *Journal of West African Languages* 5 (1): 41–50.
Aronoff, M. and R. T. Oehrle (eds.). 1984. *Language Sound Structure: Studies in Phonology presented to Morris Halle by his Teacher and Students*. Cambridge, MA: MIT Press.
Bearth, T. and H. Zemp. 1967. The phonology of Dan (Santa). *JAL* 6 (1): 9–29.
Bichakjian, B. H. 1986. A new feature for the specification of four-height vowel systems. In L. Wetzels and H. Jacobs (eds.), *Niet-lineaire Fonologie, een Theorie 'in SPE'* (Gramma 10.2), 105–117. Instituut Nederlands, University of Nijmegen.
Bosch, A., B. Need, and E. Schiller (eds.). 1987. *Parasession on Autosegmental and Metrical Phonology* (Papers from the 23rd Annual Meeting of the Chicago Linguistics Society, Part 2), Chicago: Linguistic Society, University of Chicago.
Bothorel, A. 1982. *Etude phonétique et phonologique du breton parlé à Argol (Finistère-Sud)*, Atelier National Reproduction des Thèses, Université Lille III, Lille.
Bothorel, A., P. Simon, F. Wioland, and J.-P. Zerling. 1986. *Cinéradiographie des voyelles et consonnes du français*, Travaux de l'Institut de Phonétique de Strasbourg, Strasbourg.
Brichler-Labaeye, C. 1970. *Les voyelles françaises: mouvements et positions articulatoires à la lumière de la radiocinématographie*. Paris: Klincksieck.

Bruce, G. 1970. Diphthongization in the Malmö dialect. *Working Papers of the Phonetics Laboratory* 3: 1–19.
Calabrese, A. 1987. The interaction of phonological rules and filters in Salentino. In J. McDonough and B. Plunkett (eds.), *Proceedings of NELS 17,* GLSA. Amherst, MA: University of Massachusetts.
Capo, H. B. C. 1985a. Determining the third person singular object pronoun in Gbe. In K. Williamson (ed.), *West African Languages in Education*, 106–131. Vienna: Afro-Pub.
Capo, H. B. C. 1985b. Vowel features in Gbe. *JWAL* 15 (1): 19–30.
Capo, H. B. C. 1986. Vowel rounding in Gbe: a pandialectal approach. *JWAL* 16 (1): 15–36.
Catford, J. C. 1988. *A Practical Introduction to Phonetics*. Oxford: Clarendon Press.
Chomsky, N. and M. Halle. 1968. *The Sound Pattern of English*. New York: Harper and Row.
Clements, G. N. 1974. Vowel harmony in Ewe. *Studies in African Linguistics* 5 (3): 281–301.
Clements, G. N. 1983. The hierarchical representation of tone features. In I. R. Dihoff (ed.), *Current Approaches to African Linguistics*, vol. I, 145–176. Dordrecht: Foris Publications.
Clements, G. N. 1985a. The geometry of phonological features. *Phonology Yearbook* 2: 225–252.
Clements, G. N. 1985b. Akan vowel harmony: a nonlinear analysis. In D. L. Goyvaerts (ed.), *African Linguistics: Essays in Honor of W.M.K. Semikenke,* 55–98. Amsterdam: John Benjamins.
Clements, G. N. 1986. Compensatory lengthening and consonant gemination in Luganda. In L. Wetzels and E. Sezer (eds.), *Studies in Compensatory Lengthening*, 37–77. Dordrecht: Foris Publications.
Clements, G. N. 1987a. Phonological feature representation and the description of intrusive stops. In A. Bosch, B. Need, and E. Schiller (eds.), *Parasession on Autosegmental and Metrical Phonology* (Papers from the 23rd Annual Meeting of the Chicago Linguistics Society, Part 2), 29–50. Chicago: Linguistic Society, University of Chicago.
Clements, G. N. 1987b. Toward a substantive theory of feature specification. In *Papers from the 18th Annual Meeting of the North Eastern Linguistic Society (NELS 18)*, 79–93. Amherst, MA: Dept. of Linguistics, University of Massachusetts.
Clements, G. N. 1989a. A unified set of features for consonants and vowels (preliminary version). Ms., Cornell University.
Clements, G. N. 1989b. A Theory of formal phonology. Ms., Cornell University.
Clements, G. N. 1989c. Secondary articulation in a unified feature framework. Ms., Cornell University.
Clements, G. N. 1989d. A remark on Icelandic preaspiration. Ms., Cornell University.
Clements, G. N. and E. Sezer. 1982. Vowel and consonant disharmony in Turkish. In H. van der Hulst and N. Smith (eds.), *The Structure of Phonological Representations*, parts 1 and 2, 213–255. Dordrecht: Foris Publications.
Cole, D. T. 1949. Notes on the phonological relationships of Tswana vowels. *African Studies* 8 (3): 109–131.
Cole, D. T. 1955. *An Introduction to Tswana Grammar*. London & Cape Town: Longmans, Green & Co.
Delattre, P. 1968. La radiographie des voyelles françaises et sa correlation acoustique. *The French Review* 42 (1): 48–65.
Doke, C. M. 1954. *The Southern Bantu Languages:* London: Oxford University Press.
Doke, C. M. and S. M. Mofokeng. 1957. *Textbook of Southern Sotho Grammar*. Johannesburg: Longman.

Dumas, D. 1981. Structure de la diphtongaison québécoise. *Canadian Journal of Linguistics* 26: 1–61.
Durand, J. 1990. *Generative and Non-linear Phonology*. London & New York: Longman.
Emenau, M. B. 1955. *Kolami: a Dravidian Language,* University of California Publications in Linguistics, vol. 12. Berkeley & Los Angeles: University of California Press.
Fant, G. 1970. *Acoustic Theory of Speech Production, with Calculations based on X-ray Studies of Russian Articulations*, 2nd edition. The Hague: Mouton.
Fischer-Jørgensen, E. 1985. Some basic vowel features, their articulatory correlates, and their explanatory power in phonology. In V. A. Fromkin (ed.), *Phonetic Linguistics: Essays in Honor of Peter Ladefoged*, 79–99. New York: Academic Press.
Gay, T., B. Lindblom and J. Lubker. 1981. Production of bite-block vowels: acoustic equivalence by selective compensation. *Journal of the Acoustical Society of America* 69 (3): 802–810.
Goldsmith, J. 1976. *Autosegmental Phonology*. MIT PhD dissertation, published 1979 by Garland Publishing, New York.
Goldsmith, J. 1979. The aims of autosegmental phonology. In D. Dinnsen (ed.), *Current Approaches to Phonological Theory*, 202–222. Bloomington: Indiana University Press.
Goldsmith, J. 1987. Vowel systems. In A. Bosch, B. Need, and E. Schiller (eds.), *Parasession on Autosegmental and Metrical Phonology* (Papers from the 23rd Annual Meeting of the Chicago Linguistics Society, Part 2), 116–133. Chicago: Linguistic Society, University of Chicago.
Guthrie, M. 1967. *Comparative Bantu*, vol. 1. Farnborough, Hants: Gregg International Publishers.
Hall, B. L. and R. M. R. Hall. 1980. Nez Perce vowel harmony: an Africanist explanation and some theoretical questions. In R. M. Vago (ed.), 201–236. *Issues in Vowel Harmony*, Amsterdam: John Benjamins.
Halle, M. 1959. *The Sound Pattern of Russian*. The Hague: Mouton.
Halle, M. and K. P. Mohanan. 1985. The segmental phonology of modern English. *Linguistic Inquiry* 16 (1): 57–116.
Harris, J. 987. Non-structure-preserving rules in lexical phonology. *Lingua* 72 (4): 255–292.
Harris, J. W. 1969. *Spanish Phonology*. Cambridge, MA: MIT Press.
Harris, J. W. 1985. Spanish diphthongization and stress: a paradox resolved. *Phonology Yearbook* 2: 31–45.
Hayes, B. 1985. *A Metrical Theory of Stress*. New York: Garland Publishing.
Hayes, B. 1986. Inalterability in CV phonology. *Language* 62 (2): 321–351.
Hayes, B. 1988. Diphthongization and coindexing. Ms., UCLA.
Herzallah, R. 1990. *Aspects of Palestinian Arabic Phonology: A Non-Linear Approach*. PhD dissertation, Cornell University, Ithaca, N.Y.
Hulst, H. van der. 1989. Atoms of segmental structure: components, gestures, and dependency. *Phonology Yearbook* 6 (2): 253–284.
Hulst, H. G. van der, M. Mous, and N. Smith. 1986. The autosegmental analysis of reduced vowel harmony systems: the case of Tunen. In F. Beukma and A. Hulk (eds.), *Linguistics in the Netherlands 1986*, 105–122. Dordrecht: Foris Publications.
Hulst, H. van der and N. Smith (eds.). 1982. *The Structure of Phonological Representations*, parts 1 and 2, Dordrecht: Foris Publications.
Hume, E. 1990. [Draft study of Maltese phonology], unpublished Ms., Cornell University, N.Y.
Hyman, L. M. 1986. The representation of multiple tone heights. In K. Bogers, H. van der Hulst, and M. Mous (eds.), *The Phonological Representation of Suprasegmentals*, 109–52. Dordrecht: Foris Publications.

Hyman, L. M. 1988. Underspecification and vowel height transfer in Esimbi. *Phonology* 5 (2): 255–273.

Hyman, L. M. 1989. Advanced tongue root in Kinande. Ms., U.C. Berkeley

Hyman, L. (to appear). Register tones and tonal geometry. In K. Snider and H. van der Hulst (eds.), *The Representation of Tonal Register*. Dordrecht: Foris Publications.

Inkelas, S. 1989. Register tone and the phonological representation of downstep. In I. Haïk and L. Tuller (eds.), *Current Approaches to African Linguistics*, vol. 6. Dordrecht: Foris Publications.

Inkelas, S. and W. R. Leben. 1990. Where phonology and phonetics intersect: the case of Hausa intonation. In J. Kingston and M. Beckman (eds.), *Papers in Laboratory Phonology 1: Between the Grammar and the Physics of Speech*. Cambridge: Cambridge University Press.

Jackson, M. T. 1988. Phonetic theory and crosslinguistic variation in vowel articulation. *UCLA Working Papers in Phonetics* 71: 1–184.

Jacobson, L. 1980. Voice-quality harmony in Western Nilotic Languages. In R. Vago (ed.), *Issues in Vowel Harmony*. Amsterdam: John Benjamins.

Jessen, M. 1990. The nature of diphthongization in Southern Swedish. Unpublished research report, Cornell University.

Jones, D. 1909. *The Pronunciation of English*. Cambridge: Cambridge University Press.

Katamba, F. 1989. *An Introduction to Phonology*. London & New York: Longman.

Kaye, J., J. Lowenstamm, and J.-R. Vergnaud. 1985. The internal structure of phonological elements: a theory of charm and government. *Phonology Yearbook* 2: 305–328.

Keating, P. 1988. Underspecification in phonetics. *Phonology* 5 (2): 275–292.

Kenstowicz, M. 1982. Gemination and spirantization in Tigrinya. *Studies in the Linguistic Sciences* 12: 103–122.

Kenstowicz, M. and C. W. Kisseberth (1979) *Generative Phonology: Description and Theory*, Academic Press, New York.

Kenstowicz, M. and C. Pyle. 1973. On the phonological integrity of geminate clusters. In M. Kenstowicz and C. W. Kisseberth (eds.), *Issues in Phonological Theory*. The Hague: Mouton.

Khabanyane, K. E. 1986. Southern Sotho vowel raising. Unpublished research notes, Cornell University.

Khabanyane, K. E. 1991. The five phonemic vowel heights of Southern Sotho: an Acoustic and Phonological Analysis. To appear in *Working Papers of the Cornell Phonetics Laboratory*, no. 5.

Kiparsky, P. 1968. Metrics and morphophonemics in the *Kalevala*. In C. Gribble (ed.), *Studies Presented to Professor Roman Jakobson by his Students*, 137–148. Cambridge, MA: Slavica.

Kunene, D. P. 1961. *The Sound System of Southern Sotho*. Doctoral dissertation, University of Cape Town.

Labov, W., M. Yaeger, and R. Steiner. 1972. *A Quantitative Study of Sound Change in Progress*, 2 vols., Philadelphia: U.S. Regional Survey.

Ladefoged, P. 1968. *A Phonetic Study of West African Languages*, 2nd edition: London & New York: Cambridge University Press.

Ladefoged, P. 1971. *Preliminaries to Linguistic Phonetics*. Chicago: The University of Chicago Press.

Ladefoged, P. and I. Maddieson. 1990. Vowels of the world's languages. Ms., Department of Linguistics, UCLA, Los Angeles.

Liljencrants, J. and B. Lindblom. 1972. Numerical simulation of vowel quality systems: the role of perceptual contrast. *Language* 48: 839–862.
Lindau, M. 1978. Vowel features. *Language* 54 (3): 541–563.
Lindau, M. 1979. The Feature Expanded. *Journal of Phonetics* 7: 163–176.
Lindblom, B. E. F. and J. E. F. Sundberg. 1971. Acoustical consequences of lip, tongue, jaw, and larynx movement. *Journal of the Acoustical Society of America* 50 (4; part 2): 1166–1179.
McCarthy, J. 1981. A prosodic theory of nonconcatenative morphology. *Linguistic Inquiry* 12: 373–418
McCarthy, J. 1984. Theoretical consequences of Montañes vowel harmony. *Linguistic Inquiry* 15: 291–318.
McCarthy, J. 1986. OCP effects: gemination and antigemination. *Linguistic Inquiry* 17: 207–263.
McCarthy, J. 1988. Feature geometry and dependency: a review. *Phonetica* 43: 84–108.
McCarthy, John. 1989. Guttural phonology. Ms., University of Massachusetts at Amherst.
Mabille, A. and H. Dieterlen. 1961. *Southern Sotho-English Dictionary*, 8th revised and enlarged edition. Morija: Morija Sesuto Book Depot.
Maddieson, I. 1984. *Patterns of Sounds*. Cambridge: Cambridge University Press.
Maeda, S. in press. Compensatory articulation during speech: evidence from the analysis and synthesis of vocal-tract shapes using an articulatory model. In W. J. Hardcastle and A. Marchal (eds.), *Speech Production and Speech Modelling*. Dordrecht: Kluwer Academic Publishers.
Malkiel, Y. 1984. Old Spanish resistance to diphthongization, or previous vowel lengthening. *Language* 60: 70–114.
Meinhof, C. 1932. *Introduction to the Phonology of the Bantu Languages* (revised and enlarged English translation of the original German edition of 1899), D. Reimer and E. Vohsen, Berlin.
Menéndez Pidal, R. 1973. *Manual de Gramática Histórica Española*, 14th edition. Madrid: Espasa-Calpe S.A.
Meyer-Lübke, W. 1890. *Grammaire des Langues Romanes*, French translation by E. Rabiet, vol. 1: *Phonétique*. Paris: H. Welter.
Milliken, S. 1988. *Protosyllables: A Theory of Underlying Syllable Structure in Nonlinear Phonology*. PhD dissertation, Cornell University, Ithaca, N.Y.
Mutaka, N. 1986. Vowel harmony in Kinande. Ms., University of Southern California.
Odden, D. 1989a. Vowel geometry. Unpublished Ms., Ohio State University [revised version of "Dorsal geometry," paper presented at the annual meeting of the LSA, New Orleans, December 1988].
Odden, D. 1989b. Kimatuumbi phonology and morphology. Unpublished Ms., Ohio State University.
Oyelaran, O. O. 1970. *Yoruba Phonology*. PhD dissertation, Stanford University, Stanford.
Perkell, J. 1971. Physiology of speech production: a preliminary study of two suggested revisions of the features specifying vowels. *Quarterly Progress Report* 102: 123–139, Research Laboratory of Electronics, MIT, Cambridge, MA.
Peterson, G. E. and I. Lehiste. 1960. Duration of syllable nuclei in English. *Journal of the Acoustical Society of America* 32 (6): 693–703.
Pierrehumbert, J. 1980. *The Phonology and Phonetics of English Intonation*. PhD dissertation, MIT, Cambridge.
Pierrehumbert, J. and M. Beckman. 1988. *Japanese Tone Structure*. Linguistic Inquiry Monograph 15. Cambridge, MA: MIT Press.

Plénat, M. 1987. On the structure of rime in Standard French. *Linguistics* 25 (5): 867–887.

Prince, A. 1984. Phonology with tiers. In M. Aronoff and R. T. Oehrle (eds.), *Language Sound Structure: Studies in Phonology presented to Morris Halle by his Teacher and Students*, 234–244. Cambridge, MA: MIT Press.

Rennison, J. R. 1984. On tridirectional feature systems for vowels. *Wiener Linguistische Gazette* 33/34: 69–94; also in J. Durand (ed.), 1986, *Dependency and Non-linear Phonology*, 281–303: London: Croom-Helm.

Sagey, E. 1986. *The Representation of Features and Relations in Nonlinear Phonology*. PhD dissertation, MIT, Cambridge, MA.

Schane, S. 1968. *French Phonology and Morphology*. Cambridge, MA: MIT Press.

Schane, S. 1973. [back] and [round]. In S. R. Anderson and P. Kiparsky (eds.), *A Festschrift for Morris Halle*, 174–184. New York: Holt, Rinehart and Winston.

Schane, S. 1984a. Two English vowel movements: a particle analysis. In M. Aronoff and R. T. Oehrle (eds.), *Language Sound Structure: Studies in Phonology presented to Morris Halle by his Teacher and Students*, 32–51. Cambridge, MA: MIT Press.

Schane, S. 1984b. The fundamentals of particle phonology. *Phonology Yearbook* 1: 129–155.

Schane, S. 1987. The resolution of Hiatus. In A. Bosch, B. Need, and E. Schiller (eds.), *Parasession on Autosegmental and Metrical Phonology* (Papers from the 23rd Annual Meeting of the Chicago Linguistics Society, Part 2), 279–290. Chicago: Linguistic Society, University of Chicago.

Schein, B. and D. Steriade. 1986. On geminates. *Linguistic Inquiry* 17 (4): 691–744.

Schlindwein, D. 1987. P-bearing units: a study in Kinande vowel harmony. *Proceedings of NELS 17*, Graduate Students' Linguistic Association, University of Massachusetts, Amherst, MA.

Sebeok, T. and F. Ingemann. 1961. *An Eastern Cheremis Manual, Indiana University*, Uralic and Altaic Series vol. 5. Bloomington: Indiana University Press.

Selkirk, E. O. 1988a. A two-root theory of length. Presented at NELS 19; to appear in *UMOP* 14.

Selkirk, E. O. 1988b. Dependency, place, and the notion 'tier'. Unpublished Ms., University of Massachusetts, Amherst, MA.

Sluyters, W. A. M. 1992. *Representing Diphthongs*. Unpublished doctoral dissertation, Catholic University of Nijmegen.

Smith, N. S. H. In press. Consonant place features. In H. van der Hulst and N. Smith (eds.), *Features, Segmental Structure, and Harmony Processes*, parts 1 and 2. Dordrecht: Foris Publications.

Snider, K. 1988. Towards the representation of tone: a three-dimensional approach," ms., University of Leiden.

Solé Sabater, M.-J. (n.d.). Experimentos sobre la percepción del acento. *Estudios de Fonética Experimental* I: 131–242. Laboratorio de Fonética, Facultad de Filología, Universidad de Barcelona.

Stallcup, K. L. 1980a. A brief account of nominal prefixes and vowel harmony in Esimbi. In L. Bouquiaux (ed.), *L'expansion bantoue*, vol. 2, 435–441. Paris: SELAF.

Stallcup, K. L. 1980b. Noun Classes in Esimbi. In L.M. Hyman (ed.), *Noun Classes in the Grassfields Bantu Borderland*, SCOPIL 8, 139–153.

Stampe, D. 1972. On the natural history of diphthongs. *Chicago Linguistic Society* 8, 578–590. University of Chicago.

Steriade, D. 1982. *Greek Prosodies and the Nature of Syllabification*. PhD dissertation, MIT, Cambridge, MA.

Steriade, D. 1987a. Redundant values. In A. Bosch, B. Need, and E. Schiller (eds.), *Parasession on Autosegmental and Metrical Phonology* (Papers from the 23rd Annual Meeting of the Chicago Linguistics Society, Part 2), 339–362. Chicago: Linguistic Society, University of Chicago.
Steriade, D. 1987b. Locality conditions and feature geometry. In J. McDonough and B. Plunkett (eds.), *Proceedings of NELS 17*, 595–617. Amherst, MA: Department of Linguistics, University of Massachusetts.
Stevens, K. N. 1989. On the Quantal Nature of Speech," *Journal of Phonetics* 17: 3–46.
Stevens, K. N. and A. S. House. 1955. Development of a quantitative description of vowel articulation. *Journal of the Acoustical Society of America* 27 (3): 484–493.
Stevens, K., S. J. Keyser, and H. Kawasaki. 1986. Toward a phonetic and phonological theory of redundant features. In J. Perkell and D. Klatt (eds.), *Symposium on Invariance and Variability of Speech Processes*, 432–469. Hillsdale: Lawrence Erlbaum.
Stewart, J. M. 1967. Tongue Root Position in Akan Vowel Harmony. *Phonetica* 16: 185–204.
Stewart, J. M. 1983. The High Unadvanced Vowels of Proto-Tano-Congo. *Journal of West African Languages* 13 (1): 19–36.
Traill, A. 1985. *Phonetic and Phonological Studies of !Xóõ Bushman*. Hamburg: Helmut Buske.
Trubetzkoy, N. S. 1939. *Grundzüge der Phonologie*. Göttingen: Vandenhoeck and Ruprecht. English edition: *Principles of Phonology*, tr. Christiane A. M. Baltaxe, University of California, Berkeley and Los Angeles.
Wang, W. S.-Y. 1968. Vowel features. *Language* 44: 695–708.
Weidert, A. 1981. *Tonologie: Ergebnisse, Analysen, Vermutungen*. Tübingen: Max Niemeyer.
Westermann, D. 1930. *A Study of the Ewe Language*. London: Oxford University Press.
Wood, S. 1975. Tense and lax vowels – degree of constriction or pharyngeal volume? *Lund University Working Papers* 11: 109–134.
Yip, M. 1980a. Why Scanian is not a Case for Multivalued Features. *Linguistic Inquiry* 11: 432–436.
Yip, M. 1980b. *The Tonal Phonology of Chinese*. PhD dissertation, MIT, Cambridge, MA.
Yip, M. 1988. The obligatory contour principle and phonological rules: a loss of identity. *Linguistic Inquiry* 19 (1): 65–100.
Ziervogel, D. (ed.). 1967. *Handbook of the Speech Sounds and Sound Changes of the Bantu Languages of South Africa*, UNISA Handbook Series No. 3, University of South Africa, Pretoria.

George N. Clements and Rajesh Khatiwada
# Cooccurrence constraints on aspirates in Nepali

## 1 Introduction

This paper examines cooccurrence constraints on aspirated consonants in Nepali, an Indo-Aryan language. As is well known, aspiration is a prominent feature of Indo-Aryan languages, which typically have as many as four series of stops: voiceless unaspirated, voiced unaspirated, voiceless aspirated, and voiced aspirated, the latter also referred to in the phonetic literature as breathy voiced. Most Indo-Aryan languages also have voiced or voiceless /h/, and several have aspirated nasals and/or liquids.

It has been noted that aspirated sounds are often restricted in their distribution. Within Indo-Aryan, several types of constraints have been observed in languages of the Rajasthani group (Masica 1991, MacEachern 1999):

- just one aspirate per word (Harauti, South Mewari, and some forms of Marwari)
- voiced aspirates and /h/ restricted to initial position (Harauti, Mewari of Udaipur)
- all aspirates restricted to initial position (South Mewari)
- just one aspirated stop per word unless the stops are identical (Gojri/Gujiri)

Also, Sanskrit limits aspirated stops to at most one per root (Whitney 1889, 1885). These examples are probably not exhaustive. Outside Indo-Aryan, constraints on aspirated and other laryngeally marked sounds, such as glottal stops and ejectives, have been noted in a number of languages, including the following (MacEachern 1999):

- Europe: Souletin Basque
- Western Asia: Old Georgian
- Africa: Hausa
- North America: Ofo (extinct), Shuswap (endangered)
- Central America: several Mayan languages including Tzutujil, Tsotsil, Chontal, and Yucatec
- South America: Cuzco Quechua (Peru), Aymara (Bolivia, Peru)
- Such constraints apply within the morpheme or the word.

Our goal in this study is to examine word-level laryngeal sequences in Nepali in order to discover whether similar restrictions exist, and if so, exactly what they consist of. At first sight, Nepali might seem an unlikely place to look. Previous studies of Nepali have not, as far as we are aware, discussed this topic. Indeed, earlier work has shown that aspirated stops occur with remarkable freedom in Nepali where, in contrast to many other languages, they occur contrastively before consonants and word-finally, showing only limited contextual neutralizations (Bandhu et al. 1971). Closer study has revealed, however, that Nepali has a rather strict constraints on aspirated sounds within the word, and it is this that will be the focus of our paper.

Our discussion is organized as follows. We first present an overview of some of the main features of Nepali phonology (section 2). We then turn to an examination of constraints on aspirated sounds (section 3). In the next section (4), we discuss several issues raised by the patterns we have brought to light. Section 5 places our results in a typological perspective, comparing Nepali with Sanskrit, Basque, and other languages exhibiting cooccurrence constraints on nonadjacent laryngeal features. Section 6 offers a formal analysis, and section 7 concludes.

## 2 Nepali phonology: a brief overview

Nepali is the official language of Nepal and one of the official languages of India. More than 11 million Nepalese and 2 million Indians claim this language as their mother tongue.[1] However, there exists relatively little published or easily accessible first-hand work on Nepali phonology. The main references on phonology and phonetics, respectively, are Bandhu et. al (1971) and Acharya (1991). Some further information can be found in pedagogical manuals such as Matthews (1998) and Hutt & Subedi (1999), grammars such as Acharya (1991) and Manders (2007), and dictionaries such as Turner (1931) and Schmidt (1993). Khatiwada (2009) presents a brief overview of Nepali phonetics. Michailovsky (1988) places Nepali phonology within the context of other languages of Nepal.

We begin with a brief sketch of Nepali word-level phonology. It will be useful to distinguish between the core vocabulary, consisting of native words and old, phonologically integrated loanwords, and the expanded vocabulary, which includes more recent loanwords, compounds, reduplications, and echo-words.

---

[1] According to the 2001 population censuses of Nepal and India, respectively. There are also over 150,000 speakers in Bhutan, as well as several million more in the Nepalese diaspora.

This distinction is not always clear-cut, but serves to separate out the clear cases, which are the large majority. Except where otherwise noted, the following description concerns the core vocabulary only.

The modern Nepali sound system has 38 contrastive consonants and vowels in its core vocabulary. A summary is given below.

## 2.1 Consonants

Nepali has 27 contrastive consonants in its core vocabulary, as shown below.[2]

(1) p    t     ʈ     ts     k
    pʰ   tʰ    ʈʰ    tsʰ    kʰ
    b    d     ɖ     dz     g
    bʰ   dʰ    ɖʰ    dzʰ    gʰ
                s            h
    m    n           ŋ
         l
    [w]  r           [j]

It will be seen that Nepali, like other Indo-Aryan languages, has a contrastive series of retroflex stops /ʈ ɖ ʈʰ ɖʰ/ in addition to its dental and affricated alveolar stops. These sounds involve a lesser degree of retroflexion than the corresponding stops in some other South Asian languages, and usually involve alveolar rather than post-alveolar contact (Pokharel 1989, Khatiwada 2007). /ɖ/ is realized as the voiced retroflex flap [ɽ] postvocalically (that is, intervocalically, pre-consonantally and word-finally). /ɖʰ/ may be realized as [ɽʰ] in the same contexts, but tends to be weakened to [ɽ] as we discuss just below.

(2) ɖãɖo   [ɖãɽo]   'hill'
    oɖʰne  [oɽne]   'wrap' (n.)
    haɖ    [haɽ]    'bone'

The flap allophones are transcribed with separate symbols in the traditional Devanāgarī syllabary and the standard Roman transliteration.

/bʰ dʰ ɖʰ dzʰ gʰ/ are voiced aspirated stops. While the phonetically more exact terms "breathy voiced" or "murmured" are also used for such sounds, the

---

[2] Older sources also list aspirated sonorants written *mh, nh, rh, lh*. These have mostly disappeared from the modern language.

term "voiced aspirate" is more appropriate for phonological description since, as we will see below, these sounds form a natural class with voiceless aspirates. Aspiration in breathy voiced stops tends to be weakened or eliminated intervocalically (3a), finally (3b), and preconsonantally (3c), leading to partial or full neutralization of the breathy vs. plain voiced distinction in natural speech. (We use the ellipsis "..." to indicate gradient variation.)

(3) a. sadzʰa ... sadza       'partnership'
       sãɖʱe ... sãɽe          'uncastrated, wild buffalo bull'
       sadʰa ... sada          'simple'
    b. bagʰ ... bag            'tiger'
       bãdʰ ... bãd            'dam'
       sãdʰ ... sãd            'boundary, limit'
    c. pʌndʰrʌ ... pʌndrʌ      'fifteen'
       ugʰrio ... ugrio        'opened'

In the latter two contexts, speakers rarely produce any aspiration unless they are aware of minimal pairs, or are producing the word in citation form. In addition to deaspiration, /b/, /bʰ/, /g/, and /gʰ/ are usually fricativized in intervocalic position (Pokharel 1989, 128).

In contrast, voiceless aspirated consonants keep their aspiration in most contexts, including final position, where we find minimal pairs such as [ruk] 'stop!' and [rukʰ] 'tree' (4a). However, in intervocalic and final position, /pʰ/ tends to reduce to [ɸ] and /kʰ/ to [kˣ] or [x]. Examples are shown in (4):

(4) a. sʌpʰa ... sʌɸa          'clean'
       sʌbʰa ... sʌβa          'meeting'
       sakʰa ... saxa          'branch'
    b. bapʰ ... baɸ            'steam'
       rukʰ ... rukˣ           'tree'

The processes illustrated in (2)–(4) can be related to a general tendency toward lenition in postvocalic position, which primarily affects voiced stops and aspirated stops (voiced and voiceless).

The aspirate /h/, when pronounced, is usually realized as voiced [ɦ]. It is an unstable phoneme which is normally elided intervocalically in unemphasized words, yielding rearticulated vowels and vowel clusters that do not otherwise occur. Rearticulated vowels may simplify to long vowels. (The period indicates a syllable break between vowels.)

(5) mʌhʌ ~ mʌ.ʌ ~ mʌ      'honey'
    paha ~ pa.a           'a large frog'
    loha ~ lo.a           'iron'
    lehi ~ le.i           'paste, glue'
    dohʌri ~ do.ʌri       'two folds'

The presence of such vowels and vowel sequences is a cue to the presence of underlying /h/.

All consonants occur as geminates except /h/ and the glides. Following Nepali tradition, we treat geminates here as sequences of two identical consonants,[3] except that the geminate counterpart of an aspirate such as /tʰ/ is treated as a plain stop followed by its aspirated counterpart, i.e., /ttʰ/ rather than /tʰtʰ/. This analysis is consistent with the phonetic realization, in which aspiration usually occurs only at the release of the second member. Not only aspiration but voicing is neutralized on the first member, which is realized with the voicing of the second member. As a result, just as there is no contrast between /tʰtʰ/ and /ttʰ/, there is no contrast between /td/ and /dd/, etc. These constraints create regular alternations in the verb paradigm, e.g. /dzot-do/ 'ploughing' is realized [dzoddo] by regressive voicing assimilation.

In addition to the consonants described so far, Nepali has two glides, palatal [j] and bilabial [w], which occur in complementary distribution with the vowels [i] and [u]. These sounds occur word-initially, intervocalically, and postconsonantally.

(6) jo        'this'
    wʌrʌ      'near'
    caja      'curf, dandruff'
    tawa      'chapati grill'
    tjo       'that'
    lwaŋ      'clove'

We follow the standard practice of representing the glides with separate symbols, though since they never contrast with /i/ and /u/, they can be treated as nonphonemic. Like vowels, glides do not occur as geminates. However, they provoke gemination of preceding stops (Pokharel 1989).

---

[3] An analysis as true geminates, e.g. a single stop associated with two syllable positions, might be preferable. This choice has no direct consequences for the present discussion.

## 2.2 Vowels

Nepali has eleven contrastive oral and nasal vowels, as follows:

(7)     oral                nasal
    i       u           ĩ       ũ
    e       o           ẽ       õ
        ʌ                   ʌ̃
        a                   ã

For one native speaker we have consulted, the high vowels /i/ and /u/ and their nasal counterparts are lower than IPA [i] and [u] and could be more narrowly transcribed as [ɪ] and [ʊ]. The symbol /ʌ/ represents a mid-open or raised-low vowel with two variants, [ʌ] and [ɒ̝], occurring at least partly in free variation. The nasalized vowels are less heavily nasalized than in some other languages, such as French, but are nevertheless contrastive. Notably, nasalization is a mark of the first person singular in several verb tenses, as shown by the contrast between *gʌrẽ* '(I) did' and *gʌre* '(they) did'. Nasality does not occur contrastively with the vowel quality /o/.

Nepali also has a series of breathy voiced vowels, one for each of the oral and nasal vowels shown above. These are phonetic variants of modally voiced vowels occurring after voiced aspirated stops (and for some speakers, voiceless aspirated stops; see Clements & Khatiwada 2007).

Nepali does not have an underlying length contrast in vowels. Surface long vowels arise from two main sources: h-deletion as described above, and concatenation of vowels across root-suffix boundaries, as in the following examples:

(7a)  /di-i-i/     [di.i] ~ [di:]         'she gave'     (-i 'perfective' + -i '3P-SG-FEM')
      /li-i-i/     [li.i] ~ li:]          'she took'
      /tsʰo-o/     [tsʰo.o] ~ [tsʰo:]     'touch!'       (2P-PL-IMP)
      /ro-o/       [ro.o] ~ [ro:]         'weep!'        (2P-PL-IMP)

In such cases, the long vowel is either [i:] or [o:] (Pokharel 1989: 105).

Nepali has a number of vowel sequences. We can distinguish between those that are *nonderived*, that is, which occur within single roots, and those that are *derived*, that is, created by h-deletion or morpheme combination as discussed above. Examples of nonderived vowel sequences are shown in (8); it will be noted that none contain identical vowels, and all end in a high vowel (an isolated exception is *jao* 'oats'). These are usually pronounced as single syllables, though each vowel receives its full value.

(8) nonderived vowel sequences
    a.  /i/ final

| | | |
|---|---|---|
| /ui/ | suiro | 'needle' |
| /ei/ | teis | 'twenty-three' |
| /ʌi/ | pʌisa | 'coin; money' |
| /ai/ | aimai | 'woman, wife' |
| /oi/ | poi | 'husband' |
| /aĩ/ | tʌpaĩ | 'you' (honorific) |
| /eĩ/ | tsiseĩ | 'dampness' |

    b.  /u/ and /ũ/ final

| | | |
|---|---|---|
| /iu/ | biu | 'seed' |
| /eu/ | (j)euṭa | 'one' (ADJ) |
| /ʌu/ | nʌu | 'nine' |
| /au/ | nau | 'boat' |
| /aũ/ | naũ | 'name; reputation' |
| /ʌũ/ | ʌũlo | 'finger' |

Some derived vowel sequences across root-suffix boundaries are shown in (9). (See also the examples of h-deletion in (5).)

(9)
| | |
|---|---|
| [tsʰo.e] | 'they touched' |
| [a.e] | 'they came' |
| [kʰa.ẽ] | 'I ate' |
| [gʌ.i] | 'she went' |
| [gʌ.e] | 'they went' |
| [dʰo.u] | 'wash!' (2P-SG-INF) |
| [de.o] | 'you (PL) give!' |
| [a.o] | 'you (PL) come!' |

Most derived vowel sequences may be pronounced as two syllables in careful speech, but are usually pronounced as one syllable in faster speech. Such differences in syllabification do not appear to be contrastive, and we have found no words differing only in that the same vowel sequence is monosyllabic in one and bisyllabic in the other.

    Sequences of three vowels occur only rarely and are usually syllabified as two syllables. Most of these are derived and have alternate pronunciations (for example, *piai ~ pijai* 'drinking', cf. *piu-nu* 'to drink'). The syllabification of vowel sequences is a complex subject that requires further study.

## 2.3 Adaptation of borrowed sounds

Nepali has a large number of loanwords, some of which introduce non-native phonemes. The most important component consists of loanwords from Sanskrit, which are used extensively by cultivated speakers. Nepali grammarians distinguish between words directly borrowed from Sanskrit with little or no change, called *tatsam* words, and those that have become Nepalized, called *tadbhaw* words. Turner (1931: xii–xviii) also recognizes old Nepali words which have Sanskrit cognates, which he treats as part of the native lexicon. We adopt this three-way distinction here, excluding *tatsam* words from the core vocabulary but retaining the others.

Examples of Sanskrit loanwords containing non-Nepali phonemes are shown in (10). While some speakers attempt to produce the original Sanskrit sounds, most Nepali speakers use the adaptation patterns shown in (10).[4]

(10) adaptations of Sanskrit sounds in loanwords from Sanskrit

| | | | |
|---|---|---|---|
| retroflex | ṇ > n | ban [ban] 'arrow' | (< Sk. bāṇáḥ 'reed') |
| retroflex | ṣ > s *or* kʰ | bʰasa ~ bʰakʰa 'language, tune' | (< Sk. bhāṣā) |
| | kṣ > tsʰ | bʰʌttsʰe 'edible' | (<Sk. bhakṣya) |
| palatal | ś > s | ades 'order, instruction' | (< Sk. ādeśa-) |
| labiodental | v > b | bʌrsa ~ bʌrkʰa 'monsoon' | (< Sk. varṣā) |
| | v > w | biswas 'confidence' | (< Sk. viśvāsa-) |

Languages bordering on the Nepali-speaking region are also important sources of loanwords. These include Hindi, Urdu, Maithili, Newari, Portuguese, and more recently English. There are also many Arabic and Persian loanwords used mostly in the commercial, legal and administrative domains, which entered the Nepali lexicon via Hindi and Urdu. All these languages contain a number of other foreign sounds, and these too are replaced by Nepali sounds by most speakers.

## 2.4 Syllable and word structure

The preferred syllabic structure in Nepali is CV(C), where C is a single consonant and V is a vowel or a nonderived vowel sequence. Table 1 illustrates the basic syllable types found in native words.

---

[4] Loanwords from Sanskrit and Hindi are transcribed as given in Turner (1931).

**Table 1.** Basic syllable types

|     | word-initial |                       | medial or final |                 |
| --- | ------------ | --------------------- | --------------- | --------------- |
| CV  | ho           | 'yes'                 | ama             | 'mother'        |
|     | nʌu          | 'nine'                | keʈi            | 'girl'          |
|     | timi         | 'you'                 | baʈʰo           | 'clever'        |
| CVC | kam          | 'work'                | tsamʌl          | 'uncooked rice' |
|     | pir          | 'sorrow'              | susar           | 'care, service' |
|     | gʰʌnʈi       | 'bell'                | gʰʌtseʈnu       | 'to push'       |
| V   | u            | 'he'                  | (only derived)  |                 |
|     | ʌsina        | 'hailstone'           |                 |                 |
| VC  | ek           | 'one'                 | (only derived)  |                 |
|     | ʌsti         | 'day before yesterday'|                 |                 |

As Table 1 shows, nonderived V-initial syllables are restricted to word-initial position. Further syllable types involve CC clusters in which the second C is one of the glides /j w/. Examples are shown in Table 2.

**Table 2.** CG-initial syllable types

|      | word-initial |                        | word-medial or final |                           |
| ---- | ------------ | ---------------------- | -------------------- | ------------------------- |
| CGV  | tjo          | '3P-SG-PRON'           | koʈjaunu             | 'to prick, to scratch'    |
|      | kwãʈi        | 'broth made of lentils'| biswasi              | 'trustworthy' < Sk.       |
| CGVC | tsjatnu      | 'to tear'              | pʌtjar               | 'confidence, trust'       |
|      | pwal         | 'hole'                 | bitjas               | 'unexpected calamity' < Sk.|

Noninitial syllables beginning with the cluster Cw, as illustrated in the second column, are found predominantly in Sanskrit loans.

Initial CGV and CGVC syllables are often simplified to eliminate the cluster. Various simplification strategies are illustrated below.

(11)  pwal ~ puwal        'hole'
      tsjatnu ~ tsetnu    'to tear'
      dzju ~ dziu         'life'

Initial Cr clusters occur in Sanskrit loanwords. These clusters are produced as clusters by some speakers, but are broken up by an epenthetic vowel by most, as shown in (12).

(12) priti ~ pirʌti        'love, affection'    < Sk. prīti
     prem ~ pʌrem          'love'               < Sk. preman-
     kranti ~ kʌranti      'surmounting'        < Sk. krānti
     srap ~ sʌrap          'curse'              < Sk. śāpa-, with added r

Both CG and Cr clusters are commoner word-internally. Here, too, Cr clusters tend to be broken up by epenthesis.

(13) pʌtrika ~ pʌtʌrika    'journal, magazine' (< Sk. pattrikā 'leaf')
     sastrʌ ~ sastʌrʌ      'religious book' (< Sk. śāstra)

Most consonants occur with great freedom in intervocalic clusters and word-finally, as is shown by the many examples collected by Bandhu et. al (1971).

A monosyllabic word consists of any of the syllable types given above. However, monosyllabic CV words are mostly function words, including pronouns, interrogatives, adverbs, and *nipat* words such as /po, rʌ, tʌ/ which have no proper sense, but give a certain expressiveness to the sentence. There are no monosyllabic words of the form CrV even in the loanword vocabulary (an exception is the Sanskrit loanword *śrī* 'prosperity, happiness', usually adapted as /siri/).

A polysyllabic word has the form of an initial syllable followed by one or more noninitial syllables as described above.

## 2.5 Prosodic features

Nepali has been described by Acharya (1991) and Matthews (1998) as having predictable, nonphonemic stress. However, these writers give conflicting statements of the stress rules. This area requires further study.[5]

Although Nepali does not have distinctive tone, breathy voiced vowels have been found to have notably lowered pitch (Clements & Khatiwada 2007). Studies of intonation need to be carried out.

---

[5] Matthews (1998: 17–18) classifies Nepali syllables into three types for the purposes of stress placement: final closed syllables with long vowels, other syllables with long vowels, and syllables with short vowels. For these purposes /i ʌ u/ and their nasal counterparts are classified as «short» and all other vowels and diphthongs as «long». Acharya (1991: ch. 3) draws a distinction between «short» vowels /i ʌ u/ and «long» vowels (all other vowels, diphthongs). He states that this distinction corresponds to phonetic differences in duration.

# 3 Constraints on aspirates in Nepali

With this background, we look more closely at constraints on the occurrence of aspirates in Nepali words. We use the term "aspirate" to include both aspirated stops and /h/, except where the context makes it clear that we are discussing just the stops.

## 3.1 Data source

Our primary source is *The Comparative and Etymological Dictionary of Nepali Language* written by Ralph Lilley Turner, a specialist in Indo-Aryan languages. The online version of this authoritative work, based on the paper version published in 1931, gives 26,073 Nepalese words with English glosses and etymological information. Nepali words are written in both Roman and Devanāgarī scripts. As the Roman transliteration is largely phonemic, the dictionary can be used as a tool of phonemic analysis by employing a few simple rules of letter-to-phoneme conversion. As might be expected, it is not fully suited for our purposes in all respects. For example, as the dictionary aims at comprehensiveness, it includes many dialectal variants known to few Nepali speakers. Furthermore, the search tool provided with the online edition provides no way of extracting native words only, so these must be sorted out by visual inspection of each entry. These difficulties should not be exaggerated, however. Carefully handled, this dictionary is a useful tool for lexical and phonological research work on Nepali as it was spoken in the early twentieth century.

## 3.2 Constraints on aspirates

Nepali shows strong restrictions on the cooccurrence of aspirates in its core vocabulary. We examine aspirated stops and /h/ in turn.

### 3.2.1 Aspirated stops in roots

Roots containing aspirated stops are common in the core vocabulary. However, roots containing two aspirated stops, voiced or voiceless, are virtually absent. A search through Turner reveals 264 entries containing two or more aspirated stops not separated by dashes (about 1 % of all entries). Of these, all but 7 can be easily identified as compounds, loanwords, reduplications, echo-words, proper names or variants or derivatives of words listed elsewhere.[6] These forms are shown below. Only the first four are personally known to the second author of this paper, a university-educated native speaker of the language who spent the first 24 years of his life in Nepal.

(14) apparent diaspirate roots in the core vocabulary

| | |
|---|---|
| tsʰʌtatsʰullʌ | 'overflowing (of liquids)' |
| bʰʌribʰʌnɖʌ | 'confusion, want of management' |
| bʰʌlɖʰyaŋ-bʰulʈɖʰuŋ | 'children' |
| bʰukʰʌnɖʌ | 'trouble, difficulty' (cf. kʰʌnɖʌ 'part') |
| kʰurʌndʰar | 'tenacity' |
| tʰittsʰʌ | 'two coins thrown together into the hole in the game of *khope*' |
| lakʰadʰuni | 'fatigue, exhaustion' |

None of these are monosyllabic, and only one is bisyllabic. Several of the longer words could possibly be old compounds whose component parts are no longer easily recognizable. Others have a repetitive structure suggestive of echo-words. However, we will count these as possible diaspirate roots. They are the only ones we know of in the core vocabulary.

Though Nepali has many other diaspirate roots, nearly all can be identified as loanwords, principally from Hindi and Sanskrit. Many of these are compounds in the source language and some may still be parsed as compounds in Nepali. Some examples are given in (15).

(15) diaspirate roots in the loanword vocabulary

| | |
|---|---|
| bʰʌtʰijara | 'inn-keeper' (< Hindi bhaṭhiyārā) |
| lipʰapʰa | 'envelope' (< Hindi lifāfā < Persian Arabic) |
| dzʌtʰartʰjʌ | 'truth' (< Sk. yathārthya) |
| dzʌtʰatʌtʰjʌ | 'truth' (< Sk. yathātathya) |
| dʰʌrmadʰʌrmʌ | 'right and wrong' (< Sk. dharmādharma, dharma 'duty' + ā-dharma) |

In sum, apart from the possible exceptions shown in (14), native Nepali roots have at most one aspirated stop, voiced or voiceless.

---

[6] Secondary variants do not have full listings in Turner but contain cross-references to the main entry.

One can ask whether this restriction is due to purely statistical factors. If aspirated stops are infrequent to begin with, we would expect words containing two of them to be rare, perhaps vanishingly so. To test this possibility, we examined all words of the form *CVC(V)* in Turner's Dictionary, in which C is any stop that may bear aspiration, that is, any member of the set /p b t d ṭ ḍ [ɽ] ts dz k g/ or their aspirated counterparts, and V is any vowel or vowel sequence.[7] There were 1,224 such words. These fall into four sets: those with the sequence C...C, those with the sequence C...C$^h$, those with the sequence C$^h$...C, and those with the sequence C$^h$...C$^h$ ("diaspirates"). On the null hypothesis, the frequency of C$^h$... C$^h$ words in the dictionary should be about what we would expect on the basis of the individual frequencies of each phoneme in the full lexicon.

Table 3 shows the results. Frequencies predicted by the null hypothesis are shown in parentheses.

**Table 3.** Distribution of aspirated stops and unaspirated stops in CVC(V) words in Turner's Dictionary.

|  | ... C ... | ... C$^h$ ... |
|---|---|---|
| C ... | 594 (662) | 216 (148) |
| C$^h$ ... | 406 (338) | 8 (76) |

In this table, the numbers expected under the null hypothesis are shown in parentheses. We see that 594 CVC(V) words contain a C...C sequence, 216 contain a C... C$^h$ sequence, 406 contain a C$^h$...C sequence, and 8 contain a C$^h$...C$^h$ (diaspirate) sequence. The point of interest is that 76 diaspirates are expected under a theory of free combination but only 8 are actually found. This difference is significant at the p<.0001 level (c$^2$ = 112.103). Our test is a conservative one, since our sample does not entirely exclude words from the extended vocabulary, in which diaspirate roots are more frequent. Of the 8 diaspirate words recorded in Table 3, one is a reduplication (*b$^h$ub$^h$u* 'the noise of humming'), two are echo-words (*p$^h$up$^h$a* 'exorcising', *ts$^h$aĩts$^h$uĩ* 'exhaustion of funds'), and the rest are variant forms of Sanskrit loanwords. None of these belong to the core vocabulary.

Since Turner lists all verbs with the infinitive suffix *-nu*, the count shown in Table 3 does not include verb stems. To examine verbs, we ran a new count on words of the form *CVC(V)nu*. This sample has the special advantage of nearly excluding non-core vocabulary items altogether. The result is shown in Table 4.

---

[7] The search was restricted to CVC(V) words in order to maximize the number of core vocabulary items.

**Table 4.** Distribution of aspirated stops and unaspirated stops in CVC(V)nu words in Turner's Dictionary. (All are verbal infinitives.)

|     | ... C      | ... Cʰ   |
| --- | ---------- | -------- |
| C... | 165 (195) | 75 (45)  |
| Cʰ... | 158 (128) | 0 (30)   |

30 diaspirate verb stems are expected on a statistical basis, but none occur. Overall, we find an even greater disproportion between expected and observed numbers.

We conclude that the near-absence of diaspirate roots in the Nepali core vocabulary is not a statistical effect, but reflects a significant constraint on lexical form.

### 3.2.2 Aspirated stops in affixes

There are no affixes with aspirated stops in the core vocabulary. Some examples of loanword affixes with aspirates are shown below.

(16) ʌbʰi- ('excess')   ʌbʰiman       'arrogance' < Skt. abhimāna-
                        ʌbʰibʰut      'defeated, overcome' < Skt. abhibhūta-
     ʌdʰi- ('elevated') ʌdʰikʌrma     'superintendance' < Skt. adhikarman-
                        ʌdʰikār       'authority, power' < Skt. adhikāra-
     -dʰari ('holder of') dʰʌnudʰari  'archer' < Skt. dhanudhārin-
                        dzʌṭadʰari    'having long matted hair' < Sk. jaṭā-dhārin
     -dʰʌr ('possessor') pʌktsʰʌdʰʌr  'partisan' < Sk. pakṣa 'side' (pakṣa linu 'to take sides')
                        bʌnsidʰʌr     'piper' (Krishna) < Skt. vaṁśīdhara-
     -kʰor ('consumer') gʰuskʰor      'bribe-taker' (gʰus 'bribe' < H. gʰūs)
                        napʰakʰor     'profiteer' (napʰa 'profit' < H. naf' < Ar.)

Superficial exceptions occur in the verbal paradigm. The examples in (17) show present and past tense forms of the verb root /kʰʌn-/ 'dig'. (hon. = honorific)

(17) a.  present tense

         *singular*                                    *plural*
         kʰʌn-tsʰu         '(I) dig'                   kʰʌn-tsʰʌũ         '(we) dig'
         kʰʌn-tsʰʌu        '(you) dig'                 kʰʌn-tsʰʌu         '(you) dig'
         kʰʌn-tsʰʌ         '(he) digs'                 kʰʌn-tsʰʌn         '(they) dig'
         kʰʌnnu-hun-tsʰʌ   '(you) dig' (hon.)          kʰʌnnu-hun-tsʰʌ    '(you) dig' (hon.)

b. past tense

| singular | | plural | |
|---|---|---|---|
| kʰʌn-tʰẽ | '(I) dug' | kʰʌn-tʰjʌũ | '(we) dug' |
| kʰʌn-tʰjʌu | '(you) dig' | kʰʌn-tʰjʌu | '(you) dug' |
| kʰʌn-tʰjo | '(he) digs' | kʰʌn-tʰe | '(they) dug' |
| kʰʌnnu-hun-tʰjo | '(you) dig' (hon.) | kʰʌnnu-hun-tʰjo | '(you) dug' (hon.) |

These apparent suffixes, however, are inflected forms of the verb /tsʰʌ/ 'to be (locational)' and /ho/ 'to be (definitional)', and can be regarded as inflected verbs functioning as auxiliary verbs. Other forms of these auxiliaries include *bʰajo, -tʰis*. As the examples in (17) show, all these forms can be added to stems with aspirated stops. In such cases, neither the aspirate of the base nor that of the suffix loses its aspiration, and the resulting words are diaspirate.

Nepali differs from Sanskrit in that it does not use reduplication in the verbal conjugation. However, expressive reduplications and echo-words are very common, and aspirated stops occur frequently in these words. Such words can be regarded as a form of compounding in which a word or stem is compounded with itself. A few examples are given in (18).

(18) expressive reduplications and echo-words with aspirated stops

| tsʰap-tsʰapti | 'with a close search' |
| dzʰar-dzʰur | 'shaking, flapping' |
| tʰʌk-tʰʌkjaunu | 'to knock against' |
| tʰʌr-tʰʌr | 'trembling' |
| dʰuk-dʰuki | 'palpitation, throbbing' |
| bʰun-bʰun | 'buzzing of a fly' |

### 3.2.3 Summary: aspirated stops in roots and affixes

Our observations up to this point can be summarized as follows:

(18a) Within the core vocabulary,
    a. aspirated stops do not occur in affixes
    b. roots contain at most one aspirated stop

The net effect of these two constraints is that roots and affixed stems (root + affixes) contain at most one aspirated stop.

## 3.2.4 Constraints on /h/

We now turn to the status of /h/. As /h/ is an aspirate, it is natural to ask whether it participates in the constraints discussed above. The answer is: yes, to a degree.

/h/ is subject to strict distributional restrictions. In the core vocabulary, it occurs only initially and intervocalically. It does not occur in consonant clusters except in loanwords (brʌhmʌ ~ brʌmhʌ, from Sanskrit *brahma*), a few reduplications (*hal-hali* 'flourishingly'), and, in the Eastern dialect, before /j/ and /w/ (Pokharel 1989: 154).

Unlike the aspirated stops, however, /h/ occurs in several suffixes. These include *-aha* which is used to form agentive nouns (19). As the last four examples show, this suffix combines freely with roots containing /h/ or other aspirates, voiced and voiceless. In such cases, both aspirates are preserved (though an intervocalic /h/ is subject to gradient h-deletion as mentioned earlier).

(19)　mitsaha　　'oppressor'　　　　(< mits- 'press')
　　　bokaha　　 'one who carries'　(< bok- 'carry')
　　　huljaha　　 'violent fellow'　　(< hul- 'mob')
　　　hepaha　　 'insolent fellow'　　(< hep- 'grow insolent')
　　　gʰitsaha　　'glutton'　　　　　(< gʰits- 'eat greedily')
　　　kʰodzaha　 'seeker'　　　　　 (< kʰodz- 'seek')

We have found no affixes with more than one /h/.

/h/ also occurs at most once per root. A search through Turner turns up only one apparent exception, *hʌttehʌran*, whose parts are homophonous with independent words (20a). Other examples are derivatives (20b), loanwords (20c), and reduplications (20d).

(20) a.　hʌttehʌran　　'strong insistence' (cf. hʌtya ~ hʌtte 'murder' < Sk. hatyā;
　　　　hʌran　　　　'tired; fatigue' < Hindi ḥairān 'distracted' < Arabic)
　　 b.　huljaha　　　 'violent fellow' (hul 'mob' + aha)
　　　　hʌpkjahʌt̪　　 'threat, abuse' (hʌpkau + ahʌt̪)
　　 c.　honʌhar　　　'fate' < Hindi honhar
　　　　hahakar ~ haha 'panic' < Sk. hāhākāra-
　　 d.　hʌrohʌr　　　'absolutely nothing'
　　　　hihi　　　　　'neighing'

/h/ does not occur in core vocabulary roots before an aspirated stop, adjacent or not, though as usual, we find a number of exceptions in loanwords, mostly from Sankskrit. In contrast, there is a fair number of core vocabulary roots in which

/h/ occurs *after* an aspirated stop. Some examples are shown in (21). It will be noted that in all cases, the stop is voiceless (T$^h$).

(21) kʰʌhʌrinu    'to be destroyed, be lost, be spoilt'
    kʰʌhʌre    'steep hill stream'
    tsʰʌhʌro    'waterfall, rapids'
    tsʰihilinu    'to pass the limits of decorum'
    t̪ʰʌhʌrʌi    'immediately, at once'
    t̪ʰʌhʌrnu    'to stop, remain'
    t̪ʰihi    'very cold'
    t̪ʰʌhʌr    'leaf folded up and used as a plate'
    t̪ʰʌrʌhʌri    'trembling'
    t̪ʰaha    'knowledge, information'
    pʰʌhʌraunu    'to raise a flag'

This pattern must therefore be considered regular. It might be related to the large number of derivatives formed with h-suffixes; as we saw in (19) earlier, h-suffixes can be added to roots with aspirated stops, creating diaspirate sequences in derived lexical stems. A few more examples from the core vocabulary are shown in (22).

(22) pʰʌṭaha    'prattler, babbler; one who exaggerates'
        (pʰʌṭṭi 'funny; liar' + -aha)
    kʰodzaha    'seeker' (khodz- 'seek' + -aha)
    kʰokaha    'one who is always coughing' (kʰok- 'cough' + -aha)
    girkʰjaha    'having swellings on the face or body'
        (girkʰo 'swollen gland' + -aha)
    gʱusjaha    'one who accepts bribes' (gʱus 'bribe' + -aha)
    dzʱurjahʌt    'dryness' (dzʱuryau- 'dry up' + -ahʌt)
    dudʱahar ~ dudahar    'yielding much milk' (dudʱ ~ dud 'milk' + -aha)
    bʱãgaha    'smoker of hemp' (bʱãg 'hemp' + -aha)
    dʱutaha    'crook' (dʱut- 'extort')

It might at first sight seem that these forms could have set a precedent for T$^h$...h sequences in nonderived roots as well, protecting them from eventual regularization by loss of one of the aspirates. However, this explanation would not explain why only *voiceless* aspirated stops are allowed before /h/. Voiced aspirated stops are regularly excluded before /h/, even though they occur in roots before -*aha*, as shown by several examples above. We will consider a different explanation when we take up the formal analysis in section 6. For the moment, we note that these roots constitute the sole class of regular exceptions to the exclusion of diaspirate roots.

We therefore revise our informal statement of cooccurrence restrictions on aspiration as follows:

(23) Within the core vocabulary,
    a. aspirated stops do not occur in affixes
    b. some roots contain $T^h$...h sequences ($T^h$ = any voiceless aspirated stop)
    c. otherwise, roots contain at most one aspirate (i.e., aspirated stop or /h/)

# 4 Constraints on aspirates: further questions

In this section we examine a number of further questions related to the distribution of aspirates.

## 4.1 Does /s/ pattern with aspirates?

Sanskrit phoneticians used the terms *ūṣman* 'spirant' for the fricatives and *soṣman* 'with spirance' for the aspirated stops (Allen 1957, who adds that the later grammarians abandoned this terminology). Some historical grammarians group /s/ with aspirates in a class of *aspirata*. Vaux (1998), citing a range of evidence, suggests that /s/ bears a phonologically redundant aspiration feature in some languages. One might ask, then, whether /s/ patterns with aspirates in Nepali.

A search through Turner shows that it does not. First, native roots with s...s sequences are well represented in the core vocabulary. If /s/ were an aspirate we would expect such sequences to be excluded. Examples include the following:

(24) sʌsura   'wife's or husband's father'
     sʌsto    'cheap'
     sas      'breath'
     sahʌs    'support, assistance'
     sisnu     'nettle'
     susar     'care, service'

Second, /s/ occurs freely in native roots with /h/, in both orders.

(25) sahʌsi   'venturesome, bold'
     sahʌs    'support, assistance'

sʌrʌhʌ    'equality'
sʌhʌ      'help; plenty'
sʌhi      'signature, acceptance'

Third, /s/ occurs freely with aspirated stops, in both orders.

(26) kʰʌsnu         'to fall; slip'
     gʰʌsnu         'to rub; rub on'
     dʰusi          'mildew'
     sakʰ           'one's own'
     satʰ ~ sathʌ   'together, as well'
     sugʰʌr         'neat, clean' (emphatic *suggʰʌr*)
     sudʰarnu       'to repair, mend'
     sodʰnu         'to ask, ask about'

We conclude that the constraints on aspirates do not include /s/.

## 4.2 Is the location of aspiration predictable in Nepali roots?

Aspiration has a prosodic status in Nepali, in the sense that it occurs at most once per root (with the exception of Tʰ...h sequences as noted). In other prosodic systems, the location of the prosodic feature is often predictable. For example, tone or stress may map regularly to the first, penultimate, or final vowel of the stem, according to the language. In other cases, as in a common type of nasal harmony, the prosodic feature falls on all segments licensed to bear them. In all these cases, the location of the prosodic feature need not be specified in underlying representations. Morphemes, or words, can be marked as either [+F] or [–F] for the feature in question, and mapping rules can distribute it to the segments that bear it phonetically.

Aspiration in Nepali does not behave this way. Given a root with two stops, either may bear aspiration. See the examples in (27).

(27) Cʰ is first in the sequence:        Cʰ is second in the sequence:
     pʰak    'handful'                   pitʰo    'flour'
     tʰãt    'fashion, nattiness'        katsʰ    'edge, hem'
     tʰok    'thing, matter'             gʌdʰ     'fortress'
     bʰat    'boiled rice'               madzʰ    'middle'
     dzʰuk-  'bend'                      kakʰ     'lap'
     tʰits-  'press'                     kãdʰ     'shoulder'

In this respect, Nepali aspiration is less "autonomous" as a feature than tone, or the features that underlie vowel and nasal harmony systems.

## 4.3 Underlying diaspirate roots in Nepali?

This question arises because certain patterns of alternation in Sanskrit, usually discussed under the term «Grassman's Law», have sometimes been thought to motivate underlying diaspirate roots in that language.[8] These patterns involve roots with two stops in which the first stop in aspirated in one context and the second is aspirated in another context. There is no context in which both are aspirated. Such alternations could be held to arise from underlying diaspirate roots in which aspiration is lost by two separate processes, one applying to the first stop in one context and the other to the second stop in another context.

We have found no such patterns in Nepali. A possible test case is the following. Bandhu et al. (1971) observe that /ṭʰ/ loses its aspiration before morphemes beginning with voiceless stops. They give the following examples, showing an alternation involving the verb root /tsuṭʰ/ (for the status of /-tʰjo/, see (17)):

(28) tsuṭʰ-nu    'to wash hands after eating' (/tsuṭʰ/ + /-nu/, infinitive suffix)
    tsuṭ-tʰjo    '(he) used to wash hands after eating' (/tsuṭʰ/ + /-tʰjo/, auxiliary verb)

In the first example, the root appears in a neutral environment in which the underlying aspiration of /ṭʰ/ is preserved. In the second example, /ṭʰ/ loses its aspiration before the voiceless stop /tʰ/, surfacing as a voiceless apico-alveolar flap. Now suppose Nepali had a diaspirate root such as /tsʰuṭʰ/. Before a formative like -tʰjo, the second aspiration would be lost, giving tsʰuṭ-tʰjo. Before a formative like –nu, one would expect both aspirates to appear, but as diaspirates do not surface as such in Nepali, a separate rule would be needed to delete the aspiration of the first, giving tsuṭʰ-nu. These two rules would yield the alternation tsuṭʰ ~ tsʰuṭ. We could not derive both alternates from underlying /tsuṭʰ/, since, as shown in (28), roots with final aspirates do not show this pattern of alternation. The simplest account would posit the diaspirate root /tsʰuṭʰ/.

However, while such a situation is imaginable, we have found no such pattern of alternation in Nepali, and so have no evidence, at present, that might support the recognition of underlying diaspirate roots in Nepali. The constraint against diaspirates appears to hold both underlyingly and on the surface.

---

**8** This view is no longer widely held (Collinge 1985).

## 4.4 Productivity

The large number of diaspirate words in the expanded vocabulary of Nepali suggests that the constraint is not active at the word level. It is not extended to loanwords, even those which are otherwise regularized. We have found no synchronic repair strategies used to eliminate underlying violations of the constraint against diaspirates. Moreover, in a number of cases the adaptive substitutions of *tsʰ* for Sanskrit *kṣ* or of *kʰ* for Sanskrit *ṣ* (see (10)) create diaspirate roots that did not exist in the source words. For example, the Sanskrit word *bhakṣya* 'edible' is adapted as *bʰattsʰe* by replacement of *kṣ* by *tsʰ*, marking it as a loanword (Turner 1931: xiii). If a constraint against diaspirate sequences were active in the loanword stratum, we would expect adaptations with diaspirate sequences to be blocked.

Even if there is no direct evidence that the constraint against diaspirate roots is phonologically productive at the word level, it is possible that Nepali speakers recognize diaspirate roots as phonologically "foreign", tolerating them in the loanword stratum but not in what is felt to be the native stratum. This possibility could be directly tested by devising tests on the production and categorization of pseudo-roots involving both regular forms and diaspirates.

# 5 Typological considerations

Let us compare the Nepali pattern with typologically similar patterns found in other languages. To do this, we will make use of the typological framework of MacEachern (1999), which is based on a survey of cooccurrence restriction on laryngeally marked sounds across a broad variety of languages.

One of MacEachern's discoveries was that constraints on aspirates fall into a larger pattern involving constraints on glottalic sounds (ejectives, glottal stop) as well. She also found that in her survey languages, constraints on nonidentical laryngeally marked sounds could be arrayed on a scale such that if a language has a constraint operating at a higher level of the hierarchy, it has all relevant constraints occurring at a lower level. The hierarchy is shown in Table 5 below, which includes a number of illustrative languages from MacEachern's sample, including Sanskrit. (We have not listed constraints involving implosives, which are included in the full hierarchy. Constraints on identical sounds are treated separately, see below.)

**Table 5.** Cooccurrence restrictions on nonidentical laryngeally marked sounds, after MacEachern (1999). A cooccurrence constraint for a given pair of sounds in a language, indicated by the asterisk (*), implies cooccurrence constraints for all relevant pairs of sounds below it. Languages are ordered from those whose constraints are the strictest (at left) to those whose constraints are most lax (at right).

|    |                          | BA | SK | CQ | GJ | HA | TZ | SH |
|----|--------------------------|----|----|----|----|----|----|----|
| 1  | $t^h \leftrightarrow \text{ʔ}$ |    |    | ✓  |    | ✓  |    |    |
| 2  | $t' \leftrightarrow h$   |    |    | ✓  |    | ✓  | ✓  |    |
| 3  | $h \leftrightarrow \text{ʔ}$ |    |    | ✓  |    | ✓  |    |    |
| 4  | $t^h \leftrightarrow h$  | *  | *  | *  | ✓  | ✓  |    |    |
| 5  | $d^ɦ \leftrightarrow h$  |    | *  |    |    |    |    |    |
| 6  | $t' \leftrightarrow k^h$ |    |    | *  |    | ✓  |    |    |
| 7  | $t^h \leftrightarrow g^ɦ$ |   | *  |    |    |    |    |    |
| 8  | $d^ɦ \leftrightarrow g^ɦ$ |  | *  |    |    |    |    |    |
| 9  | $t^h \leftrightarrow k^h$ | * | *  | *  | *  | ✓  |    |    |
| 10 | $t^h \leftrightarrow d^ɦ$ |   | *  |    |    |    |    |    |
| 11 | $t' \leftrightarrow \text{ʔ}$ |    |    | *  |    | *  | ✓  | ✓  |
| 12 | $t' \leftrightarrow k'$  |    |    | *  |    | *  | *  | *  |
| 13 | $t' \leftrightarrow t^h$ |    |    | *  |    | *  |    |    |

Languages: BA = Basque (Souletin dialect), SK = Sanskrit, CQ = *Cuzco Quechua, GJ = Gojri, HA = Hausa, TZ = Tzutujil, SH = Shuswap

In this table, expressions of the form "A ↔ B" can be read as the question "does sound A cooccur with sound B (in either order)"? A check mark to the right means that it does, while an asterisk means that it does not. The phonetic symbols stand for general classes of sounds. Thus, in row 1, the expression "$t^h \leftrightarrow \text{ʔ}$" can be read "do voiceless aspirated stops cooccur with glottal stops?" The expression "$t' \leftrightarrow k^h$" stands for the cooccurrence of any ejective stop with any nonhomorganic voiceless aspirate, while the expression "$t' \leftrightarrow t^h$" stands for the cooccurrence of an ejective stop with a homorganic voiceless aspirate. Shaded cells indicate configurations that are independently ruled out due to inventory considerations or distributional restrictions. For example, the shaded cells for Basque and Sanskrit in rows 1–3, 6, and 11–13 are due to the absence of glottalic sounds in these languages.

What do we learn from this table? Let us consider the three languages having no glottalic sounds, Basque, Sanskrit and Gojri.

Basque (BA) has only voiceless aspirated stops and /h/ in its inventory, so cells involving other sounds are shaded. Basque excludes any combination of aspirated stops with /h/ (row 4) or any combination of nonhomorganic aspirated stops among themselves (row 9).

Sanskrit (SK) also has voiced aspirated stops and /h/ in its inventory, so cells corresponding to these sounds (5, 7, 8, 10) are active. Sanskrit excludes any combination of aspirates, including /h/, within the root (rows 4–5, 7–10).[9]

Gojri (GJ), like Basque, has only voiceless aspirated stops and /h/ in its inventory, so other cells are shaded. Gojri differs from Basque and Sanskrit in allowing sequences of voiceless aspirated stops and /h/ (row 4).

The pairs of consonants mentioned in the constraints of Table 5 do not include homorganic consonants, such as two occurrences of /tʰ/, of /kʰ/, of /h/ or of /ʔ/. One might have assumed that such pairs, being maximally similar, would be most subject to cooccurrence restrictions and so would occur at the bottom of the hierarchy, where they would be excluded if any pairs higher in the table are excluded. It turns out, however, that this is not always the case; languages often give a "free pass" to homorganic pairs while excluding the analogous homorganic pairs. For example, Hausa allows homorganic ejectives while excluding nonhomorganic ejectives. For this reason, the option of allowing homorganic sequences is treated as an independent parameter, and a separate table is given for constraints on homorganic consonants. This is shown in Table 6 for the same languages seen earlier.

**Table 6.** Cooccurrence restrictions on identical laryngeally marked sounds, after MacEachern (1999). Languages are the same as those shown in Table 5.

|    |          | BA | SK | CQ | GJ | HA | TZ | SH |
|----|----------|----|----|----|----|----|----|----|
| 14 | h ↔ h    | *  | *  | *  |    |    |    |    |
| 15 | ʔ ↔ ʔ    |    |    |    |    |    | ✓  | ✓  |
| 16 | tʰ ↔ tʰ  | *  | *  | *  | ✓  | ✓  |    |    |
| 17 | dʱ ↔ dʱ  |    | *  |    |    |    |    |    |
| 18 | t' ↔ t'  |    |    | *  |    | ✓  | ✓  | *  |

The constraints in this table do not form part of the hierarchy shown in Table 5. This is because there is no place in Table 5 where the rows of Table 6 can be

---

9 Whitney (1889: 53) states a "euphonc law" which "forbids a root to both begin and end with an aspirate", by which he means an aspirated stop (voiceless or voiced). Neither the Sanskrit Index in Whitney (1889) nor the more complete list of verb roots in Whitney (1885) give any root with two aspirates in this sense, whatever their location, nor of any root with two occurrences of *h*. But Whitney (1885) lists the verb root *hūrch* 'fall away', in which *h* precedes the voiceless aspirate *ch*.

inserted without creating violations of the implicational pattern (compare e.g. Tzutujil and Shuswap).

As far as the three languages discussed earlier are concerned, Table 6 shows that Basque and Sanskrit do not exercise the option of allowing identical aspirates of any type (rows 14, 16, 17). Gojri, however, allows sequences of identical aspirated stops (row 16).

Let us now ask how Nepali fits into the pattern. We have extracted from Tables 4 and 5 just the rows that are relevant for Sanskrit, Nepali, and Gojri. These are shown in Table 7.

**Table 7.** Cooccurrence restrictions on aspirates in three Indo-Aryan languages, Sanskrit (SK), Nepali (NP), and Gojri (GJ).

|  |  | SK | NP | GJ |
|---|---|---|---|---|
| 4 | $t^h \leftrightarrow h$ | * | ✓ | ✓ |
| 5 | $d^h \leftrightarrow h$ | * | * |  |
| 7 | $t^h \leftrightarrow g^h$ | * | * |  |
| 8 | $d^h \leftrightarrow g^h$ | * | * |  |
| 9 | $t^h \leftrightarrow k^h$ | * | * | * |
| 10 | $t^h \leftrightarrow d^h$ | * | * |  |
| 14 | $h \leftrightarrow h$ | * | * |  |
| 16 | $t^h \leftrightarrow t^h$ | * | * | ✓ |
| 17 | $d^h \leftrightarrow d^h$ | * | * |  |

Nepali has the same types of laryngeally marked sounds as Sanskrit, and like Sanskrit, disallows any combination of aspirated stops, identical or not, within the root (rows 7–10 and 16–17). Also as in Sanskrit, no root may contain two occurrences of /h/ (row 14), and no root may contain sequences of voiced aspirated stops and /h/, in either order (row 5). But consider row 4. As we have seen (cf. (21)), Nepali allows sequences of voiceless aspirated stops and /h/, as long as they occur in just that order. Therefore, Nepali has a check mark in row 4. In this respect, Nepali is different from Sanskrit. However, it conforms to the general typology in that this check mark, the only one in Nepali, occurs higher in the hierarchy than the asterisks; in other words, the one sequence permitted in Nepali is higher in the hierarchy than all the disallowed sequences. In this respect, it confirms a theoretical ranking that was not actually attested in MacEachern's original survey languages.

But why should the row 4 constraint be crucially ordered above the row 5 constraint? MacEachern suggests that the order of constraints in Table 5 reflects increasing similarity, in some sense, as we pass from top to bottom. In other words, constraints on sequences become tighter as the sequences become more similar. In this view, the pair {t$^h$ h} would be more dissimilar than any pair listed underneath. We speculate that its dissimilarity might reside in the three phonological dimensions that distinguish {t$^h$ h} from all other pairs: 1) obstruent vs. nonobstruent, 2) supralaryngeal vs. laryngeal, and (in Nepali) voiceless (th) vs. voiced (h = [ɦ]). On these three dimensions, no lower-ranked pair is so dissimilar.[10]

## 6 Theoretical analysis

Let us finally consider how the constraints in Nepali might be stated in the grammar. In most current theory, dissimilatory constraints are expressed in terms of a family of constraints termed the OCP, or Obligatory Contour Principle, which rules out successive identical segments or features (see e.g. MacEachern 1999: 71–81, for a review and references). Let us consider first what feature or segmental subconstituent is targeted by the OCP as it applies in Nepali.

There is a surprising implication of MacEachern's hierarchy, not pointed out by MacEachern herself, that we have not yet commented on. This is that in languages having both aspirated and glottalic segments, OCP-driven constraints cannot apply only to segments bearing the feature [constricted glottis] or only to segments bearing the feature [spread glottis]. Rather, such constraints must apply to the full set of laryngeally marked consonants.

To see this more clearly, consider Table 5 again. Let us suppose that a language having both aspirated and glottalic sounds placed an OCP-driven constraint against successive occurrences of [constricted glottis]. In this case, rows 11 and 12 would bear an asterisk while row 13 would have a checkmark, contrary to the implicational hierarchy. To avoid this situation, such a language would have to impose an additional constraint on the row 13 sequence "t' ↔ t$^h$". This, strikingly, is just what Hausa, a language of this type, does. It follows, however, that the Hausa constraints do not target the feature [constricted glottis] alone.

This example may not be crucial, since MacEachern provides no empirical data supporting the ranking of row 13 after rows 11 and 12. Consider, however, the analogous case in which a language places an OCP-driven constraint only against [spread glottis] sounds. In this case, rows 4–5 and 7–10 would bear aster-

---

**10** As not all crucial rankings in MacEachern's hierarchy are supported by language data, we do not attempt to speculate on its overall physical or psychoacoustic basis in this study.

isks but row 6 and rows 11–13 would be checked. Note that rows 11–13 cannot be reordered above row 7 due to the Hausa pattern.

The hierarchy thus predicts that constraints cannot apply to the features [constricted glottis] and [spread glottis] individually, but must apply to the set comprising these two features. In other words, languages cannot rule out successive occurrences of aspirated segments without also ruling out successive occurrences of glottalic segments corresponding to lower positions on the hierarchy, and vice versa. It remains to be seen, as we examine more cases, whether this rather strong claim will prove strictly true, or whether it represents a tendency at best.

The important point for our purposes is that OCP-type constraints must be able to refer to the features [spread glottis] and [constricted glottis] as a group if they are to account correctly for the languages in MacEachern's sample that have both aspirated and glottalic consonants. In a feature geometry model, it has been proposed for independent reasons that these features are grouped under a Glottal Width node (Avery & Idsardi 2001, Yip 1995). Under such an analysis, phonological statements can refer directly to this pair of features to the exclusion of all others. Avery & Idsardi's model is shown below.

(29)

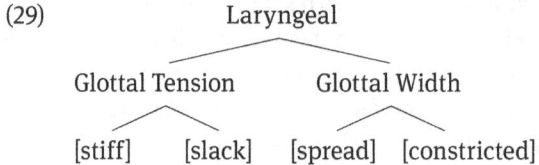

The Glottal Tension node groups the features of vocal cord tension and the Glottal Width node groups the features [spread glottis] and [constricted glottis].[11]

It may now be proposed that the constraint driving the Nepali cooccurrence constraints is a form of the OCP applying to Glottal Width nodes. We call this constraint OCP(GW). It states that the occurrence of two GW nodes is prohibited.

This constraint applies quite generally in Nepali. In order to express the special exemption of /Tʰ...h/ roots, we must adopt a constraint stating that sequences of the form /Tʰ...h/ must be preserved. In standard Optimality Theory, this would be a member of the family of faithfulness constraints. If it is crucially ranked above OCP(GW) it will exempt this special class of roots from its effect.

---

[11] Another way of referring to these two features as a group would be to invoke the Laryngeal node (Clements 1985, McCarthy 1988, Sagey 1990). In such an analysis, all constraints involving voicing would have to be higher-ranked in the hierarchy than those involving aspiration and glottalization. It remains to be seen how constraints on voicing interact with constraints on aspiration and glottalization across languages.

On this basis, the grammar of laryngeal cooccurrence restrictions in Nepali can be expressed as three constraints, applying to the core vocabulary, as shown in (30).

(30) constraints on the core vocabulary in Nepali
  a. *AspStop/AFF: aspirated stops are prohibited in affixes
  b. Preserve(T$^h$...h): sequences consisting of an aspirated stop followed by /h/ must be preserved
  c. OCP(GW): the occurrence of two GW nodes is prohibited.

As remarked above, (30b) is ranked above (30c). Note that the latter prohibits all sequences of aspirated sounds, including those containing identical aspirates such as t$^h$...t$^h$ or h...h. Unlike Gojri, Nepali does not activate further constraints that would exempt sequences of identical aspirates from the effect of OCP(GW).

The grammar summarized in (30) does not express the hierarchical entailments of the laryngeal cooccurrence scale (Table 5). If we assume such a scale on the basis of MacEachern's evidence, we could formulate these entailments in terms of a universal ranking of "Preserve" constraints, as follows:

(31) P1 ≪ P2 ≪ ... ≪ Pn

where each Pi stands for the correspondingly numbered constraint in Table 5. This ranking entails that a grammar activating any particular constraint P will also activate all constraints ranked above it in the hierarchy. For example, a language activating P4, namely P(t$^h$ ↔ h), will activate constraints P1, P2, and P3, if they are relevant. These happen to be irrelevant in Nepali, which lacks glottals and ejectives. But in Hausa, where P1 and P2 are relevant, the activation of P4 entails the activation of these two higher-ranked constraints. (P3 is not relevant in Hausa due to the fact that /ʔ/ and /h/ do not occur medially in native words.)

Finally, we must ask what domain the constraints (30b,c) apply to. Let us consider three candidates:

– the root
– the morpheme (root, affix)
– the derived stem (root + derivational affix(es))

The constraints apply to unproblematically to roots. There are no examples of core vocabulary affixes with aspirated stops, or with two occurrences of /h/. It follows that constraints (30b,c) hold over the full class of morphemes, roots and affixes alike.

However, these constraints do not, as they stand, generalize correctly to derived stems. The crucial case is the sequence /h...h/, which is prohibited in roots and affixes but which, as we saw in (19), arises in derived stems through the addition of suffixes with /h/ to roots with /h/. The OCP(GW), if applied to derived stems, would prohibit perfectly well-formed stems having the sequence /h...h/ across root-suffix boundaries. No other constraint in the system rescues them. As there is no further reason to apply the constraints in (30) to derived stems, we conclude that they apply at the level of the morpheme.

# 7 Conclusion

We briefly summarize the main results of this study. An exhaustive search of Turner's Comparative and Etymological Dictionary of the Nepali Language has brought to light the following generalizations, holding over morphemes in the core vocabulary:

- aspirated stops are absent in affixes
- some roots contain $T^h$...h sequences ($T^h$ = any voiceless aspirated stop)
- otherwise, roots and affixes contain at most one aspirate

These descriptive statements follow from the constraint system in (30).

A comparison of Nepali with other languages, including Sanskrit and Gojri, shows that Nepali is consistent with an implicational pattern discovered in a variety of languages by MacEachern (1999). This shows that the Nepali system, though apparently rare, is not atypical among languages. This paper takes a first step toward extending MacEachern's typology. It remains to be seen how our understanding of it can be improved by the study of further languages with restrictions on laryngeal features.

# References

Acharya, J. 1991. *A descriptive grammar of Nepali and an analyzed corpus*. Washington, D.C.: Georgetown University Press.
Allen, W. S. 1957. Aspiration in the Hāṛautī Nominal. In *Studies in Linguistic Analysis*, 68–86. Special Volume of the Philological Society. Oxford: Basil Blackwell.
Avery, P. & W. J. Idsardi. 2001. Laryngeal dimensions, completion and enhancement. In T. A. Hall (ed.), *Distinctive Feature Theory*, 41–70. Berlin & New York: Mouton de Gruyter.
Bandhu, C., B. M. Dahal, A. Holzhausen & A. Hale. 1971. *Nepali segmental phonology*. Kathmandu: Tribhuvan University and Summer Institute of Linguistics.
Clements, G. N. 1985. The Geometry of Phonological Features. *Phonology Yearbook* 2: 225–252.
Clements, G. N. & R. Khatiwada. 2007. Phonetic realization of contrastively aspirated affricates in Nepali. *Proceedings of ICPhS 16*, 629–632, Saarbrücken, Germany.
Collinge, N. E. (1985). *The laws of Indo-European*. Amsterdam: J. Benjamins.
Hutt, M. & A. Subedi. 1999. *Teach Yourself Nepali: A complete course in understanding, speaking and writing*. London: Hodder and Stoughton
Khatiwada, R. 2007. Nepalese retroflex stops: a static palatography study of inter- and intra-speaker variability. *INTERSPEECH* 2007: 1422–1425. Belgium: Antwerp.
Khatiwada, R. 2009. Illustrations of the IPA: Nepali. *Journal of the International phonetic Association* 39 (3): 373–380.
Manders, C. J. 2007. *A Foundation in Nepali Grammar*. Indiana: Authorhouse.
Masica, C. P. 1991. *The Indo-Aryan Languages*. Cambridge: Cambridge University Press.
MacEachern, M. R. 1999. *Laryngeal Cooccurrence Restrictions*. (Published version of *Laryngeal Dissimilatory Conditions* UCLA PhD dissertation 1997) London: Routledge.
Matthews, D. 1998. *A Course in Nepali* (3rd edition). London: School of Oriental and African Studies.
McCarthy, J. 1988. Feature Geometry and Dependency: a Review. *Phonetica* 45: 84–108.
Michailovsky, B. 1988. Phonological typology of Nepal languages. *Linguistics of the Tibeto-Burman Area* 11 (2): 25–50.
Pokharel, M. P. 1989. Experimental analysis of Nepali sound system. Doctoral dissertation. Pune, Pune University.
Sagey, E. 1990. *The Representation of Features in Nonlinear Phonology: the Articulator Node Hierarchy*. New York: Garland. (Published version of 1986 MIT PhD dissertation.)
Schmidt, R. L. 1993. *A Practical Dictionary of Modern Nepali*. Delhi: Ratna Sagar
Turner, R. L. 1931. *A Comparative and Etymological Dictionary of the Nepali Language*. University of Chicago. http://dsal.uchicago.edu/dictionaries/turner/.
Vaux, B. 1998. The laryngeal specifications of fricatives. *Linguistic Inquiry* 29: 497–511.
Whitney, W. D. 1889. *Sanskrit Grammar*. 2nd edition. Cambridge, MA: Harvard University Press.
Whitney, W. D. 1885. *The roots, verb-forms and primary derivatives of the Sanskrit language*. (A supplement to his Sanskrit grammar.) Leipzig. Reprinted 2006 by Low Price Publications, Delhi.
Yip, M. 1995. Tone in East Asian languages. In John Goldsmith (ed.), *Handbook of Phonological Theory*, 476–494. Oxford: Basil Blackwell.

Part 3

**Contributions on individual features**

Hyunsoon Kim and George N. Clements
# The feature [tense]

## 1 Main sources

Jakobson, Fant & Halle (1952: 36–9), Jakobson & Halle (1956: 30, 1971: 740), Fant (1960: 223–225), Jakobson & Waugh (1987), C.-W. Kim (1965), Chomsky & Halle (1968), Malecot (1970), Jessen (1998, 2001), Stevens (1998: 294–299), Durand (2005), H. Kim et al. (2005, 2010a,b, 2011), and H. Kim (2008, 2009, 2011a, 2012).

## 2 Overview

The feature [tense] was originally proposed by Jakobson et al. (1952: 36–39) in their auditory/perceptual perspective of distinctive features. According to them, "tense phonemes are articulated with greater distinctness and pressure than the corresponding lax phonemes." An important acoustic or auditory correlate of the Jakobsonian feature [tense] is long vs. short duration in consonants and vowels. For example, as shown in (1a), English voiceless obstruents are considered as tense and voiced ones as lax due to their relatively long vs. short closure duration. In the same vein, French long vowels are considered as tense and relatively short ones as lax, as in (1b) (the phonetic transcriptions in (1b) are taken from Tranel 1987).

(1) Tense and lax phonemes (Jakobson, Fant & Halle 1952: 36–37)

    a. tense vs. lax consonants   b. tense vs. lax vowels
       (English)                     (French)
       pill  –  bill           saute [soːt] 'jumps'– sotte [sɔt] 'fool' (fem.)
       till  –  dill           pâte [pɑːt] 'paste' – patte [pat] 'paw'
       kill  –  gill           jeûne [ʒøːn] 'fast' – jeune [ʒœn] 'young'
       chill –  gill
       fill  –  vill
       sip   –  zip

In the production of tense phonemes, "the muscular strain affects the tongue, the walls of the vocal tract and the glottis" (Jakobson et al. 1952: 38), but as for the articulatory definition of the feature [tense], Jakobson & Halle (1956: 43) noted that it "requires further investigation." It is C.-W. Kim (1965) who provided phonetic data on muscular tension in support of the Jakobsonian *tenseness*. From his articulatory, aerodynamic and acoustic data on the Korean plosives /p pʰ p' t tʰ t' k kʰ k'/, he observed that the fortis /p' t' k'/ and aspirated /pʰ tʰ kʰ/ consonants are longer not only in closure duration but also in linguo-palatal contact as well as higher in air pressure and in burst and that there is a larger amount of airflow following the release of the fortis and aspirated plosives than that of their lenis counterparts /p t k/. Moreover, the distance between the two onsets of glottal pulses (i.e. the duration of one full cycle: $1/F_0$) at the beginning of a following vowel is longer in lenis than in the other series. That is, $F_0$ is higher at the release of the fortis and aspirated plosives, which indicates that the glottis gets tenser in the consonants than their lenis counterparts (e.g. Hardcastle 1976; Stevens 1998). In addition, his EMG data on the labial plosives showed that lip muscle activity is less in /p/ than in /pʰ, p'/. C.-W. Kim (1965: 355) considered these phonetic properties as resulting from "the tension of the articulation" in the sense of Jakobson et al. (1952, 1956). It is also proposed that the Korean consonants are classified in terms of tenseness primarily: Korean fortis and aspirated consonants are classified as tense ([+tense]) with the two series consonants being distinguished secondarily by their different aspiration duration ([±asp.] short for [aspiration]) and lenis ones as lax ([−tense]).

Similar to C.-W. Kim (1965), Hardcastle (1973) considered the term tenseness as muscular tension. In his acoustic and aerodynamic data on the Korean word-initial plosives /p pʰ p' t tʰ t' k kʰ k'/ taken from a single native speaker of Seoul Korean, Hardcastle (1973) notes the double-peak configuration in the vowel onset, the sharper formant structure and the better defined harmonic partials following aspirated and fortis consonants than following lenis ones. This has led Hardcastle (1973: 264) to speculate that tenseness is "used in a specific sense referring to an increase in isometric muscular tension, primarily in the vocal cords and the pharynx." Recently, based on MRI data on the Korean obstruents taken from two native speakers of Seoul Korean, H. Kim et al. (2010a, 2011) have suggested that the feature [tense] denotes muscular tension in the primary articulator (i.e. lips, tongue tip/blade or dorsum) and the vocal folds, as later discussed in detail.

However, in Chomsky & Halle (1968), the Jakobsonian feature [tense] is replaced by the two features: [tense] for the tensing of the supralaryngeal musculature and [heightened subglottal pressure] (henceforth, [hsp]) for subglottal pressure, that is, the tensing of the sublaryngeal musculature. Chomsky & Halle (1968: 324) suggested that "The feature 'tenseness' specifies the manner in which the entire articulatory gesture of a given sound is executed by the supraglottal musculature. Tense sounds are produced with a deliberate, accurate, maximally distinct gesture that involves considerable muscular effort; nontense sounds are produced rapidly and somewhat indistinctly." Hence, "in tense sounds, both vowels and consonants, the period during which the articulatory organs maintain the appropriate configuration is relatively long, while in nontense sounds the entire gesture is executed in a somewhat superficial manner." In addition, the feature [hsp] is suggested "in the production of a speech sound without involving tenseness (in the supraglottal musculature)" (Chomsky & Halle 1968: 326). Thus, it is used for the representation of aspiration on the assumption that aspirated stops are produced with more subglottal pressure than unaspirated stops. For example, both aspiration in voiceless aspirated and in voiced aspirated stops in Hindi are represented by [+hsp].

The notion of the feature [hsp] in Chomsky & Halle (1968) is later developed for the 'fortis-lenis' distinction for consonants in the literature. According to Malecot (1970: 1591), "Force of articulation ... is primarily a synesthetic response to intrabuccal air-pressure impulse, with closure duration perphaps playing a secondary role." Malecot's aerdynamically-based account is elaborated as the account of the fortis vs. lenis consonants indicating "increased respiratory energy" by Ladefoged and his colleagues (e.g. Ladefoged 1971, 1989; Henton et al. 1992; Ladefoged & Maddieson 1996). For example, in the case of Korean consonants, Henton et al. (1992: 89) suggested that "heightened subglottal pressure accompanies the more constricted glottis and tenser walls of the vocal tract" in that the increase in pressure is suggested by Dart (1987) to be due to an increase in respiratory effort. However, more empirical data are needed in support of their fortis-lenis distinction. This is because Dart's (1987) results from a computer implemented aerodynamic modeling are based on her data on intraoral air pressure and air flow of the Korean fortis /p'/ and lenis /p/ (not including the aspirated /pʰ/). From the results, Dart (1987) inferred tenser vocal tract walls for the Korean labial fortis plosive /p'/, and a more rapid increase in respiratory muscle force than its lenis counterpart /p/.

A different view of the fortis-lenis distinction comes from Kolher (1984), according to whom the feature [±fortis] is considered as a cover term for [±voice], [±tense] and [±aspiration] in phonatory characteristics as well as long-short duration distinction ([±long]) in articulatory timing. Furthermore, it is suggested that the feature [±fortis] may be used as language universal if used only for an articulatory timing such as "the speed of stricture formation and release," or as language specific if a language uses a phonatory characteristics such "as aspiration, voicing or glottalization" (Kolher 1984: 168). For example, in his account, Finnish belongs to the first type in that it has the opposition of geminates, short obstruents and very short obstruents with no contrast in the larynx component, whereas Korean is a case of the second type in that it has two laryngeal contrasts for fortis stops, i.e. tension ([+tense]) and aspiration ([+asp.]), which it opposes to lenis counterparts that are less tense ([–tense]) and less aspirated ([–asp.]). But it is reported that the long vs. short duration in Korean consonants is closely associated with laryngeal tension of the consonants driven independently of glottal opening (H. Kim et al. 2005, 2010a,b, 2011).

## 3 Phonological use

### 3.1 [tense] in segment inventories

In segment inventories, this feature has been used in both vowels and consonants:

1. to distinguish tense vowels from lax ones (e.g. English: /i u e o / vs. /ɪ ʊ ɛ ɔ/; German: /iː eː aː oː uː yː øː/ vs. /ɪ ɛ a ɔ ʊ ʏ œ/; French /o: a: ɔ:/ vs. /ɔ a œ/);
2. to distinguish long consonants from short ones (e.g. voiceless vs. voiced in English, French and German; aspirated and fortis [pʰ tʰ tsʰ kʰ p' t' ts' k' s'] vs. lenis [p t ts k s] in Korean).

### 3.2 [tense] in phonological systems

It was Chomsky & Halle (1968) who used the feature [tense] in their discussion of English stress. As shown in (2), main stress falls on the penultimate vowel in the English verbs in column I, whereas it falls on the final vowel in columns II and III.

(2) Stress in English verbs (Chomsky & Halle 1968: 69)

| I. | II. | III. |
|---|---|---|
| astónish | maintáin | collápse |
| édit | eráse | tormént |
| consíder | caróuse | exháust |
| imágine | appéar | eléct |
| intérpret | cajóle | convínce |

As for the stress distribution in (2), Chomsky & Halle (1968: 70) generalized that "the verbs with penultimate stress end in a nontense vowel followed by a single consonant, while the verbs with final stress have a tense vowel or a diphthong in the last syllable (column II) or they end in two consonants (column III)." The stress distribution is formalized with the use of the feature value [−tense] for the last lax vowel in column I, as shown in (3).

(3) $\quad V \longrightarrow [1\ \text{stress}]\ /\ \underline{\quad} \ C_0\ (\begin{bmatrix} -\text{tense} \\ V \end{bmatrix} C'_0)$

(Chomsky & Halle 1968: 71)

Recently, Jessen (1996, 1998, 2001) has suggested that the tense vs. lax distinction is necessary in German vowels and consonants. German has a phonotactic constraint that a sequence of a lax vowel followed by a lax obstruent is phonotactically ruled out in German native vocabulary (e.g. Kloeke 1982). In his survey of the pronouncing dictionaries Duden and WdA, Jessen (1996, 1998) has found that sequences of a lax vowel (/ɪ ɛ a ɔ ʊ ʏ ø/) followed by a lax fricative (/v z ʒ j/) have a very marginal status in the phonotactic structure of German, occurring only in loans from languages such as English, French, Dutch or Yiddish, as in (4).

(4) [ɛz] Baiser, Fraiseur, Liaison, Maisonnette, Saison, Slezak
    [ɪz] Blizzard
    [ʊz] Puzzle
    [av] Bonaventura, Covercoat, Jawlenski, ravvivando,
    [ɔv] Paulownia, Sowjet, Wlassowa
    [ɛv] clever, Cheviot, Evergreen, evviva, Lewa, Reverie, Trevrizent, Zarewna
    [ɪv] Livingstonefalle, Przywara
    [ʊv] Struwwelpeter
    [ɛj] Crayon, Marseillaise, Rayon
    [œj] Feuilletonist

The constraint that disallows sequences of a lax vowel (/ɪ ɛ a ɔ ʊ ʏ œ/) followed by a lax fricative (/v z ʒ j/) is called the Puzzle Constraint by Jessen (1996). Under his assumption that phonetic parameters of the tense-lax distinction in consonants and vowels in German are based on duration, Jessen (1996: 319) suggests that the constraint is due to the OCP whereby "the feature [−tense] is ruled out to be adjacent to another instance of [−tense] on the same tier." In addition, Jenssen (1998) pointed out that the phonetic realization of the prosodic category of word stress in German corresponds to that of the feature [tense]. As duration of the segmental system of German is important as one of the correlates of the feature [tense], duration is also crucial in the realization of word stress.

Some of the strongest evidence for the feature [tense] in consonants, distinct from features of voicing or aspiration, comes from Korean. In order to support his phonetic study that Korean aspirated and fortis consonants are tense ([+tense]) and that their lenis counterparts are lax ([–tense]) in the sense of Jakobson et al. (1952, 1956), C.-W. Kim (1965) provides evidence from so-called intensified expressions in Korean, as in (5). When emphasized, lenis consonants alternate with fortis (5a) or aspirated (5b) or with both fortis and aspirated consonants (5c).[1]

(5) Korean sound symbolism

    a.   kʌm.ɨn      'black'                 k'ʌm.ɨn        'pitch black'
        pan.ts'ak     'glittering'          p'an.ts'ak     'glittering very brightly'
        tal.laŋ.tal.laŋ.  'ringing'            t'al.laŋ.tal.laŋ.  'ringing very hard'
        tsiŋ.tsiŋ.     'whining'            ts'i.tŋs'iŋ.    'whining hard'
    b.   pʌ.lʌŋ      'waving'               pʰʌ.lʌŋ       'fluttering'
        toŋ.toŋ      'stamping one's feet'  tʰo.tŋʰoŋ     'stamping one's feet hard'
        tsʌl.tsʌl      'overflowing'       tsʰʌl.tsʰʌl    'overflowing much'
    c.   piŋ.piŋ ~     pʰiŋ.pʰiŋ ~     p'iŋ.p'iŋ    'round and round'
        (slowly)      (fast and roughly)   (fast and tightly)
        tæŋ.tæŋ ~    tʰæŋ.tʰæŋ ~    t'æŋ.t'æŋ    'ding-dong'
        tsol.tsol ~    tsʰol.tsʰol ~    ts'ol.ts'ol    'trickling'

The sound pattern that Korean fortis and aspirated consonants group together in opposition to lenis ones in (5) can be expressed by virtue of the feature [tense]: fortis and aspirated as [+tense] and lenis as [–tense].[2]

The same sound pattern can be found in the Korean adaptation of French and Japanese words (H. Kim 2003, 2005, 2008, 2011a, 2012). As shown below, French voiceless stops are borrowed into Korean as either aspirated or fortis (6a) across the board, and voiced ones as lenis (6b).

(6)   French words      Korean adapted forms

    a.   Paris             **pʰa.ri**    ~   **p'a.ri**
        Toulon           **tʰul.loŋ**  ~   **t'ul.loŋ**
        boutique       **pu.tʰi.kʰɨ**  ~   **pu.t'i.k'ɨ**
        conte             **kʰoŋ.tʰɨ**  ~   **k'oŋ.t'ɨ**

---

[1] Throughout the text, we transcribe Korean affricates as alveolar, not postalveolar, in line with H. Kim (1999, 2001, 2004).
[2] Usually in the literature, an account has been given of the semanticization of aspirated and fortis consonants which intensify the expression containing the lenis ones (e.g. Kim-Renaud 1974).

b. baguette     pa.kɛ.tʰɨ ~ pa.kɛ.t'ɨ
    Bordeaux     po.lɨ.to
    début     tɛ.pwi
    De Gaulle     tɨ.kol

As H. Kim (2005, 2006, 2011a) has proposed, we can straightforwardly account for the Korean adaptation of French voicing contrast by virtue of the feature [±tense]. French voiceless (or tense) plosives, whose closure duration is relatively longer than voiced ones, are mapped into the feature [+tense] in Korean and are realized as either fortis or aspirated, in free variation. Voiced (or lax) plosives are mapped into [−tense] and are lenis. Thus, the Korean adaptation of French voicing contrast in (6) indicates that fortis and aspirated consonants, which are [+tense], group together as a natural class in opposition to lenis ones which are lax, that is, [−tense].

# 4 Phonetic definition

The current definition of the feature [tense] is mainly based on the Jakobsonian *tenseness* in vowels and consonants. Articulatory parameters and acoustic correlates of the feature [tense] are given below.

## 4.1 [±tense] for vowel quantity and quality

Tense and lax vowels in the sense of Jakobson et al. (1952) are differentiated in vowel quantity and quality. As in (1b), differences in vowel length are accompanied by qualitative differences. Vowel quality differences usually manifest themselves as peripheralization of tense vowels and centralization of short vowels. That is, Jakobson et al. (1952) noted in the case of tense vowels that the sum of the deviation of the formants from the neutral position is "always greater than that of the corresponding lax vowels," and that "the higher tension is associated with a greater deformation of the entire vocal tract from its neutral position."

As shown in Figure 1, the English tense vowels [u] and [i] have more extreme positions of the tongue body and lips than the lax counterparts [ʊ] and [ɪ]. The constriction is narrower in the tense vowels than that in the lax vowels and the cross-sectional area is larger for the tense vowels in the (lower) pharyngeal region behind the constriction. Thus, it is noticeable that the tense vowels have a widened pharynx with the tongue dorsum pushed upward. In the case of the lax vowels [ʊ] and [ɪ], the lower pharyngeal region does not widen that much as in their tense counterparts, and the tongue dorsum lowers.

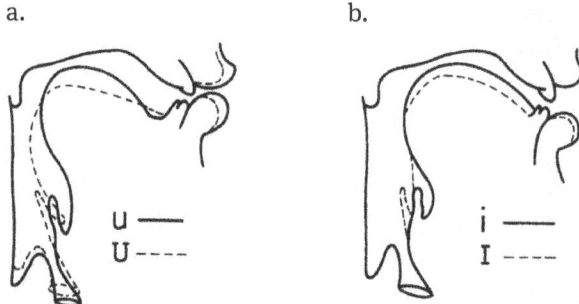

**Figure 1.** Midsagittal vocal tract configurations for tense [u i] (marked with a solid line) and lax [U I] (marked with a dotted line) high vowels for a speaker of American English in Perkell (1969) (Data from Stevens 1998).

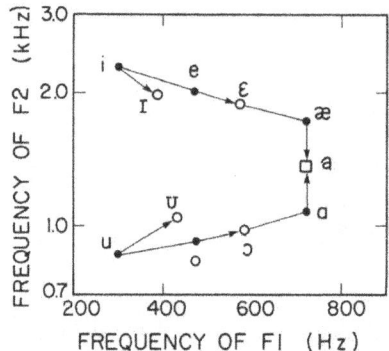

**Figure 2.** Comparison of the values of $F_1$ and $F_2$ for the basic set of six tense vowels (closed circles) and the four non-low lax vowels (open circles). Arrows point from tense vowels to corresponding lax vowels. Data are appropriate for adult male speakers. For the high vowels, data are from American English (Peterson & Barney 1952) (Data from Stevens 1998).

The less extreme constriction and the smaller volume of the cavity in the pharyngeal region in the lax vowels lead to the first and second formants shifting toward the center of the $F_1$–$F_2$ plot, especially for the high vowels. As shown in Figure 2, the formant frequencies in the $F_1$–$F_2$ plane for tense (/i e o u/) and lax (/ɪ ɛ ɔ ʊ/) vowels in English show that "the net acoustic effect of moving from the tense to the lax cognate for the high vowels is an upward shift in $F_1$ and a tendency for an inward movement of $F_2$ within the outer quadrilateral defined by the tense vowels" (Stevens 1998: 296).

The more/less extreme position of the tongue or constriction usually leads to long/short distinction because the more extreme position/constriction takes more time to reach the target of a sound than the less extreme position/constriction. Yet, this is not always the case. In Australian English (Mannell 2008), for example, vowels are classified in terms of the feature [±tense]: the tense vowels /iː eː ɜː ɐː oː uː ɪə æɪ ae ɔɪ æɔ/ are long, whereas the lax vowels /æ e ɪ ʊ ɔ ɐ/ are short. Among the Australian English vowels, the two low vowels /ɐː ɐ/ have the same tongue position ([–high, +low, –front, –back, –round]) but are different in duration.

Tense and lax vowels have different distribution properties, specifically in the Germanic languages. For example, in English, lax vowels must be followed by a consonant, as in *bid, bed, bad, good, bud*, whereas tense vowels have no such restriction, as in *bee, bay, low, boo, buy, boy, cue*.[3] Given that the lax vowels have a stable aperture and the tense ones have a movable degree of aperture except for the vowels /ɑ ɔ/ which have a stable degree of aperture, Trubetzkoy (1939) termed the difference in aperture between lax and tense vowels in the Germanic languages including English as "checked" for lax vowels and "unchecked" for tense vowels.

## 4.2 [±tense] for consonantal duration and phonatory characteristics

We suggest that [+tense] consonants are produced by longer closure or constriction duration and [–tense] consonants by shorter duration in line with Jakobson et al. (1952). It is language-specific whether both glottal tension and opening are associated with long vs. short consonantal duration.

German is one of the cases where long vs. short duration in [±tense] consonants is accompanied with laryngeal characteristics such as glottal tension and opening (e.g. Jessen 1998, 2001). According to Jessen (1998), German [+tense] obstruents have a higher $F_0$ in a vowel following the obstruents than in a vowel following [–tense] ones (see also Dixit 1989; Löfqvist 1990, 1992). Not only $F_0$-perturbation for glottal tension but also glottal opening is different between tense and lax obstruents in German (e.g. Ní Chasaide & Gobl 1993; Jessen 1998) (see also Gobl & Ní Chasaide 1988 for English, Swedish and French). Jessen (1998) has found that tense and lax obstruents show the difference between the amplitude of the first and second harmonics ($H_1$–$H_2$): tense obstruents accompany a higher value of $H_1$–$H_2$ around the first period of a following vowel than lax ones.

---

[3] The English words are taken from Ladefoged (2006). See also the English words in (2) for the lax vs. tense vowels' distribution.

In contrast, Korean shows that both long vs. short duration and glottal tension are closely assoicated with [±tense] consonants.[4] As shown in Table 1, the Korean plosives /tʰ t' pʰ p' kʰ k'/ are longer in closure duration (a) and higher in vertical larynx movement (b) than their lenis counterparts /t p k/, sometimes with the same glottal height in the aspirated and fortis ones (H. Kim et al. 2010a).

**Table 1.** The oral closure duration is determined by counting the number of consecutive frames where the tongue apex/blade and velar contact against the mouth roof for /t tʰ t'/ and /k kʰ k'/, respectively and where the lips come together for /p pʰ p'/. The duration in ms is calculated by multiplying the number of frames with 18.46 ms (the inverse of the frame rate). Glottal height is expressed as distance from the hard palate to the "center" of the thyroid cartilage measured at the most raised instance during oral closure.[5] All the consonants are embedded in /ta_a/. Source: H. Kim et al. (2010a).

|  | a. closure duration (ms) | | b. glottal height (mm) | |
|---|---|---|---|---|
|  | (i) female speaker | (ii) male speaker | (i) female speaker | (ii) male speaker |
| /t/ | 83.5 | 83.5 | 156.4 | 162.2 |
| /tʰ/ | 183.7 | 133.6 | 153.6 | 159.2 |
| /t'/ | 200.4 | 183.7 | 150.8 | 156.4 |
| /p/ | 66.8 | 66.8 | 162.2 | 165 |
| /pʰ/ | 133.6 | 116.9 | 159.2 | 162.2 |
| /p'/ | 183.7 | 133.6 | 156.4 | 162.2 |
| /k/ | 83.5 | 66.8 | 153.6 | 167.8 |
| /kʰ/ | 150.3 | 116.9 | 150.8 | 165 |
| /k'/ | 183.7 | 133.6 | 150.8 | 162.2 |

As for the cooccurrence of closure duration and glottal position in Table 1, H. Kim et al. (2010a) suggest that the feature [±tense] is defined in terms of the tensing of both the primary articulator (i.e. lips, tongue blade or dorsum) and the vocal folds. Therefore, much longer closure duration in the aspirated and fortis consonants in Table 1 can be regarded as more tension of the primary articu-

---

**4** H. Kim et al. (2005, 2010a, 20011) note that Korean consonants are characterized by the two independent patterns: a) the tensing of the primary articulator and the vocal folds, and b) glottal opening. Given this, Korean is different from German among others in which both glottal tension and opening accompany long vs. short duration difference.
**5** In the MRI studies (H. Kim 2004; H. Kim et al. 2005, 2010a), measured data in midsagittal images was multiplied by 1.422 instead of 2.844 (=256 mm/90 mm). In order to get correct data adjustments in these studies, we ask readers to multiply midsagittal measurements by 2, as in Table 1.

lator than in their lenis counterparts. In support of this, we can refer to C.-W. Kim's (1965) EMG data of the three labial plosives /p pʰ p'/. According to him, the aspirated and fortis labial stops have 'significantly more' lip activity than their lenis counterpart. In addition, as closure duration is longer in the aspirated and fortis consonants, so the glottis rises higher. Vertical larynx movements (that is, glottal height) are associated with "a generalized stiffening or slackening of the vocal folds and of the soft tissue surfaces of the vocal tract above the glottis" (Stevens 1998: 251) (see also Honda 1995, 1999; Honda et al. 1991, 1999). According to Honda (1995), vertical larynx movements have an effect on vocal fold length: when the larynx moves up, the vocal folds get longer since the thyroid and cricoid cartilage tend to follow the curvature of the cervical spine. A lengthening of the vocal folds in turn stiffens them, which results in higher intrinsic $F_0$ of vowels (Honda et al. 1999). So, higher glottal position in the aspirated and fortis consonants in Table 1 means that the vocal folds get more tense in the consonants than in their lenis counterparts. This is also supported by previous EMG data on muscular stiffness of the larynx in the articulation of Korean consonants (e.g. Hirose et al. 1974, 1983; Hong et al. 1991).

The tensing of the primary articulator and the vocal folds also characterizes the laryngeal properties of the Korean lenis and fortis fricatives /s s'/. In MRI, acoustic and aerodynamic data of the fricatives, H. Kim et al. (2010b, 2011) have found that oral constriction is longer and narrower in the fortis /s'/ than in the lenis /s/; the pharyngeal width is longer in /s'/ than in /s/; the highest tongue blade and glottal height is sustained longer in the fortis fricative /s'/ than in /s/ and that airflow resistance (the Pio (intra-oral air pressure) /U (airflow) ratio) is consistently higher in the fortis fricative than in /s/. This corresponds to the stronger (narrower and longer) oral constriction in /s'/ than in /s/.

The systematic pattern in glottal height in association with the laryngeal characterization of the Korean stop consonants in the above MRI studies can be acoustically correlated with that in $F_0$ values after a consonantal release. According to previous studies, $F_0$ of a following vowel after stop consonants varies systematically in the order lenis < aspirated, fortis in Korean, with the difference in $F_0$ between aspirated and fortis ones being very slight (e.g. C.-W. Kim 1965; Han & Weitzman 1970; Hardcastle 1973; Kagaya 1974; see also H. Kim et al. 2005 for recent references). Acoustic closure duration, which corresponds to articulatory closure duration of stop consonants, also shows that it is longer in Korean aspirated and fortis consonants than in their lenis counterparts across contexts. For example, both in word-medial and in word-initial position, acoustic closure duration of the coronal stops /t' tʰ t' ts tsʰ ts'/ varies from short to long in the order lenis < aspirated < fortis with the latter two being significantly longer than the former, when examined from ten speakers of Seoul Korean (H. Kim 2002).

A recent perception study on pitch variation in Korean speakers' categorization of Japanese plosives (H. Kim 2010, 2011b, 2012, 2013) has shown that the long vs. short duration difference is a primary auditory cue to the feature [tense] in word-medial position. In the study, native speakers of Seoul and Kyungsang Korean perceived word-medial Japanese voiced plosives as lenis ([–tense]) and voiceless ones as either aspirated or fortis ([+tense]), based on the duration difference in closure duration between Japanese voiced and voiceless plosives, regardless of whether a following vowel has H or L. Yet, when duration difference is not available in word-initial position, pitch variation in Japanese vowels after voiced and voiceless plosives is parsed for cues to the feature [tense].

In short, the common main articulatory parameter of the feature [tense] in vowels and consonants are the long vs. short duration difference. In vowels, the duration difference and vowel quality gives rise to the tense vs. lax distinction, as in English and German. The duration difference between tense and lax consonants could be accompanied with both glottal tension and opening, as in German. In the case of Korean consonants, however, it is suggested by H. Kim et al. (2010a, 2011) that the tensing of both the primary articulator and the vocal folds is denoted by the feature [±tense] with glottal opening denoted by the feature [±spread glottis].

## 4.3 alternatives

Since Chomsky & Halle (1968), the feature [tense] has rarely been maintained in feature theories. With the introduction of Autosegmental Phonology (Goldsmith 1976) into studies of English stress (i.e. Metrical phonology by Liberman & Prince 1977; Hayes 1981, 1982, 1984), the feature [tense] has never been used in the formalization of the English stress distribution. Most recent studies of English vowels have replaced [tense] with the short/long distinction, represented in terms of weight distinction on the phonological skeleton or mora tier (e.g. Anderson & Jones 1977; Halle & Mohanan 1985; Durand 2005). According to Durand (2005), the correspondence between tense vowels, diphthongs and VC sequences in English stress would be missed if the feature [tense] is used.

What is more noteworthy is that, for the feature specification of consonants, the feature [tense] has usually been replaced, in recent literature, with Halle & Stevens' (1971) laryngeal features all of which denote only the glottal status. That is, based on two dimensions of laryngeal control- a) the stiffness-slackness of the vocal cords and b) their spread-constricted positioning, Halle & Stevens (1971) proposed their four binary *articulator-bound* features -- [±stiff vocal cords], [±slack vocal cords] for glottal tensing, [±constricted glottis] and [±spread glottis] for glottal opening (henceforth, [±stiff], [±slack], [±c.g.] and [±s.g.], respectively).

See, for example, Clements (1985), Sagey (1986) and Lombardi (1994) among others for the use of the Halle & Stevens' (1971) laryngeal features.

Furthermore, the feature [voice] has been suggested for voicing (e.g. Chomsky & Halle 1968; Stevens et al. 1986, 2006; Kingston & Diehl 1994; Keyser & Stevens 2001; Wetzels & Mascaró 2001). For example, when English nouns end in tense vowels, diphthongs, sonorant or voiced consonants except for voiced strident ones, the voiced plural suffix [z] is added. The natural group of the English noun ending sounds would be captured by virtue of the feature [+voice], not [+tense].

Note also that often in the literature, the terms 'tense' and 'lax' in vowels are used for phonatory characteristics in languages spoken in China and Southeast languages (e.g. Maddieson & Ladefoged 1985; Maddieson & Hess 1986). But the attributes can be denoted by other features rather than [tense]. For example, according to Maddieson & Hess (1986), tense (/a̱ ɔ̱ ɣ̱ ɛ̱/) and lax (/a ɔ ɣ ɛ /) vowels in Wa, one of the Mon-Khmer family do not have length or quality difference but show a statistically significant difference in amplitude between the second harmonic ($H_2$) and fundamental frequency ($F_0$) in their three native subjects. In addition, they noted that Yunnanese Jingpho, one of the languages spoken in China (Liu 1964) also has tense (a̱ o̱) and lax (a o) vowels whose quality or quantity is not discerned, and that the difference in $H_2-F_0$ between tense and lax vowels is more significantly different than that in Wa.[6] According to Maddieson & Hess (1986: 106), "the lax vowels have a somewhat more breathy quality than the tense vowels" in these languages.[7] Later, Henton et al. (1992) suggest that the Chinese vowels are specified for the feature [stiff] in the sense of Halle & Stevens (1971).

Moreover, in certain African languages (e.g. Painter 1973; Lindau 1978, 1979), vowels are characterized by an advancement vs. retraction of the tongue root, not by a duration difference (e.g. Hess 1992). In this case, the feature [Advance Tongue Root] (henceforth, [ATR]) is used, because an advancement vs. retraction of the tongue root is a primary factor independent of vowel quality in the sense

---

[6] Tones in Jingpho vowels with high pitch indicated by 5 and low by 1 are not specified here and Maddieson & Hess (1986) differentiated lax vowels from tense ones in Jingpho with the former underlined (e.g. ka³¹ 'speech' vs. ka̱³¹ 'dance'; kaŋ³³ 'pull' vs. ka̱ŋ³³ 'tense' ; tom³¹ 'draw back' vs. to̱m³¹ 'conclude' ; ko³³ 'lay bricks' vs. ko̱³³ 'give'). In contrast, they underlined tense vowels in Wa. In order to keep readers from confusion in the use of underlines for the tense and lax vowels in the two languages, we underlined the tense vowels in Jingpho, as in Wa.

[7] It has been reported in the literature that vowels articulated with advanced tongue root are often produced with a breathy voice quality, whereas vowels articulated with retracted tongue root are often produced with a creaky voice quality. Yet, this covariation of voice quality with the position of the tongue root is not always in all languages (e.g. Lindau 1978, 1979; Denning 1989; Jackson1988). The two languages of Wa and Jingpho examined in Maddieson & Hess (1986) seem to present a case of this type.

of the Jakobsonian *tenseness*.[8] For example, in Akan (Niger-Congo, Ghana: Clements 1981 among others), vowels are classified into two series: /i e o u/ vs. /ɪ ɛ a ɔ ʊ/. Akan vowel harmony has been captured by virtue of the feature [ATR] (e.g. Archangeli & Pulleyblank 2007) (see also Beltzung et al. in this volume for Akan and other linguistic data).[9]

# 5 Enhancement

Tenseness regularly enhances differences in length and in voicing across languages. Geminate and singleton consonants in Pattani Malay, Italian and Japanese, among others, provide cases where differences in length are enhanced by tenseness. Pattani Malay, a language spoken in southern Thailand, has word-initial voiceless geminate and singleton stops whose duration differences play the most prominent role in identification (Abramson 1986). In addition, the differences in length in Pattani Malay are enhanced by intensity (i.e. RMS amplitude) and $F_0$. According to Abramson (1987), amplitude covaried with singleton vs. geminate contrast in word-initial position in Pattani Malay, such that amplitude was greater in post-geminate syllables than in post-singleton syllables. Also the amplitude of the post-stop syllable played a role in the listener's perception of the contrast in the language (Abramson 1992) (see also Hankamer et al. (1989) for a similar case in Bengali). Moreover, fundamental frequency differences following geminates and singletons helped listeners distinguish between the two types of segments (Abramson 1999).

Italian and Japanese also have geminates and singleton consonants but only in word-medial position. As in other languages which have geminate and singleton contrast, Italian geminate consonants are longer than singleton ones (e.g. Payne 2005). The durational differences in Italian geminate and singleton

---

[8] Other features such as [covered] (e.g. Painter 1973) and [expanded] (e.g. Lindau 1979) have also been suggested.
[9] See also Perkell (1971) for the proposal that tense vowels have an advanced tongue root in languages such as English and German, following Halle & Stevens (1969). Lindau (1978) measured tongue height and advanced tongue root for eight German vowels, using the radiographic data of Wängler (1961). Tongue height and tongue-root advancement were found to be highly correlated in four German tense-lax pairs. This led Lindau to suggest that the advancing and retracting of the tongue root is dependent on the height of the tongue. The data from the five speakers of American English also showed a high correlation between tongue height and advanced tongue root, as in German (Lindau 1978). Given this, Lindau (1978: 558) suggests that "the tongue-root mechanism is not used in any consistent way to distinguish between tense and lax vowels."

consonants are enhanced by tenseness, too. According to the EPG study of Payne (2006), Italian coronal geminate sonorants and stops are produced more with the tongue blade or blade and tip, whereas non-geminates are more apical. And the tongue is "flattish during the geminate articulation," whereas it "may be slightly cupped (concave) during non-geminates, particulary in stops" (Payne 2006: 92). Japanese also has word-medial geminate and singleton consonants (e.g. Shibatani 1990, Tsujimura 1996). The durational differences between Japanese geminate and singleton consonants are also enhanced by tenseness, such that fundamental frequency ($F_0$) has a greater fall after geminates than singletons (e.g. Kawahara 2006, Idemaru & Guion 2008) and greater intensity is associated with geminates than singletons (Idemaru & Guion 2008).

Differences in voicing is also enhanced by tenseness. In languages which have a phonemic voicing contrast, as in English, French and Japanese, it has been reported that the duration of a voiceless consonant is longer than that of a voiced one; a preceding vowel is longer before a voiced consonant; $F_0$ is higher after a voiceless consonant (e.g. Lisker 1957, House & Fairbanks 1953, Peterson & Lehiste 1960 and Ladefoged 2006 for English; O'Shaughnessy 1981 and Laeufer 1992 for French; and Han 1962, Homma 1981, Shimizu 1996 and Vance 2008 for Japanese). According to Whalen et al. (1990), English speakers' perception of voicing can be influenced by gradient fundmental frequency, such that the higher the $F_0$ onset, the more voiceless responses. This indicates that $F_0$ enhances the voicing contrast in the language.

In addition, French voicing assimilation provides another case. For example, Snoeren et al. (2008) investigated the effect of voicing assimilation on lexical access. In their experiments they used potentially ambiguous words such as *soute* /sut/ 'hold', which is confusable with *soude* /sud/ 'soda' if completely assimilated in voicing, that is, if pronounced close to [sud]. It was found that fully voice-assimilated forms such as *soute* pronounced as [sud] in *soute bondée* retained something of their underlying [–voice] specification. That is, though fully voice-assimilated to a following voiced consonant /b/ in *bondée*, the plosive /t/ in *soute* had a longer closure duration with lower intensity during oral closure and with higher $F_0$ at preceding vowel offset than the voiced counterpart /d/ in *soude* when followed by *brute*. On the assumption that listeners might exploit fine-grained acoustic detail to access abstract lexical representation (e.g. Goldrick & Blumstein 2006, Snoeren et al. 2008), we can say that the underlying voicing contrast is enhanced by the acoustic properties which can be captured by virtue of tenseness.

# References

Abramson, Arthur S. 1986. The perception of word-initial consonant length: Pattani Malay. *Journal of the International Phonetics Association* 26.

Abramson, Arthur S. 1987. Word-initial consonant length: Pattani Malay. *The 11th International Congress of Phonetic Sciences*. Tallinn, Academy of Sciences of the Estonian S.S.R. 6, 68–70.

Abramson, Arthur S. 1992. Amplitude as a cue to word-initial consonant length: Pattani Malay. *Haskins Laboratories Report on Speech Research* SR-109/110: 251–254.

Abramson, Arthur S. 1999. Fundamental frequency as a cue to word-initial consonant length: Pattani Malay. *Proceedings of the 14th International Congress of Phonetic Sciences*. San Francisco.

Anderson, J. M. & C. Jones. 1977. *Phonological Structure and the History of English*. Amsterdam: North-Holland.

Archangeli, D. & D. Pulleyblank. 2007. Harmony. In Paul de Lacy (ed.), *The Cambridge Handbook of Phonology*, 353–378. Cambridge: Cambridge University Press.

Chomsky, N. & M. Halle. 1968. *The Sound Pattern of English*. New York: Harper and Row.

Clements, G. N. 1981. Akan vowel harmony: a nonlinear analysis. *Harvard Studies in Phonology* II: 108–177.

Clements, G. N. 1985. The geometry of phonological features. *Phonology Yearbook* 2: 225–252.

Dart, S. N. 1987. An aerodynamic study of Korean stop consonants: measurements and modeling. *Journal of the Acoustical Society of America* 81: 138–147.

Denning, K. 1989. *The Diachronic Development of Phonological Voice Quality*. PhD dissertation, Stanford University.

Dixit, R. P. 1989. Glottal gestures in Hindi plosives. *Journal of Phonetics* 17: 213–237.

Durand, J. 2005. Tense/lax, the vowel system of English and phonological theory. In Philip C., Durand, J. & C. J. Ewen (eds.), *Headhood, Elements, Specification and Contrastivity: Phonological papers in honour of John Anderson*, 77–97. Amsterdam: John Benjamins.

Fant, G. 1960. *Acoustic Thoery of Speech Production*. The Hague: Mouton (second printing 1970).

Gobl, C. & A. N. Ní Chasaide. 1988. The effects of adjacent voiced/voiceless consonants on the vowel voice source: a cross language study. *Speech Transmission Laboratory Charterly Progress and Status Report. Royal Institute of Technology, Stockholm* 2-3: 23–59.

Goldrick, M. & S. E. Blumstein. 2006. Cascading activation from phonological planning to articulatory processes: evidence from tongue twisters. *Language and Cognitive Processes* 21: 649–683.

Goldsmith, J. 1976. *Autosegmental Phonology*. MIT PhD dissertation (published in 1979). New York: Garland.

Halle, M. & K. P. Mohanan. 1985. Segmental phonology of Modern English. *Linguistic Inquiry* 16: 57–116.

Halle, M. & K. Stevens. 1969. On the feature 'Advanced Tongue Root'. *Quarterly Progress Report* 94, 209–215. Cambridge, MA: Research Laboratory of Electronics, MIT.

Halle, M. & K. Stevens. 1971. A note on laryngeal features. *Quarterly Progress Report* 101. Cambridge, MA: Research Laboratory of Electronics, MIT.

Han, M. S. 1962. The feature of duration in Japanese. *Study of Sounds* 10: 65–75. Tokyo: Phonetic Society of Japan.

Han, M. S. & R. S. Weitzman. 1970. Acoustic features of Korean /P, T, K/, /p, t, k/ and /ph, th, kh/. *Phonetica* 22: 112–128.
Hankamer, J., A. Lahiri & J. Koreman. 1989. Perception of consonant length: voiceless stops in Turkish and Bengali. *Journal of Phonetics* 17: 283–298.
Hardcastle, W. J. 1973. Some observations on the tense-lax distinction in initial stops in Korean. *Journal of Phonetics* 1: 263–272.
Hayes, B. 1981. *A Metrical Theory of Stress Rules*. MIT PhD dissertation, distributed by Indiana University Linguistic Club (published 1985). New York: Garland.
Hayes, B. 1982. Extrametricality and English stress. *Linguistic Inquiry* 13: 227–276.
Hayes, B. 1984. The phonology of rhythm in English. *Linguistic Inquiry* 15: 33–74.
Henton, C., P. Ladefoged & I. Maddieson. 1992. Stops in the world's languages. *Phonetica* 49: 65–101.
Hess, S. 1992. Assimilatory effects in a vowel harmony system: an acoustic analysis of advanced tongue root in Akan. *Journal of Phonetics* 20: 475–492.
Hirose, H., C. Y. Lee & T. Ushijima. 1974. Laryngeal control in Korean stop production. *Journal of Phonetics* 2: 145–152.
Hirose, H., H. S. Park & M. Sawashima. 1983. Activity of the thyroarytenoid muscle in the production of Korean stops and fricatives. *Ann. Bull. RILP* 17: 73–81.
Homma, Y. 1981. Durational relationship between Japanese stops and vowels. *Journal of Phonetics* 9: 273–281.
Honda, K. 1995. Laryngeal and extralaryngeal mechanisms of $F_0$ control. In Bell-Berti, F. & Abbs, J. H. (eds.), *Producing speech: Contemporary issues*, 215–232. New York: American Institute of Physics.
Honda, K. 1999. Interactions between vowel articulation and $F_0$ control. In O. Fujimura, B. D. Joseph & B. Palek (eds.), *Proceedings of LP'98*, 517–527. Prague: Charles University.
Honda, K. & O. Fujimura. 1991. Intrinsic vowel $F_0$ and phrase-final $F_0$ lowering: phonological vs. biological explanations. In J. Gauffin & B. Hammarberg (eds.), *Vocal fold physiology: acoustic, perceptual, and physiological aspects of voice mechanisms*, 149–157. San Diego, CA: Singular Publishing Group.
Honda, K., H. Hirai, S. Masaki & Y. Shimada. 1999. Role of vertical larynx movement and cervical lordosis in $F_0$ control. *Language and Speech* 42: 401–411.
Hong, K., S. Niimi & H. Hirose. 1991. Laryngeal adjustments for Korean stops, affricates and fricatives – an electromyographic study. *Ann. Bull. RILP* 25: 17–31.
House, A. S. & G. Fairbanks. 1953. The influence of consonant environment upon the secondary acoustical characteristics of vowels. *Journal of the Acoustical Society of America* 25: 105–113.
Idemaru, K. & S. Guion. 2008. Acoustic covariants of length contrast in Japanese stops. *Journal of the International Phonetic Association* 38: 167–186.
Jackson, M. T. T. 1988. Phonetic theory and cross-linguistic variation in vowel production. *UCLA Working Papers in Phonetics* 43.
Jaeger, J. J. 1983. The fortis/lenis question: evidence from Zapotec and Jawon. *Journal of Phonetics* 11: 177–189.
Jakobson, R., G. Fant & M. Halle. 1952. *Preliminaries to speech analysis*. Cambridge, MA: MIT Press.
Jakobson, R. & M. Halle. 1956. *Fundamentals of language*. The Hague: Mouton.
Jakobson, R. & M. Halle. 1971. The revised version of the list of inherent features. *Roman Jakobson Selected Writings: Phonological Studies*, 738–742. 2nd, expanded edition. The Hague & Paris: Mouton.

Jakobson, R. & L. R. Waugh. 1987. *The sound shape of language*. Berlin & New York: Mouton de Gruyter.

Jessen, M. 1996. The relevance of phonetic reality for underlying phonological representation: the case of tense versus lax obstruents in German. In U. Kleinhenz (ed.), *Interfaces in Phonology*, 294–328. Berlin: Akademie Verlag.

Jessen, M. 1998. *Phonetics and phonology of tense and lax obstruents in German*. Amsterdam, Philadelphia: John Benjamins Publishing company.

Jessen, M. 2001. Phonetic implementation of the distinctive auditory features [voice] and [tense] in stop consonants. In T. A. Hall (ed.), *Distinctive Feature Theory*, 237–294. Berlin & New York: Mouton de Gruyter.

Kagaya, R. 1974. A fiberscopic and acoustic study of the Korean stops, affricates and fricatives. *Journal of Phonetics* 2: 161–180.

Kawahara, S. 2006. A faithfulness ranking projected from a perceptibility scale: The case of [+voice] in Japanese. *Language* 82: 536–574.

Keyser, Samuel J. & Kenneth N. Stevens. 2001. Enhancement revisited. In Michael Kenstowicz (ed.), *Ken Hale: A Life in Language*, 271–291. Cambridge, MA: MIT press.

Kim, C.-W. 1965. On the autonomy of the tensity feature in stop classification. *Word* 21: 339–359.

Kim, H. 1999. The Place of Articulation of the Korean Affricates Revisited. *Journal of East Asian Linguistics* 8: 313–347.

Kim, H. 2001. The place of articulation of the Korean plain affricate in intervocalic position: an articulatory and acoustic study. *Journal of International Phonetics Association* 31: 229–257.

Kim, H. 2002. Korean tense consonants as singletons. *Proceedings of the 38$^{th}$ Chicago Linguistic Society: the Main Session*, 329–344. Chicago: The University of Chicago Press.

Kim, H. 2003. The feature [tense] revisited: the case of Korean consonants. *NELS* 34: 319–332.

Kim, H. 2004. Stroboscopic-cine MRI data on Korean coronal plosives and affricates: implications for their place of articulation as alveolar. *Phonetica* 61: 234–251.

Kim, H. 2005. The representation of the three-way laryngeal contrast in Korean consonants. In Marc van Oostendorp & Jeroen van de Weijer (eds.), *The Internal Organization of Phonological Segments*, 287–315. Berlin & New York: Mouton de Gruyter.

Kim, H. 2006. A feature-driven non-native percept in the loanword adaptation of English and French voicing contrast into Korean. Presented at the 14$^{th}$ Manchester Phonology Meeting, the University of Manchester, England.

Kim, H. 2008. Loanword adaptation between Japanese and Korean: evidence for L1 feature-driven perception. *Journal of East Asian Linguistics* 17: 331–346.

Kim, H. 2009. Korean adaptation of English affricates and fricatives in a feature-driven model of loanword adaptation. In A. Calabrese & L. Wetzel (eds.), *Loan Phonology*, 155–180. Amsterdam & Philadelphia: John Benjamins.

Kim, H. 2011a. An L1 grammar-driven model of loanword adaptation: Evidence from Korean. To appear in *Korean Linguistics* 16 (2). Amsterdam & Philadelphia: John Benjamins.

Kim, H. 2011b. Kyungsang Korean subjects' perception of Japanese pitch-accent. *Proceedings of ICPhS 17*, Hong Kong: 1058–1061.

Kim, H. 2012 (submitted). The role of $F_0$ in Korean speakers' categorization of Japanese plosives: Implications for the Korean laryngeal feature specification.

Kim, H. 2013. Seoul Korean subjects' perception of Japanese Pitch-Accent: Evidence for the absence of tonogenesis in Korean. *Japanese-Korean Linguistics* 20: 217–232. CSLI: Stanford University.

Kim, H., K. Honda & S. Maeda. 2005. Stroboscopic-cine MRI study on the phasing between the tongue and the larynx in Korean three-way phonation contrast. *Journal of Phonetics* 33: 1–26.
Kim, H., Maeda, S. & Honda, K. 2010a. Invariant articulatory bases of the features [tense] and [spread glottis] in Korean: New stroboscopic cine-MRI data. *Journal of Phonetics* 38: 90–108.
Kim, H., S. Maeda, K. Honda, & S. Hans. 2010b. The laryngeal characterization of Korean fricatives: Acoustic and aerodynamic data. In S. Fuchs, M. Toda and M. Zygis (eds.), *Turbulent sounds: An interdisciplinary guide*, 143–166. Berlin & New York: Mouton de Gruyter.
Kim, H., S. Maeda & K. Honda 2011. The laryngeal characterization of Korean fricatives: stroboscopic cine-MRI data. *Journal of Phonetics* 39: 626–641.
Kim-Renaud, Y.-K. 1974. *Korean Consonantal Phonology*. PhD dissertation, University of Hawaii.
Kingston, J. & R. L. Diehl. 1994. Phonetic knowledge. *Language* 70: 419–454.
Kloeke, W. U. S. van Lessen. 1982 Deutsche Phonologie und Morphologie. Merkmale und Markierheit. Tübingen: Niemeyer. (From Jessen 1996)
Kohler, K. J. 1984. Phonetic explanations in phonology: the feature fortis/lenis. *Phonetica* 41: 150–174.
Laeufer, C. 1992. Patterns of voicing-conditioned vowel duration in French and English. *Journal of Phonetics* 20: 411–440.
Lindau, M. 1978. Vowel features. *Language* 54: 541–563.
Lindau, M. 1979. The feature expanded. *Journal of Phonetics* 7: 163–176.
Lisker, L. 1957. Closure duration and the intervocalic voiced-voiceless distinction in English. *Language* 33: 42–49.
Lisker, L., & A. S. Abramson. 1964. Cross-language study of voicing in initial stops: acoustical measurements. *Word* 20: 384–422.
Liu, L. 1964. Jingpoyu gaikuang [Brief description of the Jingpho language]. *Zhongguo Yuwen* 132: 408–417.
Liberman, M. & A. Prince. 1977. On stress and linguistic rhythm. *Linguistic Inquiry* 8: 249–336.
Ladefoged, P. 1971. *Preliminaries to Linguistic Phonetics*. Chicago: University of Chicago Press.
Ladefoged, P. 1989. Representing phonetic structure. *UCLA Working Papers in Phonetics* 73.
Ladefoged, P. 2006. *A Course in Phonetics*. Boston, MA: Thomson Wadsworth.
Ladefoged, P. & I. Maddieson. 1996. *The Sounds of the World's Languages*. Oxford: Blackwell.
Löfqvist, A. 1990. Speech as audible gestures. In W. J. Hardcastle & A. Marchal (eds.), *Speech Production and Speech Modelling*, 289–322. Dordrecht: Kluwer.
Löfqvist, A. 1992. Acoustic and aerodynamic effects of interarticulator timing in voiceless consonants. *Language and Speech* 35: 15–28.
Lombardi, L. 1994. *Laryngeal Features and Laryngeal Neutralization*. (PhD dissertation, 1991, University of Massachusetts, Amherst, MA) New York: Garland.
Maddieson, I. & S. A. Hess. 1986. "Tense" and "lax" revisited: more on phonation types and pitch in minority lanuages of China. *UCLA Working Papers in Phonetics* 63: 103–109.
Maddieson, I. & P. Ladefoged. 1985. "Tense" and "lax" in four minority languages of China. *Journal of Phonetics* 13: 433–454.
Malecot, A. 1970. The lenis/fortis opposition: its physiological parameters. *Journal of the Acoustic Society of America* 47: 1588–1592.
Mannell, R. 2008. Distinctive features. Ms., Macquarie University.
Ní Chasaide, A. N. & C. Gobl. 1993. Contextual variation of the vowel voice source as a function of adjacent consonants. *Language and Speech* 36: 303–330.

O'Shaughnessy, D. 1981. A study of French vowel and consonant durations. *Journal of Phonetics* 9: 385–406.
Painter, C. 1973. Cineradiographic data on the feature "covered" in Twi vowel harmony. *Phonetica* 28: 97–120.
Payne, E. M. 2005. Phonetic variation in Italian consonant gemination. *Journal of the International Phonetic Association* 35: 153–181.
Payne, E. M. 2006. Non-durational indices in Italian geminate consonants. *Journal of the International Phonetic Association* 36: 83–95.
Perkell, J. S. 1969. *Physiology of Speech Production: Results and Implications of a Quantitative Cineradiographic Study*. Cambridge, MA: MIT Press.
Perkell, J. 1971. Physiology of speech production: a preliminary study of two suggested revisions of the features specifying vowels. *Quarterly Progress Report* 102: 123–138. Cambridge, MA: MIT.
Peterson, G. E. & H. Barney. 1952. Control methods used in a study of the vowels. *Journal of the Acoustical Society of America* 24: 175–184.
Peterson, G. E. & I. Lehiste. 1960. Duration of syllable nuclei in English. *Journal of the Acoustical Society of America* 32: 693–703.
Sagey, E. 1986. *The Representation of Features in Nonlinear Phonology: The Articulator Node Hierarchy*. MIT PhD dissertation (published in 1990. N.Y.: Garland).
Shibatani, M. 1990. *The Languages of Japan*. Cambridge: Cambridge University Press.
Shimizu, K. 1996. *A Cross-Language Study of Voicing Contrasts of Stop Consonants in Asian Languages*. Tokyo: Seibido.
Snoeren, N., J. Segui & P. A. Hallé. 2008. On the role of regular phonological variation in lexical access: Evidence from voice assimilation in French. *Cognition* 108: 512–521.
Stevens, K. N. 1998. *Acoustic Phonetics*. Cambridge, MA: MIT Press.
Stevens, K. N., Keyser, S. J. & Kawasaki, H. 1986. Toward a phonetic and phonological theory of redundant features. In Perkell, J. S. & Klatt, D. H. (eds.), *Invariance and variability in speech processes*, 426–447. Hillsdale, NJ: Lawrence Erlbaum.
Stevens, K. N. & Keyser, S. J. 2006. Enhancement and overlap in the speech chain. *Language* 82: 33–64.
Tranel, B. 1987. *The Sounds of French*. Cambridge: Cambridge University Press.
Trubetzkoy, N. S. 1939. *Grundzüge der Phonologie*. Göttingen: Vandenhoeck & Ruprecht. (English edition: Principles of Phonology. tr. C. A. M. Baltaxe. Berkeley & Los Angeles: University of California, 1969.)
Tsujimura, N. 1996. *An Introduction to Japanese Linguistics*. Oxford: Blackwell.
Vance, T. 2008. *The Sounds of Japanese*. Cambridge: Cambridge University Press.
Whalen, D. H., A. S. Abramson, L. Lisker & M. Mody. 1990. Gradient effects of fundamental frequency on stop consonant voicing judgments. *Phonetica* 47: 36–49.
Wängler, H.-H. 1961. *Atlas deutscher Sprachlaute*. Berlin: Akademie-Verlag. (From Lindau 1978)
Wetzels, W. L. & J. Mascaró. 2001. The typology of voicing and devoicing. *Language* 77: 207–244.

Hyunsoon Kim, George N. Clements and Martine Toda
# The feature [strident]

## 1 Main sources

Jakobson (1939), Jakobson, Fant & Halle (1952), Jakobson & Halle (1956), Chomsky & Halle (1968), Ladefoged (1971), Stevens (1983, 1985).

## 2 Overview

This widely-accepted feature, originally proposed by Jakobson (1939), was defined as follows by Jakobson, Fant & Halle (1952: 24):

> Strident phonemes are primarily characterized by a noise which is due to turbulence at the point of articulation. This strong turbulence, in its turn, is a consequence of a more complex impediment which distinguishes the strident from the corresponding mellow consonants: the labiodentals from the bilabials, the hissing and hushing sibilants from the nonsibilant dentals and palatals respectively, and the uvulars from the velars proper.

This definition covers stops as well as fricatives. It thus distinguishes not only sibilant fricatives from corresponding nonsibilant fricatives, as in English *sigh* [s] vs. *thigh* [θ], but also sibilant affricates from corresponding nonsibilant stops, as in German *reizen* [ts] 'to tease' vs. *reiten* [t] 'to ride'. The feature [strident] has been maintained in one form or another in most subsequent work. Occasional attempts to eliminate it have not been successful (see Hall 1997: 142–143 for a review).

A long controversy has surrounded the use of [+strident] to distinguish sibilant affricates from corresponding nonsibilant stops. One alternative involves the proposal to use a feature such as [delayed release] for this purpose. The motivation for this move comes from the existence of contrasts between sibilant and non-sibilant affricates. For example, the Athabaskan language Dëné Sɬiné (Chipewyan) has a phonemic distinction among three series of anterior coronals sounds: plain stops such as [t], nonsibilant affricates such as [tθ], and sibilant affricates such as [ts]. McCawley (1967) pointed out that while [strident] could distinguish the second pair of sounds, it could not distinguish the first. The problem is shown in (1a):

(1) | | t | tθ | ts
---|---|---|---|---
a. | continuant | – | – | –
 | strident | – | – | +
b. | delayed release | – | + | +
c. | distributed | – | + | –

To solve this problem, Chomsky & Halle (1968) proposed to characterize the class of affricates by the feature [+delayed release]: "affricates are stops with delayed releases" (p. 322). In their analysis, the three series of sounds were analyzed with the three features shown in (1a,b). In later work, however, evidence was brought forward that [t] and [tθ] are distinguished by the feature [distributed] in a number of Athabaskan languages (Clements 1999), including Chipewyan (Flynn 2006).[1] The addition of this feature gives the analysis shown in (1c). If this analysis is correct, the feature [+delayed release] would not be needed to distinguish the three series of coronals. Of course, [+strident] is still needed in any case to distinguish strident affricates such as [ts] from nonstrident affricates such as [tθ], so this controversy does not call into question the feature [strident] as such.

A second alternative to the analysis of affricates was proposed in CV phonology and feature geometry. In typical approaches, as shown in (2), affricates were treated as internally complex segments with either sequenced (2a,b) or simultaneous (2c) specifications for [–continuant] and [+continuant].

(2) a.        C              b.        root              c.        root
         ╱     ╲                    ╱      ╲                      ╱    ╲
        t        s                [–cont]  [+cont]          [stop]    [cont]

   (Clements & Keyser 1983)         (Sagey 1990)              (Hualde 1988)

In such analyses, the distinction between an affricate [ts] and stop [t] was simply one of complex vs. simple structure, and the feature [strident] becomes superfluous. It was subsequently shown, however, that while affricates systematically

---

[1] Darin Flynn writes: "in virtually all dialects of Dëné Sųłiné (formerly Chipewyan) the alveolar affricates and fricatives (sibilants) are apical, hence [+ant, +dist], while the interdental affricates and fricatives (thibilants) are laminal, hence [+ant, +dist]. Exceptional dialects include Cold Lake and Fort Chipewyan, Alberta: apparently due to heavy contact with Plains Cree, in which affricates and fricatives vary freely between alveolar and palatoalveolar articulations, in these particular Dëné Sųłiné dialects sibilants are variably pronounced as shibilants ([-anterior]). (In my experience, however, speakers of these dialects insist that sibilants and shibilants remain distinct...)" (personal communication, 2008).

pattern with stops, they rarely if ever pattern with fricatives, as the analyses in (2) would predict (Rubach 1994, Clements 1999, Kim 2001, Kehrein 2002). For this and other reasons, sibilant affricates are now once again treated as simple [+strident] stops by most linguists, in line with the original Jakobsonian analysis.

Another much-discussed question is whether [strident] characterizes only coronal sounds, or whether it also applies to labial and dorsal sounds, as was originally claimed by Jakobson and his colleagues. Little evidence has been found for recognizing natural classes mixing coronal and noncoronal sounds such as [f s ʃ χ] while excluding the corresponding nonstrident sounds. No assimilation rules operating across articulators (e.g. x → χ / __ s) are known. For these reasons, the most widely-held view at present is that [strident] is restricted to coronal sounds, for which reason it is sometimes also called [+sibilant] (e.g. Ladefoged 1971, 1997). One exception is Halle (1995), who states: "The feature [strident] serves to distinguish bilabial from labiodental continuants in Ewe ... It is not clear whether [strident] can also be distinctive for Dorsal obstruents...". (p. 6). In the absence of evidence from natural classes and assimilation rules, the main arguments for using [strident] to distinguish labiodentals from bilabials are plausibility (the resulting distinctions involve more vs. less noisy sounds, and are restricted to obstruents), symmetry (the p/pf distinction parallels the t/ts distinction in languages such as German), and theoretical parsimony (no other independently-required feature seems available to characterize this distinction). In historical sound shifts, changes such as t > ts are often paralled by changes like p > pf, k > kχ, as in the history of German.

The restriction of [strident] to coronal sounds would be most simply expressed by making this feature a dependent of the coronal node. In this analysis, [strident] would be treated as an articulator-dependent feature, and would function as a member of the place features (Sagey 1990):

(3)   Place
      |
      coronal
      |
      strident

This analysis predicts, correctly, that strident sounds may spread as a unit with other coronal-dependent features. For example, Shaw (1991) shows that consonant harmony in Tahltan spreads [+strident] together with other coronal features, and Rubach (1994) shows that [+strident] spreads with other coronal features in Polish. The major challenge to this analysis is the fact that processes of nasal place assimilation do not change values of the feature [strident]; thus, assimilation of [n] to [ʃ] makes it palato-alveolar, but not strident, as (3) would predict. Clements (2001) argues that this objection can be overcome if [+strident] is phonetically defined in terms of the turbulence noise associated with obstruents (see below); as [n] has no turbulence noise, it cannot be the locus of a [+strident] specification.

## 3 Phonological use

This feature is restricted to obstruents, where it has two main uses:

1. to distinguish sibilant fricatives from nonsibilant fricatives
2. to distinguish sibilant stops (i.e. affricates) from nonsibilant stops

Thus, sibilant fricatives [s z ʃ ʒ ʂ ʐ ɕ ʑ] and the corresponding affricates are classified as [+strident], and non-sibilant fricatives [θ ð ç ʝ] and stops [t d c ɟ] are classified as [–strident]. As mentioned above, this feature is usually restricted to coronal sounds. It combines freely with coronal obstruents except for the following redundancies, noted by Hall (1997):

(4) a. apical anterior fricatives are always strident (there is no nonstrident counterpart to apical [s])
b. posterior coronal fricatives are always strident (there are no nonstrident counterparts to posterior [ʃ ɕ ʂ])

The palatal fricative [ç] (the 'ich-laut' of German), universally regarded as nonstrident, is not a counterexample to (4b) if it is a front dorsal sound, as argued by Hall (1997).

We give some examples illustrating regular patterns involving [+strident] sounds below.

## 3.1 English plural formation

English provides a simple example illustrating the use of [+strident] to define natural classes. Let us consider the various realizations of the English plural suffix -(e)s. As shown in (5), the plural suffix is pronounced as [ɪz] after sibilant sounds (a), as [z] after nonsibilant voiced sounds (b), and as [s] after nonsibilant voiceless sounds (c).

(5) a. buses  b. beds  c. caps
       buzzes    caves    cats
       bushes    beans    baths
       judges    fees     giraffes

The word-final consonants in (5a) are specified as [+strident], and those in (5b, c) as [−strident]. If we assume that the underlying representation of the English plural suffix is /ɨz/, the rule of plural allomorphy can be stated as deleting [ɨ] except where it would create adjacent instances of the feature [+strident] (a violation of the Obligatory Contour Principle, cf. Yip 1989). [z] is then devoiced after a voiceless sound by the general constraint that prohibits clusters containing a voiceless obstruent followed by a voiceless one (we thus have *axe* [æks], *adze* [ædz], but not *[æds]).

## 3.2 Stop assibilation

Many languages have phonological stop assibilation – the creation of sibilants affricates or fricatives from non-sibilant plosives. This process commonly occurs before high vowels. Examples from Finnish and Korean are shown in (6) and (7), where this process applies across morpheme boundaries.

(6) Finnish (Kiparsky 1973): spirantization

　　/halut+i/　→　[halusi]　'wanted' cf. /halut+a/ 'want'
　　/hakkat+i/　→　[hakkasi]　'hewed'
　　/turpot+i/　→　[turposi]　'swelled'

(7) Korean (Kim 2001): affrication

　　/mat+i/　→　[madzi]　'first child'
　　/pʰiputʰ+i/　→　[pʰiputsʰi]　'one's own child'
　　/katʰ+i/　→　[katsʰi]　'together'

This type of phonological stop assibilation has its phonetic origin in the brief period of turbulence which occurs at the release of a plosive into a high vowel (Kim 2001, Hall et al. 2006). This turbulence is interpreted in the phonology as the insertion of the feature [+strident] into the representation of the plosive, accompanied by the loss of [−continuant] in the case of spirantization.

Many further examples of the phonological use of [±strident] are given by Flynn (2006).

# 4 Phonetic definition

The feature [strident] has been defined in articulatory, acoustic and perceptual terms. We consider these in turn.

## 4.1 Articulatory definition

Jakobson, Fant and Halle (1952: 24) offer the following articulatory account:

> A supplementary barrier that offers greater resistance to the air stream is necessary in the case of the stridents. Thus, beside the lips which constitute the sole impediment employed in the production of the bi-labials, the labiodentals involve also the teeth. In addition to the obstacles utilized in the corresponding mellow consonants, the sibilants employ the lower teeth ... and the uvulars, the uvula. The rush of air against such a supplementary barrier following the release of the strident stops yields the characteristic fricative effect that distinguishes these from the other stops.

This definition is intended to hold for labial, coronal and dorsal places of articulation. In this account, no single gesture implements the feature [+strident].

Chomsky & Halle (1968) offer an aerodynamic definition:

> When the airstream passes over a surface, a certain amount of turbulence will be generated depending on the nature of the surface, the rate of flow, and the angle of incidence. A rougher surface, a faster rate of flow, and an angle of incidence closer to ninety degrees will all contribute to greater stridency. (p. 329)

This rather complex definition, unlike the previous one, does not relate stridency to the presence of an obstacle.

An updated definition, reviving the notion of obstacle, is proposed by Stevens (1983: 251):

> Strident consonants are produced by directing a rapid airstream against an obstacle (usually the lower teeth), giving rise to a significantly higher sound energy due to turbulence noise than the sound energy from turbulence in an unobstructed airstream. The noise generation process is qualitatively different in the two cases.

This definition is in conformity with earlier results reported by Catford (1977: 155–156), who compared spectra of the fricatives [θ s ʃ] spoken by subjects with and without their false teeth (both upper and lower). He found that [s] and [ʃ] change drastically, losing much high-frequency energy when the teeth are removed, while [θ] changes only slightly.

Stevens' definition will restrict strident sounds to coronals if the obstacle is required to be the teeth, or more precisely the incisors. The incisors can be modelled as an obstacle positioned downstream from the constriction. When the airstream is obstructed by such an obstacle, a dipole source is generated and the amplitude of the turbulence is enhanced, especially at higher frequencies (Shadle 1985, Pastel 1987, Stevens 1998). In contrast, no such obstacle is present in [θ], which is produced by directing the airstream through the narrow slit between the upper incisors and the flat upper surface of the tongue. Here the teeth form the constriction itself.

In coronal sounds, only the incisors can produce strident noise. We therefore propose the following revised definition:

(8) Strident consonants are produced by directing a rapid airstream against the incisors. Nonstrident sounds are produced without this obstacle.

This definition is inherently asymmetrical, as it turns on the presence vs. the absence of an articulatory property: the presence vs. absence of an obstacle. This asymmetry is reflected in the phonological behavior of this feature: [+strident] commonly behaves as an active feature, defining sound classes relevant for rules (as in the English plural rule discussed above) or engaging in spreading (see Polish examples in Rubach 1994). Furthermore, in many phonological rules, as well as in a common type of speech error, [+strident] sounds assimilate or dissimilate to each other, as in familiar tongue-twisters such as *She sells seashells by the seashore*. In contrast, rules requiring reference to [−strident] are rare at best. Such rules would group nonstrident fricatives such as [θ] and [ð] together with nonstrident stops such as [t d]. Considering this question, Hall (1997: 36–37) fails to find any convincing examples of such natural classes. However, a number are reported in Mielke's survey of natural classes (2004).

## 4.2 Acoustic definition

Strident sounds have typically been defined in terms of their greater noisiness, but such definitions conceal an inherent ambiguity: are strident sounds noisier because they are more irregular, because they have greater intensity, or because their noise component is concentrated at higher frequencies? This ambiguity can be seen in various attempts to define the acoustic correlates of strident sounds.

In the definition proposed by Jakobson, Fant & Halle (1952), strident sounds were said to have irregular waveforms, while nonstrident sounds, which they called mellow, were often found to display some regular formant structure. This definition was quickly abandoned, however, perhaps because strident sounds, especially voiced fricatives, sometimes show well-defined formant structure especially at lower frequencies. In their subsequent work, Jakobson and Halle (1956) place the emphasis on high vs. low intensity: "Strident / mellow ; acoustically- higher intensity noise vs. lower intensity noise" (p. 31).

A new definition of [strident], emphasizing the importance of higher-frequency noise, is proposed by Stevens (1983: 249–251). This definition is paraphrased below:

> In [+strident] sounds, the amplitude of the noise in high-frequency regions exceeds the spectral amplitude of an adjacent vowel in the same frequency region. Thus as the sound pattern proceeds from a strident consonant to a vowel, there is a fall in the amplitude of the spectrum at high frequencies.

Stevens' definition is based on a comparison of the English voiceless sibilants [s z ʃ ʒ tʃ dʒ] with nonstrident sounds. Stevens illustrates this definition with the graphs in Figure 1, showing the spectra of English [s] and [θ] (solid lines) overlaid on the spectrum of a following vowel (dashed lines).

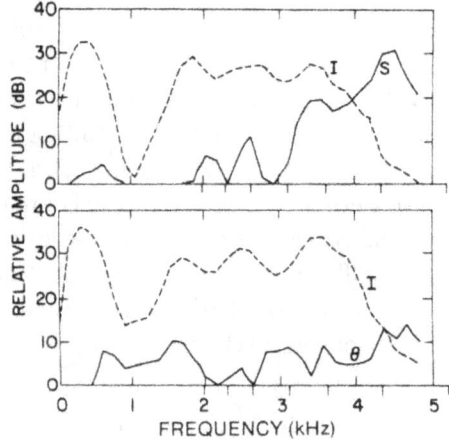

**Figure 1.** Short-time spectra sampled in the consonants [s] (upper panel) and [θ] (lower panel) in the words *sin* and *thin*. Dashed curves show spectra of the vowel immediately following the onset of voicing. In the highest critical band in the frequency range (above 4 kHz in this example), the spectral amplitude for [s] is well above that for the adjacent vowel, whereas for [θ] it is not. The speech has been preemphasized at high frequencies. (After Stevens 1983)

In [–strident] fricatives, the spectral amplitude is lower than that of the strident fricatives at most frequencies, including frequencies above 5 kHz range (not shown in Figure 1), where strident sounds continue to show high energy.

In addition to the comparison noted by Stevens, a difference in spectral profile can be observed when we compare strident fricatives to their nonstrident counterparts: [s] shows an abrupt rise in amplitude at about 3 kHz, as shown in

Figure 1, while [θ] shows a relatively flat, low-amplitude profile. A study of the spectra of other sibilant sounds shows that all typically involve a sharp increase in amplitude across a broad band of higher frequencies (about 2 kHz or above). In contrast, spectra of labial and nonsibilant dental fricatives are relatively flat, and spectra of dorsal fricatives such as [ç x] show a compact mid-frequency peak which drops off sharply at higher frequencies. Spectra of pharyngeal fricatives such as [χ ħ] are unique in showing a high peak at low frequencies (around 1 kHz). Spectra of various fricative types illustrating these differences are reproduced in Ladefoged & Maddieson (1996: 176–177) and Johnson (2002: 121). However, some nonstrident fricatives show a profile similar to that of strident fricatives: in experiments conducted with native speakers of German, we found no abrupt acoustic boundary between postalveolar strident [ʃ] and predorsal nonstrident [ç]. The latter, however, fails to meet the articulatory definition of [+strident].

On the basis of this discussion, we state the main acoustic cue associated with [strident] as follows:

(9) Strident consonants are characterized by a strong noise component over a broad range of higher frequencies. Nonstrident sounds lack this high-frequency component.

## 4.3 Perceptual definition

Experimental testing has attempted to find the properties involved in the hearer's ability to discriminate strident sounds as a class from nonstrident sounds. Stevens (1985) reports a perceptual experiment designed to test the acoustic definition given above. A series of eight fricative + vowel stimuli was synthesized in which the fricative varied along an [θ]-to-[s] continuum and the vowel was [ɑ]. Amplitude of turbulence noise in the $F_5$–$F_6$ region was gradually increased in 5 dB steps from –18 dB to +17 dB relative to the vowel. C-to-V transitions had values intermediate between those typical of the two fricatives. The stimuli were presented to four American English speakers. The results showed a rather abrupt shift from *th* responses to *s* responses very close to the point at which the noise amplitude of the fricative became equal to that of the vowel formant in the same region ($F_5$). In other words, listeners appeared to identify the consonant as [θ] if the high-frequency noise amplitude *rises* into the vowel and as [s] if the high-frequency noise amplitude *falls* into the vowel. Stevens points out that from the point of view of auditory psychophysics and physiology, a rise in amplitude from one segment to another gives a response that is qualitatively different from a fall in amplitude. This fact, together with the qualitative difference between strident and nonstrident turbulence noise, establishes a quasi-categorical distinction between strident and nonstrident sounds.

Stevens' definition of [strident] applies only in CV or VC contexts. However, strident fricatives can be distinguished from corresponding nonstrident fricatives even when spoken in isolation, where the identification rate, for experimental stimuli, can be as good as that in CV utterances (Hedrick & Ohde 1993). This fact suggests that listeners may also be using inherent spectral cues to distinguish /s/ and /θ/, such as the differences in spectral profile noted above. Abdelatty Ali et. al. (2001) find that a measure of maximum normalized spectral slope allows an 85–99 % correct detection rate for sibilants as a class and for nonsibilants as a class. Other studies have found that spectral tilt allows one fricative to be distinguished from another (Nissen & Fox 2005).

## 4.4 Is [strident] an "auditory feature"?

In the view taken here, features are defined in terms of an articulatory configuration and a related acoustic/perceptual product. Thus there are no separate sets of articulatory and acoustic (or auditory) features. However, some writers have held that certain features are best defined in acoustic or auditory terms, and [strident] is sometimes offered as an example.

Thus, Ladefoged (1997) argues that [+sibilant], his term for the feature [+strident] restricted to coronals, is better classified as an auditory feature than an articulatory feature. Noting that sibilant sounds are always produced with the jaw raised, he reasons as follows:

> ...the fact that sibilant sounds have an articulatory attribute in common is an unlikely cause for their acting together in historical changes and morphological alternations. There is no evidence showing that jaw position is a salient characteristic of sounds causing them to be grouped together, whereas the auditory grouping of these sounds is evident in the perceptual confusion data of Miller and Nicely (1955) and its re-analysis by Shepard (1972). (Ladefoged 1997: 613)

However, as Goldstein (1994) has pointed out, jaw position does appear to group sounds together into linguistically significant classes. Specifically, Goldstein suggests that the class of guttural consonants (or [pharyngeal] consonants in the sense of McCarthy 1994), which comprises uvular, tongue root and glottal articulations, involves coordinative structures in which the jaw is not involved, while in nonguttural consonants (including sibilants) the jaw serves to directly raise or lower the articulators toward their constriction goal. Experimental evidence supporting this proposal is presented in Zéroual (2007).

## 4.5 Labial fricatives

We return briefly to the status of labial fricatives. The Jakobsonian classification of the labiodentals [f v] as [+strident] and the bilabials [ɸ β] as [−strident] was based on the fact that the former have greater noise amplitude than the latter. In support of this claim, Utman & Blumstein (1994) found that labiodental [f] has substantially higher intensity (especially above 6 kHz) than bilabial [ɸ] in Ewe, a language in which these two fricatives contrast. However, the acoustic and perceptual studies reviewed earlier in this section do not generally support the classification of labiodental fricatives as [+strident] sounds, as they have no rise in noise amplitude at higher frequencies. In further work, Behrens & Blumstein (1988) showed that in terms of overall amplitude, [f] is more similar to nonstrident [ɸ] than to strident [s] or [ʃ]. They found that decreasing the overall amplitude of the sibilant [s] increased the number of [θ] responses by their listeners, but the opposite was not true: increasing the amplitude of [θ] did not increase [s] responses. (Readers may test this effect informally on themselves.) As Behrens & Blumstein suggest, this may be because the two sounds have different spectral profiles, which remain distinct even when overall amplitude is varied. They conclude that relative overall amplitude is a useful, but not sufficient, cue for detecting sibilants; rather, "spectral properties rather than amplitude properties are the predominant determinants in the perception of place of articulation in fricative consonants" (p. 866). This result is consistent with those of Stevens (1985), who manipulated only high-frequency amplitude, and thus modified spectral profile rather than overall amplitude. Similar results were found in Abdelatty Ali et al. (2001), who found that not only relative amplitude but also "maximum normalized spectral slope" is necessary for the discrimination of sibilants from nonsibilants. See Nartey (1982) for further acoustic arguments against the extension of [+strident] to labials.

If labiodental fricatives are not [+strident] sounds, we must ask what feature distinguishes them from bilabial fricatives. A feature [+labiodental] is proposed by Palmada (1995). K. N. Stevens and S. J. Keyser (personal communication) have suggested a feature [+dental], referring to the upper teeth, which would group labiodental sounds such as [f] together with nonsibilant dental sounds such as [θ], accounting for their similar acoustic properties and frequent confusion in perceptual studies and sound shifts.

## 5 Temporal alignment of the feature [+strident]

Given the phonetic account of [strident] above, the restriction of this feature to coronal obstruents follows from its phonetic definition: [+strident] sounds are coronal because only the tongue front, in conjunction with jaw raising, is physiologically capable of directing the airstream against the lower teeth. Furthermore, this feature is restricted to obstruents because only obstruents, by definition, are produced with turbulent noise; sonorant sounds have no noise component in which the cues to stridency can be implemented. Thus the constraint *[+strident, +sonorant] is phonetically motivated.

However, an important difference in the alignment of [+strident] emerges when we compare the behavior of fricatives and stops. In fricatives, the cues to stridency are present in the fricative noise itself, and are therefore temporally coextensive with the fricative. In stops, however, the cues to [+strident] cannot be realized during the closure. If the feature [+strident] is to be implemented, its cues must be aligned with the turbulence noise that follows a stop's release. This is of course exactly how affricates are produced (Stevens 1993). These considerations help explain the apparent absence of what we might call "reversed affricates" across languages: stops in which sibilant noise is realized just *prior* to the stop closure, as in a hypothetical sound [ˢt]. These sounds are ill-formed since the closing phase of stops is not associated with turbulence noise.

## 6 Is [strident] a quantal feature?

As the reader will recall, a quantal feature definition identifies an articulatory continuum associated with an acoustic discontinuity, and specifies the range within this continuum that corresponds to relatively stable regions in the acoustic output. The articulatory values associated with the stable regions provide the articulatory definition of each term of the contrast, and the acoustic properties of the stable regions provide the acoustic definition. The question at issue, then, is: can we identify an articulatory continuum between e.g. [θ] and [s], or [t] and [ts], that corresponds to a stable region bounded by an unstable region?

While no strict modelling has yet been carried out, to our knowledge, the considerations discussed earlier suggest that the boundary between strident and nonstrident fricatives is at least qualitative (i.e., categorical), depending on the presence of an obstacle in the airstream and its associated acoustic effects. As we have seen, the high-intensity noise which is the acoustic cue to the class of sibilant fricatives [s, ʃ] is attributed to an articulatory configuration in which the incisors play the role of an obstacle. This view explains the typically high jaw target of the strident fricatives [s, ʃ], which is higher than expected given their place of articulation. It is in fact the highest among coronal consonants, suggesting that the placement of the teeth in such a way as to create a stronger noise source is essential to the production of a strident sound (see also Lee et al. 1994, Howe and McGowan 2005, Mooshammer et al. 2007).

The articulatory continuum required for a quantal definition of [+strident], in this view, involves variation along the parameter that separates [θ] from [s]. What movements does this parameter consist of? Since both sounds can be produced at either dental or alveolar places of articulation, place of articulation cannot be the main factor. As Pétursson (1971) has shown in his discussion of the sibilant and nonsibilant alveolar fricatives of Icelandic, several simultaneous continua are involved, which we summarize after Ladefoged & Maddieson (1996):

**Table 1.** Alveolar fricatives of Icelandic (Pétursson 1971)

| Continuum | non sibilant θ | sibilant s |
|---|---|---|
| articulator | tongue blade | tongue tip |
| place of articulation | advanced | less advanced |
| upper tongue surface | flat | curved |
| constriction at teeth | large channel | narrow channel |

Other studies have found considerable variation in the production of sibilant fricatives from one speaker to another, which may be due to individual differences in anatomy. What seems to be essential for the configuration of a strident sound is that the airstream is directed against the teeth, however this goal is achieved.

# 7 Enhancement

Due to its salient acoustic properties, [+strident] is often used as an enhancing feature. A common use across languages is to enhance the feature [+continuant] in coronal fricatives, further increasing their auditory distance from stops. The contrast /s/ vs. /t/, for example, is auditorily more robust than the contrast /θ/ vs. /t/, and is much more frequent across languages (Maddieson 1984). [+strident] may also enhance the feature [−anterior] in stops: if a language has two voiceless coronal stops, the posterior one is likely to be an affricate, as in English. In addition, [+strident] is sometimes used to enhance the feature [spread glottis] in aspirated vs. plain stop contrasts; in a number of languages, including Nama, aspirates are realized with heavy but phonologically redundant affrication. Similarly, palatalized stops often shift to affricates in sound change: tʲ > tʃ.

It might not seem that contrasts between strident and nonstrident sounds would require enhancement themselves. However, Keating (1991: 45) suggests that [+strident] is enhanced by the specific tongue blade and tongue body configurations that help achieve its acoustic target. For example, an apical articulation, as in typical grooved fricatives, is more conducive to stridency than a laminal articulation. [+strident] is enhanced in some languages by [+round], as in Hupa Athabascan, where final /ʃ/ has evolved into /ʍ/ (Flynn & Fulop 2005). As for the negative value of this feature, Keyser & Stevens (2006) have suggested that [−strident] may be enhanced by tongue backing in English, since the resulting lowering of $F_2$ in /θ ð/ helps to distinguish these sounds from /f v/ on the one hand, and from /t d/ and (in nasalizing contexts) /n/ on the other.

# References

Abdelatty Ali, Ahmed M., Jan Van der Spiegel & Paul Mueller. 2001. Acoustic-phonetic features for the automatic classification of fricatives. *Journal of the Acoustical Society of America* 109 (5.1): 2217–2235.

Behrens, Susan & Sheila E. Blumstein. 1988. On the role of the amplitude of the fricative noise in the perception of place of articulation in voiceless fricative consonants. *Journal of the Acoustical Society of America* 84: 861–867.

Catford, Jan C. 1977. *Fundamental Problems in Phonetics*. Edinburgh: University Press and Bloomington: Indiana University Press.

Chomksy, Noam & Morris Halle. 1968. *The Sound Pattern of English*. New York: Harper and Row.

Clements, George N. 1999. Affricates as noncontoured stops. In O. Fujimura, B. D. Joseph & B. Palek (eds.), *Proceedings of LP '98: Item Order in Language and Speech*, 271–299. Prague: The Karolinum Press.

Clements, George N. 2001. Representational economy in constraint-based phonology. In T. Alan Hall (ed.), *Distinctive Feature Theory*, 71–146. Berlin & New York: Mouton de Gruyter.

Clements, GeorgeN. 2005. The role of features in phonological inventories. In Eric Raimy & Charles Cairns (eds.), *Contemporary Views on Architecture and Representations in Phonological Theory*. Cambridge, MA: MIT Press.

Clements, George N. & Samuel J. Keyser 1983. *CV Phonology: a Generative Theory of the Syllable*. Cambridge, MA: MIT Press.

Flynn, Darin. 2006. Articulator theory. Unpublished Ms., University of Calgary. http://ucalgary.ca/dflynn/files/dflynn/Flynn06.pdf

Flynn (Howe), Darin & Fulop, Sean. 2005. Acoustic features in Athabascan. Ms., University of Calgary and CSU-Fresno. *Paper presented at the Annual Meeting of the Linguistic Society of America*, Oakland, CA, Jan. 9, 2005.

Goldstein, Louis. 1994. Possible articulatory bases for the class of guttural consonants. In Patricia A. Keating (ed.), *Papers in Laboratory Phonology III: Phonological Structure and Phonetic Evidence*, 234–241. Cambridge: Cambridge University Press.

Hall, T. Alan. 1997. *The Phonology of Coronals*. Amsterdam: Benjamins.
Hall, T. Alan, Silke Hamann & Marzena Zygis. 2006. The phonetic motivation for phonological stop assibilation. *JIPA* 36 (1): 59–81.
Halle, Morris. 1995. Feature Geometry and Feature Spreading. *Linguistic Inquiry* 26 (1): 1–46.
Hedrick, Mark S. & Ralph N. Ohde. 1993. Effect of relative amplitude of frication on perception of place of articulation. *Journal of the Acoustical Society of America* 94 (4): 2005–2026.
Howe, Michael S. & Richard S. McGowan. 2005. Aeroacoustics of [s]. *Proceedings of the Royal Society A 461*: 1005–1028.
Hualde, José I. 1988. Affricates are not Contour Segments. *WCCFL* 7: 143–157.
Jakobson, Roman. 1939. Observations sur le classement phonologique des consonnes. *Proceedings of ICPhS 3*, Geneva. Reprinted in R. Jakobson, *Selected Writings 1*, 272–279. [Second expanded edition. The Hague: Mouton, 1971.]
Jakobson, Roman, Gunnar M. Fant & Morris Halle. 1952. *Preliminaries to Speech Analysis: the Distinctive Features and their Correlates*. Cambridge, MA: MIT Press.
Jakobson, Roman & Morris Halle. 1956. *Fundamentals of language*. The Hague: Mouton.
Johnson, Keith. 1997. *Acoustic and Auditory Phonetics*. Oxford: Blackwell.
Keating, Patricia. 1991. Coronal Places of Articulation. In C. Paradis & J.-F. Prunet (eds.), *Phonetics and Phonology*, vol. 2: *The Special Status of Coronals: Internal and External Evidence*, 29–48. San Diego: Academic Press.
Kehrein, Wolfgang. 2002. *Phonological Representation and Phonetic Phasing: Affricates and Laryngeals*. Tübingen: Max Niemeyer.
Keyser, Samuel Jay & Kenneth N. Stevens. 2006. Enhancement and overlap in the speech chain. *Language* 82 (1): 33–63.
Kim, Hyunsoon. 2001. A phonetically based account of phonological stop assibilation. *Phonology* 18 (1): 81–108.
Kiparsky, Paul. 1973. Abstractness, opacity, and glottal rules. In O. Fujimura (ed.), *Three Dimensions of Linguistic Theory*, 57–86. Tokyo: Taikusha.
Ladefoged, Peter. 1971. *Preliminaries to Linguistic Phonetics*. Chicago: University of Chicago Press.
Ladefoged, Peter. 1997. Linguistic phonetic descriptions. In W. J. Hardcastle & J. Laver (eds.), *The handbook of phonetic sciences*, 589–618. Oxford: Blackwell.
Ladefoged, P. and I. Maddieson. 1996. *The Sounds of the World's Languages*. Oxford: Blackwell Publishers.
Lee, Sook-hyang, Mary E. Beckman & Michel Jackson. 1994. Jaw targets for strident fricatives. *Proceedings of the International Conference on Spoken Language Processing (ICSLP)*: 37–40.
McCarthy, John J. 1994. The Phonetics and Phonology of Semitic Pharyngeals. In P. Keating (ed.), *Papers in Laboratory Phonology 3*, 191–233. Cambridge: Cambridge University Press.
McCawley, John J. 1967. Le rôle d'un système de traits phonologiques dans une théorie du langage. *Langages* 8: 112–123. (Reprinted 1972 in the original English as "The Role of a Phonological Feature System in a Theory of Language" in V. B. Makkai (ed.), *Phonological Theory: Evolution and Current Practice*, 522–528. New York: Holt, Rinehart and Winston.)
Maddieson, Ian. 1984. *Patterns of Sounds*. Cambridge: Cambridge University Press.
Mielke, Jeff. 2004. *The Emergence of Distinctive Features*. PhD dissertation, Ohio State University.
Miller, George A. & Patricia E. Nicely. 1955. An analysis of perceptual confusions among some English consonants. *Journal of the Acoustical Society of America* 27: 338–352.

Mooshammer, Christine, Philip Hoole & Anja Geumann. 2007. Jaw and order. *Language & Speech* 52: 145–176.

Nartey, Jonas N.A. 1982. On Fricative Phones and Phonemes: Measuring the Phonetic Difference within and Between Languages. *UCLA Working Papers in Phonetics* 55.

Nissen, Shawn L. & Robert A. Fox. 2005. Acoustic and spectral characteristics of young children's fricative productions: a developmental perspective," *Journal of the Acoustical Society of America* 118 (4): 2570–2578.

Palmada, Bianca. 1995. From place to continuity. In Harry van der Hulst & Jerome van der Weijer (eds.), *Leiden in Last. HIL Phonology Papers I*, 299–313. The Hague: Holland Academic.

Pastel, Leah M. P. 1987. Turbulent noise sources in vocal tract models. MS thesis, Cambridge, MA: MIT.

Pétursson, Magnus. 1971. Etude de la réalisation des consonnes islandaises þ, ð, s dans la prononciation d'un sujet islandais à partir de la radiocinématographie. *Phonetica* 23: 203–216.

Rubach, Jerzy. 1994. Affricates as Strident Stops in Polish. *Linguistic Inquiry* 25 (1): 119–144.

Sagey, Elizabeth. 1990. *The Representation of Features in Nonlinear Phonology: the Articulator Node Hierarchy*. New York: Garland. [1986 MIT PhD dissertation.]

Shadle, Christine H. 1985. The Acoustics of Fricative Consonants. *Technical Report* 506, Research Laboratory of Electronics. Cambridge, MA: MIT.

Shaw, Patricia. 1991. Consonant harmony systems: the special status of coronal harmony. In Paradis, Carole, & Jean-François Prunet (eds.) *Phonetics and Phonology*, vol. 2: *The Special Status of Coronals: Internal and External Evidence*. San Diego: Academic Press, 125–157.

Shepard, Roger N. 1972. Psychological representations of speech sounds. In E. E. David & P. B. Denes (eds.), *Human communication: A unified view*. New York: McGraw-Hill.

Stevens, Kenneth N. 1983. Design features of speech sound systems. In Peter F. MacNeilage (ed.), *The Production of Speech*, 247–261. New York: Springer-Verlag.

Stevens, Kenneth N. 1985. Evidence for the role of acoustic boundaries in the perception of speech sounds. In Victoria A. Fromkin (ed.), *Phonetic Linguistics: Essays in Honor of Peter Ladefoged*, 243–255. Orlando: Academic Press.

Stevens, Kenneth N. 1993. Modelling affricate consonants. *Speech Communication* 13 (1–2): 33–43.

Stevens, Kenneth N. 1998. *Acoustic Phonetics*. Cambridge, MA: MIT Press.

Utman, Jennifer Aydelott & Sheila E. Blumstein. 1994. The influence of language on the acoustic properties of phonetic features: a study of the feature [strident] in Ewe and English. *Phonetica* 51: 221–238.

Yip, Moira. 1988. The Obligatory Contour Principle and Phonological Rules: a Loss of Identity. *Linguistic Inquiry* 19 (1): 65–100.

Zéroual, Chakir. 2007. [Pharyngeal]. Talk presented to the Workshop "Phonetic bases of distinctive features", Paris, October 6, 2007. Ms., Faculté pluridisciplinaire de Taza, Morocco.

George N. Clements, Jacqueline Vaissière, Angélique Amelot and Julie Montagu
# The feature [nasal]

## 1 Main sources

Trubetzkoy 1939, Jakobson, Fant & Halle 1952, Fujimura 1962, Chomsky & Halle 1968, Ferguson, Hyman & Ohala 1975, Huffman & Krakow 1993, Cohn 1993a.

## 2 Overview

The existence of [nasal] as a phonological feature is not controversial. Nasality was recognized as a distinctive feature at least as early as Trubetzkoy (1939). In Trubetzkoy's system, nasality was an example of a privative opposition: a phonemic contrast between two members, one of which is characterized by the presence of a mark and the other one by its absence. The nasal member of the nasal/oral opposition is defined as the marked member. This feature was taken up with little change in Jakobson, Fant & Halle (1952).

Chomsky & Halle (1968), being committed to a binary analysis, considered [nasal], like all other features, as a binary feature. Other linguists have nonetheless continued to consider [nasal] as a privative feature, noting that the negative value [−nasal] posited by Chomsky & Halle's model is rarely if ever found to spread or to define a natural class. However, a few arguments for recognizing the negative value are summarized by Hall (2007). In any case, there is an important similarity between the privative and binary analyses: the value [+nasal] is considered as the marked value under both approaches. There is indeed a variety of reasons for adopting this viewpoint, such as the facts that:

- nasal vowels are often absent in inventories, whereas oral vowels are always present
- nasal sounds are less frequent than oral sounds in speech sound inventories
- in any language, nasal sounds have lower lexical and text frequencies than oral sounds
- the value [+nasal] is much more frequently observed to spread to other segments than the value [−nasal].

[Nasal] is usually considered a dependent of the root node in feature geometry models, either immediately (McCarthy 1988, Clements & Hume 1995) or through an intervening velic or soft palate node (Sagey 1990, Halle 1995). This choice is justified by the fact that this feature typically fails to show solidarities with other features. However, Hayes (1986) cites evidence that [+nasal] may spread along with [+voiced] in certain languages, and Piggott (1992) and Rice (1993) have proposed to link this feature under a "sonorant voicing" node.

# 3 Phonological use

Nasality is a widely occurring feature, commonly used to distinguish nasal vs. oral consonants and vowels. General surveys of the phonology and phonetics of nasals and nasalization have been conducted by Ferguson et al. (1975), Maddieson (1984), Huffman & Krakow (1993), and Hajek (1997).

## 3.1 Nasality in segment inventories

There are four different ways in which languages use the feature "nasal" in surface-distinctive segment inventories (cf. Cohn 1993a), as shown in Table 1.

**Table 1.** A sketchy typology of the place of nasal sounds in phonemic systems, with indications of frequency among a broad sample of the world's languages.

| Type | Distinctive consonantal nasality | Distinctive vocalic nasality | Summary in words – nasality distinctive on: | Number of languages in the expanded UPSID database (Maddieson 1991) |
|---|---|---|---|---|
| A | + | + | vowels and consonants | 97 |
| B | + | − | consonants only | 345 |
| C |   | + | vowels only | 5 |
| D |   | − | neither vowels nor consonants | 4 |

The figures in Table 1 reveal that type B systems – as exemplified by English and Arabic – are the commonest, while Type A systems such as French and Bengali take the second place. Type C languages, having distinctive nasal vowels but not consonants, are rare; these include West African languages such as Ewe, Kpelle, and Bwamu; South American languages such as Barasana, Tucano, and Warao; and North American languages such as Mandan (Siouan family; see

Mixco 1997). Type D languages, making no distinctive use of nasality at all, are also rare; these include Quileute and the Salishan languages (North America), Pirahã and Mura (South America), and Rotokas (Papua New Guinea).

The feature [+nasal] combines easily with most other features in phonemic segment inventories. Nasal sounds are most often modally voiced, but voiceless, breathy voiced, and creaky voiced or glottalized nasals occur distinctively in some languages. As far as place of articulation is concerned, the commonest nasal stops across languages, all positions combined, are the dental or alveolar /n/, the bilabial /m/, the velar /ŋ/, and the palatal /ɲ/, in that order (Maddieson 1984). The labiodental [ɱ] arises mainly through coarticulation with a following labiodental sound, as in common pronunciations of the English word *emphasis*. A possible exception is Southern Teke (otherwise known as Kukuya), a Bantu language reported to have a contrast between bilabial and labiodental nasals. However, the latter sound involves considerable lip protrusion (Christiane Paulian, p.c.) and might be regarded as rounded /m$^w$/ at the phonological level. The uvular nasal /ɴ/ is rare, but has been reported to occur distinctively in Western Greenlandic Inuit and Klallam. Nasalized glottal stops are usually considered to be phonetically impossible sounds, since the glottal occlusion prevents any airflow. However, a contrast between oral and nasal glottal stops has been reported in certain varieties of Sui (Dell 1993: 182), in which nasal glottal stops, unlike their oral counterparts, are always followed by nasalized vowels, which do not otherwise occur in the language.

Partially nasal stops such as /mb/, patterning as single segments in the phonology, are less common, and their feature analysis is not altogether clear. They are sometimes analyzed as nasalized obstruents, but more commonly as some kind of sequence: for example, as single segments containing internally sequenced nasal and oral features (Anderson 1976), successive nasal and oral segments "contouring" under a single segmental timing unit (Clements & Keyser 1983), two tautosyllabic segments (Feinstein 1979), or ordinary nasal stops with an oral release (Steriade 1993). In languages such as Fijian, where partly nasal stops such as /mb/ do not contrast with voiced stops such as /b/, they may be analyzed as simple voiced stops with a phonetically predictable prenasalization phase.

Nasalized continuants, combining oral and nasal airstreams, are uncommon (Cohn 1993b). Thus nasalized fricatives are rare, though reliably documented in a small number of languages such as MBundu, spoken in Angola, which has a phonemically contrastive fricative /ṽ/ (Schadeberg 1982). It is possible that some reported cases of voiced nasalized fricatives, when more carefully studied, may prove to be frictionless approximants. Phonemic nasalized liquids are rare, but /l̃/ occurs again in MBundu, and nasalized glides such as /j̃/ and /w̃/ have phonemic status in a number of languages such as Lua and Yakut. A phonemically nasalized glottal continuant /h̃/ contrasts with oral /h/ in Kwangali and ThiMbukushu, spoken in northern Namibia (Ladefoged & Maddieson 1996). In the latter language, vowels are noncontrastively nasalized after nasal and nasalized consonants, including /h̃/, so that the contrast between /h̃/ and /h/ is reinforced by a nasality contrast in the following vowel.

Many languages have what is known as a nasalized glide or nasal mora, unspecified for any place of articulation of its own (Trigo 1988). Its place of articulation is usually acquired by assimilation from neighboring segments or supplied by default. The best-known example is the nasal mora /N/ of Japanese, realized as a nasal homorganic to the following stop, if there is one, and as a uvular nasal [N] utterance-finally (Vance 1987). Portuguese nasal vowels can be viewed as sequences of an oral vowel followed by a nasal mora (Wetzels 1997).

Nasal vowels are found in close to a quarter of the UPSID vowel inventories. It appears that any vowel quality can be phonemically nasalized, and that the crosslinguistic frequency of a nasal vowel tends to correspond to the frequency of its oral counterpart. Thus, for example, /ĩ ũ ã/ are the commonest nasal vowels in UPSID, just as /i u a/ are the commonest oral vowels. Among UPSID languages with nasal vowels, oral vowels outnumber nasal vowels in 55% and are equal in number in the remaining 45%. It has been claimed that nasal vowels never outnumber oral vowels in an inventory (Jakobson, Fant & Halle 1952), and no exception to this statement is known to us.

## 3.2 Nasals in phonological systems

Among segmental features, [+nasal] is one of those that are most prone to engage in phonological assimilation. Nasal vowels often arise historically through a process in which a vowel is contextually nasalized by a following nasal coda consonant, which is then lost. Such a process seems to be in progress in English, where the loss of preconsonantal nasals may give rise to surface contrasts like *can't* [kæ̃t] vs. *cat* [kæt] (Malécot 1956). Nasal assimilation often extends over the syllable or longer domains, and may spread progressively, regressively, or bidirectionally. In a number of languages, especially in South America, nasality spreads across the entire word. For example, in Guaraní, a Tupí language of Paraguay, nasality spreads bidirectionally across the word from stressed nasal vowels, nasalizing voiced sounds. Any intervening voiceless sounds are skipped. Some examples are given below, after Walker (2000).

(1) a. /ⁿdo-ɾoi-ⁿdu'pã-i/ realized [nõ-r̃õĩ-nũ'pã-ĩ] 'I don't beat you'
    b. /ɾo-ᵐbo-po'ɾã/ realized [r̃õ-mõ-põ'r̃ã] 'I embellished you'
    c. /aˌkãɾa'ɯʷe/ realized [ãˌkãr̃ã'ɯʷe] 'hair (of the head)'

The first two examples show that all voiced sounds in the spreading domain are replaced by their nasal counterparts. The third example shows that assimilation does not extend to stressed syllables in words with multiple stresses. Walker is careful to show that voiceless stops such as /k/ in nasalized words do not have the acoustic properties of nasal segments. On the view that speech sounds must bear both the articulatory and acoustic attributes of a feature in order to be considered as bearing that feature, these sounds remain phonologically [−nasal] sounds.

A broad survey of nasalization patterns across languages shows that segment types can be arrayed along a scale of susceptibility to nasalization, with vowels, laryngeals and glides at the high (most susceptible) end and obstruents, especially oral stops, at the low (most resistant) end (Clements & Osu 2003). We have just seen that voiceless stops resist nasalization in Guaraní. However, even these sounds can be nasalized in some languages. In French, for example, both voiceless as well as voiced stops undergo nasalization after nasal vowels in colloquial speech styles if they are followed by another consonant across a syllable boundary. Thus we find optional nasalization of the voiceless stop /t/ in *vingt-deux* 'twenty-two', which can be realized as either [vɛ̃t.dø] or [vɛ̃n.dø].

As far as their phonotactics is concerned, nasal sounds are more favored in some positions than in others. Labial and coronal nasal stops generally occur freely in initial and intervocalic position, while velar nasals are often restricted to syllable-final position, as in Cambodian and Mandarin (Anderson 2005). Nasals are also favored preconsonantally, where they may assimilate in place of articulation to the following consonant. Nasals occur commonly in word-final position, and in a number of languages, such as Mandarin, nasals are the *only* consonants that occur word-finally. Nasals are also a favored type of syllabic consonant across languages, as in English where /n/ is syllabic in words like *button* [bʌtn̩]. Nasal vowels generally have the same distribution as oral vowels, except for gaps that reflect their historic origin. In French, for example, whose nasal vowels arose historically from the deletion of N in tautosyllabic /vN/ sequences, nasal vowels do not occur before NC sequences in underlying representations. Surface exceptions are created by the nasalization process described just above, in which e.g. underlying /vɛ̃tdø/ 'twenty-two' is optionally realized as [vɛ̃ndø].

# 4 Phonetic definition

## 4.1 Articulatory definition

The articulatory aspect of the nasal feature is rather simple: the velopharyngeal port opens for the production of the nasal phonemes. Nasal sounds are of two types according to the way the airstream is channeled. Figure 1 shows the cross-sectional configuration of the vocal tract for a nasal stop (left) and a nasal vowel (right). In nasal stops, the whole of the airstream passes through the nasal cavity, since the oral cavity is blocked by a complete constriction somewhere between the uvula and the lips. In nasal and nasalized vowels and approximants, part of the airstream also passes through the oral cavity. The amount of air which is shunted through the velopharyngeal port depends on the impedance in the oral cavity.

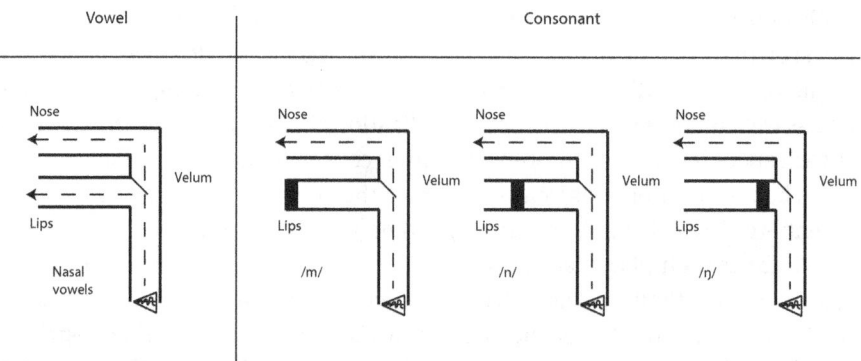

**Figure 1.** Schematic cross-sectional configuration of the vocal tract in nasal vowels (left) and nasal consonants /m/, /n/ and /ŋ/ (right). Black bars indicate closure in oral cavity. Arrows show direction of airflow.

The nasal feature is primarily implemented by relaxing the levator palatini muscle, among other adjustments (Bell-Berti 1993), generally as early as during the phoneme preceding the nasal phoneme. The lack of activity allows the velum to lower, opening the velopharyngeal port and linking the nasal cavity to the oral cavity. Figure 2 left illustrates the "ideal" temporal alignment between velopharyngeal opening and supralaryngeal closing gestures for a consonant, with the mechanistic coarticulation, but without planned coarticulation phenomena. The velum slides along the posterior pharyngeal wall for a while (a-b) before the velopharyngeal port opens (b), and starts to rise (d) before the velopharyngeal port opens again (e). Ideally, the velopharyngeal port opens when the supralaryngeal tract closes (3): all the air goes through the nose and there is no oral airflow. electromyographic studies (Bell-Berti 1976, Benguerel et al. 1977, Ushijima & Hirose 1977) and fiberscopic data (Benguerel et al. 1975, Amelot 2004) favor the conclusion of a large anticipation of velic opening. Conversely, aerodynamic data generally report more extensive carry-over phenomena than anticipatory (Benguerel 1974, Basset et al. 2001).

There may be lateral opening of the velopharyngeal port as the velum is in an overall high position (Serrurier & Badin 2008). Velum height, opening of the velopharyngeal port and aerodynamic data, when taken simultaneously (Amelot et al. 2003), seldom display a perfect correlation and symmetry. The point of maximal airflow often appears at the beginning of an obstruent consonant following a nasal vowel, because of airflow resistance in the oral cavity (at a point in time when the velum has almost achieved closing). Acoustic data suggest a velum gesture of equivalent amplitude in "tent" as compared to "tend" in American English, but with an earlier initiation of the gesture in the unvoiced-stop-final word than in the voiced-stop-final word (Beddor 2007); Ohala's nasographic data (1971) argue for a small difference in velum gesture, but X-ray Microbeam data points to a much larger difference (Vaissière 1988) for the same sequences.

We may define nasalized sounds as those in which the velopharyngeal opening is large enough to ensure a perceptible coupling between the oral and nasal cavities. It is assumed that other necessary conditions, such as the presence of airflow across the glottis (except in the case of nasalized glottal stops), are satisfied as well.

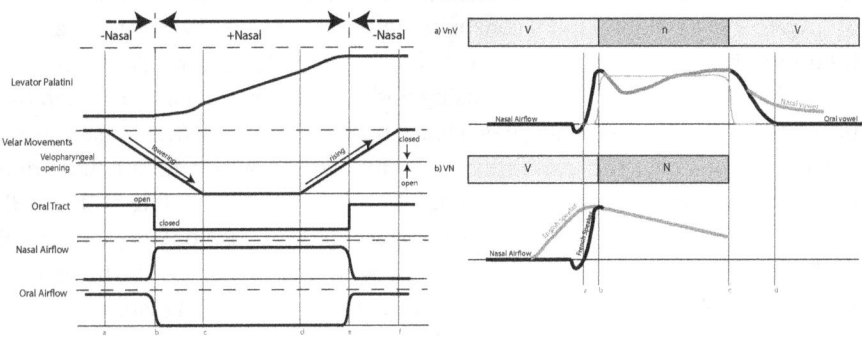

**Figure 2.** left: consonant, ideal case, right: differences generally observed between a consonant in initial position (top) and in coda position (bottom).

There are important differences in the articulatory realization of the nasal feature according to the segment involved. The velum is lower for nasal vowels than nasal consonants (Benguerel et al. 1975); no convincing explanation is available for this observation. Velum height and levator palatini activity in vowels vary according to vowel height, the velum being lower for high vowels (Clumeck 1976), even when oral. Velum height is also different for the oral consonants: for example, the nonobstruents /r/ and /l/ and the consonant clusters containing /r/ and /l/ are relatively more affected than obstruents by nasal codas, and velar obstruents consonants are less affected than labial and coronal obstruents in the same context (Vaissière 1988).

The position of the nasal consonant within the syllable plays a major role. Prosodic influences on vowel nasalization include greater nasalization in tautosyllabic than heterosyllabic sequences. The velum is lower for the oral and nasal consonant in syllable-initial position (represented here as /n/) than in coda (represented here as /N/). EMG data (on Japanese: Kiritani et al. 1980; on English: Bell-Berti & Hirose 1973), fiberscopic data (on Japanese: Ushijima & Sawashima, 1972), velotrace data (on English: Krakow 1989; Bell-Berti & Krakow 1991), nasographic data (on English: Ohala 1971), X-ray Microbeam data (on Japanese; Kiritani et al. 1975; on English: Vaissière 1988; on Japanese and English: Fujimura et al. 1977), aerodynamic data (Fougeron 1998) all bring out the decisive importance of the position of the nasal consonant within the syllable: onset or coda. Ceteris paribus, the coda nasal is phonetically "more" nasalized, as compared to the onset nasal: longer suppression of the levator palatini activity, larger lowering, lower velum height, longer low plateau. Few studies take the position of the nasal consonant within the syllable into account, as it should be done. Figure 1 (right) illustrates what is generally observed in the case of an initial nasal consonant (right top) and of a nasal consonant in coda (right bottom). First, in the case of /nV/, that is a syllable-initial consonant followed by an oral vowel (part a–b in figure 3 right), an anticipatory nasal airflow is generally observed; it is favoured by the fact that the vocal tract is closing and the airflow is pushed through the nasal cavity as the velopharyngeal port opens. The carry-over nasalisation always extends over the beginning of the following vowel, velum being often the most open at the nasal release (part c-d on the right hand-side of figure 3). Second, in the case of /–N/ (a nasal consonant in coda position), the amount of anticipatory nasalisation depends on the language (Clumeck 1976). The preceding oral vowel tends to be completely nasalized in case of English, and much less in French (Cohn 1990) and Spanish (Solé & Ohala 1991). Using a photoelectric device, Clumeck (1976) showed that the degree of coarticulated nasality is language-specific. Among the languages tested, American English and Brazilian Portuguese speakers exhibited the greatest amount of assimilatory nasalization on vowels, whereas Amoy speakers showed the least. These observations make it clear that the fact that a language uses nasalization to contrast between vowels (as in Portuguese) does not necessarily inhibit coarticulatory nasalization. Using the same device, Solé & Ohala (1991) argued that vowel nasalization in Spanish is unintended, while American English speakers intentionally implement it. Third, in the case of CVNC, the temporal alignment is fuzzier, as one would expect from the less clear phonotactic status of the nasal consonant in this sequence.

There are also important differences depending on other prosodic considerations. For example, the velum is higher for consonants (both oral and nasal) in word-initial position (a strong position) than word-final position (for English: Ohala 1971 and Krakow 1989; for Japanese: Ushijima and Hirose 1974). The velum has been found to be lower in stressed 'CVN syllables than in unstressed CVN syllables (Vaissière 1988, for English). The velum is higher for consonants and nasal vowels in French not only in word-initial position, but also in initial position within a higher prosodic domain (Fougeron 1998). See also Krakow 1993. Note that the presence of pauses also plays a large role. After a pause, the exact timing of the speech ready gesture (which concerns all articulators) relatively to the acoustic beginning of speech is random for a given speaker and it may greatly vary from one repetition to the next (Vaissière 1986). Before a pause, in / nV/ + pause sequence, the oral vowel tends to be strongly nasalized, as much as in /nVN/ sequence (the pause acts as a nasal phoneme) (Vaissière 1988). Some studies overestimated the extent of carry-over nasalization in NV, when the sequence is followed by a pause (such as in Ouvaroff & Rossato 2003). Even when the logatoms under study are placed in a frame sentence, the researcher should mention the absence/presence of a pause adjacent to the logatoms.

## 4.2 Acoustic definition

The acoustic definition of the [nasal] feature is rather complicated, unlike its articulatory definition. From the acoustic point of view, it is necessary to treat consonants and vowels separately. Acoustic information is useful in giving us primary descriptive data, but to obtain a deeper understanding we also require further methods such as vocal tract modelling (e.g. Fant 1960), articulatory synthesis (e.g. Maeda 1993), and sweep tone measurements (e.g. Fujimura 1962, Fujimura & Lindqvist 1971).

The acoustics of nasal consonants is rather well understood. The main tube in nasal consonants is formed by the combined pharyngeal + nasal cavity, from the glottis to the nostrils (see Figure 1 above). The main tube has a fixed formant structure for all places of articulation. The combined pharyngeal + nasal cavity is longer than the oral cavity tube alone (as it is shaped for the realization of the neutral vowel [ə]). As a result, its natural resonances are more numerous and lower in frequency than those of the oral cavity. Furthermore, its formants have a wider bandwidth, due to the larger surface area. Its natural frequencies are relatively stable and said to occur in the region of 250–300 Hz, 1000 Hz, 2000 Hz, and 3000 Hz (Fant 1960, Fujimura 1962, Stevens 2000). The broad peak at 250–300 Hz, which corresponds to a natural frequency of the main tube, has a wider bandwidth than the otherwise comparable peak found for the lateral /l/ (produced in the oral cavity). This difference is due to energy loss. This peak in the spectrum of nasal resonances has constant amplitude; its strong energy often equals or surpasses the energy found in the same low-frequency region for neighboring vowels (Stevens 1983). The oral cavity anterior of the constriction acts as a side cavity and introduces zeroes (antiresonances) in the formant structure, which weaken the nasal formants. Their frequencies depend on the length, and to a lesser degree on the shape, of the oral cavity anterior of the constriction, and is thus indicative of the place of constriction. They are normally located between about 750 Hz and 1250 Hz for /m/, between 1450 Hz and 2200 Hz for /n/, and above 3000 Hz for /ŋ/ (Fujimura 1962).

The acoustics of the nasal consonants are much less influenced by the vocalic context than those of the other sonorant consonants (the lateral and the approximant consonants). There are also antiformants in the laterals, since the lateral cavities act as side cavities, but the first antiformant is located between $F_2$ and $F_3$ for the laterals and under $F_2$ for the nasals, and the average spacing of the formants is larger in laterals than it is in nasals.

In sum, nasal consonants can be defined acoustically as having a relatively high concentration of energy in the region 250–300 Hz, and substantially reduced energy at higher frequencies. No oral consonant displays this structure.

The acoustics of the nasal or nasalized vowels are somehow more difficult to understand than the acoustics of the nasal consonants, because of the complexity of the varying coupling between the two cavities. Our knowledge of the acoustic structure of nasal and nasalized vowels comes mainly from formant and articulatory synthesis. In articulatory synthesis, taking oral vowels as the point of departure, an acoustic coupling is introduced gradually as the velum is lowered, and the transfer function at each step can be analyzed. As the coupling increases, the addition of these new formants and antiformants to the spectrum of the oral cavity creates a very complex spectrum, varying over time (House & Stevens 1956, Fant 1960, Stevens 1997, Maeda 1993). The exact size of the opening required to achieve the acoustic coupling varies somewhat according to the oral tract configuration. In the case of synthesized /i/, for example, the simulation of a small amount of velopharyngeal opening leaves the oral formants $F_1$ and $F_2$ unchanged, but leads to the appearance of an additional formant between $F_1$

and $F_2$, to which the ear is very sensitive; on the other hand, the same amount of velopharyngeal opening has not perceptual effect on the open vowel /a/ (Maeda 1993).

There is no regular correspondence between the oral cavity formants in oral vowels, on the one side, and the spectral peaks visible on spectrograms in nasal and nasalized vowels, on the other side. This is because the spectral peaks in nasal and nasalized vowels are the combined result of the oral cavity formants and the nasal formants and anti-formants. Following the release of an oral stop, the oral cavity formants are seen in spectrograms in the first milliseconds of a following nasal vowel. This is exemplified in Figure 3; the consonant chosen is a labial, /b/, because the formant transitions for labial consonants are limited, as compared with consonants whose realization involves tongue movements. It is thus easier to observe the spectral characteristics that are due to nasalization. Unlike nasal consonants, nasal and nasalized vowels have a spectral structure that evolves in time, especially when the nasal vowels are surrounded by oral consonants. It is nonetheless possible in many cases to single out a point where acoustic changes take place rather abruptly; the vertical line in Figure 3 represents this time point.

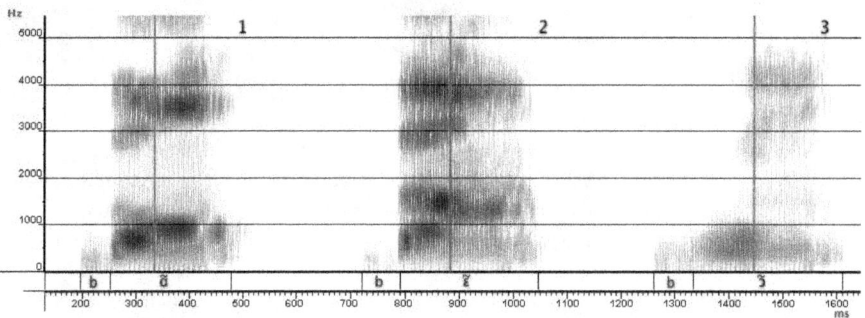

**Figure 3.** Spectrograms of the French syllables [bɑ̃], [bɛ̃], [bɔ̃]. The red line indicates approximately the point in time where the nasal vowel becomes heavily nasalized acoustically. The first part of the vowel is phonetically oral. The logatoms were spoken by a female French native speaker.

The primary attribute of nasality in vowels can be interpreted as a spectral flattening of the peaks in the region of $F_1$ and $F_2$ (Maeda 1993, see also Stevens 1985). This flattening takes the form of a broadening of the first peak of the oral vowel (as in the case of /a/) or the addition of a distinct formant in its vicinity (as in the case of /i/), and can be attributed to the addition of nasal formants and zeroes. Figure 4 shows different allophones of the oral vowel /a/ (1 to 4) and the nasal vowel /ɑ̃/ (5). The position of the tongue and lips is most likely similar during the realization of the vowel /a/ in /bababa/ (1) and /mamama/ (3) and the F-pattern (in the sense of Fant 1960) is expected to be very similar. In the illustrated example, the first peak in the nasalized case has a much weaker energy that the first formant in the oral vowel, as expected, due to the presence of an antiformants in the low frequency region; $F_2$ is left unchanged and the third peak in the nasalized version is raised as compared to the third formant, due to the presence of another antiformant, and not due to a change in the tongue or lip configuration. The acoustics of the nasal vowel /ɑ̃/ is different in French from the nasalized version of the oral vowel /a/, as seen for the vowel /a/ in Figure 4, and the differences are due in part to the fact than the nasal vowel is a posterior vowel (with lower $F_2$), closed to the articulation of /a/ in the sequence /rarara/ (4) and the lips are less open in the case of the nasal (Zerling 1984).

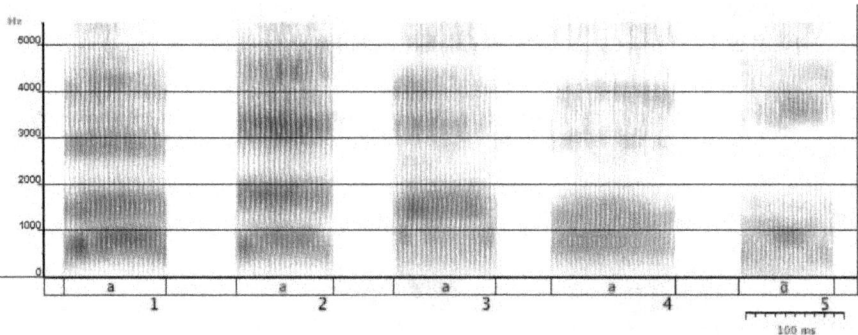

**Figure 4.** Spectrograms the vowel [a] and [ɑ̃]. Each vowel corresponds to the middle vowel of CVCVCV sequences uttered in isolation, [bababa], [dadada], [mamama], [rarara] and [mɑ̃mɑ̃mɑ̃] respectively. The logatoms were spoken by a female French native speaker. [a] may be considered as close to its target in /bababa/, fronted in /dadada/, and backed in /rarara/. It is phonetically nasalized in /mamama/, and the nasal vowel, phonemic /ɑ̃/, corresponds to the backed version of the vowel.

Note that the nasal sound pressure is not simply a function of the degree of nasal coupling: it obviously also reflects vocal intensity. Thus, an increase of intranasal sound intensity might represent nothing more than increased phonatory effort. Something of a solution to the last problem can be achieved by separately and simultaneously measuring intranasal and oral sound pressure levels and comparing them. As vocal intensity changes, the oral and nasal signals would presumably change together, maintaining a constant relationship (Baken 2000: 464).

In a nutshell, this overview provides abundant justification for the observation mentioned at the outset, namely that it is necessary to recognize distinct acoustic attributes for nasal consonants and nasal vowels: (i) for consonants, the dominant low-frequency resonance in the nasal murmur, and (ii) for vowels, low-frequency spectral flattening (and often weakening) in the case of nasal vowels, often accompanied by a decrease of energy in the low frequency as compared to their closest counterpart among oral vowels. Although the low-frequency spectral region is involved in both cases, the effect of nasal coupling differs.

## 4.3 Perceptual correlates

Here we discuss the perceptual properties that correspond to the acoustic properties we have just discussed.

### 4.3.1 Consonants

The conditions for the presence of audible nasality in consonants depends, much more than in vowels, on the context in which they occur. A fricative context does not favor the perception of nasality of the consonant in the context of nasal+fricative sequences (Ohala & Busà 1995).

Here we discuss two contexts: /nV/ (word-initial nasal consonant followed by vowel) and /vN/ (vowel followed by syllable- or word-final nasal unreleased consonant), which correspond, as seen before (paragraph 4.1), to two different strategies on the articulatory level.

For what concerns the initial nasal consonants, acoustic evidence of nasal coupling is only required at the vicinity of release of the nasal consonant for the nasality to be perceived; a short duration of acoustic coupling is sufficient. No anticipation on the preceding vowel is perceptually necessary for the consonant to be perceived as nasal. Also, the nasal murmur before release needs not be long for nasality to be perceived. A consonant is heard as nasal if the low-frequency nasal resonance $FN1$ is present for a minimum of 20-odd msec in the vicinity of the consonant release, and if the amplitude of the spectral peak corresponding to this lowest resonance is at least as high as the spectral amplitude at about 250 Hz in the adjacent vowels (Stevens 1981). Although the very beginning of the vowel is actually nasalized in NV sequences (low velum and consistent nasal air flow), the listeners do not appear to attribute the nasalization of the vowel to the presence of a nasal consonant.

In vN contexts, when N in coda position is unreleased (a situation abbreviated as vN#), acoustic evidence has to last for a longer time than is strictly needed for an onset nasal. The very beginning of the consonant is masked by the vowel: the consonant in coda position is heard as nasal only if the nasal murmur is long enough. If the nasal murmur is short, no consonant at all is heard. Anticipation of nasality in the preceding vowel allows the perception of the nasality of the consonant with a shorter murmur (Vaissière 2008), confirming that the listeners would be sensitive to the total nasalization in VN# sequence (Beddor 2007).

### 4.3.2 Vowels

It seems rather easy to create the sensation of nasality for a vowel through manipulation of the audio signal: for instance, an artificial weakening of $F_1$ intensity for /a/ leads to the perception of nasality (Delattre 1954). However, it is actually difficult to do so in a principled way. It is not necessary for a vowel to be completely nasalized acoustically for being perceived as a nasal vowel, only the second part has to be nasalized (see Figure 2), at least in French. The beginning of a nasal vowel located after an oral consonant is almost always phonetically oral (at least in French, Montagu 2007), the mid part and last of the nasal vowel phonetically nasal. The extent of carry-over of nasalisation depends in the following consonant (Delvaux 2003). For Portuguese nasal diphtongs represented as two moras, nasality aligned with the second one (Wetzels 1997). For nasalized vowels, in American English, nasalization aligned with vowel regardless of speech rate and in Spanish, nasalization has fixed duration, and the vowel is less nasalized in slow speech (Solé & Ohala 1991). The listeners tend to judge the relatice nasality of vowels depending in their native languages (for English and Thai, Beddor & Krakow 1999).

## 5 Temporal alignment

The realisation of the nasal feature is rather sluggish. Nasality tends to spread over several segments and the nasal feature is prone to transphonologization. Nasal vowels often originate in a former nasal coda, the latter disappearing in the process. Less frequently, the feature of nasality may transphonologize from an initial cluster to the following vowel. This process is well-established in a certain number of unrelated languages: Kam-Sui (Tai-Kadai family; see Ferlus 1996: 255), Goidelic and Breton (Jackson 1986: 801–803); and the East Asian languages Mon, Yao, Yi, Tamang, Naxi, Na and Laze (Michaud et al. 2012). In languages that lack contrastive nasal consonants, these phonemes may arise from the influence of a following nasal vowel, as happened in a majority of Siouan languages (ibid.)

Alignment depends also on style. From aerodynamic data, Basset et al. (2001) showed that in spontaneous speech as compared to read speech, the nasal flow propagates more, both before and after the nasal phoneme. They found several voiced stop consonants produced with nasal airflow during the burst in spontaneous speech but not in read speech. Spontaneous speech favors the propagation of nasalization, but conversely, it also allows a denasalization of nasal vowels – again, at least in French. Moreover, from articulatory data obtained by fiberscopic measurement, Amelot (2004) showed that the velar movements are less steep in spontaneous speech: the maximum of lowering is of smaller amplitude during the nasal in spontaneous speech than in read speech.

# 6 Variability

There are temporal and spatial variations in the realization of the [nasal] feature. It varies depending on the speaker's gender and anatomy (Clarke 1975; Amelot 2004), speaker strategy (Croft et al., 1981; Skolnick et al., 1973; Vaissière 1988), the language (Clumeck 1976), the speaking style (Basset et al. 2001), the speaking rate (Bell-Berti & Krakow 1991), and as seen before, the speech sound type, on the position of the nasal phoneme within the syllable and word, the phonetic context and prosodic structure.

# 7 Enhancement

We have not found compelling evidence for the notion of enhancement in the case of nasal consonants. In noise, the nasals are confused with one another, but rarely with any of the other consonants (Miller & Nicely 1953). It could perhaps be said that anticipatory nasalization on the preceding vowel enhances the nasality of a nasal coda consonant. Beddor (2007) has shown that the contexts that trigger shorter nasal coda consonants (such as "tent" versus "tend") have concomitantly longer anticipatory vowel nasalization, contributing to the realization of their [nasal] feature in an adverse context.

## 7.1 Nasality and voicing

One could build an argument about nasality as an enhancer of voicing. In a number of languages, plain voiceless stops contrast with prenasalized voiced stops. As noted before, voiced stops are often phonetically prenasalized, in a number of languages. The articulatory-acoustic cause of this phenomenon is clear: voicing is difficult to maintain during stop closure, as air pressure builds up inside the oral cavity, reducing the transglottal pressure drop which is necessary to voicing. Lowering the velum early on in the articulation of the stop allows for a portion of sustained voicing, so that voicing can be identified even if it is hardly realized during the final part of the consonant, when the velum is raised again. The preference for prenasalised (or implosive) stops over plain voiced stops has been explained on the grounds that prenasalised and implosive stops are more distinct phonetically from voiceless stops (cf. Iverson & Salmons 1996).

## 7.2 Nasal and sonorant

As a final note about the affinities between [nasal] and other features, the [+nasal] feature should be implemented together with [+sonorant] in order to enhance the acoustic manifestations of continuant and coronal sounds. For [+continuant, +sonorant] consonants, the feature coronal is more strongly implemented when accompanied by the feature [−nasal] because nasalization tends to perturb the ideal rising or falling spectrum shape respectively for the [+coronal] and [−coronal] consonant. Evidently, then, the representation of [−continuant] is enhanced for the [+ nasal] versions of the combination of primary features such as [continuant, sonorant, coronal]. Enhancement of the abruptness of the release presumably also enhances the representation of the feature [coronal] when [+nasal] is implemented (Stevens & Keyser 1989).

# 8 Is [nasal] a quantal feature?

Somewhat paradoxically, nasality may be considered as a quantal feature for consonants but not for vowels. In nasal phonemes, there is no direct correspondence between the observed spectra and the underlying oral formants: while the lowering of the velum is progressive, the acoustic effect of the opening of the velopharyngeal port is abrupt. It creates a nasal-oral coupling, resulting in the sudden addition of nasal formants and antiformants. Furthermore, the maximum amplitude of velic opening observed during the nasal consonants is rather quickly reached and remains level, giving relatively stable regions in the related acoustic output during /m/ and /n/. The feature [nasal] effectively distinguishes segments bearing this feature from otherwise similar consonants that do not, and it is resistant to noise. In the case of vowels, a similar claim could be made on the basis of acoustic data: the nasal-oral coupling sets apart nasal vowels from oral vowels in that the relationship of formant amplitude to formant frequency is predictable for oral vowels whereas it is unpredictable for nasal vowels (due to the introduction of nasal formants and antiformants): see Vaissière 2007. However, this acoustic difference, which in principle could appear as a textbook example of a quantal phenomenon, appears less than ideally clear from a perceptual point of view, calling into question the usefulness of this concept for the [nasal] feature in its most general phonological understanding.

# Acknowledgments

This chapter has much benefited from insights gained from conversations with Alexis Michaud, who has also greatly improved the latest English version.

# References

Amelot, A. 2004. *Etude aérodynamique, fibroscopique, acoustique et perceptive des voyelles nasales du français*. Thèse de doctorat, Paris III – Sorbonne Nouvelle, Paris, France.
Amelot, A., L. Crevier-Buchman & S. Maeda. 2003. Observations of the velopharyngeal closure mechanism in horizontal and lateral directions from fiberscopic data. *The 15th International Congress of Phonetic Sciences, Barcelona*: 3021–3024.
Anderson, G. 2005. Areal and phonotactic distribution of /***NG/. In Marc van Oostendorp and Jeroen van de Weijer (eds.), *The Internal Organization of Phonological Segments*, 217–234. Berlin & New York: Mouton de Gruyter.
Anderson, S. R. 1976. Nasal consonants and the internal structure of segments. *Language* 52: 326–344.
Baken, R. J. 1987. Clinical measurement of speech and voice. London: Taylor and Francis.
Basset, P., A. Amelot, J. Vaissière & B. Roubeau. 2001. Nasal airflow in French spontaneous speech. *The Journal of the International Phonetic Association* 31: 87–100.
Beddor, P. S. 2007. Nasals and nasalization: the relation between segmental and coarticulatory timing. *The Proceedings of the 16th International Congress of Phonetic Sciences*, Saarbrucken, 249–254.
Beddor, P. S. & R. A. Krakow. 1999. Perception of coarticulatory nasalization by speakers of English and Thai: evidence for partial compensation. *Journal of the Acoustical Society of America* 106 (5): 2868–2887.
Bell-Berti, F. 1976. An electromyographic study of velopharyngeal function in speech. *Journal of Speech and Hearing Research* 19: 225–240.
Bell-Berti, F. 1993. Understanding velic motor control: studies of segmental context. In M. K. Huffman & R. A. Krakow (eds.), *Nasals, Nasalization, and the Velum*, 63–85. San Diego: Academic Press.
Bell-Berti, F. & H. Hirose. 1973. Patterns of Palatoglossus Activity and their Implications for Speech Organization. *Speech Research* 30: 203–209.

Bell-Berti, F. & R. A. Krakow. 1991. Anticipatory velar lowering: A coproduction account. *Journal of the Acoustical Society of America* 90: 112–123.

Benguerel, A. P. 1974. Nasal airflow patterns and velar coarticulation in French. *Speech Wave Processing and Transmission* 2: 105–112. Stockholm: Almqvist & Wiksell.

Benguerel, A. P., H. Hirose & M. Sawashima. 1975. Velar height and its timing in French: A fiberscopic study. *Annual Bulletin Research Institute of Logopedics and Phoniatrics* 6: 67–78.

Benguerel, A. P., H. Hirose & M. Sawashima. 1977. Velar coarticulation in French: An electromyographic study. *Journal of Phonetics* 5: 159–168.

Chomsky, N. & M. Halle. 1968. *The sound pattern of English*. New York: Harper and Row.

Clarke, W. M. 1975. The measurements of the oral and nasal sound pressure levels of speech. *Journal of Phonetics* 3: 257–262.

Clements, G. N. & E. Hume. 1995. The internal organization of speech sounds. In John Goldsmith (ed.), *Handbook of Phonological Theory*, 245–306. Oxford & Cambridge, MA: Basil Blackwell.

Clements, G. N. & S. J. Keyser. 1983. *CV phonology: a generative theory of the syllable*. Cambridge, MA: MIT Press.

Clements, G. N. & S. Osu. 2005. Nasal harmony in Ikwere, a language with no phonemic nasal consonants. *Journal of African Languages and Linguistics* 26 (2): 165–200.

Clumeck, H. 1976. Patterns of Soft Palate Movements in Six Languages. *Journal of Phonetics* 4: 337–351.

Cohn, A. C. 1993a. A survey of the phonology of the feature [+nasal]. *Working Papers of the Cornell Phonetics Laboratory* 8: 141–203. Ithaca: Cornell University.

Cohn, A. C. 1993b. The status of nasalized continuants. In M. K. Huffman & R. A. Krakow (eds.), *Nasals, Nasalization, and the Velum*, 329–367. San Diego: Academic Press.

Cohn, A. C. 1999. Phonetic and phonological rules of nasalisation. PhD dissertation, UCLA.

Croft, C. B., R. J. Shprintzen & S. J. Rakoff. 1981. Patterns of velopharyngeal valving in normal and cleft palate subjects: A multi-view videofluoroscopic and nasendoscopic study. *Laryngoscope* 91: 265–271.

Delattre, P. C. 1954. Les attributs acoustiques de la nasalité vocalique et consonantique. *Studia Linguistica* 8 (2): 103–110.

Dell, F. 1993. Assimilations supralaryngales dans deux parlers de la Chine méridionale. In B. Laks & A. Rialland (eds.), *L'architecture des représentations phonologiques*, 173–185. Paris: CNRS Editions.

Delvaux, V. 2003. *Contrôle et connaissance phonétique: Les voyelles nasales du français*. Thèse de doctorat. Bruxelles: Phonétique-Phonologie.

Fant, G. 1960. *Acoustic theory of speech production*. The Hague: Mouton.

Feinstein, M. 1979. Prenasalization and syllable structure. *Linguistic Inquiry* 10: 245–278.

Ferguson, C. A., L. M. Hyman & J. J. Ohala. 1975. *Nasálfest: Papers from a symposium on nasals and nasalization*. Stanford: Department of Linguistics, Stanford University.

Ferlus, M. 1996. Remarques sur le consonantisme du proto kam-sui. *Cahiers de linguistique – Asie Orientale* 25 (2): 235–278.

Fougeron, C. 1998. *Variations articulatoires en début de constituants prosodiques de différents niveaux en français*. Thèse de doctorat, Université Paris III – Sorbonne Nouvelle, Paris, France.

Fujimura, O. 1962. Analysis of nasal consonants. *Journal of the Acoustical Society of America* 34 (12): 1865–1875.

Fujimura O. & J. Lindqvist. 1971. Sweep-tone measurements of vocal-tract characteristics. *Journal of the Acoustical Society of America* 49 (2): 541–558.

Fujimura, O., J. E. Miller, S. Kiritani. 1977. A computer-controlled X-Ray microbeam study of articulatory characteristics of nasal consonants in English and Japanese. *The Proceedings of the 9th International Congress on Acoustics*, Madrid, 461.
Hajek, J. 1997. *Universals of sound change in nasalization*. Oxford: Blackwell Publishers.
Hall, T. A. 2007. Segmental features. In Paul de Lacy (eds.) *Handbook of Phonology*, 311–334. Cambridge: Cambridge University Press.
Halle, M. 1995. Feature geometry and feature spreading. *Linguistic Inquiry* 26: 1–46.
Hayes, B. 1986. Assimilation as spreading in Toba Batak. *Linguistic Inquiry* 17: 467–499.
House, A. S. & K. N. Stevens. 1956. Analog Studies of the Nasalization of Vowels. *Journal of Speech and Hearing Disorders* 21: 218–232.
Huffman, M. K. & R. A. Krakow (eds.). 1993. *Phonetics and Phonology 5: Nasals, Nasalization and the Velum*. London: Academic Press.
Iverson, G. & J. C. Salmons. 1996. Mixtec prenasalization as hypervoicing. *International Journal of American Linguistics* 62 (2): 165–175.
Jackson, K. H. 1986. *A historical phonology of Breton*. Dublin: Dublin Institute for Advanced Studies.
Jakobson, R., G. Fant & M. Halle 1952. *Preliminaries to Speech Analysis: The Distinctive Features and Their Correlates*. Cambridge, MA: MIT Press.
Kent, R. D. & C. Read. 1992. *The Acoustic Analysis of Speech*. San Diego: Singular Publishing Group.
Kiritani, S., H. Hirose & M. Sawashima. 1980. Simultaneous X-ray microbeam and EMG study of velum movement for Japanese nasal sounds. *Annual Bulletin Research Institute of Logopedics and Phoniatrics* 14: 91–100.
Kiritani, S., K. Itoh & O. Fujimura. 1975. Tongue-pellet tracking by a computer controlled X-ray microbeam system. *Journal of the Acoustical Society of America* 57: 1516–1520.
Krakow, R. A. 1989. *The Articulatory Organization of Syllables: A Kinematic Analysis of Labial and Velar Gestures*. Doctoral Dissertation, Yale University, New Haven, CT.
Krakow, R. A. 1993. Nonsegmental influences on velum movement patterns: syllables, sentences, stress, and speaking rate. In M. K. Huffman & R. A. Krakow (eds.), *Phonetics and Phonology vol. 5: Nasals, Nasalization, and the Velum*, 87–116. New York: Academic Press.
Ladefoged, P. & I. Maddieson. 1996. *The sounds of the world's languages*. Oxford: Blackwell.
Maddieson, I. 1984. Nasals. Chapter 4 in *Patterns of Sound*: 59–72. Cambridge: Cambridge University Press.
Maddieson, I. 1991. Testing the universality of phonological generalizations with a phonetically-specified segment database: results and limitations. *Phonetica* 48 (3): 193–206.
Maeda, S. 1993. Acoustics of vowel nasalization and articulatory shifts in French nasal vowels. In M. K. Huffman & R. A. Krakow (eds.), *Phonetics and Phonology 5: Nasals, Nasalization and the Velum*, 147–167. London: Academic Press.
Malécot, A. 1956. Acoustic cues for nasal consonants: an experimental study involving tape splicing techniques. *Language* 32: 274–284.
McCarthy, J. 1988. Feature geometry and dependency: a review. *Phonetica* 45: 84–108.
Michaud, A., G. Jacques & R. L. Rankin. 2012. Historical transfer of nasality between consonantal onset and vowel: from C to V or from V to C? *Diachronica* 29 (2): 201–230.
Miller, G. A. & P. E. Nicely. 1955. An analysis of perceptual confusions among some English consonants. *Journal of the Acoustical Society of America* 27: 338–352.
Mixco, M. 1997. *Mandan*. Munich: Lincom Europa.
Montagu J. 2007. *Étude acoustique et perceptive des voyelles nasales et nasalisées du français parisien*. Thèse de doctorat, Université Paris III – Sorbonne Nouvelle, Paris, France.

Ohala, J. J. 1971. Monitoring soft palate movements in speech. *Journal of the Acoustical Society of America* 50 (1): 140.

Ohala, J. J. & M. G. Busà. 1995. Nasal loss before voiceless fricatives: a perceptually-based sound change. *Rivista di Linguistica* 7: 125–144.

Ouvaroff, T. & S. Rossato. 2006. Nasalité consonantique et coarticulation: étude perceptive. *Revue Parole* 39–40: 233–257

Piggott, G. 1992. Variability in feature dependency: the case of nasality. *Natural Language and Linguistic Theory* 10: 33–77.

Rice, K. 1993. A reexamination of the feature [sonorant]: the status of 'sonorant obstruents'. *Language* 69 (2): 308–344.

Sagey, E. 1990. *The representation of features in nonlinear phonology: the articulator node hierarchy*. New York: Garland.

Schadeberg, T. 1982. Nasalization in UMbundu. *Journal of African Languages and Linguistics* 4: 109–132.

Serrurier, A. & P. Badin. 2008. A three-dimensional articulatory model of the velum and nasopharyngeal wall based on MRI and CT data. *Journal of the Acoustical Society of America* 123 (4): 2335–2355.

Skolnick, M. L., G. L. McCall & M. Barnes. 1973. The sphincteric mechanism of velopharyngeal closure. *Cleft Palate Journal* 10: 286–305.

Solé, M. & J. J. Ohala. 1991. Differentiating between phonetic and phonological processes: the case of nasalization. *The 12th International Congress of Phonetic Sciences*, Aix-en-Provence, 19–24.

Steriade, D. 1993. Closure, release, and nasal contours. In M. K. Huffman & R. A. Krakow (eds.), *Phonetics and Phonology vol. 5: Nasals, Nasalization, and the Velum*, 401–470, New York: Academic Press.

Stevens, K. N. 1981. Evidence for the role of acoustic boundaries in the perception of speech sounds. *Journal of the Acoustical Society of America* 69 (1): 116.

Stevens, K. N. 1983. Design features of speech sound systems. In Peter F. MacNeilage (eds.), *The Production of Speech*, 247–261. New York: Springer.

Stevens, K. N. 1985. Evidence for the role of acoustic boundaries in the perception of speech sounds. In V. Fromkin (ed.), *Phonetic Linguistics: Essays in honour of Peter Ladefoged*, 243–255. New York: Academic Press.

Stevens, K. N. 1997. Articulatory-acoustic-auditory relationships. In William J. Hardcastle and John Laver (eds.), *The Handbook of Phonetic Sciences*, 462–506. Oxford: Blackwell Publishers.

Stevens, K. N. 2000. Diverse acoustic cues at consonantal landmarks. *Phonetica* 57: 139–151.

Stevens, K. N. & S. J. Keyser. 1989. Primary features and their enhancement in consonants. *Language* 65 (1): 81–106.

Trigo, L. 1988. *On the Phonological Derivation and Behavior of Nasal Glides*. Unpublished PhD dissertation, MIT, Cambridge, MA.

Trubetzkoy, N. S. 1969. *Principles of phonology*. (Translation of *Grundzüge der Phonologie*, 1939, by Christiane A. M. Baltaxe) Berkeley: University of California Press.

Ushijima, T. & H. Hirose. 1974. Electromyographic study of the velum during speech. *Journal of Phonetics* 2: 315–236.

Ushijima, T. & M. Sawashima. 1972. Fiberscopic examination of velar movements during speech. *Annual Bulletin of the Research Institute of Logopedics and Phoniatrics* 6: 25–38.

Vaissière, J. 1986. Variance and invariance at the word Level. In J. S. Perkell & D. H. Klatt (eds.), *Invariance and variability in speech processes*, 534–539. Hillsdale: Lawrence Erlbaum.

Vaissière, J. 1988. Prediction of velum movement from phonological specifications. *Phonetica* 54: 122–139.

Vaissière, J. 2007. Area functions and articulatory modeling as a tool for investigating the articulatory, acoustic and perceptual properties of the contrast between the sounds in a language. In P. S. Beddor, M. J. Solé and M. Ohala (eds.), *Experimental Approaches to Phonology*, 54–72. Oxford: Oxford University Press.

Vaissière, J. 2008. Perceptual explanations of articulatory variability in the realisation of the nasal feature for the consonants. *Journal of the Acoustical Society of America* 123: 3459.

Vance, T. J. 1987. *An introduction to Japanese phonology*. Albany: State University of New York Press.

Walker, R. 2000. *Nasalization, neutral segments, and opacity effects*. New York: Garland.

Wetzels, W. L. 1997. The lexical representation of nasality in Brazilian Portuguese. *Probus* 9: 203–232.

Zerling, J.-P. 1984. Phénomènes de nasalité et de nasalisation vocalique: Étude cinéradiographique pour deux locuteurs. *Travaux de l'Institut de phonétique de Strasbourg* 16: 241–266.

Jean-Marc Beltzung, Cédric Patin and George N. Clements
# The feature [ATR]*

> *Is the [ATR] feature restricted to vowel harmony systems, and if it is, why do we find this curious coincidence?*
>
> (Nick Clements, personal communication)

## 1 Introduction

The [Advanced Tongue Root] feature ([ATR]) is one of the most discussed vocalic features in the phonological literature. The term *Advanced Tongue-Root* first appears in Stewart (1967). However, the importance of the tongue-root position in phonological processes was recognized as early as Pike (1947: 21) who accounted for the particular quality of advanced vowels in African languages by "fronting of the tongue so that the root of the tongue is farther from the wall of the throat", suggesting that [+ATR] vowels are produced by a combination of tongue-root advancement and larynx lowering. Stewart (1967) captured Pike's observations by introducing a new feature, [ATR], that has been largely accepted in the phonological literature.

Nonetheless, various terms have been used in the literature to distinguish advanced and retracted vowels such as open, lax, light, hard, creaky, narrow or dull for [–ATR] vowels and close, tense, heavy, hollow, breathy, wide or bright for [+ATR] vowels (Tucker 1964, Lindau 1978, Rottland 1980, Ladefoged & Maddieson 1996, Clements 2000, among others). Moreover, Chomsky & Halle (1968: 314–315) suggest a feature [±covered], which refers to the position of the pharyngeal walls. [+covered] sounds are produced with the pharyngeal walls narrowed and tensed, while [–covered] sounds are produced without such a configuration. Cineradiographic data collected by Painter (1973) on Twi (Akan, Niger-Congo, Ghana) reveal that the feature [±covered] does not improve phonetic description more than [±tense] and [±lax] features and that tensed vowels in Twi are pronounced with a *widened pharynx*. Based on articulatory correlates of [±ATR] vowel sets, Lindau (1975, 1978) proposed the feature [expanded] instead of [open] (Tucker 1964) or [ATR] (Stewart 1967, Halle & Stevens 1969), since larynx

---

* We wish to thank Douglas Pulleyblank for his insightful comments and suggestions of corrections and Laura Downing, Alexis Michaud, Kathleen O'Connor, Annie Rialland, Rachid Ridouane, Alex Vaxman, Lucille Wallet and all the members of the ACI project "Phonetic Bases of Distinctive Features: Quantal Theory" for helpful comments, suggestions and corrections throughout the writing of this paper. All remaining errors are, of course, entirely our own.

lowering is somewhat involved and since [ATR] and [open] only refer to a part of the articulation involved. Finally, Svantesson (1985: 299) introduces the feature [pharyngeal] to explain Khalkha Mongolian vowel harmony.[1] In the rest of this paper, we give preference to the commonly accepted [ATR] and use it as cover term for all the features discussed above.

The first section of this paper is devoted to the phonological use of the [ATR] feature. Here, we discuss common vowel harmony processes (stem-controled vs. dominant-recessive) involving the spreading of the [+ATR] feature. Privativity and markedness reversal are also discussed and we then explore the tongue-root specification for consonants. In the second section we explore the phonetic definition of the feature [ATR]. Here, both articulatory and acoustic correlates of this feature are examined. Finally, we show that the tongue-root movement may also be analyzed in terms of enhancement gesture.

# 2 Phonological use

Phonologically, the feature [ATR] is mainly involved in *cross-height vowel harmony* processes. Broadly speaking, a language is claimed to undergo vowel harmony if there are two or more vowels that agree with respect to some feature(s) within a domain such as the word.[2] The analyses of [ATR] harmony in African languages made a significant contribution to linguistic theory. They also shed light on vowel harmony processes in languages elsewhere. For example, vowel harmony in Nez Perce (Hall & Hall 1980), Khalkha Mongolian (Rialland & Djamouri 1984, Svantesson 1985), Tungusic languages such as Oroqen (Zhang 1995) or Menomini (Archangeli & Pulleyblank 1994) should be analyzed in terms of *cross-height harmony* (i.e. the process of harmonization across vowels of different height).

Before we discuss [ATR] vowel harmony, we thought it useful to provide the reader with a vocalic feature chart for the most common vowels of the world's languages. In this chart, we have reported the [ATR]/[tense] contrast for all vowels:

---

[1] The articulatory correlates of this feature involve the activity of hyoglossi and pharyngeal constrictors muscles.

[2] However, languages where the harmony is restricted to two adjacent syllables also exist. Lango (Nilotic, Uganda, Noonan 1992) for example, has a restricted harmony domain where the feature [+ATR] spreads from the first vowel of the suffix to the root-final vowel or from a root-final vowel to the following suffix vowel: /bònɔ́-ní/ → [bòŋóní] "your dress", /àmók-ní / → [àmúkkí] "your shoe". In this case, harmony may be analyzed as *non-iterative*.

(1) Feature specifications for 16 common vowels including [ATR] contrast

|  | i | ɪ | ɨ | y | u | ʊ | e | ɛ | ə | ʌ | ø | œ | o | ɔ | a | æ |
|---|---|---|---|---|---|---|---|---|---|---|---|---|---|---|---|---|
| high | + | + | + | + | + | + | – | – | – | – | – | – | – | – | – | – |
| low | – | – | – | – | – | – | – | – | – | – | – | – | – | – | + | + |
| back | – | – | + | – | + | + | – | – | + | + | – | – | + | + | + | – |
| round | – | – | – | + | + | + | – | – | – | – | + | + | + | + | – | – |
| ATR/tense | + | – | + | + | + | – | + | – | + | – | + | – | + | – | – | – |

In chart (1), it is interesting to note that crosslinguistically the feature [ATR] appears to be in complementary distribution with the feature [tense].[3] Although these two features are not known to co-occur distinctively in any language (Halle & Stevens 1969, Clements 1981), Lindau-Webb (1987), who explicitly states that [ATR] and [tense] are not the same acoustically, reports that Agwagwune, a Lower Cross River Language of Nigeria with [ATR] harmony, has also a rule of vowel centralization/laxing in closed syllables that can be accounted for in terms of [tense] feature rather than the [ATR] feature. Unfortunately, except for the small abstract of Lindau-Webb (1987), no sources are currently available for this language. Finally, based on phonetic evidence and distributional restrictions within vowel inventories, Goad (1991) argues that the feature [ATR] and [tense] should be conflated.

A thorough discussion of the relation between [ATR] and [tense] is beyond the scope of the present paper. For this reason, we do not consider this topic here any further. Indeed, we will assume that the features [ATR] and [tense] are simply variant implementations of a single feature.

## 2.1 Vowel harmony processes

Regarding [ATR] harmony systems, it has been assumed that vowel harmony processes can be either *stem-controlled* (also root-controlled) or *dominant-recessive* (van der Hulst & van de Weijer 1995, Baković 2000 among others). In stem-controlled [ATR] harmony systems, affix vowels must agree with the [ATR] specification of the stem. In dominant-recessive [ATR] harmony systems, both the stem and the affixes must agree with the dominant specification of [ATR]. Both types of systems are discussed below.

---

[3] Tense vowels are produced with a tongue body or tongue-root configuration involving a greater degree of constriction than that found in their lax counterpart. This greater degree of constriction is frequently accompanied by greater length, as in English.

### 2.1.1 Stem-controlled harmony

Akan (Niger-Congo, Ghana; Schachter & Fromkin 1968, Clements 1981 among others) is perhaps the most cited stem-controlled language in the literature. Akan vowels are paired with respect to the feature [±ATR], except the low vowel /a/ which is unpaired: /i, e, o, u/ vs. /ɪ, ɛ, a, ɔ, ʊ/. In this language, affix vowels must agree with the [ATR] value of the root vowels (in the following forms, roots are underlined):

(2) Akan: [±ATR] stem-controlled harmony (Archangeli & Pulleyblank 2007)

| Advanced | | Retracted | |
|---|---|---|---|
| [e-bu-o] | "nest" | [ɛ-bʊ-ɔ] | "stone" |
| [o-kusi-e] | "rat" | [ɔ-kɔdɪ-ɛ] | "eagle" |
| [o-be-tu-i] | "he came and dug (it)" | [ɔ-bɛ-tʊ-ɪ] | "he came and threw (it)" |

Since the Akan segment inventory lacks advanced low vowels, the examples below show that /a/ does not participate in [ATR] harmony (where [a̘] is the advanced counterpart of [a]):

(3) Akan: neutrality of the low vowel /a/ (Archangeli & Pulleyblank 2007)

| [wa-tu] | "he has dug it" | *[wa̘-tu] |
|---|---|---|
| [ba-yi-e] | "witchcraft" | *[ba̘-yi-e] |

Igbo (Niger-Congo, Nigeria; Zsiga 1992 among others) is also a well-known stem-controlled language with [ATR] harmony. Igbo has eight vowels paired with respect to the feature [±ATR]:

(4) Igbo: vowel inventory (Zsiga 1992: 102)

|  | i | ɪ | u | ʊ | o | ɔ | e | a |
|---|---|---|---|---|---|---|---|---|
| high | + | + | + | + | − | − | − | − |
| round | − | − | + | + | + | + | − | − |
| ATR | + | − | + | − | + | − | + | − |

Contrary to Akan, in this language, the low vowel /a/ is paired with the mid vowel /e/ since these vowels are only distinguished by the [ATR] feature. In Igbo, [+ATR] and [−ATR] vowels do not cooccur within a stem. All the vowels within the stem are either [+ATR] or [−ATR], as in (5a). Moreover, the [ATR] value of the stem determines the [ATR] value of the affixes (see 5b–d) (stems are underlined):

(5) Igbo: [±ATR] stem-controlled harmony (Zsiga 1992: 103)

| *Retracted* | | *Advanced* | |
|---|---|---|---|
| a. [ʊzɔ̀] | "road" | [ozu] | "corpse" |
| [akpî] | "scorpion" | [ùbe] | "pear" |
| [ɔ̀jɪ] | "kola nut" | [obî] | "heart" |
| b. [sɪ-a] | "tell!" | [si-e] | "cook!" |
| [sɪ-ghɪ] | "did not tell!" | [si-ghi] | "did not cook" |
| c. [ɪ-sɪ́] | "to tell" | [i-sí] | "to cook" |
| [ɔ́-sɪ] | "the teller" | [ò-si] | "the cook" |
| d. [a-zʊ-ɔla] | "has bought" | [è-ri-ele] | "has eaten" |

Both Akan and Igbo cross-height harmony can be analyzed as an assimilation of the feature [+ATR] from a stem vowel to affix vowels within the word.

## 2.1.2 Dominant-recessive harmony

Maasai (or Maa, Eastern Nilotic, Kenya; Tucker & Mpaayei 1955, Cole & Trigo 1988, Archangeli & Pulleyblank 1994) has nine distinct vowels based on the [ATR] feature distinction. [+ATR] vowels are /i, u, e, o/ and [–ATR] vowels are /ɪ, ɛ, a, ɔ, ʊ/. The two sets of vowels participate in cross-height vowel harmony. As in some other Nilotic languages, the [+ATR] value is *dominant* and the [–ATR] value is *recessive* (or adaptive), which means that a [–ATR] vowel can become [+ATR], but a [+ATR] vowel cannot become [–ATR].[4] In Maasai cross-height harmony, all vowels within a word surface as [+ATR] if there is a morpheme in that word which contains an underlying [+ATR] vowel. This is illustrated in (6) (where the roots are underlined and target segments are set in bold).

(6) Maasai: dominant-recessive harmony
(Archangeli & Pulleyblank 1994: 305–306)

/kɪ-norr-ʊ/ → [kiɲorru] "we shall love"
/kɪ-ɪdɪm-ʊ/ → [kɪdɪmʊ] "we shall be able"
/mɪ-kɪ-itoki/ → [mikintoki] "let us not do again"

---

[4] Since the [–ATR] value seems to be assigned by a default rule in Maasai (Cole & Trigo 1988), [–ATR] may be considered as the unmarked feature value while [+ATR] is the marked feature value. It is interesting to note that [+ATR] vowels are cross-linguistically unmarked but they are marked in [±ATR]-based systems. This "ATR paradox" is discussed in Kaye et al. (1988: 117–118).

/mɪ-kɪ-ran/ → [mɪkɪraɲ] "let us not sing"
/ɪsʊj-ɪʃɔ-re/ → [isujiʃore] "wash with something"
/ɪsʊj-ɪʃɔ/ → [ɪsʊjɪʃɔ] "wash!/do the washing"

In the first forms of (6a) and (6b), the affix vowels specified with the recessive [−ATR] value are harmonized with the dominant [+ATR] root vowels. Contrary to the preceding forms, the first form in (6c) shows a case where a recessive [−ATR] root vowel is harmonized with a dominant [+ATR] suffix vowel. In the second forms of (6a–c), both root and affix vowels are specified for a negative recessive value of [ATR] in the underlying representation and, therefore, [ATR] harmony cannot be initiated.

### 2.1.3 Opacity and transparency

In Maasai, the low vowel /a/ is unpaired, meaning that [+low] vowel has no [+ATR] counterpart (*/ą/). Thus, it fails to harmonize with [+ATR] vowels and *blocks* the harmonic feature. Such disharmony is called *opacity*. In Maasai, harmony does not affect nor does it skip the low vowel[5] (the opaque low vowel is underlined in surface forms):

(7) Maasai: low vowel blocks harmony
(Archangeli & Pulleyblank 1994: 306ff, Baković 2000: 197)

a. /kɪ-ta-dot-ʊn-ie/ → [kɪtadotuɲie] "we pulled it out with s.t."
/kɪ-dot-ʊn-ie/ → [kidotuɲie] "we shall pull it out with s.t."
b. /ɪ-as-ɪʃɔ-re/ → [ɪasiʃore] "you work"
/ɪ-dun-ɪʃɔ-re/ → [iduɲiʃore] "you cut with s.t."
c. /kɪ-nar-ie/ → [kɪɲarie] "we share with s.o."
/kɪ-dun-ie/ → [kiduɲie] "we cut with s.t."

The first form in (7a–c), respectively, shows that the low vowel blocks [+ATR] harmony whereas absence of the low vowel, as in the second form of (7a–c), fully allows harmony. Thus, the harmonic feature neither propagates through the low vowel (*[kitądotuɲie]) nor skips it (*[kitadotuɲie]).

---

[5] In fact, Maasai harmony is much more complicated. Harmony is blocked by a low vowel encountered to the left of a harmonic trigger. But when the low vowel appears to the right of a harmonic trigger, the low vowel is raised to [o] as for example in /ɪn-mudon-a/ → [imudoŋo] "kinship". Low vowel raising has been described as a [−low] assimilation rule at a distance by Cole & Trigo (1988: 29–35) and not as a [−ATR] feature manipulation.

In some cases, *transparency* is found instead of opacity. That is, an intervening segment is skipped and the harmonic feature appears to pass through it. According to Baković (2001), opacity and transparency have the same basis: they involve harmonically unpaired vowels. However, in Menomini (Algonquian, Northeastern Wisconsin; Bloomfield 1962, Cole & Trigo 1988, Steriade 1987, Archangeli & Pulleyblank 1994 among others) both transparency and opacity effects seem to occur although Menomini has [±ATR] contrast in low vowels. Menomini has an iterative leftward [+ATR] harmony process triggered by and targeting only the non-low vowels (i.e. /i, ɪ, u, ʊ/). Moreover, only [+high,+ATR] vowels /i, i:, u, u:/ are possible triggers and only long [+high,–ATR] vowels /ɪ:, ʊ:/ are possible targets (see 8a,b). Short [+high,–ATR] vowels /ɪ, ʊ/ and long or short [+low,–ATR] vowels /a, a:/ are transparent, as in (8c,d). Conversely, [+low,+ATR] vowels /ą, ą:/ are opaque (see 8e) (triggers are underlined and targets are set in bold):

(8) Menomini: [+ATR] harmony (Archangeli & Pulleyblank 1994: 377–383)

a. si:p**i**ah          "river-LOC"
   cf. sɪ:pɪ:w          "river"
b. ʊ**tu**:hpuakanɪw    "he has X as a pipe"
   cf. ʊtʊ:ta:mɪw       "he has X as a totem"
c. wɪ:nɪpʊw             "he dirties his mouth"
   nɪw**i**:nɪp**i**m   "I dirty his (my?) mouth"
d. nɪs**i**:kah**i**:qim "I put drops in my eyes"
   cf. sɪ:kahɪ:ʔkʊw     "he puts drops in his eyes"
e. nʊ:nɪhpąni:w         "he digs potatoes" (*nu:nɪhpąni:w)
   cf. pɪ:htąhki:ʔtaw   "he sticks his head in" (*pi:htąhki:ʔtaw)

Archangeli & Pulleyblank (1994) explain the opacity in Menomini harmony through an A-condition,[6] __<+ATR & ATR/LO>, which broadly states that [+ATR] may only spread from a non-low vowel. The grounded condition ATR/LO is an implicational statement and may be read: *if* [+ATR] *then not* [+low] or *if* [+low] *then* [–ATR]. Since /ą/ is [+ATR] and also [+low], it violates the A-condition and harmony is blocked.

---

[6] Archangeli & Pulleyblank (1994) introduce a grounding theory that regulates the well-formedness of feature combination in tongue-root harmonic systems. Constraints regulating the well-formedness of high and low vowels are (i) HI/ATR: If [+high] then [ATR] and (ii) LO/RTR: If [+low] then [RTR]. See also the marking statements of Calabrese (2005) that prohibit feature combinations *[+HI,–ATR] and *[+LO,+ATR].

## 2.2 Markedness reversal and privativity

While the feature value [+ATR] is active (or marked) in some languages, some other languages have cross-height harmony wherein the active feature value is [–ATR]. The existence of such languages raises the issue of markedness reversal and, consequently, has prompted some authors to assume two privative antagonistic features such as [ATR] and [RTR] (for Retracted Tongue-Root) instead of one binary tongue-root feature (either [±ATR] or [±RTR]).

### 2.2.1 Markedness reversal

In all the languages examined so far, [+ATR] was the active feature value involved in cross-height harmony. Nevertheless, in some other languages the active harmonic feature value appears to be the negative value of the feature [ATR], hence [–ATR]. Yoruba (Niger-Congo, Nigeria; Archangeli & Pulleyblank 1989, 1994) is a perfect example of a harmony system involving the feature [–ATR]. In this language, the vowel system is /i, e, ɛ, a, ɔ, o, u/ and it is commonly accepted that only [–ATR] values are active. Mid vowels are either [+ATR] or [–ATR] and sequences of mid vowels agree in their value for [ATR]:

(9) Yoruba: mid vowels agree for an [ATR] value
(Archangeli & Pulleyblank 1994: 86)

|    |     |                  |     |           |
|----|-----|------------------|-----|-----------|
| a. | ebè | "heap for yams"  | ekpo| "oil"     |
|    | olè | "thief"          | owó | "money"   |
| b. | ɛsɛ̀ | "foot"          | ɛkɔ́ | "pap"     |
|    | ɔbɛ̀ | "soup"          | ɔkɔ̀ | "vehicle" |

In Yoruba, [–ATR] harmony, which applies from right to left (cf. Archangeli & Pulleyblanck 1994: 86), targets mid vowels and is triggered by some mid (i.e. {ɛ, ɔ}) and all low vowels (see 10a). When low vowels occur to the left of the mid vowels, as in (10b), no [–ATR] agreement takes place. Finally, high vowels, which are also [+ATR], do not have any harmonic effect on the mid vowels which are to the right (10c) or to the left (10d):

(10) Yoruba: low and high vowels (a)symmetry
(Archangeli & Pulleyblank 1994: 86ff)

|    |          |             |          |          |
|----|----------|-------------|----------|----------|
| a. | ɛ̀kpà (*èkpà) | "groundnut" | ɔjà ( *ojà) | "market" |
| b. | ate      | "hat"       | àwo      | "plate"  |
|    | àjɛ̀     | "paddle"    | aʃɔ      | "cloth"  |

|   |   |   |   |   |   |
|---|---|---|---|---|---|
| c. | ilé | "house" | igò | "bottle" |
|   | ilɛ̀ | "land" | itɔ́ | "saliva" |
| d. | ebi | "hunger" | orí | "head" |
|   | ɛ̀bi | "guilt" | ɔkín | "egret" |

In addition to Yoruba, Kenstowicz (1979) analyses Chukchee (Chukotko-Kamchatkan, Siberia) vowel harmony in terms of [–ATR] spreading as do Hall & Hall (1980) in Nez Perce (Penutian, Northern Idaho), Johnson (1975) in Coeur d'Alene, and Rialland & Djamouri (1984) pointed out that Khalkha Mongolian vowel harmony may actually involve [–ATR] spreading.

Based on markedness principles originally introduced by Trubetzkoy (1931: 97) — more specifically, the principle stating that the marked term of an equipollent opposition bears a positive mark —, a great body of work has re-analyzed harmonic systems in which [–ATR] is active with the feature [+RTR] instead.[7] Hence, the [RTR] feature has been basically used in languages in which the dominant feature is tongue-root retraction. A representative example of an analysis involving this feature may be found in Oroqen, a Tungusic language spoken in Northern China (Xunke dialect; Zhang 1995). Oroqen has nine vowels paired with respect to the feature [RTR]: the vowels /i, e, ə, o, u/ are [+RTR] and the vowels /ɛ, a, ɔ, ʊ/ are [–RTR]. The high front vowel /i/ has no retracted counterpart. Both sets are involved in stem-controlled harmony: all vowels of the root must agree in [±RTR] and suffix vowels must agree in [±RTR] with the last vowel of the root[8] (IPA transcription is ours, triggers are underlined and targets are set in bold):

(11) Oroqen: cross-height harmony (Zhang 1995: 166)

*Retracted*      *Non-retracted*

| | | | | |
|---|---|---|---|---|
| a. | ma:tɕʰu̱-ɕal | "mother's brother-PL" | nəku̱n-ɕəl | "younger brothers-PL" |
|    | kakara̱-ɕal | "chicken-PL" | bəja̱-ɕəl | "person-PL" |
|    | ta:lʊ̱:-ja | "birch bark-indef.OBJ" | n̪un̪uku̱-jə | "bear-indef.OBJ" |
|    | tɕaphu̱n-dʊ | "eight-DAT" | uta̱-du | "son-dative" |
|    | buwa̱-dʊ | "place-DAT" | ənu̱:-du | "illness dative" |
| b. | mu̱ri-ma | "horse-def.OBJ" | ku̱ni-mə | "daughter-in-law-def.OBJ" |
|    | ɕa̱gdi-tɕʰa | "become old-PERF" | u̱li-tɕʰə | "save-PERF" |
| c. | dɔ̱:ldi-tɕʰa | "listen-PERF" | i̱t-tɕʰə | "rippen-PERF" |
|    | gɔrɔ̱-tɕʰira | "far-DIM" | nili̱:-tɕʰirə | "fishy-DIM" |

---

[7] Gussenhoven & Jacobs (1998: 77) underline that [±RTR] feature may be seen as a phonetic variant of the phonological feature [±ATR].
[8] Note that Oroqen also has a rightward rounding harmony (cf. [nɔjɔ-ɕɔl] "official-PL" vs. [morgo-ɕol] "carp-PL"). Nowadays, Oroqen [±RTR] vowel harmony is lost.

The forms in (11b) show that the high front vowel /i/ is transparent to the harmony. Hence, the high front vowel neither undergoes nor blocks the rightward spreading of [+RTR]. Moreover, when a stem contains only the high front vowel /i(ː)/, as in (11c), the suffix appears with a [−RTR] vowel. In sum, vowel harmony in Oroqen involves spreading of [+RTR].[9] In this case, [−RTR] appears as the unmarked feature value in Oroqen vowel inventory.

In the languages such as Oroquen or Yoruba, ATR harmony requires reference to [−ATR] as the active value (i.e. marked) while in other systems [+ATR] must be assumed to be active (cf. Akan and Igbo cited above). This kind of distribution, in which one value of a feature is marked in some languages and the other one in other languages, is called *markedness reversal*.

On theoretical grounds — and contra Archangeli's (1988: 193–196) proposal —, Steriade (1995: 131ff) argues "that parametrization is clearly involved in the Yoruba and Akan [ATR] systems" but it is not obvious "[...] that what is being parametrized is markedness". On cross-linguistic grounds, it seems impossible to claim that one or the other [ATR] value is marked since this feature "[...] displays a cross-linguistic distribution that does not involve the sort of context-free implicational relations upon which claims of markedness are normally based". For example, we usually say that an ejective stop such as /t'/ is marked in a given system since its presence always implies the presence of the corresponding plain one (i.e. /t/). However, cross-linguistically, the presence of either [+ATR] or [−ATR] vowels does not imply the presence of the other value. Nevertheless, it is obvious that only some combinations between [ATR] and height values can be said to be marked in some languages (cf. Menomini). Following these observations, Steriade (1995) eventually concludes that markedness reversal must be rejected, as it would make wrong predictions concerning other features.

### 2.2.2 The privative view of the tongue-root features

Based on the markedness reversal problem inherent to the feature [±ATR], Czaykowska-Higgins (1987), Goad (1991), Steriade (1995) and van der Hulst and van der Weijer (1995), among others, have assumed two privative antagonistic features for tongue-root position ([ATR] *and* [RTR]) instead of one binary feature (either [±ATR] *or* [±RTR]) and argue that both these features constitute a single phonological and phonetic dimension. Some languages select [ATR] for their harmony systems and others select [RTR]. A few languages select both. For example, Steriade (1995) cites Kalenjin as well as Chilcotin, van der Hust and van

---

[9] Note that Oroqen vowel harmony may be analyzed as a [−ATR] spreading rule as well.

der Weijer (1995) cite Turkana. Furthermore, van der Hulst and van de Weijer (1995: 511) clearly state that African languages seem to involve [ATR] harmony systems while Asian languages often involve [RTR] harmony systems. Casali (2008) refines this observation and argues that the tongue-root feature value active in a given language mainly depends on the structure of its vowel inventory: [ATR] is dominant in languages with tongue-root position contrast among high vowels while [RTR] is dominant in languages with tongue-root position contrast among non-high vowels.

Another argument in favor of a distinction between [ATR] and [RTR] is given by Steriade (1995: 149–151) when she argues that [ATR] and [RTR] are not phonetically identical since [ATR] involves displacement of the tongue-root forward from its neutral position while [RTR] involves displacement backward. Thus, a vowel (or a consonant) which is not marked for either one or the other (i.e. the non-ATR vowels in an ATR system and the non-RTR vowels in an RTR system) would be produced with a neutral configuration. Finally, Pulleyblank (2002), who derives harmony by prohibiting feature disharmony, also assumes that the feature [±ATR] is no longer binary but privative instead. He describes vowel harmony in Degema and Yoruba both with [ATR] and [RTR] features. According to him, harmony emerges from feature co-occurrence constraints such as *ATR RTR or *RTR ATR.

Nevertheless, the proposal advanced by Steriade (1995) – and the single-valued tongue-root feature proposal in general – suffers from a significant problem: two mutually exclusive single-valued features predict three contrastive categories, in the way that [spread glottis] and [constricted glottis] do. However, to the best of our knowledge, a language with a minimal three-way contrast among vowels (ATR, RTR, and neither one nor the other) doesn not seem to exist. For example, compare the two following sets of segments:

(12)

| | $t^h$ | t | t' | | e | ʔ | ɛ |
|---|---|---|---|---|---|---|---|
| spread | • | | | ATR | • | | |
| constricted | | | • | RTR | | • | |

If the three-way contrasts really exist among the vowels in this set, they might be found in some Nilotic languages, but we do not know any examples of such languages. At a first glance, Shilluk, which has three mid back vowels, looks like a candidate. However, according to the analysis in Gilley (1992), it involves the binary feature [±expanded pharynx]. Discovery of such a language would make a very strong case for the ATR/RTR model, while failure to discover such a language would support the binary analysis. As the burden of proof is on proponents of new features, it has to be shown that [RTR] is not just possible or useful, but necessary. Another way to argue for [RTR] might be to show that both [ATR] and [RTR] can spread in ways that remain unexplained if a binary feature is assumed (e.g. transparency effects).

Pulleyblank (1992) provides another argument against replacing one binary feature like [±ATR] with two privative features like [ATR] and [RTR]. Based on a logical consideration, the two values of one feature [F] may not cooccur within a segment since one segment cannot be simultaneously specified by [+F] and [–F]. However, two distinct privative features such as [F] and [G] may freely cooccur. Therefore, Steriade (1995: fn 36) explains the fact that a segment cannot be simultaneously specified as [ATR] and [RTR] by mutually incompatible articulatory gestures.

Finally, and perhaps implicitly in support of a privative conception of the tongue-root features, Rialland & Djamouri (1984) underline variation in tongue root position for contrasting [+ATR] and [–ATR] vowel sets as follows (where neutral tongue-root/neutral tongue-root is logically excluded):

(13) Possible contrastive tongue-root positions accross languages

| | Vowel set A | Vowel set B | Active feature | Languages |
|---|---|---|---|---|
| a. | Advanced tongue root | Neutral tongue root | ATR | Akan, Igbo |
| b. | Neutral tongue root | Retracted tongue root | RTR | Yoruba, Oroqen |
| c. | Advanced tongue root | Retracted tongue root | ATR *and* RTR | Turkana |

According to us, languages with the configuration (13a) contrastively involve the feature [ATR] while languages with the configuration (13b) contrastively involve the feature [RTR]. Moreover, some languages, like Turkana (Noske 2000), may display a configuration where both [ATR] and [RTR] are contrastively involved (13c).

Two articulatory studies nicely illustrate the view defended in (13). Both these works, based on ultrasound investigations used with reference to the inter-utterance speech rest position (ISP) – an articulatory parameter defined as "language-specific speech posture to which the articulators return between utterances" (Gick et al. 2004: 229) – had shown that the tongue-root position is the main articulatory parameter of the features [ATR] and [RTR]. For example, St'at'imcets, a Salish language spoken in British Columbia (Canada), has a set of inherently retracted consonants (/ʕ, ʕʷ, ʕ', ʕ'ʷ, q, qʷ, q', χ, χʷ/) and a set of retracted coronals (/tṣ, tṣ', ṣ, ɬ̣, l̡'/) that both affect the articulation of the neighbouring vowels (adjacent or at a distance). Namdaran (2006) has shown that retracted consonants in that language cause preceding high vowels /i/ and /u/

to lower and retract to [ɛ] and [ɔ] respectively (e.g. /tʃ[ê]qtn/ "spear" and /ʃtʃ[ɔ̂]ʕʷ/ "stripe", Namdaran 2006: 151). He concludes that the active feature responsible for the vowel retraction in St'at'imcets is tongue-root retraction ([RTR]) and that non-retracted vowels are produced near the neutral tongue-root rest position (ISP). Hudu (2010) shows that the dominant [+ATR] harmonic feature of Dagbani (Gur, Ghana) has a tongue-root position anterior to the neutral tongue-root position (ISP) while the recessive [−ATR] vowels are realized with a tongue-root position near ISP. According to him, "the dominant phonological harmonic feature has a distinct articulatory position compared to a neutral position of the tongue-root" and the phonologically inactive recessive feature, either [ATR] or [RTR], "is generally not expected to correspond to a distinct tongue-root position" (Hudu 2010: 222ff).

## 2.3 Tongue-root position in consonants

Since the feature [±ATR]/[±RTR] (or the two privative features [ATR] and [RTR]) is involved in cross-height harmony processes, one may ask whether a tongue-root position feature may be active in the consonant inventory as well. According to Halle & Stevens (1969: 43), "The so-called heavy consonants of Javanese have this acoustic characteristic [i.e. lowering the $F_1$ of the following vowel], and are presumably characterized by the feature advanced tongue-root. [...] The "slightly aspirated" Korean stop consonants may also have this feature, particularly in intervocalic position" (but cf. Kim (this vol.) who analyzes Korean fortis stops in terms of the [tense] feature). Trigo (1986) claims that voiced obstruents of Buchan Scots are [+ATR]. Similarly, Vaux (1992, 1996) shows that the back vowels /a, ɔ, u/ of the Kirzan dialect of Armenian (northern Azerbaijan) surface as [æ, œ, y] immediately after a voiced obstruent in an initial syllable (triggers are underlined and targets are in boldface):

(14) Kirzan: consonant-vowel interaction (Vaux 1996: 177–178)

a. <u>b</u>ah → <u>b</u>**æ**h "spade"
<u>b</u>ɔłk → <u>b</u>**œ**χk "radish"
<u>b</u>urd → <u>b</u>**y**rd "snowstorm"
b. takʰ → takʰ "hot"
toron → toron "madder (plant)"
puk → puk "throat"

According to Vaux (1992, 1996), the non-structure-preserving allophones of the vowels /a, ɔ, u/ in (14a) result from assimilation of the feature [+ATR] triggered by the syllable-initial voiced obstruent. Hence, he concludes that voiced stops are specified for [+ATR] in Kirzan.

Ćavar (2007), building notably upon phonotactic constraints, distinguishes between [+ATR] consonants /ɕ, ʑ, tɕ, dʑ/ and their [–ATR] counterparts /ʂ, ʐ, tʂ, dʐ/ in Polish.

Lindau (1978: 553) has pointed out that the same mechanism is involved in pharyngealization and [ATR] harmony. In fact, tongue-root position has been used to characterize pharyngealization (i.e. emphatic consonants, tˤ, sˤ...) and the natural class formed by guttural consonants (q, ɢ, χ, ʁ, ħ, ʕ) in languages such as Arabic. McCarthy (1994) for example, argues that emphatic and guttural consonants share a [pharyngeal] place of articulation. According to Rose (1996), both emphatic and guttural consonants share the feature [RTR]. The main motivation for this proposition is based on the quite widespread process of *vowel lowering* in the neighborhood of emphatic and guttural consonants. For example, in West Greenlandic Eskimo (Eskimo-Aleut; Schultz-Lorentzen 1945), the high vowels /i/ and /u/ are lowered to [ɛ] and [ɔ], respectively, when they precede an uvular consonant /q/ or /ʁ/ (triggers are underlined and targets are in boldface):

(15) Vowel lowering in West Greenlandic Eskimo (Schultz-Lorentzen 1945)

a. sɛʁmi-t "glaciers" b. sɛʁm[ɛ]-q̲ "glacier"
   uvdlu-t "days"       uvdl[ɔ]-q̲ "day"
   iki-t "your wound"   ik[ɛ]-ʁ̲put "our wound"

However, one may analyse this process in terms of [–high] feature spreading from uvular to a nearby vowel instead of spreading of [RTR].[10]

Conversely, vowels may lower a consonant. For example, in Classical Mongolian (Altaic; Odden 1980 among others), velar consonants are lowered to uvulars when they are adjacent to a back vowel (triggers are underlined and targets are set in bold):

(16) Classical Mongolian: vowel-consonant harmony (Odden 1980: 288)

a. keü-**ken** "little child"  qar<u>a</u>-**q**an "little black"
   ine-**ken** "little this"   n<u>o</u>yi-**q**an "little prince"

---

**10** Note that in classical generative phonology, velar and uvular consonants are distinguished by the feature [±high]. Velar consonants are [+back,+high] while uvular consonants are [+back,–high].

b. üje-**g**de "to be seen"  tayil**u**-ɢda "to be explained"
   biči-**g**de "to be written"  al**a**-ɢda "to be killed"
c. ide-**g** "bribe"  jil**u**-ɢ "picture"
   büji-**g** "dance"  q**o**ri-ɢ "forbiddance"
d. jimis-li**g** "orchard"  miq**a**-liɢ "corpulence"
   temür-lig "metal"  bay**a**-liɢ "riches"

Since both velar and uvular consonants are [+back] in a given system, the Classical Mongolian vowel to consonant harmony is best analysed in terms of [RTR] spreading from a [+RTR] vowel to a velar consonant within non-compound words. Following this line of analysis, uvular consonants must be distinguished from velar consonants by means of the contrastive values of a binary [RTR] feature: uvular consonants are [+RTR] and velar consonants are [−RTR]. It seems that the [±high] feature is somewhat redundant in the consonant system of Classical Mongolian since [+RTR] consonants are also [−high] (uvular) and [−RTR] consonants are also [+high] (velar). It is interesting to note that in Classical Mongolian the high vowel /i/ is transparent both with respect to vowel harmony and to the process just discussed. Hence, data in (16) show that the vowel system of Classical Mongolian can be split into [+RTR] vowels (/a, o, u/) and [−RTR] vowels (/e, ø, ü/), leaving /i/ unspecified for [RTR].

Chumburung, a Kwa language (Niger-Congo) spoken in Ghana (Snider 1984, Pulleyblank 2011), is another language that exhibits [ATR]-based vowel-consonant interactions. The vowel system of that language is paired with respect to [ATR], excepted the low vowel /a/ which is unpaired: /i, e, o, u/ for the [+ATR] set and /ɪ, ɛ, a, ɔ, ʊ/ for the [−ATR] set.[11] In Chumburung, the lateral consonant [l] is in complementary distribution with the so-called "lightly-retroflexed alveolar flap" [ɽ]. Thus, the established phoneme /l/ is realized as [l] in stem-initial position for all speakers (e.g. [lɔ́sɛ́] "difficult", [kà-làadaá] "libation") and, at least for some speakers, as [ɽ] in word-medial position except when the onset of the preceding syllable is [l] and the surrounding vowels are [+ATR][12] (triggers are underlined and targets are in boldface):

---

[11] In the cross-height vowel harmony of Chumburung, "all prefix vowels assimilate the [+ATR] feature of a [+ATR] noun-stem" (Snider 1984: 52, fn6).
[12] For other speakers, the lateral /l/ invariably surfaces as [ɽ] in word-medial position.

(17) Chumburung: vowel-consonant interaction (Snider 1984: 49)

| Advanced | | Retracted | |
|---|---|---|---|
| làlàkwḭ́? | "type of tuber" | kḭ-láɽámbɔ̰ | "thing which frightens" |
| láalḛ̂ | "cattle egret" | làaɽí | "waist" |
| lóolí | "deep" | lɔ̰ɔɽí | "to remove seeds" |
| àlúulá? | "red dye" | làaɽɔ̰ | "to lie accross" |

Snider (1984: 52) assumes that the "[−ATR] vowel harmony set and [ɽ] have a feature retracted tongue-root as a common denominator". Following Snider's account, it is possible to analyze the Chumburung data as resulting from an [ATR]-based vowel-consonant interaction: the lateral /l/ surfaces as a lightly-retroflexed alveolar flap [ɽ] in the neighborhood of the [−ATR] vowel set. Note that the low vowel /a/ is transparent to the vowel-consonant harmony. Consequently, the allophonic [ɽ] of Chumburung may be interpreted as the [−ATR] counterpart of the lateral [l].

Maybe the more straightforward account regarding the presence of a tongue-root feature in the consonantal inventory involves vowel-consonant harmony triggered by emphatic and guttural consonants in some languages. For example, besides a process of uvular harmony between vowels and consonants, Chilcotin, a Northern Athapaskan language (Dene) spoken in British Columbia (Krauss 1975, Cook 1993, Hansson 2001), has a secondary-articulation harmony which involves pharyngealization. In this language, alveolar sibilants contrast in pharyngealization: /sˤ, zˤ, tsˤ, tsʰˤ, ts'ˤ / (the pharyngealized set) vs. /s, z, ts, tsʰ, ts'/ (the non-pharyngealized set). In the neighborhood of a pharyngealized sibilant and/or uvular consonant (/q, qʰ, q', χ, ʁ, qʷ, qʷʰ, qʷ', χʷ, ʁʷ/), vowels are lowered and/or backed by a process of *Vowel Flattening* similar to the phonological process found in St'at'imcets. Chilcotin has also a third sibilant series /ʃ, tʃ, tʃʰ, tʃ'/ that has no effect on any vowel or on sibilant harmony. According to Cook (1993) and Hansson (2001), among others, the pharyngealization contrast among anterior sibilants and allophonic alternations of neighboring vowels must be analyzed in terms of [RTR]. Hansson (2001) underlines that the pharyngealized harmony targeting sibilants is hidden by a pharyngealized harmony in which [+RTR] spreads iteratively leftward from a pharyngealized sibilant (or a uvular consonant) to every vowel in the word[13] (the IPA transcription is ours):

---

**13** Note that the first (tautosyllabic) vowel at the right of the trigger also undergoes [+RTR] assimilation. Unlike the unbounded regressive (leftward) pharyngealized sibilant harmony, Chilcotin has also a much more restrictive progressive (rightward) pharyngealized harmony in which the neutral consonants (i.e. non-phrayngealized and non-uvular) and the high vowel /i/ block the spreading of [+RTR]. To be more precise, the high vowel /i/ undergoes vowel flattening but the spreading of [+RTR] is blocked beyond that vowel.

(18) Leftward [+RTR] vowel-consonant harmony
(Cook 1993: 160ff, Hansson 2001: 102)

kʷɛ-nɛ-tʰɛ-ʁɛ-z̙ˤɛɬ → kʷʌnʌtʰaz̙ˤʌɬ "it's going to get warm"
næ-tʰæ-k'ɛns̙ˤ → natʰak'ã̙s̙ˤ "he stretches himself"
ʔæ-næ-tʰɛ-s̙ˤɛ-it-t'in → ʔanatʰʌz̙ˤʌitt'in "we're started working"
tʰæ -nɛ-yˤɛ-z̙ˤɛ-tʰæn → tʰanʌyʌs̙ˤtʰan "he is drunk"

Sibilant pharyngealized harmony causes agreement in [±RTR] among all anterior sibilants within a word. The rightmost sibilant determines the [±RTR] value of all preceding [+anterior] sibilants in the word domain. When the harmonic feature value is [+RTR], consonant harmony is hidden by the vowel-consonant harmony (as in 19a) while when the harmonic feature value is [–RTR], consonant harmony is visible since no vowel flattening occurs (as in 19b):

(19) Sibilant pharyngalized harmony (Cook 1993: 160ff, Hansson 2001: 102)

a. *Pharyngealized*

næ-sɛ-næ-ʁɛ-nɛ-l-tsʰˤɛns̙ˤ → nas̙ˤʌnaʁʌ̃ĩltsʰˤã̙s̙ˤ "you're hitting me"
χæ-tʰæ-s-kɛns̙ˤ → χatʰas̙ˤkã̙s̙ˤ "I'm spinning you around"
næ-nɛ-tɛ-ʁɛ-s-ɬ-pæs̙ˤ → nanʌtas̙ˤɬpas̙ˤ "I'll twist it out"
sɛ-u-z̙ˤɛ-nɛ-s-ɬ-tʃˤæn → s̙ˤoz̙ˤʌɨɬ-tʃˤan "you listened to me"

b. *Depharyngealized*

næ-tʰɛ-s̙ˤɛ-s-t-pin → nætʰɛzɛspin "I'm swimming away"
s̙ˤɛ-i-ɬ-tʃʰæz → siɬtʃʰæz "I barbecued it"
tʰæ-nɛ-s̙ˤɛ-s-tʰæn → tʰænɛzɛstʰæn "I'm drunk"
tʰɛ-z̙ˤɛ-i-ɬ-tsʰæz → tʰɛziɬtsʰæz "I started to cook"

Krauss (1975: 35) underlines the fact that Chilcotin has a Morpheme Structure Contraint prohibiting the stems of the-form SˤVS or SVSˤ, where S represents a sibilant fricative. In that language, only stems of the form SˤVSˤ or SVS are permitted. Thus, the process of sibilant pharyngealized harmony discussed here shows that the constraint holding on lexical morphemes is also duplicated through morphological concatenation, essentially from the stem to a prefix. Beside the equipollent use of the feature [RTR] assumed by Cook (1993) and Hansson (2001), the sibilant harmony of Chilcotin may also be explained with the two privative tongue-root features [RTR] and [ATR]. Following this interpretation, pharyngealized sibilant harmony emerges from prohibited sequences *ATR RTR or *RTR ATR inside the class of sibilants, i.e. all anterior sibilants in the word must agree in tongue-root position (either ATR or RTR).

The puzzling case of Chilcotin's vowels is very interesting for any feature-based phonological theory. According to Cook (1993: 152), Chilcotin vowels are paired with respect to the feature [tense]: tense vowels are /i, u, æ/ and lax vowels are /ɪ, ʊ, ɛ/. Nevertheless, it is also possible that the underlying distinction between /i, u, æ/ and /ɪ, ʊ, ɛ/ is based on the feature [ATR]: the first vowels in the set are specified [ATR] while those in the second set are left unspecified (neutral tongue-root position). As Goad (1993) and Rose (1996) note about Turkana and Chilcotin vowels, [RTR] is not incompatible with vowels specified as [ATR]. Therefore, spreading [RTR] from pharyngealized consonants onto vowel of both sets gives rise to allophonic alternations such as [ʌi~e, o, ɑ] and [ʌɪ, ɔ, ʌ] respectively. In this way, Chilcotin [RTR] harmony produces vowels that are slightly lowered and backed.

# 3 Phonetic definition

This section is devoted to the phonetic definition of the feature [ATR]. Here, we examine both articulatory parameters and acoustic correlates of the feature [ATR] and show that, on the one hand, the main articulatory implementation of the feature [ATR] involves the horizontal tongue-root position and, on the other hand, the direct acoustic correlate of the tongue-root position involves the height of the first formant. Finally, in the last part of this section, we explore the possibility for the feature [ATR] to act as an enhancement gesture for other features, notably the features [±high] and [±voice].

## 3.1 Articulatory parameters

### 3.1.1 Tongue-root position

The basic articulatory correlate of the feature [ATR] involves, as its name suggest, the tongue-root position. The X-ray cinematography data collected by Ladefoged (1964, 1968) on various languages of West Africa, and especially on Igbo (Niger-Congo, Nigeria), show that the advanced tongue-root position is the main articulatory correlate of [+ATR] vowels while the retracted tongue-root position is associated with [ATR] vowels.[14] Similar results were recently obtained using ultrasound data on Kinande (Gick et al. 2006). According to Halle & Stevens

---

[14] He also discovered that the lips, the jaw and the highest point of the tongue body are in the same position for each member of the pair.

(1969: 37ff), the movement of the tongue-root occurs "in the vicinity of the lower pharynx, the epiglottis, and the hyoid bone", and is driven by the contraction of the mylohyoid, geniohyoid and genioglossus muscles.

### 3.1.2 Pharyngeal expansion/constriction

Advancing the tongue-root results in a greater pharyngeal cavity, while retracting the tongue-root leads to a smaller pharyngeal cavity (cf. Figure 1). Ladefoged (1975: 226) claims that "what matters for the distinction between the two sets of vowels [i.e. +ATR *vs* –ATR] is that one should have a comparatively large pharyngeal cavity, and the other a comparatively small one".

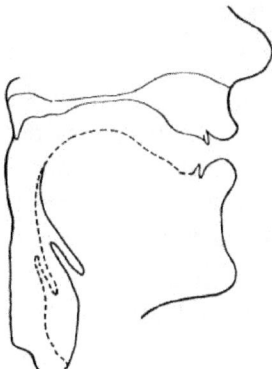

**Figure 1.** The movement of the tongue associated to the pharynx width (where the plain line represents the neutral tongue-root configuration and the dashed line a backward movement of the tongue-root leading to a smaller pharyngeal cavity, from Ladefoged 1980: 492).

### 3.1.3 Larynx lowering/raising

According to Lindau (1978: 552), "the articulatory correlate of vowel harmony involves the tongue-root and the larynx, working together to accomplish variation of pharyngal size". Then, the advancing of the tongue-root position is most of the time associated with the lowering of the larynx (e.g. in Akan, Ladefoged 1975) while the retraction of the tongue-root is often associated with the raising of the larynx. Both of these articulatory parameters — tongue-root/larynx movements — combine to expand or constrict the pharyngal cavity, as pointed out by Painter (1973) on Twi or Lindau (1975).

However, Lindau (1979: 173) later stated that there are "no intrinsic connections between the larynx and the tongue-root that would necessitate the larynx to move vertically down, as the tongue moves horizontally forward". She argues that this strong correlation is not triggered by phonological necessity: "by combining the advanced tongue-root with a lower larynx position and the retracted tongue-root with a raised larynx, the speaker accomplishes a larger variation of the size of the pharyngal cavity, than if he varied just the tongue-root position alone". Then, the lowering of the larynx has to be considered as an enhancement gesture (see Section 3.3 for a similar discussion about the height of the tongue). It would also be the case for other articulatory parameters, such as the widening of the pharyngeal walls or the raising of the velum. All these supplementary adjustments would support the continued use of [±ATR].

### 3.1.4 Tongue height

Laver (1994: 141–142, 289–290), in line with Ladefoged (1975: 203), states that "the articulatory mechanism is probably better described as a longitudinal bunching of the whole tongue". Specifically, [ATR] vowels are associated to a specific, "tighter-than-neutral", curve of the tip and the blade of the tongue (figure 2). However, he agrees with the idea that the different articulatory strategies lead to an expanded pharynx.

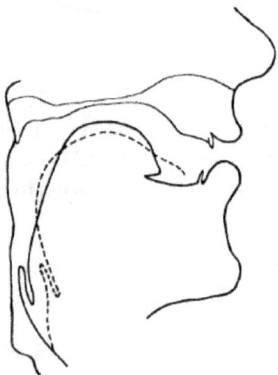

**Figure 2.** The movements of the tongue associated with tongue bunching (where the plain line represents an upward movement of the tongue body leading to a smaller pharyngeal cavity and the dashed line a neutral tongue body configuration, from Ladefoged 1980: 492).

So far, the articulators involved in the production of [+ATR] vowels are summarized in figure 3, where the sympathetic movements of tongue body and larynx had also been included:

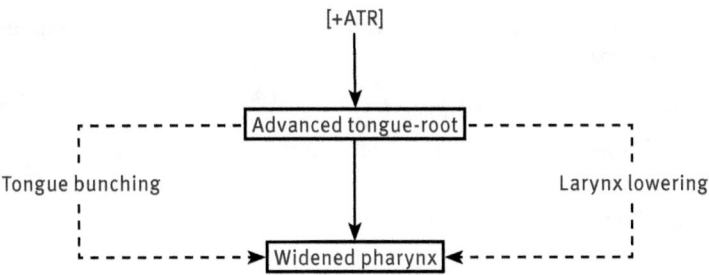

**Figure 3.** Diagram of articulators involved in production of advanced tongue-root vowels (dashed lines represent sympathetic movements).

### 3.1.5 Voice quality

In many African languages with ATR vowel harmony, the [±ATR] distinction is also accompanied — or enhanced — by voice quality distinctions (Kingston & al. 1997), which have been described in various ways. It is sometimes said that [+ATR] vowels are more 'breathy', while a non-advanced tongue-root involves a more creaky voice. Electroglottographic (EGG) analysis of Maasai vowels (Guion et al. 2004) shows that [+ATR] vowels tend to have smaller closure quotient (CQ) values than their [−ATR] counterparts, suggesting that the production of [+ATR] vowels involves somewhat less contact between the vocal folds than that of their [−ATR] counterparts. Laver (1994: 411) observes that "a setting which involves an advanced tongue-root tends to sound rather "hollow", whereas the one with a retracted tongue-root sounds rather 'muffled'". However, it is normally the [+ATR] vowels that are described as breathy or muffled, especially in Nilotic languages, and [−ATR] vowels that are brassy, harsh. This is true in Anywa (Reh 1996), in Shilluk and in Maasai (Tucker and Mpaayei 1955: 51), where the [+ATR] counterparts of [−ATR] vowels are breathy voiced. Thus, Reh (1996: 36–37) reports that in Anywa breathiness decreases from the low vowel /ʌ/ to high vowels /i/ and /u/ although there is an increase of tenseness from low to high vowels. Moreover, he clearly states that "the presence of tenseness suggests that breathy vowels are pronounced with the 'advanced tongue-root', i.e. they have the feature [+ATR]":

(20) Anywa: relashionship between voice quality and advanced tongue-root
(Reh 1996: 36–37)

| *Retracted* | | *Advanced* | |
|---|---|---|---|
| wàrɔ̀ | "shoe" | wa̠rò | "cow-dung" |
| dɔ̄ɔl | "voice" | du̠ol | "royal grave" |
| ɲwέɲ | "barb" | ɲwè̠ɲ | "metals" |

The same report has been made in Akan (Berry 1957) and Ikpɔsɔ (Kwa, Anderson 1999). However, Ladefoged & Maddieson (1996: 302) point out that "in most cases [...], the West African languages using [ATR] do not have markedly different voice qualities".

## 3.2 Acoustic correlates

### 3.2.1 Height of the first formant

Most acoustic studies have shown that the first formant is the main accoustic correlate of the ATR feature. For example, Halle & Stevens (1969: 38) note that "the clearest and most consistent acoustic consequence of widening the vocal tract in the vicinity of the tongue-root is a lowering of the first-formant frequency". Similarly, Archangeli & Pulleyblank (1994: 7) state that "The primary acoustic correlate of tongue-root advancement is a lowering of the first formant frequency, while tongue-root retraction correlates with a raising of the same formant". According to Guion et al. (2004), [+ATR] high and mid vowels have significantly lower $F_1$ values than their [–ATR] counterparts. Creider (1991) finds that the height of the first formant of the Dholuo (Nilotic) vowels is the main acoustic correlate within [ATR] contrasts. Larsen (1991: 271ff) also states that in the Koony dialect of Saboat (Nilotic, Kalenjin), the first formant frequency of [+ATR] vowels is significantly lower than it is for [–ATR]. Maddieson (2003) found that Kinande [–ATR] vowels have "a substantially higher first formant [...] than [their] harmonic conterpart[s]".

### 3.2.2 Height of the second formant

It is sometimes also said (e.g. Halle & Stevens 1969: 39) that $F_2$ is involved but Lindau (1979: 173) argues that the differences between F1 frequencies are larger than the differences between F2 frequencies, and concludes that the change of the pharyngeal cavity affects $F_1$ more than $F_2$. Ladefoged (1964, 1968), cited by

Halle & Stevens (1969: 39), has not noted any modification of the $F_2$ of back/+ATR vowels of Igbo. Larsen (1991: 271ff) has noted that the second formant frequency is relatively constant in the Koony dialect of Saboat, and Guion et al. (2004) have obtained roughly the same results with Maa. Hess (1988, 1992) has shown however that formant height in Akan does not distinguish [+ATR] vowels from [−ATR] vowels in a quite convincing way.

Moreover, Casali (2003) and Guion et al. (2004) among others, underline the fact that [−ATR] high vowels /ɪ/ and /ʊ/ and [+ATR] mid vowels /e/ and /o/ tend to overlap in acoustic space since they have similar formant structures. In Ijo, the upper mid vowels even have a lower $F_1$ value than the lower high vowels (Ladefoged & Maddieson 1996: 305). This fact has also been underline by Creider (1991) in Dholuo, where a smaller acoustic distance is found between first formant frequency of [−ATR] high vowels /ɪ, ʊ / and [+ATR] mid vowels /e, o/:

(21) Dholuo: $F_1$ means for [−ATR] high vs. [+ATR] mid vowels (Creider 1991: 181)

| Vowel | [ATR] | $F_1$ mean (Hz) |
|---|---|---|
| ɪ | − | 399.67 |
| e | + | 443.97 |
| ʊ | − | 426.5 |
| o | + | 448.33 |

Despite this variability, Ladefoged & Maddieson (1996: 304) insist on the fact that "in virtually all cases the [+ATR] vowel appears to be raised and advanced in the acoustic space" and that "the high back retracted tongue-root vowel is always further back than its counterpart, rather than further forward, as in the case for the traditional lax back vowels. Lax vowels of all kinds are normally taken to be more centralized. Retracted tongue-root vowels do not always have this characteristic".

### 3.2.3 First formant bandwidth

Hess (1988) argues on the contrary that the first formant bandwidth is the relevant acoustic correlate. She is followed by Ladefoged & Maddieson (1996: 301–302), for whom "there is a noticeable difference in the bandwidths of the formants; those of the advanced tongue-root vowel are narrower, probably because there is a greater tension of the vocal tract walls and fewer acoustic losses in the region of the resonances". Creider (1991), on Dholuo, and Kingston et al. (1997), however, state that formant bandwidth is not a salient clue.

## 3.2.4 Acoustic energy

According to Guion et al. (2004), acoustic analysis of Maasai (Nilotic) vowels shows that [+ATR] vowels display somewhat *less* energy in the higher frequency than their [−ATR] counterparts. This lack of energy was also noticed by Halle & Stevens (1969: 41) – "as a consequence of the normal relationship between formant frequencies and formant amplitudes" –, and Fulop et al. (1998), about Degema (Edoid, Nigeria).

Strangely, Ladefoged & Maddieson's (1996: 301) own analyses of the same language lead them to say the exact opposite: "the advanced tongue-root vowel [of Degema] sounds 'brighter' because of the greater amount of energy in the higher part of the spectrum". The strangeness of this claim is increased by the fact that [−ATR] vowels are most of the time presented as 'brighter' (Guion et al. 2004 cite Berry 1955, Stewart 1967 and Jacobson 1980).

Other correlates have been proposed. For instance, Kingston et al. (1997) find that the difference between the first and fourth harmonics ($H_1$–$H_4$) is the main acoustic correlate that distinguishes vowel sets.

## 3.3 [ATR] as an enhancement feature

### 3.3.1 Tongue height enhancement

Halle & Stevens (1969: 40) note that there is a strong relashionship between the tongue-root position and the height of the tongue. According to Halle & Stevens (1969: 38), Ladefoged et al. (1972) and Archangeli & Pulleyblank (1994: 172), among others, this relation has its origin in the *incompressability of the tongue* since, as it was pointed out by Jackobson (1980: 185), "if the tongue is constricted in one area it will expand in another." In other words, the constriction of the tongue in a specific area leads to its expansion in another and reciprocally. Then, the advance of the tongue-root position leads to the compression of the tongue, which is therefore raised. "Conversely, as the tongue-root is retracted, the tongue body is pulled down and therefore lowered." (Hall & Hall 1980: 207). So, most of the authors commonly assume that the "movement of the tongue-root tends to be accompanied by a sympathetic movement of the tongue body" (Archangeli & Pulleyblank 1994: 175). This correlation is also supported by accoustic correlates, since the height of the first formant is the prime acoustic correlate of both tongue-root position and tongue body raising and lowering (Archangeli & Pulleyblank 1994: 7).

However, the correlation between the position of the tongue-root and the height of the body is not automatic. Ladefoged & Maddieson (1996) explain that the difference of the height of the body in ATR sets is limited in Akan, and does not occur in Igbo. They conclude that ATR movement is a separated gesture in those languages (Ladefoged & Maddieson 1996). Archangeli & Pulleyblank (1994: 175) consider that "the interdependancy between tongue-root and tongue body movements constitutes a tendency, not an absolute correlation".

Consequently, the tongue-root movement may be considered an enhancement feature (Keyser & Stevens 2001, Clements 2005, Clements & Ridouane 2006, among others) of the [±high] feature since, as it is stated by Jackobson (1980: 185), "it is not an unusual expectation for higher vowels to have a tongue-root which is more advanced [than] that for lower vowels", and reciprocally: "one could say that tongue-root advancement *enhances* tongue body lowering (see Halle & Stevens 1969)" (Archangeli & Pulleyblank 1994: 174). This claim has been made for English (see among others Ladefoged & Maddieson 1996: 304; Ladefoged 1975: 203; Halle & Stevens 1969; Perkell 1971; MacCay 1976). The [±tense] feature would then be analysed as the combination of tongue-root and height movements.

### 3.3.2 Voicing enhancement

Keyser & Stevens (2006) argue that advanced tongue-root is used in order to enhance voicing distinction in American English words such as *ri*[s]*ing* vs. *ri*[z]*ing*. In these words, the first formant frequency of a vowel preceding a voiceless obstruent is lower and the second formant frequency is higher than that of the same vowel preceding a voiced obstruent. According to Keyser & Stevens (2006: 14), this effect may be due to the advanced tongue-root since "advancing of the tongue results in a raising of the tongue body. Consequently, the pharynx is more fully extended, and little further expansion is possible during the consonantal portion of the gesture. This fully extended pharynx, therefore, prevents further airflow through the glottis and, consequently, inhibits consonantal voicing". Nevertheless, authors underline that such enhancement appears only when a vowel is followed by an offglide with high tongue body position.

# 4 Summary

In summary, the [ATR] feature has been mainly used in the phonological literature for explaining cross-height vowel harmony processes in some african and asiatic languages, where a vowel set A is distinguished from a vowel set B according to this feature. Nevertheless, we have seen that a great body of works has assumed a privative position regarding the tongue-root feature. Following this view, markedness reversal — the fact that some ATR harmony systems require reference to [−ATR] as the active value (i.e. marked) while other systems require reference to [+ATR] as the active value — must be rejected and the tongue-root feature must be split into two single-valued features: either [ATR] or [RTR]. Finally, the tongue-root feature has also been used to distinguish the natural class formed by guttural consonants (mainly uvular and pharyngeal(ized) consonants).

Turning to the phonetic side, it is widely accepted that the main articulatory correlates of the [ATR] feature are the tongue body position, on the one side, and the height of the larynx, on the other side, even if the latter is not claimed to be automatic. Both these parameters are used to enlarge or reduce the size of the pharyngeal cavity. While a voice quality difference frequently helps to distinguish the [+ATR] and the [−ATR] vowel sets, this parameter seems to be an enhancement feature rather than an inherent property of the feature.

There is no agreement on the acoustic correlates of feature [ATR]. The heigth of the first formant is frequently mentioned, but several authors claimed that this parameter is in some languages irrelevant. Alternative proposals include the $F_1$ bandwidth, energy in the higher frequencies or the difference between the first and the fourth harmonics.

Finally, the feature [ATR] may sometimes constitute an enhancement gesture. A tongue-root position difference may notably help to distinguish between [+tense] and [−tense] vowel sets.

# References

Anderson, Coleen G. 1999. ATR vowel harmony in Akposso. *Studies in African Linguistics* 28: 186–214.
Archangeli, Diana. 1988. Aspects of underspecification theory. *Phonology* 5: 183–207.
Archangeli, Diana & Douglas Pulleyblank (1989). Yoruba vowel harmony. *Linguistic Inquiry* 20: 173–217.
Archangeli, Diana & Douglas Pulleyblank. 1994. *Grounded phonology*. Cambridge, MA: MIT Press.
Archangeli, Diana & Douglas Pulleyblank. 2007. Harmony. In Paul de Lacy (ed.), *The Cambridge Handbook of Phonology*, 353–378. Cambridge: Cambridge University Press.
Baković, Eric. 2000. *Harmony, Dominance and Control*. PhD thesis, Rutgers University, New Brunswick, NJ.
Baković, Eric. 2001. Vowel harmony and cyclicity in Eastern Nilotic. In *27th Annual Meeting of the Berkeley Linguistics Society*. Berkeley, California: Berkeley Linguistics Society.
Berry, J. 1955. Some notes on the phonology of the Nzema and Ahanta dialects. *Bulletin of the School of Oriental and African Studies* 17: 160–165.
Bloomfield, Leonard. 1962. *The Menomini language*. New Haven, CT: Yale University Press.

Calabrese, Andrea. 2005. *Markedness and Economy in a Derivational Model of Phonology*. Berlin & New York: Mouton de Gruyter.
Casali, Roderic F. 2002. Nawuri ATR harmony in typological perspective. *Journal of West African Languages* 29: 3–43.
Casali, Roderic F. 2003. [ATR] value asymmetries and underlying vowel inventory structure in Niger-Congo and Nilo-Saharan. *Linguistic Typology* 7: 307–382.
Casali, Roderic F. 2008. ATR harmony in African languages. *Language and Linguistics Compass* 2: 496–549.
Ćavar, Małgorzata E. 2007. [ATR] in Polish. *Journal of Slavic Linguistics* 15: 207–228.
Chomsky, Noam & Morris Halle. 1968. *The Sound Pattern of English*. New York: Harper and Row.
Clements, G. N. 1981. Akan vowel harmony: a nonlinear analysis. In Clements G. N. (ed.), *Harvard Studies in Phonology*, volume II, 108–177. Bloomington, IN: I.U.L.C.
Clements, George N. 2000. Phonology. In Bernd Heine & Derek Nurse (eds.), *African Languages: An Introduction*, 123–160. Cambridge: Cambridge University Press.
Clements, George N. 2005. The role of features in speech sound inventories. In Eric Raimy & Charles Cairns (eds.), *Contemporary Views on Architecture and Representations in Phonological Theory*, 19–68. Cambridge, MA: MIT Press.
Clements, George N. & Rachid Ridouane. 2006. Distinctive feature enhancement: a review. In Antonis Botinis (ed.), *Proceedings of the ISCA Tutorial and Research Workshop on Experimental Linguistics*, 97–100. Athens: University of Athens.
Cole, Jennifer & Loren Trigo. 1988. Parasitic Harmony. In N. Smith & H. van der Hulst (eds.), *Features, Segmental Structures and Harmony Processes*, 19–38. Dordrecht: Foris.
Cook, Eung-Do. 1993. Chilcotin flattening and autosegmental spreading. *Lingua* 91: 149–174.
Czaykowska-Higgins, Ewa. 1987. Characterizing tongue root behavior. Unpublished Ms.
Edmondson, Jerold A. & John H. Esling. 2006. The valves of the throat and their functioning in tone, vocal register and stress: Laryngoscopic case studies. *Phonology* 23: 157–191.
Fulop, Sean A., Ethelbert Kari & Peter Ladefoged. 1998. An acoustic study of the tongue root contrasts in Degema vowels. *Phonetica* 55: 80–98.
Gick, Bryan, Douglas Pulleyblank, Fiona Campbell & Ngessimo Mutaka. 2006. Low vowels and transparency in Kinande vowel harmony. *Phonology* 23 (1): 1–20.
Gick, Bryan, Ian Wilson, Karsten Koch & Clare Cook. 2004. Language-specific articulatory settings: Evidence from inter-utterance rest position. *Phonetica* 61: 220–233.
Gilley, Leoma G. 1992. *An autosegmental approach to Shilluk phonology*. Dallas, Texas: Summer Institute of Linguistics.
Goad, Heather. 1991. [Atr] and [rtr] are different features. In D. Bates (ed.), *Proceedings of the West Coast Conference on Formal Linguistics* 11: 163–173.
Goad, Heather. 1993. *On the Configuration of Height Features*. PhD thesis, University of Southern California, Berkeley.
Guion, Susan G., Mark W. Post & Doris L. Payne. 2004. Phonetic correlates of tongue root vowel contrasts in Maa. *Journal of Phonetics* 32: 517–542.
Gussenhoven, Carlos & Haike Jacobs. 1998. *Understanding Phonology*. London: Arnold.
Hall, Beatrice L. & R. M. R. Hall. 1980. Nez Perce vowel harmony: An Africanist explanation and some theoretical consequences. In R. Vago (ed.), *Issues in Vowel Harmony*, 201–236. Amsterdam: John Benjamins.
Halle, M. & K. Stevens. 1969. On the feature advanced tongue root. *Quarterly Progress Report (MIT Research Laboratory of Electronics)* 94: 209–215.
Hansson, Gunnar O. 2001. *Theoretical and Typological Issues in Consonant Harmony*. PhD thesis, University of California, Berkeley, CA.

Harris, John & Geoff Lindsey. 1995. The elements of phonological representation. In *Frontiers of phonology: atoms, structures, derivations*, 34–79. Harlow, Essex: Longman.
Hess, Susan. 1988. Acoustic characteristics of the vowel harmony feature and vowel raising in Akan. *UCLA Working Papers in Phonetics* 70: 58–72.
Hess, Susan. 1992. Assimilatory effects in a vowel harmony system: An acoustic of advanced tongue root in Akan. *Journal of Phonetics* 20: 475–492.
Hudu, Fusheini Angulu. 2010. *Dagbani Tongue-Root Harmony: A Formal Account with Ultrasound Investigation*. PhD thesis, The University of British Columbia.
Hulst, Harry G. van der & Jeroen M. van de Weijer. 1995. Vowel Harmony. In John A. Goldsmith (ed.), *Handbook of Phonological Theory*, 495–534. Oxford: Blackwell.
Jacobson, Leon C. 1978. DhoLuo vowel harmony. *UCLA Working Papers in Phonetics* 43.
Jacobson, Leon C. 1980. Voice-quality harmony in Western Nilotic languages. In R. Vago (ed.), *Issues in Vowel Harmony*, 183–200. Amsterdam: John Benjamins.
Johnson, Robert. 1975. *The Role of Phonetic Detail in Coeur D'Alene Phonology*. PhD thesis, Washington State University.
Kaye, Jonathan, Jean Lowenstamm & Jean-Roger Vergnaud. 1988. La structure interne des éléments phonologiques: une théorie du Charme et du Gouvernement. *Recherches Linguistiques de Vincennes* 17: 109–134.
Kenstowicz, Michael. 1979. Chukchee vowel harmony and epenthesis. In P. Clyne, W. Hanks & C. Hofbauer (eds.), *Chicago Linguistic Society 15: The Elements: Parasession on Linguistic Units and Level*, 402–412. Chicago: Chicago Linguistic Society.
Keyser, Samuel J. & Kenneth N. Stevens. 2001. Enhancement revisited. In Michael Kenstowicz (ed.), *Ken Hale: a Life in Language*, 271–291. Cambridge, MA: MIT Press.
Keyser, Samuel J. & Kenneth N. Stevens. 2006. Enhancement and Overlap in the Speech Chain. *Language* 82: 33–63.
Kingston, John, Neil A. Macmillian, Laura Walsh Dickey, Rachel Thorburn & Christine Bartels. 1997. Integrality in the perception of tongue root position and voice quality in vowels. *Journal of the Acoustical Society of America* 101: 1696–1709.
Krauss, Michael E. 1975. Chilcotin phonology, a descriptive and historical report, with recommendations for a Chilcotin orthography. Alaskan Native Language Center (unpublished Ms.).
Ladefoged, Peter. 1964. A phonetic study of West African languages. In *West African Language Monograph 1*. Cambridge.
Ladefoged, Peter. 1968. *A Phonetic Study of West African Languages*. Cambridge: Cambridge University Press.
Ladefoged, Peter. 1971. *Preliminaries to Linguistic Phonetics*. Chicago: University of Chicago Press.
Ladefoged, Peter. 1975. *A Course in Phonetics [3rd ed.]*. Orlando: Harcourt Brace.
Ladefoged, Peter. 1980. What are linguistic sounds made of? *Language* 56: 485–502.
Ladefoged, P. 1999. Linguistic phonetic descriptions. In Hardcastle W. & J. Laver (eds.), *Handbook of Phonetic Sciences*, 589–618. Oxford: Blackwell.
Ladefoged, Peter., J. De Clerk, M. Lindau & G. Papgun. 1972. An auditory-motor theory of speech production. *UCLA Working Papers in Phonetics* 22: 48–75.
Ladefoged, Peter. & Ian Maddieson. 1996. *The Sounds of the World's Languages*. Oxford: Blackwell.
Larsen, Iver A. 1991. A puzzling dissimilation process in Southern Nilotic. In M. Lionel Bender (ed.), *Fourth Nilo-Saharan Colloquium, Nilo-Saharan Linguistics Analyses and Documentation*, volume 7, 263–272. Hamburg: Helmut Buske.

Laver, John. 1994. *Principles of Phonetics*. Cambridge: Cambridge University Press.
Lindau, Mona. 1975. Features for vowels. *UCLA Working Papers in Phonetics* 30: 16–21.
Lindau, Mona. 1978. Vowel features. *Language* 54: 541–563.
Lindau, Mona. 1979. The feature EXPANDED. *Journal of Phonetics* 7: 163–177.
Lindau-Webb, Mona. 1987. Acoustic correlates of TENSE-LAX vowels and ATR vowels. *The Journal of the Acoustical Society of America* 82: S116–S116.
MacCay, Ian R. A. 1976. *Ultrasonic investigation of Anterior Pharyngeal Wall (Tongue Root) Position in Syllables Containing Tense and Lax Vowels*. Doctoral dissertation, University of Cincinnati.
Maddieson, Ian. 2003. The sounds of the Bantu languages. In D. Nurse & G. Philippson (eds.), *The Bantu Languages*, 15–41. London, New York: Routledge.
McCarthy, John J. 1994. The phonetics and phonology of Semitic pharyngeals. In Patricia Keating (ed.), *Papers in Laboratory Phonology III: Phonological Structure and Phonetic Form*, 191–233. Cambridge: Cambridge University Press.
Namdaran, Nahal. 2006. *Retraction in St'át'imcets: An Ultrasonic Investigation*. Master's thesis, The University of British Columbia.
Noonan, Michael. 1992. *A Grammar of Lango*. Berlin & New York: Mouton de Gruyter.
Odden, David. 1980. The irrelevancy of the relevancy condition: evidence for the feature specification constraint. *Linguistic analysis* 6: 261–394.
Painter, Colin. 1973. Cineradiographic data on the feature 'Covered' in Twi vowel harmony. *Phonetica* 28: 97–120.
Perkell, Joseph S. 1971. Physiology of speech production: a preliminary study of two suggested revisions of he features specifying vowels. *Quarterly Progree Report of the Research Laboratory of Electronics* 102: 123–139.
Pike, Kenneth L. 1947. *Phonemics*. Ann Arbor: University of Michigan Press.
Pulleyblank, Douglas. 1992. *International Encyclopedia of Linguistics*, volume 4, chapter Yoruba, 261–266. Oxford: Oxford University Press.
Pulleyblank, Douglas. 2002. Harmony drivers: no disagreement allowed. In *Twenty-eighth Annual Meeting of the Berkeley Linguistics Society*, 249–267. Berkeley, CA: Berkeley Linguistics Society.
Pulleyblank, Douglas. 2011. Vowel height. In Marc Van Oostendorp, Colin J. Ewen, Elizabeth V. Hume & Keren Rice (eds.), *The Blackwell Companion to Phonology*, 491–518. Oxford: Wiley-Blackwell.
Reh, Mechthild. 1996. *Anywa Language: Description and Internal Reconstruction*. Köln: Köppe.
Rialland, Annie & Redouane Djamouri. 1984. Harmonie vocalique, consonantique et structures de dépendance dans le mot en mongol khalkha. *Bulletin de la Société de Linguistique de Paris* 79: 333–383.
Rose, Sharon. 1996. Variable laryngeals and vowel lowering. *Phonology* 13: 73–117.
Rottland, Franz. 1980. Vowel harmony in Southern Nilotic. Ms., University of Nairobi.
Schachter, P. & V. A. Fromkin. 1968. A phonology of Akan: Akuapem, Asante, Fante. In *UCLA Working Papers in Phonetics*, volume 9. Los Angeles: Phonetics Laboratory, University of California.
Schultz-Lorentzen, Christian. 1945. *A Grammar of the West Greenland Language*. Copenhagen: C. A. Reitzels.
Snider, Keith L. 1984. Vowel harmony and the consonant l in Chumburung. *Studies in African Linguistics* 15: 47–57.

Steriade, Donca. 1987. Redundant Values. *Chicago Linguistic Society* 23: 339–362.
Steriade, Donca. 1995. Underspecification and markedness. In J. A. Goldsmith (ed.), *Handbook of Phonological Theory*, 149–152. Oxford: Blackwell.
Stewart, John M. 1967. Tongue root position in Akan vowel harmony. *Phonetica* 16: 185–204.
Svantesson, Jan-Olaf. 1985. Vowel harmony shift in Mongolian. *Lingua* 67: 283–327.
Tiede, Mark K. 1996. An MRI-based study of pharyngeal volume contrasts in Akan and English. *Journal of Phonetics* 24: 399–421.
Trigo, Loren. 1986. Voicing and pharyngeal expansion: ATR harmony in Buchan and Madurese. Unpublished Ms.
Trubetzkoy, Nikolaï S. 1931. Die phonologischen Systeme. In *Travaux du Cercle Linguistique de Prague* 4: 96–116.
Tucker, Archibald N. 1964. Kalenjin phonetics. In D. Abercrombie, D. B. Fry, P. A. D. Mac-Carthy, N. C. Scott & J. L. M. Trim (eds.), *In Honour of Daniel Jones*, 445–470. London: Longmans.
Tucker, Archibald N. & John T. O. Mpaayei. 1955. *A Maasai Grammar with Vocabulary*. London: Longmans, Green & Co.
Vaux, Bert. 1992. Adjarian's Law and Consonantal ATR in Armenian. In J. Greppin (ed.), *Proceedings of the Fourth International Conference of Armenian Linguistics*. Delmar, NY: Caravan.
Vaux, Bert. 1996. The Status of ATR in Feature Geometry. *Linguistic Inquiry* 27: 175–182.
Zhang, Xi. 1995. Vowel harmony in Oroqen (Tungus). *Toronto Working Papers in Linguistics* 14: 161–174.
Zsiga, Elisabeth C. 1992. A mismatch between morphological and prosodic domains: Evidence from two Igbo rules. *Phonology* 9: 101–135.

Chakir Zeroual and George N. Clements
# The feature [pharyngeal]

## Main sources

McCarthy (1989ab, 1991, 1994), Herzallah (1990), Halle (1989, 1992, 1995), Halle et al. (2000), Clements (1989, 1990, 1993), Clements and Hume (1995), Catford (1968, 1977), Rose (1996), Ladefoged and Maddieson (1996), Esling (1996). Bin-Muqbil (2006), Zeroual (1999, 2000, 2003), Zeroual et al. (2007ab, 2011abc[1]), Zeroual and Crevier-Buchman (2002).

## 1 Overview

Place features have always held a central position in the debate over the lexical representations of segmental contrasts and phonological processes. Indeed, they are often involved in phonological assimilations, and the shift from the feature bundle representations to the Feature Geometry was in part motivated by incoherencies mainly induced by these feature types (Clements 1985, Sagey 1986, McCarthy 1988). Sagey (1986) was the first to have argued for a hierarchical representation of features based on the 'articulatory node' notion (i.e. [labial], [coronal], [dorsal] considered as privative features. Each "articulatory node" dominates the SPE binary place features that it executes. [labial], [coronal], and [dorsal] under the abstract Place node have been adopted by the majority of the post-SPE phonologists.

**Table 1.** The main SPE place features.

|                 | [±anterior] | [±coronal] | [±high] | [±low] | [±back] |
|-----------------|-------------|------------|---------|--------|---------|
| Labial          | +           | −          | −       | −      | −       |
| Alveolar        | +           | +          | −       | −      | −       |
| Palato-alveolar | −           | +          | +       | −      | −       |
| Velar           | −           | −          | +       | −      | +       |
| Uvular          | −           | −          | −       | −      | +       |
| Pharyngeal      | −           | −          | −       | +      | +       |
| Laryngeal       | −           | −          | −       | +      | −       |

---

[1] More recent references (e.g. Zeroual et al. 2011abc) were added by the first author because the data and analyses they provide are consistent with the hypotheses discussed in earlier versions of this paper.

Several studies have pointed out that SPE places features (Table 1) are also not adapted to represent back articulations and to characterize the natural class of gutturals (/χ ʁ ħ ʕ ʔ h/). Indeed, SPE [−anterior, −high] could isolate these gutturals (McCarthy 1989ab, 1991, 1994); while Feature Geometry hypotheses predicts that [−anterior] is specified only for consonants executed by the articulator [coronal].[2] [−high] refers to neither a raised nor lowered tongue body position, which contradicts its high position during the production of uvulars. The process of high vowel lowering induced by gutturals (section 2.1.1) seems to validate their [+low] specification, but the strong coarticulation between the laryngeals and the following high vowels invalidates this specification for all the gutturals (section 3.2.3; Zeroual and Crevier-Buchman 2002).

In fact, even post-SPE analyses fail to propose quite similar representations for these back articulations. These phonological divergences are due to the different and sometimes opposite phonetic characterizations retained for these back consonants, as well as to some variable phonological behaviors of these consonants. They are also attributed to the theoretical hypotheses on which these hierarchical feature models and especially their secondary articulation representations are based.

In this presentation, we distinguish between two main and opposite approaches. Hypothesis 1: The Place node dominates a fourth place feature [pharyngeal] which explains the guttural grouping, as well as many phonological processes involving back segments (McCarthy 1989ab, 1991, 1994; Herzallah 1990, Rose 1996, Clements 1989, 1993). Hypothesis 2: Only [labial], [coronal] and [dorsal] features are dominated by the Place node (Halle 1989, 1992, 1995). Given that the phonological representations of the back consonants are still debated, we discuss some phonological and phonetic arguments provided for these two hypotheses based on phonetic descriptions of the back articulations in Semitic and non-Semitic languages with special focus on those of Moroccan Arabic (MA). We try to identify phonetic correlates of a potential place feature (e.g. [pharyngeal]) shared by all the gutturals. We use as much as possible standard phonetic terms (Table 2) that we adjust progressively.

**Table 2.** Consonants with primary and/or secondary back articulation generally specified for the feature [pharyngeal]. Upper-case letters are used for emphatic consonants.

|             | Coronal emphatic | Uvular | Pharyngeal | Epiglottal | Laryngeal |
|-------------|------------------|--------|------------|------------|-----------|
| Plosive     | /T D/            | /q/    |            | /ʔ/        | /ʔ/       |
| Non-plosive | /S/              | /χ ʁ/  | /ħ ʕ/      | /ʜ ʕ/      | /h ɦ/     |

---

**2** See Sagey (1986) for more convincing pieces of evidence in favor of this analysis.

## 2 Phonological use

### 2.1 Hypothesis 1: Place node dominates the feature [pharyngeal]

[pharyngeal] was proposed initially by McCarthy (1988, 1989ab, 1991, 1994) mainly to characterize the class of gutturals. Hayward and Hayward (1989) provided evidence for a similar feature called [guttural][3] which also appears in the phonological representations of Halle and his colleagues, but with a different phonetic definition.

#### 2.1.1 [pharyngeal] in McCarthy (1989ab, 1991, 1994) and Herzallah (1990)

McCarthy (1988, 1989ab, 1991, 1994) demonstrated the limits of Sagey's (1986) model to account for several phonological processes involving the guttural /χ ʁ ħ ʕ h ʔ/. Among these processes, we have the co-occurrence restrictions in the Arabic (classic and dialectal) $C_1VC_2VC_3$ verbs, where $C_1C_2$, $C_2C_3$ and $C_1C_3$ combinations cannot be formed by two homorganic consonants[4] (Table 3). This process involves consonants that are produced, in general, by the same active articulator ([labial], [coronal] or [dorsal]); for coronals, it also requires the same values for [±continuant] and [±sonorant] features. /χ ʁ ħ ʕ h ʔ/ are restricted even though they involve three different gestures "[a...] glottal one in the [...] laryngeals; retraction of the tongue root and epiglottis and advancement of the posterior wall of the laryngopharynx in the pharyngeals; and a superior-posterior movement of the tongue dorsum in the uvulars" (McCarthy 1989a: 33, and 1994: 196). For this reason, McCarthy (1989ab, 1991, 1994) proposed characterizing the gutturals by the feature [pharyngeal][5] (Figure 1) referring to an "articulatory zone": "the feature [pharyngeal] is defined in terms of a region of the vocal tract (the pharynx) and a particular spectral property (high $F_1$)" (McCarthy 1994: 223; see

---

[3] Referring to McCarthy's (1989a) on the natural class of gutturals, Hayward and Hayward (1989: 190) outlined that "his and our work were undertaken in total independence and although differing in matters of detail, the main thrust of both is to advocate the recognition of this too-long neglected feature".
[4] See also Greenberg (1951), McCarthy (1986), Yip (1989), Pierrehumbert (1993), Elmedlaoui (1995).
[5] [pharyngeal] was also proposed by McCarthy (1988) but as an "articulator feature" that "should properly be added [...] to account for languages like Arabic where the pharynx is a major articulator" (McCarthy 1988: 102). But this definition for the feature [pharyngeal] was not adopted in his subsequent works.

also McCCarthy 1989a: 36). This zone "include[s] the inclusive region from the oropharynx to the larynx" (McCarthy 1989a: 36). Hayward and Hayward (1989) proposed the feature [Guttural] referring also to an "articulatory zone", but "which extends from the end of the oral cavity (i.e. the uvula) to the pharynx. The pharyngeals and the low vowel [ɑ] would be prototypically 'guttural' sounds, but the 'guttural' area could also include laryngeals, uvulars, and all the low vowels, the more front ones being considered to have guttural constriction with very open approximation". (Hayward and Hayward 1989: 187–188).

**Table 3.** Consonant groups involved in the Arabic co-occurrence restrictions. /T D Z/ are emphatic cognate of /t d ð/ respectively.

| Labials | /b m f/ |
|---|---|
| Coronal sonorants | /l n r/ |
| Coronal stops | /t d T D/ |
| Coronal fricatives | /s z ʃ θ ð Z ʒ/ |
| Velars | /g k q/ |
| Gutturals | /χ ʁ ħ ʕ h ʔ/ |

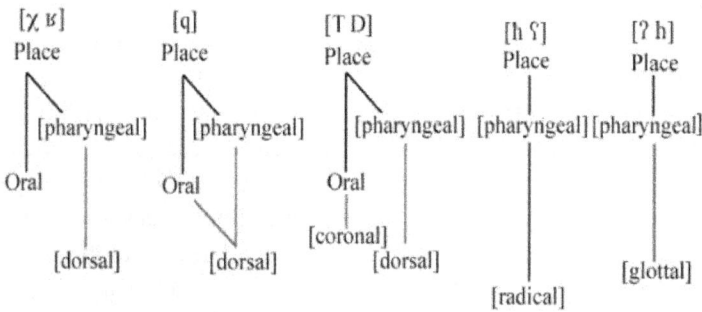

**Figure 1.** McCarthy's model (1989b) for guttural and emphatic consonant representations.

To phonetically support this [pharyngeal] feature, McCarthy (1989a, 1991, 1994) adopted Perkell's (1980) hypothesis according to which the features are "orosensory patterns corresponding to distinctive sound producing states. "These 'orosensory' patterns consist of proprioceptive, tactile and more complicated air-pressure and airflow information from the entire vocal tract" (Perkell 1980: 338). For McCarthy, "the corresponding 'distinctive sound producing state' of [pharyngeal] is high $F_1$, a property that the gutturals share" (McCarthy 1994: 199). Based on El-Halees (1985) perceptual results, McCarthy (1989a, 1991, 1994) added that $F_1$ is not sufficient to characterize gutturals since it also distinguishes pharyngeals from uvulars (see section 3.2.3 and Zeroual and Crevier-Buchman 2002).

Another phonological process can justify the feature [pharyngeal]. In classical Arabic (McCarthy 1989ab, 1991, 1994) three possible imperfective forms correspond to the perfective $C_1a_1C_2a_2C_3$ verbs (Table 4). The "$a_2 \to i$" and "$a_2 \to u$" alternations are unpredictable, whereas "$a_2 \to a$" is conditioned by consonantal context. McCarthy (1989ab, 1991, 1994) underlined that within among 436 $C_1a_1C_2a_2C_3$ verbs having "$a_2 \to a$" alternation, 411 possess a guttural in $C_2$ or $C_3$. He proposed that these $yaC_1C_2aC_3$ forms have an underlying high vowel (/i/ or /u/) that is converted to /a/ by a 'lowering' process which spreads [pharyngeal] from a guttural to these two vowels.

**Table 4.** Examples of imperfective forms of $C_1a_1C_2a_2C_3$ Arabic verbs. G = guttural.

| Perfective | Alternation | Imperfective | Examples |
|---|---|---|---|
| $C_1a_1C_2a_2C_3$ | "$a_2 \to i$" | $yaC_1C_2iC_3$ | [Daraba] vs. [jaDribu] 'beat' |
| | | | [ʒalasa] vs. [jaʒlisu] 'take a seat' |
| | "$a_2 \to u$" | $yaC_1C_2uC_3$ | [kataba] vs. [jaktubu] 'write' |
| | | | [ħadaθa] vs. [jaħduθu] 'happen' |
| | "$a_2 \to a$" | $yaC_1C_2aC_3$ | [faʕala] vs. [jafʕalu] 'do' |
| | $C_2$ or $C_3$ = G | | [baχasa] vs. [jabχasu] 'be cheap' |

McCarthy (1989ab, 1991, 1994) also provided data from several Semitic languages where only gutturals are transparent to some total vocalic harmonies. In Hebrew, for example, a schwa is inserted after a guttural coda; its quality is the same as the vowel of the preceding syllable. To represent this guttural transparency, McCarthy (1991, 1994) divided Place into two class nodes Oral and Pharyngeal (Figure 1). The guttural transparency process is analyzed as the spreading of the Oral node which is absent in the gutturals.

Co-occurrence restrictions are also significant within /q χ ʁ k g/, suggesting that uvulars are [dorsal] (McCarthy 1989ab, 1991, 1994). For McCarthy (1989ab, 1991, 1994), /q/ is an emphatic consonant, produced with a major dorsal articulator and a secondary [pharyngeal] articulation; while the guttural uvulars are "primarily [pharyngeal]s with secondary [dorsal] specification" McCarthy (1989a: 48). Since /q/ must be specified for the feature [pharyngeal], McCarthy (1989a) proposed that gutturals are [pharyngeal] and [+approximant].[6] However, his first analyses show that the guttural class can also be isolated while using place features only (Figure 1). Indeed, according to these characterizations, the gut-

---

[6] This feature was introduced by Clements (1989: draft version, 1990: published version). For this phonological feature [±approximant], Clements (1990: 293) provides the phonetic definition: "I will consider an approximant to be any sound produced with an oral tract stricture open enough so that airflow through it is turbulent only if it is voiceless".

tural class regroups the segments that have place features under the node [pharyngeal]. To distinguish the pharyngeals from the laryngeals, McCarthy (1989b) specified [radical][7] for pharyngeals and [glottal] for laryngeals placed under the node [pharyngeal] (Figure 1). For McCarthy (1989a), emphatic consonants are "primary [coronal]" and "secondary [pharyngeal]", and in McCarthy (1989b, 1991, 1994) he added [dorsal] to their representations (Figure 1).

Arabic guttural laryngeals must be specified for [pharyngeal] even though it has often been claimed that they are placeless (Clements 1985, Sagey 1986, Steriade 1987, Keating 1990).[8] To explain the variable behaviors of laryngeals, McCarthy (1989a, 1991, 1994), as well as Hess (1990) and Nolan (1995), suggested that laryngeals that pattern as gutturals are aryepiglottal. McCarthy (1989a, 1991, 1994) also adopted the Node Activation Condition (NAC) proposed by Avery & Rice (1988) to explain some variable behaviors of coronals. According to this principle, "if a feature is distinctive for a class of segments in a phonological system, then the node which dominates that feature is said to be activated for that class of segments. Active nodes must be present in underlying representation. Inactive nodes are absent in underlying representation" (McCarthy 1989a 26: 52). This principle predicts that laryngeals are specified for [pharyngeal] only in a language having several gutturals.

Herzallah's hierarchical model (1990) combined McCarthy's (1989ab) and Clements' (Clements 1989, 1990, 1993, Clements and Hume 1995) hypothesizes. Indeed, she adopted the feature [pharyngeal] that she grouped with [labial], [coronal] and [dorsal] directly under the "C-place" introduced by Clements (1989, 1993). As in Clements (1989, 1993), she analyzed the vowels and the consonants by the same articulatory nodes [labial], [coronal], [dorsal], and [pharyngeal].[9] Since the secondary articulation is generally considered, as "the superimposition of a close-vowel-like articulation on a consonant" (IPA 1999: 17), Herzallah (1990) represented it, as in Clements (1989, 1993), by a 'V-place' dominating material which varies with the nature of this secondary articulation.

---

[7] In Clements (1993: 105), [radical] "caractérise les sons produits avec une constriction formée par la racine de la langue dans la partie inférieure du pharynx". In Ladefoged (2001: 259) radical is also used "to apply as a cover term for [pharyngeal] and [epiglottal] articulations made with the root of the tongue".
[8] Indeed, laryngeals are transparent to total vocalic harmonies (Steriade 1987), and do not have invariant articulatory or acoustic targets (Keating 1990).
[9] [labial] for labial consonants and rounded vowels; [coronal] for dental, alveolar, palatoalveolar, palatal, and retroflex consonants and front vowels; [dorsal] for velar, uvular consonants and high back vowels; and [pharyngeal] for guttural consonants and low vowels. Note that in McCarthy (1989ab, 1991, 1994) and Sagey (1986) the vowels are represented by [±high, ±low, ±back] features executed by the articulator [dorsal].

Based on some preliminary analyses proposed by McCarthy (1989ab) for uvlars and emphatics, Herzallah (1990) proposed specifying, for /q χ ʁ/, "[dorsal] which refers to the articulator which is activated (or raised in this case), and [pharyngeal] which refers to the site (i.e. place) in which the activity of the dorsum takes place" (Herzallah 1990: 52). She proposed (Figure 2) identical place feature representations for /q χ ʁ/ and adopted the feature [+approximant] to isolate /χ ʁ ħ ʕ h ʔ/ considered as [pharyngeal, +approximant] (Figure 2). She also proposed exhaustive analyses for emphatic consonants arguing that their secondary articulation is a dorsopharyngealisation or uvularization and must be specified for [pharyngeal] and [dorsal][10] features placed under 'V-place' node (Figure 2).

**Table 5.** The 'imâla' process in Palestinian Arabic (Herzallah 1990: 59). [K x ɣ] are correspondent of Classical Arabic [q χ ʁ].

| Noun+i | | Noun+a | | | |
|---|---|---|---|---|---|
| [naml-i] | 'ant' | [furS-a] | 'a chance' | [samaK-a] | 'red dirt' |
| [ħilm-i] | 'dream' | [baTT-a] | 'a duck' | [farx-a] | 'a young hen' |
| [samak-i] | 'fish" | [ħaar-a] | 'neighborhood' | [marɣ+a] | 'loitering' |
| [zibd-i] | 'butter' | | | [simʕ-a] | 'reputation' |
| | | | | [walh-a] ' | 'a surprise' |

She adopted these representations (in Figure 2) to explain the 'imâla' process (Table 5) observed in Palestinian Arabic where the suffix of the feminine is realized /i/ or /e/ after an oral consonant, but /a/ after the emphatics, uvulars, pharyngeals and laryngeals. Herzallah (1990) represented this process by the propagation of the feature [pharyngeal] from the gutturals and even the emphatics and the uvular /q/. Furthermore, Herzallah (1990) noticed that Palestinian Arabic CaCaC verbs, where a radical consonant is emphatic or uvular, have in their imperfective forms /u/ instead of an expected /i/ (Table 6).[11] She considered that this alternation is trigged by the spreading of the feature [dorsal] from uvular or emphatic consonants toward the underlying thematic vowel /i/.

McCarthy (1989b, 1994) has also proposed representations that bring the emphatics closer to the uvulars: "the emphatics and q have a constriction in the upper pharynx similar to that of the uvular gutturals χ and ʁ. [...] all studies, now encompassing several different dialect areas, find that the emphatics have a constriction in the upper pharynx. The so-called pharyngealized consonants of

---

[10] These two features also appear in the emphatic representations (see Figure 1) of McCarthy (1989b).
[11] Post-palatal /k/ is not involved in this 'dorsalisation' process which is not expected.

Arabic should really be called uvularized" (McCarthy 1994: 218–219). McCarthy (1991, 1994) mentioned Arabic co-occurrence restrictions within /k g T D/ which constitute another phonological argument in favor of the specification of [dorsal] to emphatics.[12]

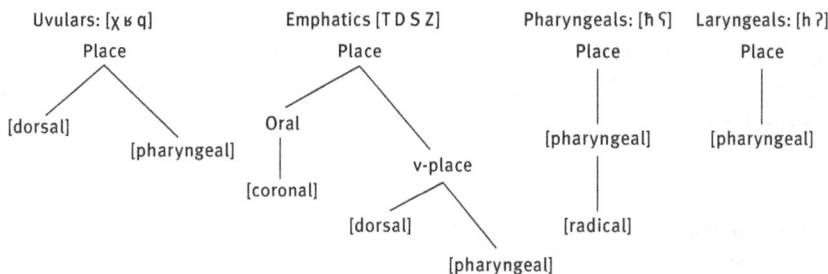

**Figure 2.** Herzallah's (1990) model for guttural and emphatic consonant representations.

To distinguish the pharyngeals from the laryngeals, Herzallah (1990) adopted the feature [Radical] under the node [pharyngeal] (Figure 2). In their formal representations for /χ ʁ q/ and emphatic consonants, Herzallah (1990) and McCarthy (1989ab, 1991, 1994) made no reference to the tongue root, which is not entirely in line with their phonetic properties. Their models, as discussed below, do not predict why uvulars and pharyngeals (and emphatics) may pattern together without laryngeals (Rose 1996).

**Table 6.** The 'dorsalisation' process in Palestinian Arabic (Herzallah 1990). [x ɣ] are correspondents of Classical Arabic [χ ʁ].

| Perfective | Imperfective | gloss |
| --- | --- | --- |
| katab | yiktib | 'he wrote/he writes' |
| malas | yimlis | 'he leveled/he levels' |
| Salab | yuSlub | 'he crucified/he crucifies' |
| ʃaTab | yuʃTub | 'he crossed out/he crosses out' |
| saxan | yusxun | 'he got hot/he gets …' |
| nabaɣ | yunbuɣ | 'he reached/he reaches' |

---

**12** Phonetics hypotheses are provided in Zeroual et al. (2007b) and Zeroual et al. (2011c) to explain MA restricted *Tk clusters.

## 2.1.2 Pharyngeal in Rose (1996)

Rose (1996) focused her analyses on some variable phonological behaviors of the laryngeals observed even in languages that have several guttural consonants. She provided data from some Semitic and non-Semitic languages where the uvulars, pharyngeals and emphatics form a natural class to the exclusion of the laryngeals. Data from Salish languages show that /i/ and /u/ become, in some paradigms, /e/ and /o/ respectively when they are in the context of emphatic, uvular or pharyngeal consonants (Table 7). According to Rose (1996), this process is different from the high vowel 'lowering' triggered by gutturals in the Semitic languages which converts /u i/ to /a/. She proposed that in Salish languages, we have a 'retraction' process that draws these high vowels backwards and downwards when they co-occur with uvulars, pharyngeals or emphatics.

**Table 7.** The 'retracting' process in the Salish Thompson language (Rose 1996).

| /ʔiq't/ | [ʔeq't] | 'scraped off' |
|---|---|---|
| /ʔuqʷeʔ/ | [ʔoqʷeʔ] | 'drink' |
| /maʕ't/ | [mʌʕ't] | 'broken' |
| /niʔhelus/ | [niʔhelus] | 'good-natured' |
| /miceʔq/ | [micæʔq] | 'sit' |
| /snəʔZ/ | [snʌʔZ] | 'mountain goat hair blanket' |

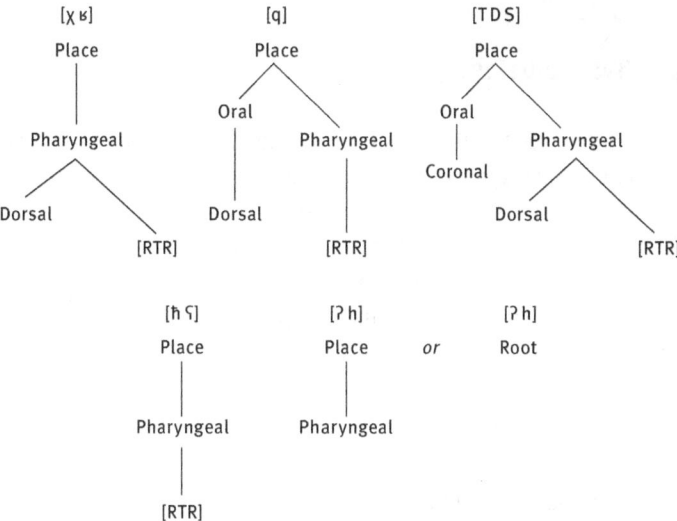

**Figure 3.** Rose's (1996) models for guttural and emphatic consonant representations.

To account for these data, Rose (1996: 86) adopted the feature Pharyngeal, but she added that: "The feature that groups emphatics, uvulars and pharyngeals together is the feature [RTR], and I conclude that this feature is responsible for emphasis and the similar retraction caused by uvulars and pharyngeals, as seen in Moroccan Arabic and Berber. This parallels conclusions reached by Goad (1991) and Davis (1992, 1995), who also argue that emphasis harmony found in Arabic dialects involves the feature [RTR]". Rose (1996) analyzed this process as the spreading of [RTR]. She added that [RTR] is different from [ATR] and is specified only for consonants, since its spreading effect is non-structure preserving. According to this analysis, the 'retraction' process in Salish does not involve the laryngeals, not because they are placeless segments, but because they do not have the [RTR] feature.[13]

Rose (1996) proposed specifying [pharyngeal], [dorsal] and [RTR] for the emphatics and the uvular /q χ ʁ/ (Figure 3). She analyzed /q/ as emphatic having a primary Dorsal and a secondary [RTR] and /χ ʁ/ as primary [RTR] and secondary Dorsal. For Rose (1996) Pharyngeals have the features [pharyngeal] and [RTR]. Rose (1996) adopted the Node Activation Condition (NAC) and predicted that laryngeals were specified for the feature [pharyngeal] only in the languages that possess several guttural consonants.[14] According to her model (Figure 3), gutturals are segments that do not have place features under the Oral node.

## 2.2 Hypothesis 2: Place node does not dominate a feature [pharyngeal]

### 2.2.1 Halle (1989, 1992, 1995)

Halle (1989, 1992, 1995) extends the articulatory node notion of Sagey (1986) to the back cavity and groups his Tongue Root and Larynx articulatory nodes under a non-terminal node called 'Guttural' (Figure 4) that is phonetically motivated: "The existence of the Guttural node dominating these two articulators formally reflects the fact that the two articulators are more intimately linked to one another phonetically and leads us to expect such inter-actions" (Halle 1995: 18). For Halle (1989, 1992, 1995), /χ ʁ/ are complex segments produced with major Tongue Root (TR) and secondary tongue back (Dorsal) articulators; the major articulator for the pharyngeals is TR whereas the major articulator for laryngeals

---
[13] See Shahin (1997, 2002) for a different phonological analysis for Salish laryngeals.
[14] Analyses of loanwords provided by Paradis and LaCharité (2001) seem to support this hypothesis.

is Larynx.[15] For Halle (1992, 1995) gutturals are thus argued to be segments produced with a major articulator dominated by the Guttural node.

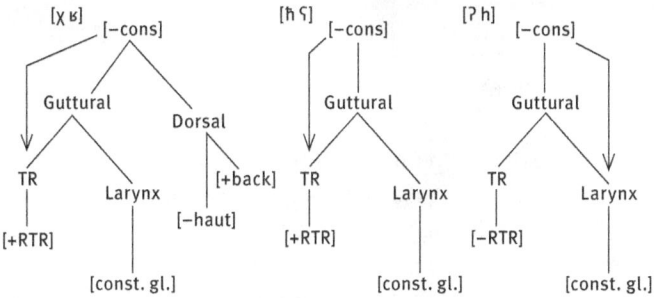

Figure 4. Halle's model (1995) for guttural consonant representations.

In fact, Halle's (1989, 1992, 1995) model is inspired by a phonological hypothesis presented in Sagey (1986) for the representation of a complex segment, which predicts that only a major articulator can have different values for the feature [±continuant]. Since the manner contrast between /χʁ/ (continuant) and /q/ (non-continuant) is implemented by the dorsum, this latter seems to be their major articulator contrary to Halle's prediction (1989, 1992, 1995; see below that this conclusion is adopted by Halle el al. 2000). Halle's model is also based on a theoretical assumption claiming that only the segments whose major articulator is [labial], [coronal] or [dorsal] can have different specifications for manner or major class features. This hypothesis predicts, for example, no possible contrast between pharyngeals in terms of the [±continuant] feature. However, phonetic evidence show that epiglottal segments may be produced with a different manner of articulation (see section 3.1).

Halle et al. (2000) proposed a modified version of Halle's (1995) model, where a secondary articulation is represented without the use of a 'pointer'. Indeed, Halle et al. (2000) proposed placing not only binary features, but also unary articulatory features (i.e., [labial], [coronal], [dorsal], [rhinal], [radical], [glottal]) under the articulatory nodes. In this model, segments with secondary articulation are specified for all the place features under the major articulator node, but only for the binary features under the secondary articulator node (Figure 5). In this model, Halle et al. (2000) claimed that only the 'designed articulator' feature (articulator that executes manner and major class features) must appear in the feature tree. Based on this hypothesis, Halle et al. (2000) proposed representations for uvulars and emphatics showing clearly that they are dorsals produced

---

15 Halle (1989, 1992; 1995) does not provide any analysis for [q].

without tongue root involvement; the dorsum is considered as a major articulator for uvulars and as secondary for emphatics. However, Halle et al. (2000) did not provide representations for the rest of gutturals.

### 2.2.2 Bin-Muqbil (2006)

Bin-Muqbil (2006) extends the model of Halle et al. (2000) to include gutturals, but began by replacing Place and Tongue Root nodes by Oral and Pharynx respectively (Figure 6). He considered Pharynx as an "active articulator"[16] that "extends from the anterior faucal pillars to the larynx, inclusively" (Bin-Muqbil 2006: 246–247). He adds that this articulator is associated with several muscles (intrinsic laryngeal muscles, pharyngeal constrictors, the palatoglossus, the soft palate muscles) which possess a source of neuronal activation that does not participate in the contraction of the muscles responsible for the oral articulations. He also considered that "tongue root-based articulations are clearly not mainly executed by any of the tongue muscles. Rather such articulations are controlled by the pharyngeal constrictors" (Bin-Muqbil 2006: 249). This neuromotoric hypothesis for Pharynx as an active articulator arises from his examination of guttural X-ray tracings and his acoustic measurements of V-to-V coarticulation. To interpret these data, Bin-Muqbil (2006: 224) admitted that "the tongue dorsum is the main articulator of vowels". He based this conclusion on some electromyographic studies (Honda et al. 1992, Maeda and Honda 1994) showing that vowel articulations are mainly achieved by the contraction of the extrinsic tongue muscles: genioglossus, styloglossus, and hyoglossus.

Based on his acoustic investigations, Bin-muqbil (2006) also showed that pharyngeals and laryngeals are less resistant to V-to-V coarticulation since they do not intrinsically involve the tongue body but the tongue root (pharyngeal constrictors) and the larynx (intrinsic laryngeal muscles) respectively. He specified Pharynx and [radical] for these consonants and considered that pharyngeals are [+RTR] and laryngeals [–RTR] (Figure 6), since only the former induce $F_1$ raising. As the emphatics are the most resistant to V-to-V coarticulation, and they do not induce important $F_1$ raising, Bin-Muqbil (2006: 241) suggested that their sec-

---

**16** Zawaydeh (2003) has also proposed that the "pharynx can also be considered an active articulator, and thus it is not just a 'place' of articulation like the teeth or the hard palate. We can consider it an active articulator because its diameter can be changed during speech. This point has been made by Hardcastle (1976)" (Zawaydeh, 2003: 280). Even in McCarthy (1988) [pharyngeal] refers not to a "place of articulation" but to "a major articulator" as in the case of [labial], [coronal] and [dorsal] features.

ondary articulation "largely employs the tongue dorsum" without tongue root involvement. He proposed a phonological representation for these emphatic segments which is more similar to the one proposed by Halle et al. (2000) (Figure 5 and Figure6).

According to Bin Muqbil (2006) uvulars have intermediate resistance magnitude to V-to-V coarticulation that varies with the degree of constriction (/q/ > /χ/ > /ʁ/), and their production seems to involve the soft palate. He suggested that their backward and upward dorsum movements are achieved "mainly by the action of the palatoglossus along with the velar depressors (for [ʁ]) and velar tensors (for [χ] and [q])" Bin Muqbil (2006: 242). He added that, during uvulars, the styglossus would be active and its degree of activation "increases in line with the degree of constriction" (Bin Muqbil 2006: 242), but the hyoglossus would be inactive to permit upward dorsum movement. He specified uvulars for both Tongue Body and Pharynx articulatory nodes, but added that they "are primarily guttural and secondarily dorsal". For Bin-Muqbil (2006), uvulars are guttural due mainly to the "active participation" of the soft palate, and [−RTR] since they do not induce important $F_1$ raising.

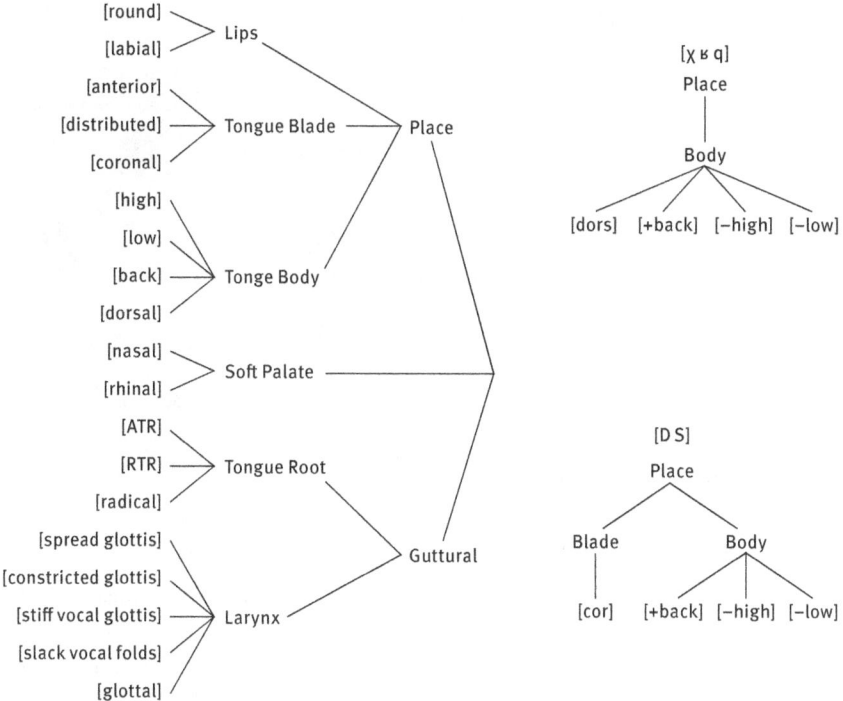

**Figure 5.** Halle et al. (2000)'s model for some guttural and emphatic consonant representations.

In order to exclude /q/ from the class of gutturals, Bin-Muqbil (2006) rejected the analysis according to which all the latter are [+approximant], since his acoustic investigations as well as some influential phonetic descriptions show that /χ ʁ/ are generally achieved as fricatives (Ladefoged and Maddieson 1996, Catford 1977). He proposes that the guttural sounds are segments specified for the articulatory [radical] and the manner [+continuant] features.

Although Bin-Muqbil (2006) tried to explain several phonological processes involving the guttural and emphatic consonants, his hierarchical model is based on two phonetic and phonological hypotheses that still remain very controversial. He adopted the main phonological assumptions of Halle et al. (2000) for the secondary articulation representation which is not the unique model for this type of articulation. He also considered that uvulars are produced with an "active participation" of the soft palate which is not a common articulatory characterization attributed to these consonants. Indeed, some previous articulatory investigations have mentioned that the uvular guttural consonants are produced with a lower position of the soft palate (Ali and Daniloff 1981[17], Zeroual 2000). Even Delattre's (1971) figures show that the velum is low during the uvular fricatives and most importantly during /q/. However, no one of these studies has explicitly claimed that this participation is active.

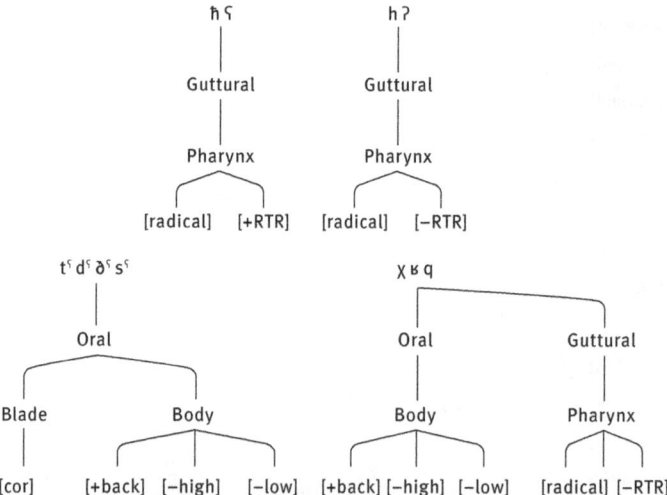

**Figure 6.** Bin-Muqbil's model (2006) for guttural and emphatic consonant representations.

---

[17] "In all [q] sequences examined, the velum approached and nearly approximated contact with the tongue during [q] production. In other words, only for [q] production is more than tongue movement alone involved in cavity constriction" Ali and Daniloff (1972: 91). In this study, only emphatics and [q] were investigated.

# 3 Phonetic definitions

## 3.1 Terminological considerations: Pharyngeal vs. epiglottal.

The characterization of the place of articulation of back consonants remains very controversial even at the phonetic level. For this reason, we define the two main and standard terms pharyngeal vs. epiglottal generally used to define these consonants phonetically.

Pharyngeal is generally associated to an articulation produced by tongue root retraction toward the posterior oropharyngeal wall (Ladefoged and Maddieson 1996, Catford 1977, Laver 1994). Catford (1977) called this articulation type "linguo-pharyngeal" and opposed it to "faucal or transverse pharyngeal" produced only by a lateral compression of the "faucal pillars". Epiglottal articulation is achieved mainly by a pronounced backward epiglottis movement toward the posterior laryngopharyngeal wall. This movement results in a first constriction between the tip of the epiglottis and the pharyngeal wall (epiglotto-pharyngeal constriction[18]), and a second constriction between the arytenoids, the base of the epiglottis and the aryepiglottic folds (aryepiglottal constriction).

For Catford (1977: 163), "[Faucal or transverse pharyngeal] appears to be the most common articulation of the pharyngeal approximants [ħ] and [ʕ]". However, several authors have demonstrated that modern Arabic dialects possess epiglottal and not pharyngeal consonants (Laufer et al. 1979; Laufer et al., 1988; Ladefoged and Maddieson 1996; Zeroual 1999, 2000; Zeroual and Crevier-Buchman 2002). In this paper we give other arguments from MA in favor of this analysis and propose using the symbol /ʜ ʢ/ instead of /ħ ʕ/ for Arabic. Agul seems to be the unique case of language that has /ħ ʕ/ which contrasts phonologically with /ʜ ʢ/ (Ladefoged and Maddieson 1996). The phonetic descriptions provided in the literature suggest that the pharyngeal articulations are often "linguo-pharyngeal" and secondary (e.g. pharyngealized vowels and consonants). Phonetic investigations of Traill (1985) showed that epiglottal articulation is also attested as a secondary articulation in Khosian languages.

Esling (1996) is the first author to propose that all the consonants considered as pharyngeal and epiglottal are generally aryepiglottal. He adds that the aryepiglottic constriction is partial during /ħ ʕ ʜ ʢ/ and total during /ʔ/, and that during /ʜ ʢ/, the aryepiglottic folds apply more strongly against the base of the epiglottis while vibrating. Esling's model predicts that all the articulations produced in the pharyngeal cavity (upper and lower parts) have an aryepiglottic constriction.

---

[18] Adapted from Catford (1968).

Taking into consideration the results of several phonetic experiments on MA back consonants, we test various articulatory and acoustic parameters that have been proposed as possible correlates for the feature [pharyngeal]. We use pharyngeal and epiglottal to characterize an articulation in the upper-part and lower-part of the pharyngeal cavity respectively, and aryepiglottal to refer to an articulation at the aryepiglottic level.

## 3.2 Possible phonetic correlates of a feature [pharyngeal]

### 3.2.1 Pharyngeal and laryngeal postures (endoscopic data)

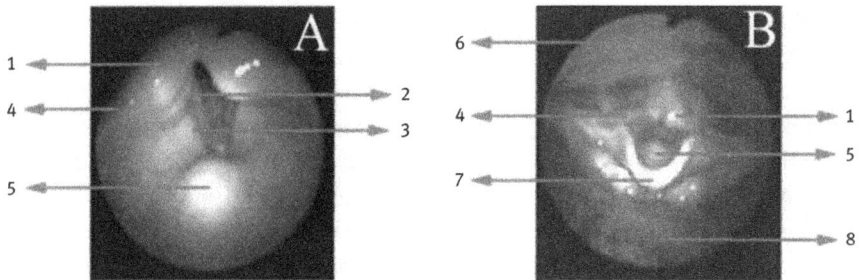

**Figure 7.** 1. Arytenoid cartilage, 2. Vocal fols, 3. Ventricular folds, 4. Aryepiglottic folds, 5. Base of the epiglottis, 6. Posterior pharyngeal wall, 7. Tip of the epiglottis, 8. Tongue back. A. Laryngeal cavity; B. Pharyngeal cavity.

To observe the postures of the pharyngeal (Figure 7B) and the laryngeal cavities (Figure 7A) we carried out a fiberscopic experiment during which an endoscope, connected to a micro camera Olympus OTV-SF (25 frames/second), was inserted through a nostril of one MA subject (34 years old). This endoscope was placed in two different positions: behind the uvula to observe the movements of the tongue, the epiglottis and the pharyngeal walls (Figure 7B), and just above the laryngeal cavity to examine the postures of glottal and supraglottal levels (Figure 7A). We used MA words where the consonants /s z S χ ʁ ʜ ʕ h/ appear in three symmetrical vocalic contexts (iCi, aCa, and uCu) with the stress on the second vowel.

/ʜ ʕ/ are produced, in VCV, by a retraction of the epiglottis, the tip of which reaches a very close position to the posterior laryngopharyngeal wall (epiglotto-pharyngeal articulation); the tongue root also moves back (Figure 10). During /χ ʁ/, the articulation in the pharyngeal cavity is achieved by a more raised[19] part

---

[19] We can infer the height of the tongue back from the degree of brightness as well as the size of the illuminated parts of the tongue (Kagaya, 1974).

of the back of the tongue, particularly in iCi and uCu compared to aCa contexts, but the epiglottis remains more distant from the posterior oropharyngeal wall. The back articulation during /S/ is very similar to the one during /χ ʁ/. During /h s/, no pharyngeal articulation is observed and the tongue root coarticulates strongly with the adjacent vowels: closer to the epiglottis in aCa than in iCi and uCu. /s S χ/ are produced (Figure 11) while the glottis is open along its entire length; this corresponds to the typical glottis posture of a voiceless segment (Ladefoged 1971, Sawashima et al. 1980, Laver 1994, Zeroual 1999, 2000, Zeroual et al. 2006). The maximal glottis opening is however larger during /χ/ compared to /s S/.[20] /ʁ/ is generally produced while the glottis is closed along its entire length which is typical for a voiced segment. However, during /h/ in /VCV/, the anterior part of the glottis is closed and its posterior part slightly open, which is in line with its breathy voice phonation mode (see Fig. 8). Only /ʜ ʕ/ have an anterior-posterior compression of the aryepiglottic sphincter that is more pronounced during /ʕ/ than /ʜ/.

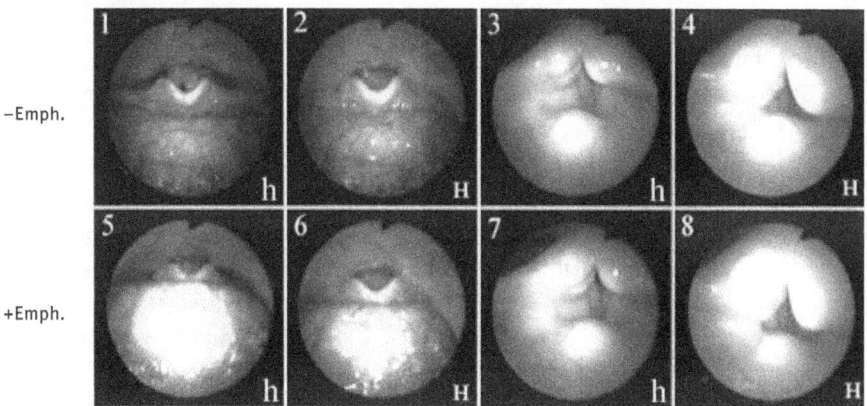

**Figure 8.** Pharyngeal and laryngeal cavity postures during MA /h/ and /ʜ/ in a non-emphatic (−Emph) or non pharyngealized and in an emphatic contexts (+Emph = before an emphatic consonant). In these contexts, /h/ is produced as [ɦ].

The epiglotto-pharyngeal constriction seems too large to generate the turbulence during /ʜ/ (Figure 10) suggesting that the major articulation for the epiglottals is at the aryepiglottic and/or glottic level. This hypothesis has also been suggested by Ghazeli (1977: 49): "Although this is highly speculative, it seems to me that the friction during /ħ/ is created by intralaryngeal adjustments rather than the relatively wide constriction between the epiglottis and the pharyngeal wall". Yeou

---

**20** This glottis difference is discussed in Zeroual (2000, 2003) and Zeroual et al. (2006).

and Maeda (1995) elaborated a three tube model for /ʜ/ based on Ghazeli's (1977) cine-radiographic data, its theoretical resonant frequencies have been compared to the ones measured during /ʜ/ produced by four MA speakers. This comparison showed that $F_2$ of /ʜ/ is associated with the Helmoltz resonator showing that, during /ʜ/, even the cavity posterior to the epiglotto-pharyngeal constriction is excited and confirming that its turbulence is generated at the laryngeal level.[21]

Epiglottal consonants are therefore closer to the laryngeals than to the uvulars. Jakobson (1957) have also made a connection between Arabic "pharyngeal" and laryngeal consonants, but he considered the former as pharyngealized (or emphatic) laryngeals.[22] This hypothesis is not confirmed by our articulatory data (Figure 8). Indeed, /ʜ/ in an emphatic context (Figure 8, pictures 6 and 8) is pharyngealized but remains epiglottal (more precisely aryepiglottal) even though the part of the tongue that retracts during its production is higher compared to its cognate placed in a non-emphatic context (Figure 8, pictures 2 and 4). Furthermore, /h/ before an emphatic consonant (Figure 8, pictures 5 and 7) is produced with a secondary articulation that is similar to the one observed during /S/ (i.e. /h/ is pharyngealized), but without any anterior-posterior aryepiglottic compression.

Based on the phonetic definitions presented in the section 3.1, we can deduce that MA /χ ʁ S/ have a pharyngeal articulation. Since this later is secondary during /S/, it must be characterized as pharyngealization. This characterization is considered here as an articulatory component and used instead of uvularisation. /χ ʁ S/ show clearly that a pharyngeal articulation can be produced without necessarily being combined with aryepiglottal constriction. MA does not have pharyngeal /ħ ʕ/ but epiglottal /ʜ ʢ/ produced with epiglotto-pharyngeal and aryepiglottal constrictions (see also Zeroual 1999, 2000, Zeroual and Crevier-Buchman 2002). MA /h/ is produced without any pharyngeal or aryepiglottal constriction.

Our fiberscopic data do not permit the isolation of articulatory correlates shared by MA guttural and emphatic consonants. Indeed, these consonants have different places of articulation: pharyngeal, epiglottal (epiglotto-pharyngeal, aryepiglottal) and glottal[23] involving different articulators (tongue root, epiglottis, and the larynx).

---

[21] Further aerodynamic arguments in favor of this conclusion are presented in Zeroual (2000, 2003).

[22] "Students endeavoring to master /ħ/ are advised by Gairdner to pronounce an ordinary glottal /h/ and "try to tighten the pharynx during its production" (p. 27). In other words, /ħ/ is essentially a pharyngealized laryngeal" (Jakobson 1957: 518).

[23] These observations do not agree with the conclusion of Laufer and Baer (1988: 193–194) according to which: "emphatic and pharyngeal consonants share the same type of articulation in the pharynx. During production of these sounds, we saw that the epiglottis forms a constric-

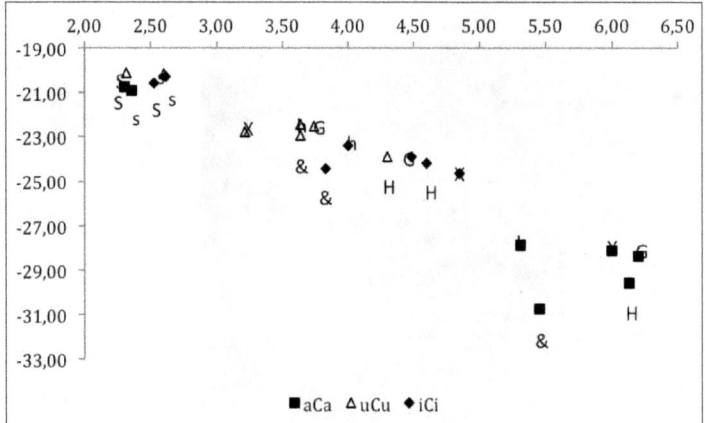

**Figure 9.** Mean values (7 tokens) of vertical (y-axis) and horizontal (x-axis) jaw positions (in mm) during MA /s S χ ʁ н ʕ h/ produced in /iCi, uCu, aCa/ within MA words and nonsense words by one MA speaker. /X G H & h/ = /χ ʁ н ʕ h/. In these contexts, MA /h/ is produced as [ɦ].

### 3.2.2 Jaw postures (EMA data)

More recent studies assume that the jaw can be actively controlled to reach the medio-sagittal targets, but the degree of its involvement varies with the segment type. Mooshammer et al., (2006) suggested that a high jaw target aligned with the release of /t/ is necessary to enhance the spectral properties of its burst. For Elgendy (1999) 'pharyngeal' consonants are produced with an active jaw lowering to help the tongue root and the epiglottis to be retracted more easily. Goldstein (1994: 238) demonstrated, however, that "the class of guttural consonants could be defined as involving Gestures that are produced with coordinative structures in which the jaw does not participate". According to Goldstein (1994), the guttural class regroups the segments shearing similar jaw patterns. To test these hypotheses, we present the vertical and horizontal positions of the jaw[24] at the midpoint of MA /s S χ ʁ н ʕ h/ produced in iCi, uCu, and aCa contexts (Figure 9) within MA words and nonsense words.

---

tion with the pharyngeal walls and that the root of the tongue, at the bottom of the pharynx, also moves backward. As we expected, the main difference between the emphatics and the pharyngeals, as seen in the pharynx, is in the degree of constriction".

[24] Our EMA data was collected at the Institut für Phonetik, Munich using 3-dimensional EMA technique (AG500 Carstens Medizinelektronik, Hoole et al. 2010).

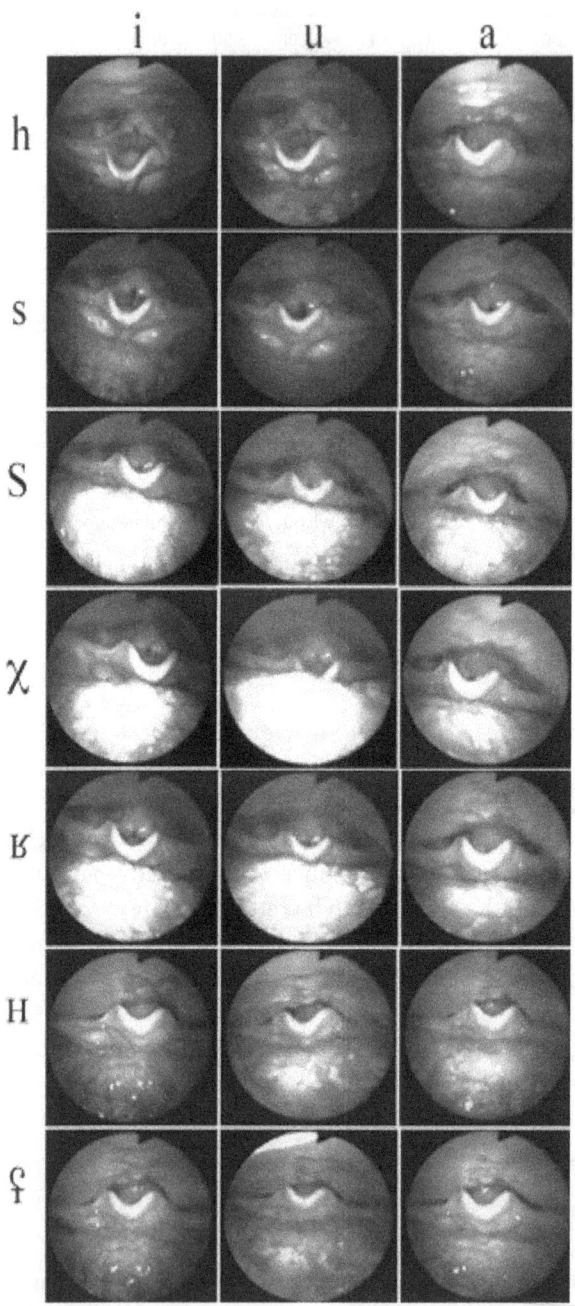

**Figure 10.** Pharyngeal cavity postures during MA /h s S χ ʁ H ʕ/ in three symmetrical aCa, iCi and uCu contexts within MA words and nonsense words. In these contexts, /h/ is produced as [ɦ].

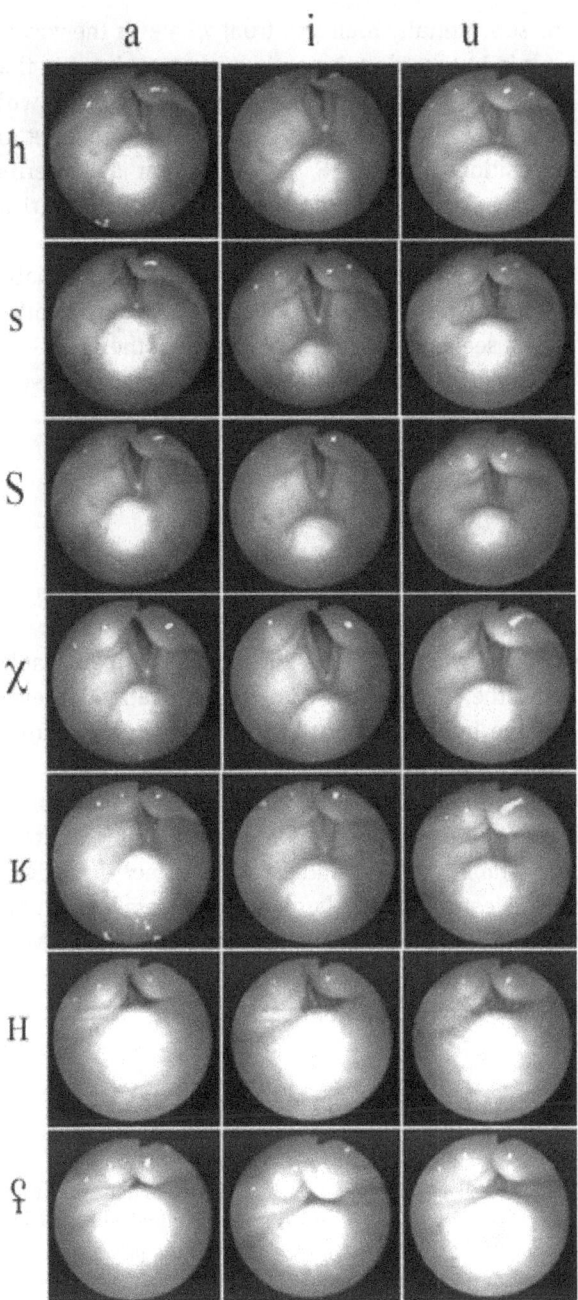

**Figure 11.** Laryngeal cavity postures during MA /h s S χ ʁ H ʕ/ in three symmetrical aCa, iCi and uCu contexts within MA words and nonsense words. In these contexts, /h/ is produced as [ɦ].

During /s S/ the jaw remains substantially high and front whatever the vocalic context (Figure 9). This result is in accord with previous studies showing that /s/ and /t/ possess the highest jaw position that coarticulates weakly with adjacent vowels (Keating et al. 1994; Mooshammer et al., 2006, Zeroual et al. 2007a).[25] Similar (high) jaw positions during /s S/ also show that jaw lowering is not required for tongue root retraction[26] during /S/. However, variable vertical and horizontal jaw positions are observed during /χ ʁ ʜ ʕ h/: mid-high and mid-retracted in iCi and uCu, but very low and more retracted in aCa. This variable jaw positions during /χ ʁ ʜ ʕ h/ can be attributed to their strong coarticulation with the adjacent vowels, which seems to confirm the main hypothesis of Goldstein (1994) according to which gutturals would be produced with a very weak degree of jaw activation.[27]

### 3.2.3 Possible acoustic correlates for the feature [pharyngeal]

Zawaydeh (2003) showed that $F_1$ at the midpoint of Jordanian Arabic /a i/ is significantly higher after guttural /χ ʁ ʜ ʕ h/ than oral /s k/. This result is in line with the acoustic study carried out by Shahin (1997, 2002) on Palestinian Arabic. Shahin (1997, 2002) attributed the raised $F_1$ to a tongue root retraction even during laryngeals. However, the hypothesis of the tongue root participation during laryngeals has not been confirmed by our endoscopic data[28] (see section 3.2.1). Zawaydeh (2003) also showed that the pharyngeal cavity width during the Jordanian Arabic laryngeal and the oral /s k/ is not significantly different. She concluded that "[...] the Arabic guttural natural class is not exclusively articulatory based; the acoustic feature [high $F_1$] unites the guttural sound, not the articulatory feature [pharyngeal Diameter]" (Zawaydeh 2003: 291). More recently, Shahin (2009 and 2011: endoscopic data) also observed that during the Arabic laryngeal consonants, the epiglottis and the aryepiglottic sphincter are not involved.

---

[25] The jaw target position is aligned with the release of /t/ (Zeroual et al. 2007a).
[26] In Zeroual et al. (2007a) we showed that jaw position during [T] is as high as during [t], even though the former is apical and has very short VOT and the latter laminal with very long VOT. We suggested that the unexpected high position of the jaw during [T] is "probably to compensate for the lowering of the [anterior part of the] tongue due to the retraction of its root to produce the emphasis" Zeroual et al. (2007a: 399).
[27] For Lee (1995: 358) the jaw may participate but in different manners for guttural vs. oral consonant: "jaw raising for orals vs. no jaw raising (lowering or no participation) for gutturals".
[28] This laryngeal property was mentioned in our works since Zeroual (1999, 2000).

Our previous acoustic results[29] (Zeroual 2000), showed that $F_1$ onset of /a/ in /CVb/ is significantly higher after /h/ than after /f t k/ but not significantly different when V = /i u/. These results clearly illustrate that, at least in MA, a raised $F_1$ is not shared by all the gutturals. Furthermore, $F_1$ onset of MA /a i u/ is significantly higher after /ħ/ than after /h/, which is in accord with El-Halees (1985) acoustic results who also provided perceptual evidence that $F_1$ perceptually distinguishes among gutturals.[30] In fact, the higher value of $F_1$ onset of /a/ after /h/ than after /f t k/ can be ascribed to the fact that during /h/ the tongue would already be in the position of the following vowels /a/ (or /i u/) due to the placeless status of the laryngeals and to their strong coarticulation with adjacent segments.[31]

Arabic emphatic consonants also induce raising of $F_1$ which is generally slight and combined with a large drop of $F_2$. Obrecht (1968) and Yeou (1995)[32] demonstrated that $F_2$ is the major acoustic correlate for the emphasis perception with trading relation between $F_1$ and $F_2$ (Yeou 1995).[33] Emphatic consonants have been differently characterized (velarized, pharyngealized, uvularized and/or labialized). Arabic emphasis is a velarization for Obrecht (1968) and uvularization for Kingston & Nichols (1987), McCarthy (1994), Shahin (1997) and Zawaydeh (2003), but the majority of phoneticians consider it as a pharyngealization.[34]

Our EMA and ultrasound data presented in Zeroual et al. (2011ab) clearly show that MA possesses velarized labial consonants which do not induce a raising of $F_1$. During these consonants, the tongue dorsum moves back and high towards the post-palatal zone; this is different from the horizontal backward movement of the tongue back in the posterior oro-pharyngeal cavity during the emphatics. MA emphasis is then not a velarization; we propose characterizing its gesture as pharyngealization. The large $F_2$ drop after emphatic consonants can be attributed not only to their (upper-)pharyngeal constriction, but also to the "simultaneous depression of the palatine dorsum" (Ali and Daniloff 1981: 100) compared to their non-emphatic cognates (see also Marçais 1948, Ghazeli 1977, Zeroual et

---

[29] In this exhaustive acoustic study (Zeroual, 2000), we measured onset, middle and offset values of $F_1$–$F_2$–$F_3$ during [a, i, u] in [CVb] MA words and nonsense words pronounced (5 tokens) in a carrier phrase by 10 Moroccan Arabic speakers. In these MA [CVb], C = [f t T k q χ ħ h].

[30] "$F_1$ [… is] sufficient to distinguish the uvular and pharyngeal places of articulation. $F_1$ transition then has a direct relationship with the place and degree of the constriction in the back cavity" El-Halees (1985: 296).

[31] Notice that Bessell (1992) and Shahin (1997, 2002) have also reported that the laryngeals in Salish languages do not induce raising of $F_1$.

[32] Obrecht (1968, Lebanese Arabic speakers) and Yeou (1995, Moroccan Arabic speakers).

[33] According to Yeou (1995), relatively small $F_2$ lowering is sufficient to perceive emphasis when $F_1$ is substantially high.

[34] Marçais (1948), Jakobson, (1957), Ghazeli (1977), Ali and Daniloff (1985), etc.

al. 2007ab). The pharyngeal articulation during MA emphatics seems not narrow enough; this can explain why they do not induce substantial raising of $F_1$.

Based on all these acoustic observations, it can be argued that $F_1$ is not a regular acoustic correlate shared by all the segments produced by an articulation in the upper and/or lower pharyngeal cavities and for which the feature [pharyngeal] can be specified.

# 4 Variability

Different phonetic realizations are predicted for the laryngeals depending on whether or not they phonologically pattern or not with gutturals. The hypothesis of the aryepiglottic involvement during laryngeals that have [pharyngeal] feature (Hess 1990, Nolan 1995) has not yet been extensively tested. Shahin (1997, 2002) predicted that such laryngeals should be produced by tongue root retraction and induce a raising of $F_1$; but until now, several physiological studies have not shown any evidence of such tongue involvement.

According to Goldstein (1994), articulatory variability between speakers, dialects, and languages is expected during the gutturals and especially the laryngeals and pharyngeals. He noticed that pharyngeal consonants have a low jaw position in MA and a relatively high position in Lebanese Arabic.[35] According to Goldstein (1994: 239), "Such inter-speaker (or inter-language) variability might be expected if the jaw were not intrinsically involved in producing these constrictions, and was free to take on speaker-preferred postures".

In the following paragraphs, we discuss the fact that the pharyngeal and especially epiglottal articulations may exhibit a raising of the anterior part of the tongue which seems to be a language-specific and not universal property.

# 5 Enhancement

Delattre (1971) established a relationship between Iraqi Arabic /ħ ʕ/ and American English /r/ and showed that /ħ ʕ/ have not only a lower-pharyngeal or epiglottal articulation, but also a raising of the anterior part of the tongue. Cineradiographic traces provided by Ghazeli's (1977)[36] and by El-Halees's (1985) also

---

[35] Data from Boff Dkhissi (1983: Moroccan Arabic speakers) and Delattre (1971: Lebanese Arabic speakers).
[36] McCarthy (1994: 194) added that: "Neither Delattre nor Ghazeli made films of pharyngeals in different vocalic contexts. Thus, although we see some raising of the anterior portion of

show a similar raising during Tunisian and Iraqi epiglottals respectively. Ladefoged & Maddieson (1996: 308) mentioned some Caucasian languages data, from Catford (ms. see also Catford 1983) and Dzhejranishvili (1959), where it clearly appears that during the voiceless epiglottal consonant in Abkhaz and pharyngealized vowels in Tsakhur and Udi, the anterior part of the tongue is also raised.

According to Lindau (1984), American English /r/ combines palatal with pharyngeal constrictions and even with lip rounding. These three constrictions are close to the pressure nodes associated with $F_3$ and should substantially lower its frequency (Ohala 1990). The raising of the anterior part of the tongue during a pharyngeal or an epiglottal consonant would enhance the lowering of $F_3$. For Delattre (1971: 135), the "3rd formant transitions lowers regularly for /ħ/ as well as for /ʕ/, much less than for American /r/ – which is comprehensive since the dorsal bulge is much less high for the 2 Arabic consonants than for the American one". Our articulatory data (Zeroual 2000, Zeroual and Crevier-Buchman 2002) showed that MA /ħ ʕ/ are produced without any raising of the anterior part of the tongue in aCa, but with a strong coarticulation of this portion of the tongue with the adjacent vowels in iCi and uCu contexts. These observations suggest that the involvement of the anterior part of the tongue in the enhancement of the spectral properties of the pharyngeal or epiglottal articulations is rather language-specific.

Several physiological analyses (Marçais 1948, Ali and Daniloff 1972, Ghazeli 1977, Zeroual et al. 2007ab) show a "depression of the palatine dorsum" during the emphatic consonants. It is not clear whether this "depression" is a passive consequence of the backward movement of the tongue root, or an active gesture to enhance the large drop in $F_2$.

# 6 Conclusion

In the first part of this chapter we presented some phonological and phonetic arguments advanced in favor of or against the use of the place feature Pharyngeal in the phonological representation of the back consonants (e.g. uvular stop, guttural and emphatic consonants). We showed that although several phonological models are proposed for these consonants, they are unable to give account for all their phonological and phonetic aspects.

---

the tongue body during the pharyngeals, we cannot know whether this is the influence of the vowel or an additional requirement of the pharyngeal consonants. In the actual tokens that Ghazeli examined, the vowel following the pharyngeal is [æ]. In Delattre's data, the tongue-body position also looks fairly [æ]-like".

In the second part of this paper, and after identifying potential phonetic correlates proposed for the feature Pharyngeal, we provided exhaustive physiological and acoustic data based mainly on MA back consonants to examine the validity of these hypotheses. Our phonetic observations seem to be in accord only with Goldstein's hypothesis (1994) related to the jaw, since they show that MA guttural consonants are produced with a lower degree of jaw participation.

Clear enough, further phonetic and phonological data are needed to contribute to deepening our understanding of the phonetic typology and the phonological behaviors of the back articulations.

## Acknowledgements

The authors are grateful to our colleagues from the "Laboratoire de Phonétique et Phonologie, CNRS-UMR7018 & Sorbonne Nouvelle" and to an anonymous reviewer for their comments and suggestions. Thanks are also due to [1]Phil Hoole, [1]Adamantios Gafos, [2]John H. Esling, [2]Lise Crevier-Buchman, [3]Cécile Fougeron, [3]Rachid Ridouane, for their scientific and technical help to collect our physiological ([1]EMA, [2]endoscopy, [3]Ultrasound) data during a period of several years. Special thanks go to John H. Esling, Phil Hoole, Adamantios Gafos and Rachid Ridouane for their financial support to the first author.

## References

Al-Ani, S. 1970. *Arabic phonology*. The Hague: Mouton.
Ali, L. H. and Daniloff, R. G. 1972. A contrastive cinefluorographic investigation of the articulation of emphatic-non emphatic cognate consonants. *Studia Linguistica* 26: 81–105.
Avery, P., and Rice, K. 1988. Underspecification theory and the coronal node. *Toronto Working Papers in Linguistics* 9: 101–119.
Avery, P. & K. Rice. 1989. Segment structure and coronal underspecification. *Phonology* 6: 179–200.
Bin-Muqbil, M. S. 2006. *Phonetic and Phonological Aspects of Arabic Emphatics and Gutturals*. PhD dissertation, University of Wisconsin-Madison.
Boff Dkhissi, M. C. 1983. Contribution à l'étude expérimentale des consonnes d'arrière de l'arabe classique (locuteurs marocains). *Travaux de l'Institut de Phonétique de Strasbourg* 15: 1–363.
Butcher, A. & K. Ahmad. 1987. Some acoustic and aerodynamic characteristics of pharyngeal consonants in Iraqi Arabic. *Phonetica* 44: 156–172.
Catford, J. C. 1968. The articulatory possibilities of man. In B. Malmberg (ed.), *Manual of Phonetics*, 309–333. Amsterdam: North-Holland.
Catford, J. C. 1977. *Fundamental Problems in Phonetics*. Edinburgh: Edinburgh University Press.

Catford, J. C. 1983. Pharyngeal and laryngeal sounds in Caucasian languages. In D. M. Bless & J. H. Abbs (eds.), *Vocal Folds Physiology: Contemporary Research and Clinical Issues*, 344-350. San Diego: College Hill Press.
Clements, G. N. 1989. A unified set of features for consonants and vowels. Ms., Cornell University, Ithaca, N.Y.
Clements, G. N. & E. Hume. 1995. The internal organization of speech sounds. In J. A. Goldsmith (ed.), The *Handbook of Phonological Theory*, 245-306. Cambridge, USA & Oxford, UK: Blackwell.
Clements, G. N. (1985). The geometry of phonological features. *Phonology Yearbook* 2: 225-252.
Clements, G. N. 1990. The role of the sonority cycle in core syllabification. In J. Kingston and M. Beckman (eds.), *Papers in Laboratory Phonology I: Between the Grammar and Physics of Speech*, 283-333. Cambridge: Cambridge University Press.
Clements, G. N. 1993. Lieu d'articulation unifié des consonnes et des voyelles. In B. Laks and A. Rialland (eds.), *L'architecture et la géométrie des représentations phonologiques*, 101-145. Paris: Editions du CNRS.
Delattre, P. 1971. Pharyngeal features in the consonants of Arabic, German, Spanish, French, and American English. *Phonetica* 23: 129-155.
El-Halees, Y. 1985. The role of $F_1$ in the place-of-articulation distinction in Arabic. *Phonetica* 13: 287-298.
Elmedlaoui, M. 1995. Géométrie des restrictions de cooccurrence de traits en sémitique et en berbère: synchronie et diachronie. *Canadian Journal of Linguistics* 40: 39-76.
Esling, J. H. 1996. Pharyngeal consonants and the aryepiglottic sphincter. *Journal of the International Phonetic Association* 26: 65-88.
Ghazeli, S. 1977. *Back Consonants and Backing Coarticulation in Arabic*. PhD dissertation, University of Texas Austin.
Goldstein, L. 1994. Possible articulatory bases for the class of guttural consonants. In P. Keating (ed.), *Papers in Laboratory Phonology III: Phonological Structure and Phonetic Form*, 234-241. Cambridge: Cambridge University Press.
Greenberg, J. 1951. The patterning of root morphemes in Semitic. *Word* 6: 162-181.
Halle, M. 1989. The intrinsic structure of speech sounds. Ms., MIT, Cambridge.
Halle, M. 1992. Phonological features. In W. Bright (ed.), *International Encyclopedia of Linguistics*, 207-212. New York & Oxford: Oxford University Press.
Halle, M. 1995. Feature geometry and feature spreading. *Linguistic Inquiry* 26: 1-46.
Halle, M., B. Vaux & A. Wolfe. 2000. On feature spreading and the representation of place of articulation. *Linguistic Inquiry* 31: 387-444.
*Handbook of the International Phonetic Association*. Cambridge: Cambridge University Press.
Hayward, K. M. & R. J. Hayward. 1989. 'Guttural': Arguments for a new distinctive feature. *Transactions of the Philological Society* 87: 179-193.
Heath, J. 1987. *Ablaut and Ambiguity: Phonology of a Moroccan Arabic dialect*. Albany, NY: State University of New York Press.
Herzallah, R. 1990. *Aspects of Palestinian Arabic Phonology: A Non-Linear Approach*. PhD dissertation, Cornell University.
Hess, S. 1990. Pharyngeal articulations in Akan and Arabic. Ms., UCLA.
Hoole, P. & A. Zierdt. 2010. Five-dimensional articulography. In B. Maassen and P. van Lieshout (eds.), *Speech Motor Control: New Developments in Basic and Applied Research*, 331-349. Oxford: Oxford University Press.

Honda, K., N. Kusakawa & Y. Kakita. 1992. An EMG analysis of sequential control cycles of articulatory activity during /əpVp/ utterances. *Journal of Phonetics* 20: 53–63.

Jakobson, R. 1957. Mufaxxama, the "emphatic" phonemes of Arabic. In E. Pulgram (ed.), *Studies presented to Jushua Whatmough on his 60th Birthday*, 105–115. The Hague: Mouton.

Kagaya, R. 1974. A fiberscopic and acoustic study of the Korean stops, affricates and fricatives. *Journal of Phonetics* 2: 161–180.

Keating, P. 1990. The window model of coarticulation: articulatory evidence. In J. Kingston & M. Beckman, (eds.), *Papers in Laboratory Phonology I*, 451–470. Cambridge: Cambridge University Press.

Keating, P., B. Lindblom, J. Lubker & J. Kreiman. 1994. Variability in jaw height for segments in English and Swedish VCVs. *Journal of Phonetics* 22: 407–422.

Ladefoged, P. & I. Maddieson. 1996. *The Sounds of the World's Languages*. Cambridge, USA & Oxford, UK: Blackwell.

Ladefoged, P. 1971. *Preliminaries to Linguistic Phonetics*. Chicago & London: The University of Chicago Press.

Ladefoged, P. 2001 [1975]. *A Course in Phonetics*. 4th edition. Fort Worth, TX: Hartcourt Brace Jovanovich.

Ladefoged, P. 2001. *Vowels and Consonants. An Introduction to the Sounds of Languages*. Massachusetts, USA & Oxford, UK: Blackwell.

Laufer, A., and T. Baer. 1988. The emphatic and pharyngeal sounds in Hebrew and in Arabic. *Language and Speech* 31: 181–205.

Laufer, A. & I. D. Condax. 1979. The epiglottis as an articulator. *UCLA Working Papers in Phonetics* 45: 60–83.

Laver, J. 1994. *Principle of Phonetics*. Cambridge: Cambridge University Press.

Lee, S. H. 1995. Orals, gutturals, and the jaw. In B. Connell and A. Arvaniti (eds.), *Papers in Laboratory Phonology IV: Phonology and Phonetic Evidence*, 343–360. Cambridge: Cambridge University Press.

Lindau, M. 1984. Phonetic differences in glottalic consonants. *Journal of phonetics* 12: 147–155.

Maeda, S. & K. Honda. 1994. From EMG to formant patterns of vowels: The implication of vowel spaces. *Phonetica* 51: 17–29.

Marçais, P. 1948. L'articulation de l'emphase dans un parler arabe maghrébin. *Annales de l'Institut d'Etudes Orientales d'Alger* 7: 5–28.

McCarthy, J. 1986. OCP effects: gemination and antigemination. *Linguistic Inquiry* 17: 207–263.

McCarthy, J. 1988. Feature geometry and dependency: a review. *Phonetica* 45: 84–108.

McCarthy, J. 1989a. Guttural phonology. Ms., University of Massachusetts, Amherst (61 pages, version date: 26 march).

McCarthy, J. 1989b. Guttural Phonology. Ms., University of Massachusetts, Amherst (version date: October).

McCarthy, J. 1991. The phonology of pharyngeal articulations in Semitic. Ms., University of Massachusetts, Amherst.

McCarthy, J. 1994. The phonetics and phonology of Semitic pharyngeals. In P. Keating (ed.), *Papers In Laboratory Phonology III: Phonological Structure and Phonetic Form*, 191–233. Cambridge: Cambridge University Press.

Mooshammer, C., P. Hoole & A. Geumann. 2006. Interarticulator cohesion within coronal consonant production. *Journal of the Acoustical Society of America* 120: 1028–1039.

Nolan, F. 1995. The role of the jaw active or passive? Comments on Lee. In B. Connell & A. Arvaniti (eds.), *Papers in Laboratory Phonology IV: Phonology and Phonetic Evidence*, 361–367. Cambridge: Cambridge University Press.
Ohala, J. 1990. The generality of articulatory binding: Comments on Kingston's paper. In J. Kingston and M. Beckman (eds.), *Papers in Laboratory Phonology I: Between the Grammar and Physics of Speech*, 435–444. Cambridge: Cambridge University Press.
Paradis, C. & D. LaCharité. 2001. Guttural deletion in loanwords. *Phonology* 18: 255–300.
Perkell, J. 1980. Phonetic Features and the Physiology of Speech Production. In B. Butterworth (ed.), *Language Production 1: Speech and Talk*. London & New York: Academic Press.
Pierrehumbert, J. 1993. Dissimilarity in the arabic verbal roots. *Proceedings of North Eastern Linguistics Society* 23: 367–381.
Rose, S. 1996. Variable laryngeals and vowel lowering. *Phonology* 13: 73–117.
Sagey, E. 1986. *The Representation of Features and Relations in Nonlinear Phonology*. PhD dissertation, MIT, Cambridge, MA.
Shahin, K. N. 1997. *Postvelar Harmony. An Examination of its Bases and Crosslinguistic Variation*. PhD dissertation, University of British Columbia. Published version (2002): *Postvelar harmony*. Amsterdam & Philadelphia: John Benjamins.
Shahin, K. 2009. The Phonology of Pharyngeals. *International Workshop on Pharyngeals and Pharyngealisation*, Newcastle (Published version: Shahin 2011).
Shahin, K. 2011. A phonetic study of guttural laryngeal consonants in Palestinian Arabic using laryngoscopic and acoustic analysis. In Z. M. Hassan and B. Heselwood (eds.), *Instrumental Studies in Arabic Phonetics* (Current Issues in Linguistic Theory 319), 129–140. Amsterdam & Philadelphia: John Benjamins.
Steriade, D. 1987. Locality condition and feature geometry. *Proceeding of NELS 17*: 595–618.
Traill, A. 1985. *Phonetic and phonological studies of !Xóõ Bushman*. Hamburg: Helmut Buske.
Yeou, M. & S. Maeda. 1995. Uvular and pharyngeal consonants are approximants: An acoustic modeling and study. *Proceedings of the XIII$^{th}$ ICPHS*, Stockholm, 586–589.
Yip, M. 1989. Feature geometry and co-occurrence restrictions. *Phonology* 6: 349–374.
Zawaydeh, B. A. 2003. The interaction of the phonetics and phonology of gutturals. In J. Local, R. Ogden and R. Temple (eds.), *Papers in Laboratory Phonology VI: Phonetic interpretation*, 279–292. Cambridge: Cambridge University Press.
Zeroual, C. 1999. A fiberscopic and acoustic study of 'guttural' and emphatic consonants of Moroccan Arabic. *XIV$^{th}$ ICPHS*, San Francisco, 997–1000.
Zeroual, C. 2000. *Propos controversés sur la phonétique et la phonologie de l'arabe marocain*. Thèse de Doctorat, Université de Paris 8.
Zeroual, C. & L. Crevier-Buchman. 2002. L'arabe marocain possède des consonnes épiglottales et non pharyngales. *XXIV$^{èmes}$ Journées d'Etude sur la Parole*, Nancy, 237–240.
Zeroual, C. 2003. Aerodynamic study of Moroccan Arabic guttural consonants. *Proceedings of the XV$^{th}$ ICPHS*, Barcelona, 1859–1862.
Zeroual, C., S. Fuchs & P. Hoole. 2006. Kinematic study of Moroccan Arabic simple and geminate obstruents: Evidence from transillumination, *Proceedings of the 7th International Seminar on Speech Production*, Ubatuba-SP, 287–294.
Zeroual, C., P. Hoole, S. Fuchs & J. H. Esling. 2007a. EMA study of the coronal emphatic and non-emphatic plosive consonants of Moroccan Arabic. *Proceedings of the XVI$^{th}$ ICPHS*, Saarbrücken, 397–340.
Zeroual C., P. Hoole & J. H. Esling. 2007b. Etude de la coarticulation au niveau des suites *Tk en arabe marocain. *Proceedings of the workshop La co-articulation: Indices, Direction et Représentation*, Montpellier, 79–82.

Zeroual, C., J. H. Esling & P. Hoole. 2011a. EMA, endoscopic, ultrasound and acoustic study of two secondary articulations in Moroccan Arabic: labial-velarization vs. emphasis. In Z. M. Hassan and B. Heselwood (eds.), *Instrumental Studies in Arabic Phonetics* (Current Issues in Linguistic Theory 319), 277–297. Amsterdam & Philadelphia: John Benjamins.

Zeroual, C., J. H. Esling, P. Hoole & R. Ridouane. 2011b. Ultrasound study of Moroccan Arabic labiovelarization. *Proceedings of the XVII[th] International Congress of Phonetic Sciences*, Hong Kong, 2272–2275.

Zeroual C., P. Hoole & J. H. Esling. 2011c. Contraintes articulatoires et acoustico-perceptives liées à la production de /k/ emphatisée en arabe marocain. In M. Embarki & C. Dodane (eds.), *La Coarticulation, des Indices aux Représentations*, (Collection Langue et Parole), 227–240. Paris: L'Harmattan.

# Index

acquisition, 7-8, 12, 38
Akan, 111-115, 172, 220, 235
Anywa, 238
Arabic, 196, 247-276
    Iraqi ~, 271
    Jordanian ~, 268
    Lebanese ~, 270
    Moroccan ~, 269-271
    Palestinian ~, 253-254
Armenian Kirzan, 229
Articulatory Phonology, 4, 9
aryepiglottal, 252, 261-262, 264
aspirate, 13, 127-154, 160-165, 168-170, 229
assimilation, 9, 27, 35, 39, 41, 43-44, 50-51, 57-77, 81, 84, 86-87, 69, 95, 112, 116-117, 131, 173, 178, 181-182, 198-199, 221-222, 230, 232, 247
Autosegmental Phonology, 5, 13-18, 20-25, 35, 45, 50, 94, 117, 119, 152, 170, 174, 243

Barasana, 196
Bengali, 196
Berber, 256
Bwamu, 196

C-Place, 50, 57, 252
Cambodian, 199
Cheremis Eastern, 57-59
Chilcotin, 226, 232-233
Chinese Mandarin, 199
Chipewyan, 179
Chukchee, 225
Chumburung, 231-232
coarticulation, 197, 200, 212, 214, 248, 258-259, 269-276
cooccurrence, 13, 36, 127-155, 168
contrast, 4, 7, 9-10, 29-30, 41-42, 44-48, 62, 66, 68, 79, 85, 116, 128-133, 161, 165, 172-173, 179, 189-192, 195, 197-198, 202, 208-209, 219-219, 223, 227-228, 231-232, 238, 247, 257, 261

denasalization, 209
Dholuo, 238-239
diphthongization, 36, 47, 92-123
dissimilation, 27, 102, 104

emphatic consonant, 116, 230, 232, 248, 250-275
English, 159, 162, 166-167, 172, 179, 182, 196, 198, 202
    American ~, 201-203
epiglottal, 248, 257, 261-264, 270-271
Esimbi, 72-76
Ewe, 60-63, 196

features
    [approximant], 6, 251, 253, 260-261
    [ATR], 28, 32, 50, 62-63, 66, 68, 70-73 77-78, 84-86, 92, 105-106, 112-118, 171-172, 217-246, 256-259
    [back], 34, 39, 47, 50, 55-56-58, 71, 73, 75, 82, 85-86, 115, 124, 167, 219, 231, 247, 257-260
    [click], 9
    [continuant], 110, 191, 257, 260
    [constricted glottis], 151-152, 170, 227, 240, 259
    [coronal], 34, 56-59, 63-65, 75, 82, 101-104, 118, 169, 181-185, 190-194, 202, 247-250, 252, 258-259, 272-274
    [distributed], 118-119
    [dorsal], 34, 57, 116, 247-249, 251-259
    [high], 28-34, 38-39, 50, 62-63, 70-74, 82, 96, 116-118, 219-220, 223, 234, 248, 259
    [labial], 27, 51, 56, 58-59, 63-66, 75, 102, 104, 118, 205, 248, 252
    [low], 28-30, 33-35, 38, 62-63, 73-74, 84-87, 95-96, 115-116, 118, 167, 219, 222-223, 259
    [nasal], 11-12, 60-61, 65, 81, 87-88, 132, 136, 145-146, 181, 195-215, 259

[open], 6, 25–118, 218
[pharyngeal], 12, 110–111, 114, 116, 188, 194, 230, 247–272
[RTR], 223–228, 255–257
[slack], 152, 169–170, 259
[sonorant], 118, 190, 210, 214, 249
[spread glottis], 151–152, 170, 173, 177, 191, 259
[stiff], 152, 169–171, 259
[strident], 12, 171, 179–194
[tap], 9
[tense], 12, 29–30, 32, 66, 77, 95–96, 105, 116–117–118, 159–178, 218–219, 229, 234, 241–242
[voiced], 82, 196
feature bundle, 5, 103, 247,
feature economy, 6–7, 15, 17, 19, 21, 192, 243
feature enhancement, 7, 10, 15–16, 21, 95, 155, 172, 176, 178, 191–193, 209–210, 214, 218, 234, 240–244, 270
feature geometry, 6, 26, 50, 152, 180, 193, 195, 213, 246–248, 273–275
feature node
    aperture node, 51, 53, 55–76, 81, 101–104, 116–117
    guttural node, 249, 256–258
    height node, 5–6
    oral node, 251, 254
    pharyngeal node, 251–252, 254
Fijian, 197
Finnish, 183
formants
    antiformant, 204, 206, 210–211
    first formant, 28, 30, 78, 93–94, 106–107, 238, 240–242
    formant bandwith, 238
    nasal formant, 204–205, 211
    second formant, 78, 93–94, 166
fortis, 160–165, 168–170, 229
French, 31, 159, 162, 173, 196, 199, 203–205

Gbe, 60–66
geminate, 131, 161, 172–17
German, 162–163, 172, 181
gesture, 9–10, 12, 29, 32, 109, 11, 116, 160–161, 184, 200–201, 203, 218, 228, 234, 236, 241–242, 249, 265, 269, 271

glide, 51–52, 99, 131, 135, 195–198, 219, 243
Gojri/Gujiri, 127
Grassman's Law, 146
Gta, 39
Guarani, 198–199
Guttural, 188, 192, 230, 232, 242, 248–272

Harauti, 127

Icelandic, 191
Igbo, 32, 66, 220, 234
intrinsic
    duration, 99
    fundamental frequency (IF0), 169, 175
    laryngeal muscles, 258
Inuit Greenlandic, 197, 230
Italian, 172–173
    Northern Salentino, 40
inventories (of phonemes), 7, 9, 11, 15, 18, 162, 192, 195–198, 219–243

Japanese, 172–173, 198, 202–203
Jingpho, 171

Kalenjin, 226
Kam-Sui, 208
Kimatuumbi, 67–69
Kinande, 69–72
Klallam, 197
Korean, 160, 164, 168, 183, 229
Kpelle, 196
Kukuya, 197
Kwangali, 198

Latin, 25, 98
lips, 10, 107, 115, 160, 165, 168, 184, 200, 205–206, 234, 259
laryngeal, 52, 128, 152–153, 161, 170, 199, 247, 249–270
lax, 29, 40, 95–97, 116, 125, 159–177, 217, 234, 239
lengthening, 97–98
Lua, 198

Maasai, 221–222, 237
Malay, 172
Mandan, 196

markedness, 38, 218, 224–226, 242–243, 246
Mbundu, 197
Menomini, 218–223
Mewari, 127
Mon, 208
Mongolian, 218, 230–231
motor theory of speech perception, 4, 9
Mura, 197

nasal mora, 198
natural class, 34, 38–41, 43, 50, 57, 62, 71, 87, 96, 117, 130, 165, 181–182, 185, 195, 230, 242, 248–249, 255, 268
Naxi, 208
Nepali, 127–155
Nez Perce, 218
Ngwe, 30–33
node fission, 100–105
node Activation Condition, 252, 256

Obligatory Contour Principle (OCP), 81–82, 102–103, 151–154, 163, 274
Oroqen, 225

Pirahã, 197
Portuguese, 198
~ Brazilian, 202
prenasalization, 207
prosodic domain, 203
prosodic feature, 113, 136, 145
prosodic word, 59

Quantal Theory, 9–12, 16, 21, 125, 190–191, 210–211, 217
Quileute, 197

redundant, 6, 10, 16, 39, 48, 53, 55, 66, 76, 103, 144, 192, 231
retroflex, 129, 134, 155, 231, 252
Rotokas, 197

Salish, 197
Sesotho, 77–92
shortening, 97
singleton, 172–173, 176
Siouan languages, 208

skeleton, 54, 97, 170
timing tier, 54–55, 97, 102
soft palate, 111, 196, 212, 214, 247, 258–260
Spanish, 47, 102, 202
spreading, 35, 40, 51–59, 61–63, 65, 71, 87, 185, 199, 213, 21, 225–226, 230–234, 243, 251, 256, 273
St'at'imcets, 228
Sui, 197
Swedish, 92–102
Syllable
coda, 198, 201–202, 207–209, 251
onset, 202, 207, 231
sonority, 5, 14–15, 19, 273
syllabic nasal, 80, 87
Tamang, 208
tenseness, 66, 95, 107, 160–161, 165, 172–173, 237
ThiMbukushu, 198
tongue
~ blade, 168–169, 173, 191–192, 259
~ body, 28, 30, 93, 108–111, 114–115, 165, 192, 219, 234, 236, 240–242, 248, 258–259, 271
~ dorsum, 165, 249, 258–259, 269
~ tip, 160, 249, 258–259, 269
transphonologization 208
Tucano, 196
Turkana, 227
Turkish, 46
Twi, 217

underspecification, 6–7, 14, 21, 43, 55, 76, 117, 119, 122, 246, 272
ultrasound, 228, 234, 269
uvula, 184, 200, 250, 262
uvular, 179, 184, 188, 197, 230–232, 242, 247–260, 269, 271, 275

V-Place, 50–51, 57–66, 85–86, 101–104, 252–254
velar, 168, 179, 197, 199, 201, 209 213–214, 230–231, 250, 259
voice onset time (VOT), 268
voice quality, 12, 171, 237–238, 242, 244
voicing, 131, 152, 161, 163, 165, 171–173, 176, 186, 196, 209–210, 213, 241

vowel harmony, 5–6, 14, 16–18, 20–22, 32, 38, 46, 63, 66, 78, 112–125, 145–146, 172, 217–246
vowel shift, 97, 102

Wa, 171
Warao, 196

Yakut, 198
Yao, 208
Yi, 208
Yoruba, 224–226

www.ingramcontent.com/pod-product-compliance
Lightning Source LLC
Chambersburg PA
CBHW070822170426
43200CB00007B/866